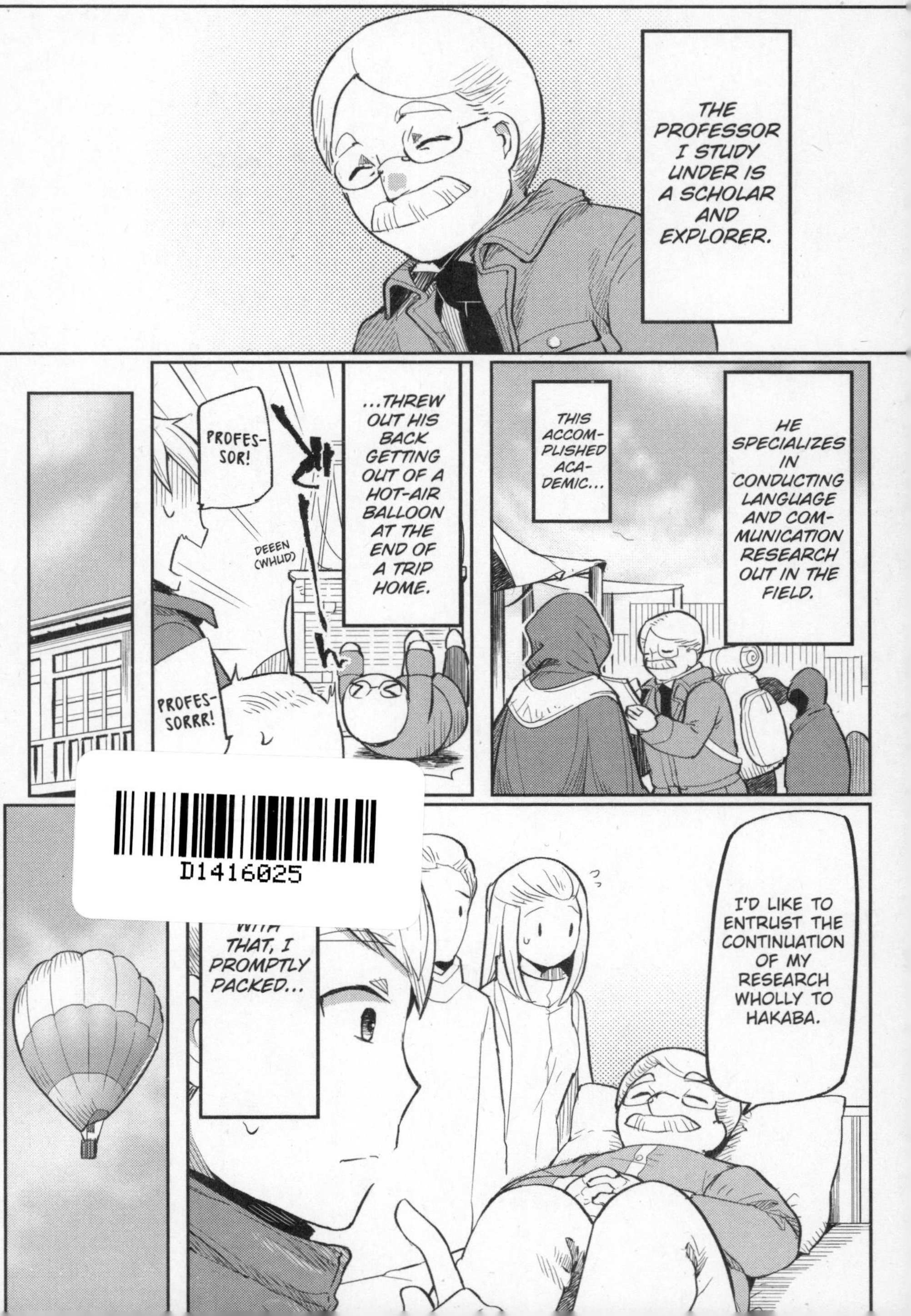
THE PROFESSOR I STUDY UNDER IS A SCHOLAR AND EXPLORER.
HE SPECIALIZES IN CONDUCTING LANGUAGE AND COMMUNICATION RESEARCH OUT IN THE FIELD.
THIS ACCOMPLISHED ACADEMIC...
...THREW OUT HIS BACK GETTING OUT OF A HOT-AIR BALLOON AT THE END OF A TRIP HOME.
PROFESSOR!
DEEEN (WHUD)
PROFESSORRR!
I'D LIKE TO ENTRUST THE CONTINUATION OF MY RESEARCH WHOLLY TO HAKABA.
WITH THAT, I PROMPTLY PACKED...

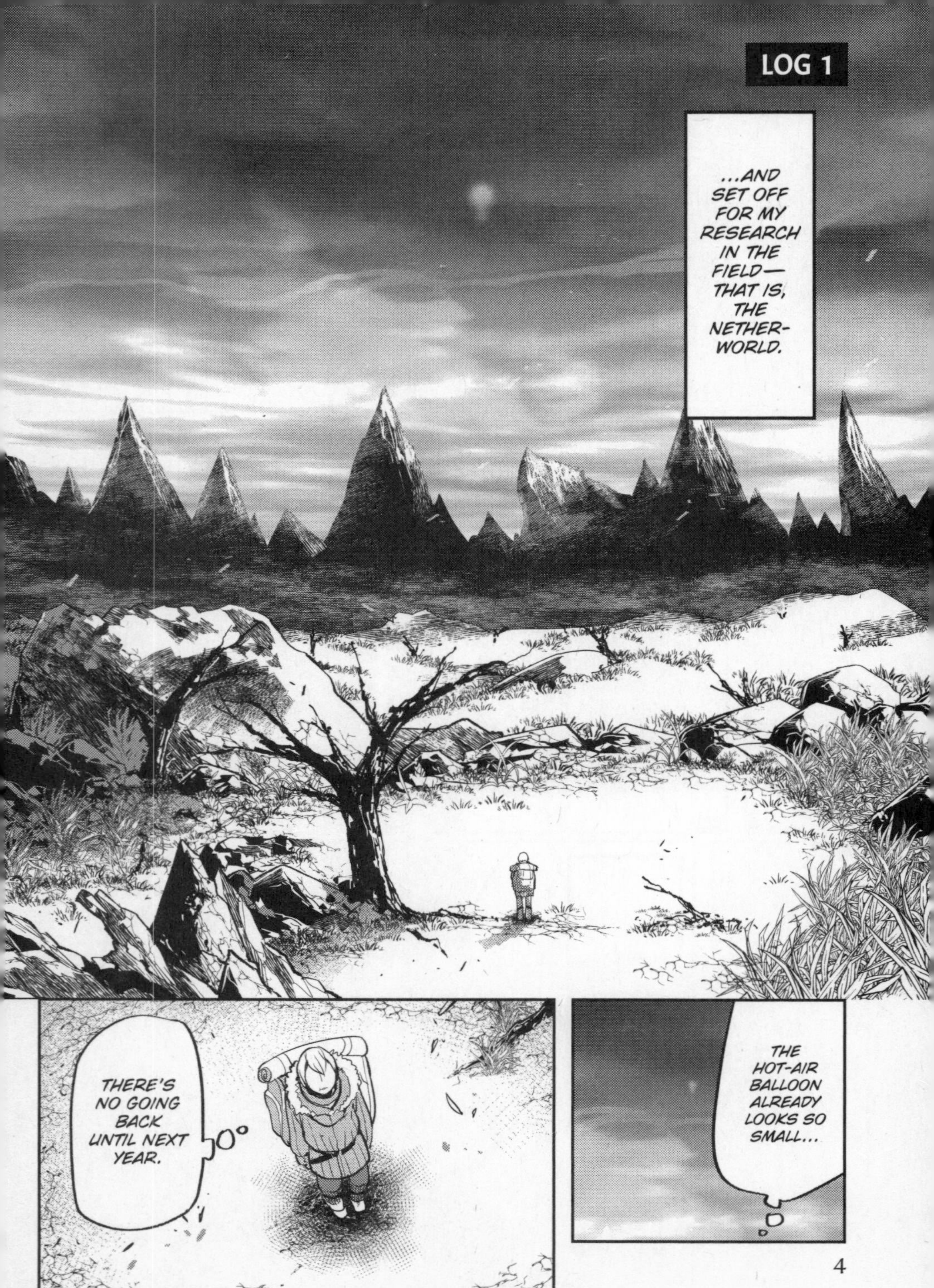
LOG 1
...AND SET OFF FOR MY RESEARCH IN THE FIELD— THAT IS, THE NETHER-WORLD.
THE HOT-AIR BALLOON ALREADY LOOKS SO SMALL...
THERE'S NO GOING BACK UNTIL NEXT YEAR.

HETEROGENIA LINGUISTICO

An Introduction to Interspecies Linguistics

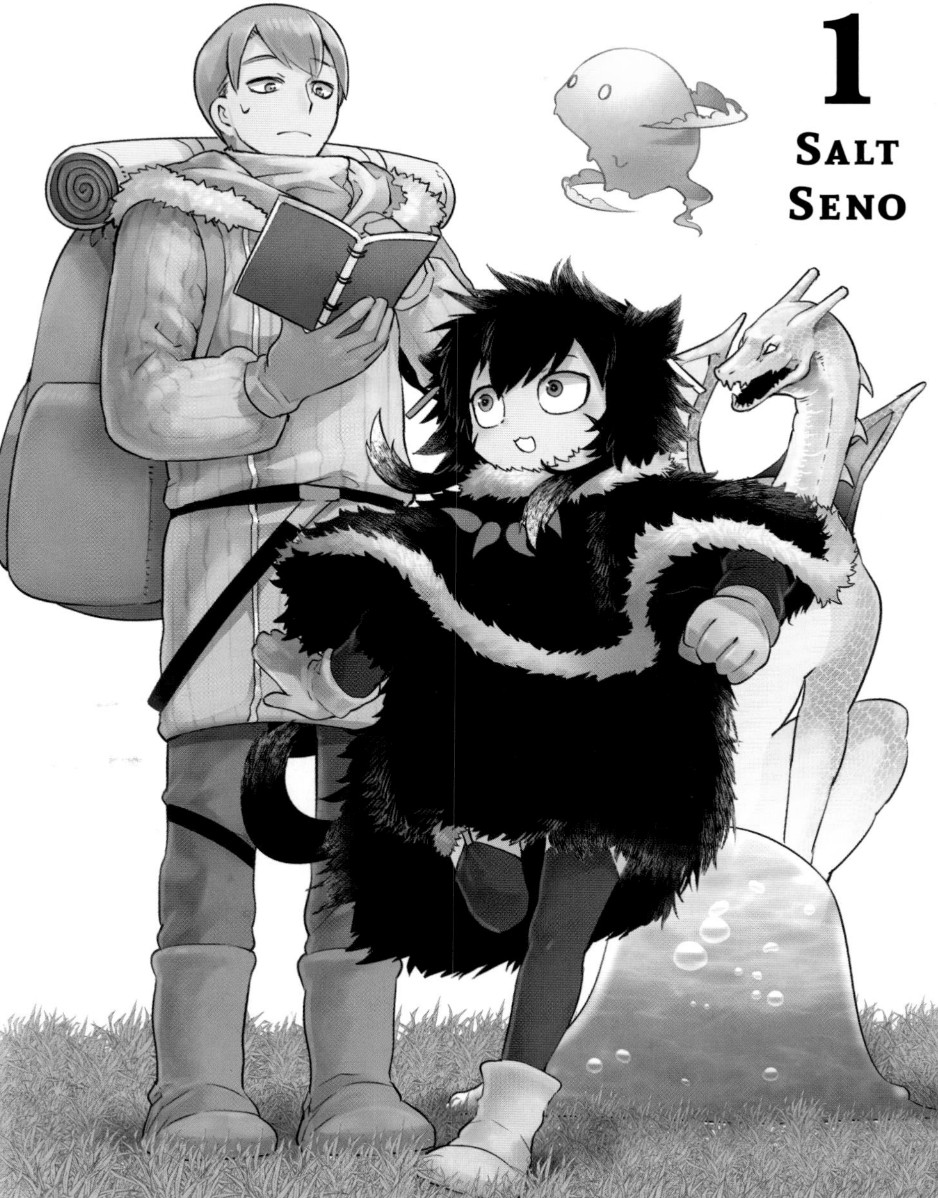

1

SALT SENO

Contents

HETEROGENIA LINGUISTICO

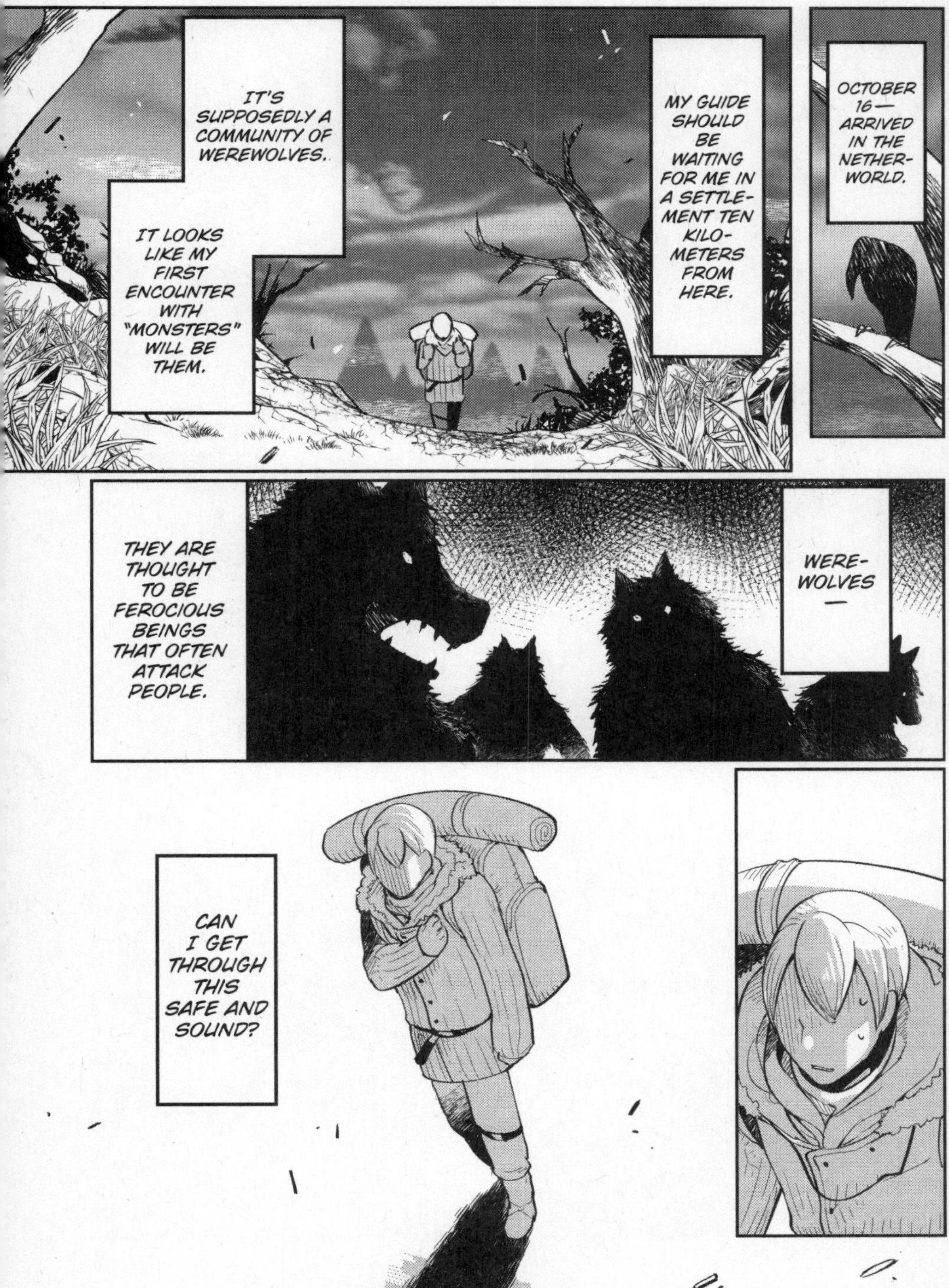
OCTOBER 16— ARRIVED IN THE NETHER-WORLD.
MY GUIDE SHOULD BE WAITING FOR ME IN A SETTLE-MENT TEN KILO-METERS FROM HERE.
IT'S SUPPOSEDLY A COMMUNITY OF WEREWOLVES.
IT LOOKS LIKE MY FIRST ENCOUNTER WITH "MONSTERS" WILL BE THEM.
WERE-WOLVES —
THEY ARE THOUGHT TO BE FEROCIOUS BEINGS THAT OFTEN ATTACK PEOPLE.
CAN I GET THROUGH THIS SAFE AND SOUND?

Answer: No.

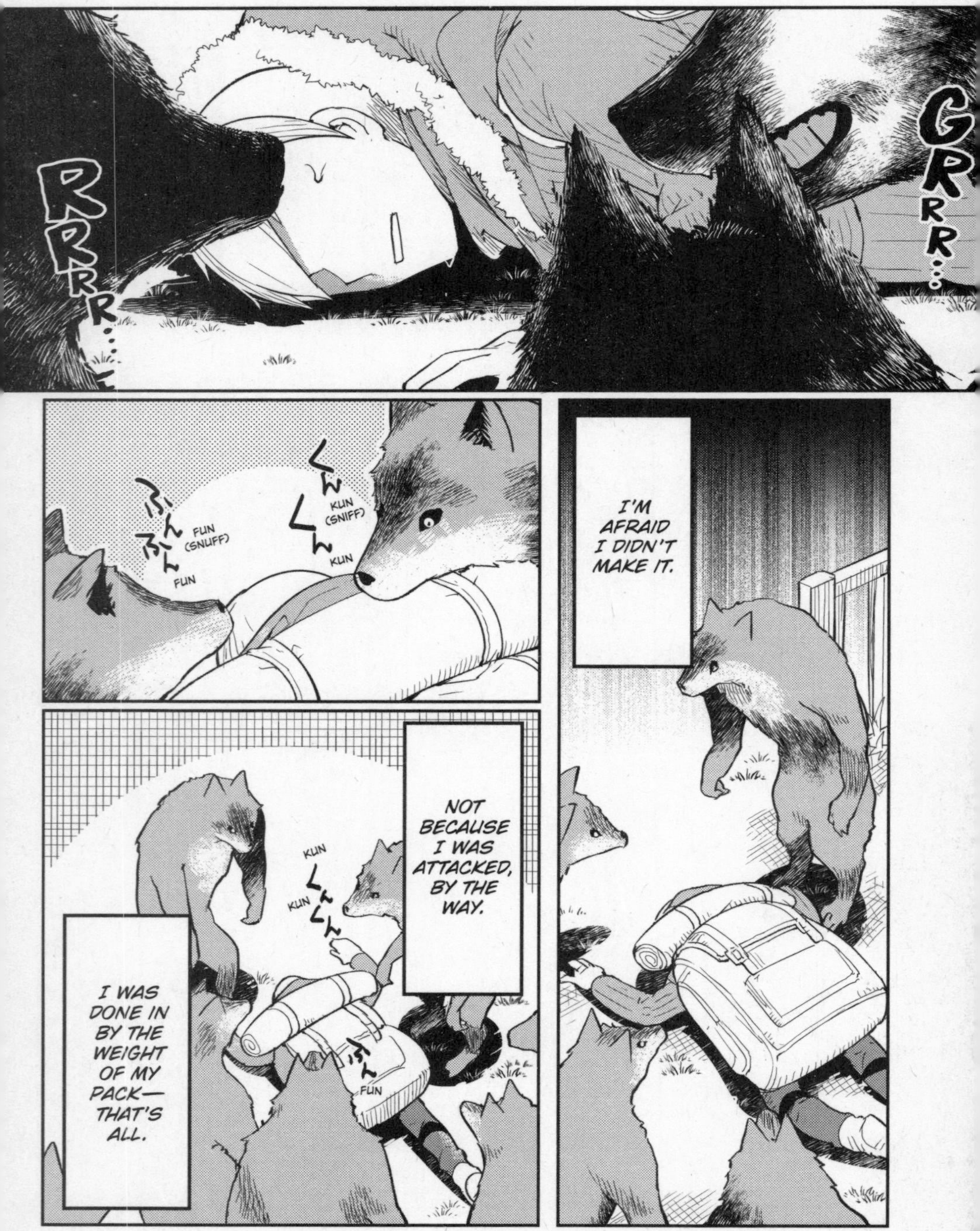
GRRR...
RRRRR...
I'M AFRAID I DIDN'T MAKE IT.
くんくん
KUN (SNIFF)
KUN
ふんふん
FUN (SNUFF)
FUN
NOT BECAUSE I WAS ATTACKED, BY THE WAY.
くんくん
KUN
KUN
I WAS DONE IN BY THE WEIGHT OF MY PACK—THAT'S ALL.
ふん
FUN

Native Speakers

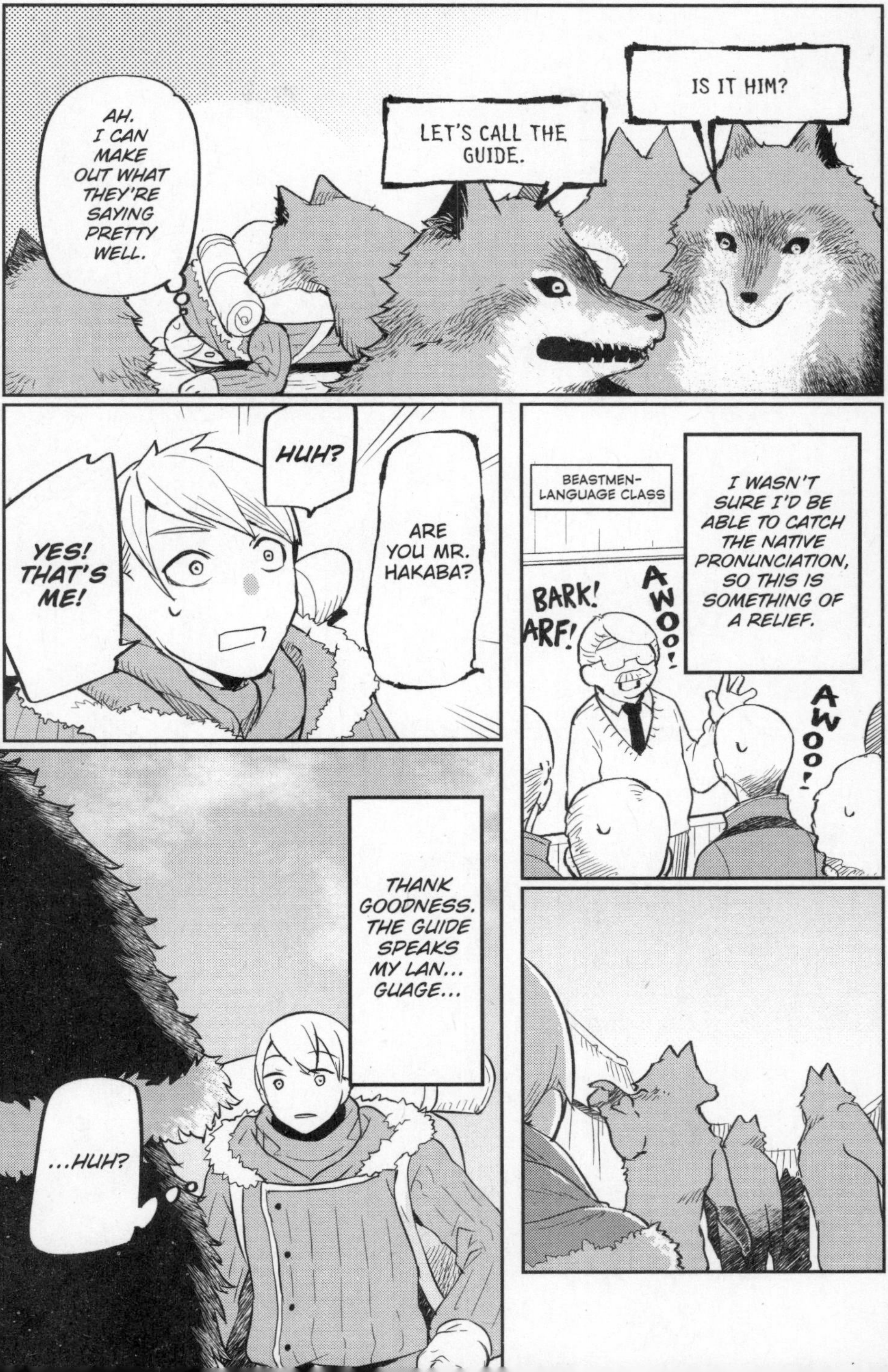
IS IT HIM?
LET'S CALL THE GUIDE.
AH. I CAN MAKE OUT WHAT THEY'RE SAYING PRETTY WELL.
BEASTMEN-LANGUAGE CLASS
I WASN'T SURE I'D BE ABLE TO CATCH THE NATIVE PRONUNCIATION, SO THIS IS SOMETHING OF A RELIEF.
AWOO!
BARK! ARF!
AWOO!
HUH?
ARE YOU MR. HAKABA?
YES! THAT'S ME!
THANK GOODNESS. THE GUIDE SPEAKS MY LAN... GUAGE...
...HUH?

Local Guide

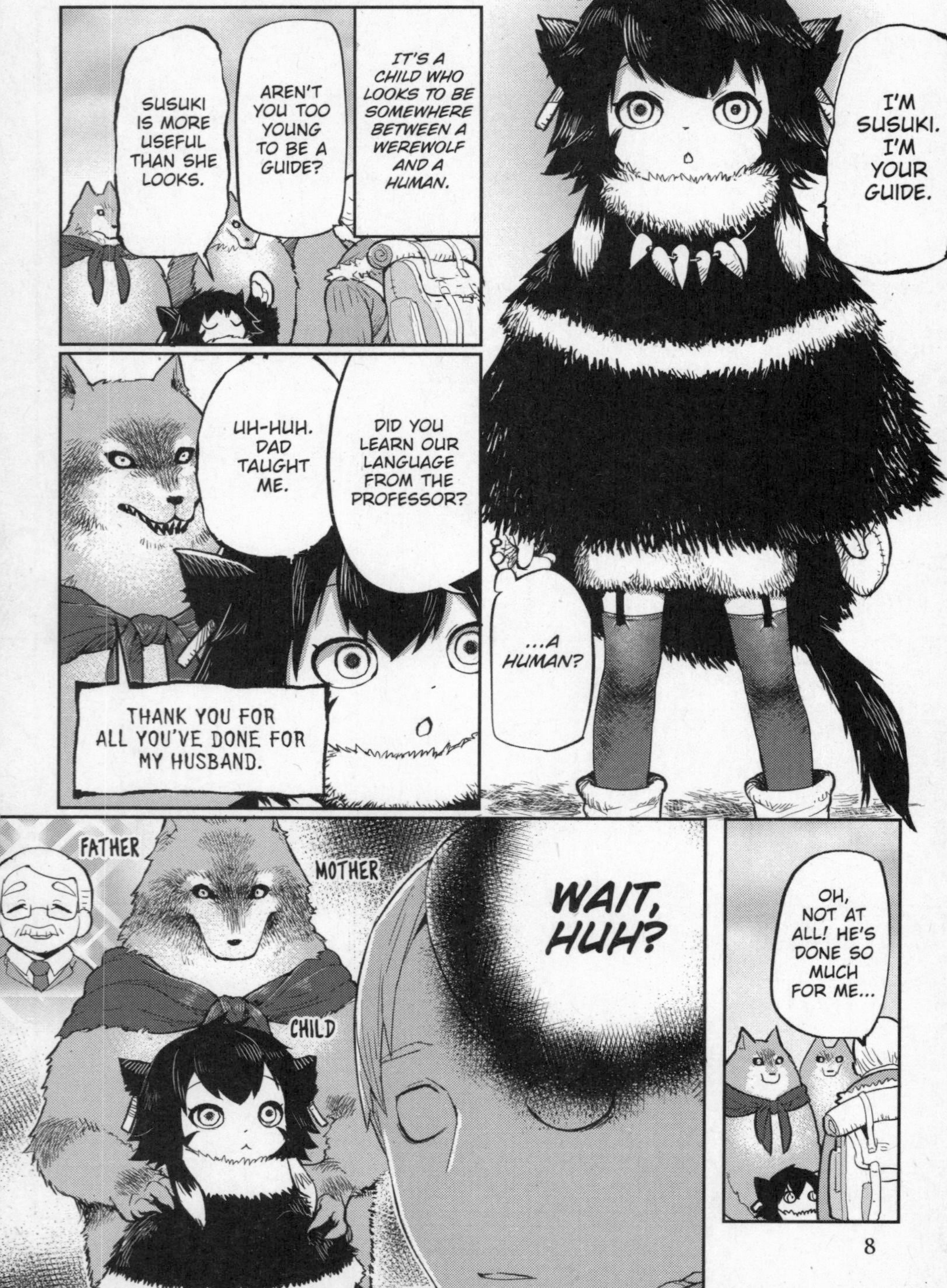
I'M SUSUKI. I'M YOUR GUIDE.
...A HUMAN?
IT'S A CHILD WHO LOOKS TO BE SOMEWHERE BETWEEN A WEREWOLF AND A HUMAN.
AREN'T YOU TOO YOUNG TO BE A GUIDE?
SUSUKI IS MORE USEFUL THAN SHE LOOKS.
DID YOU LEARN OUR LANGUAGE FROM THE PROFESSOR?
UH-HUH. DAD TAUGHT ME.
THANK YOU FOR ALL YOU'VE DONE FOR MY HUSBAND.
OH, NOT AT ALL! HE'S DONE SO MUCH FOR ME...
WAIT, HUH?
MOTHER
FATHER
CHILD

Research Begins

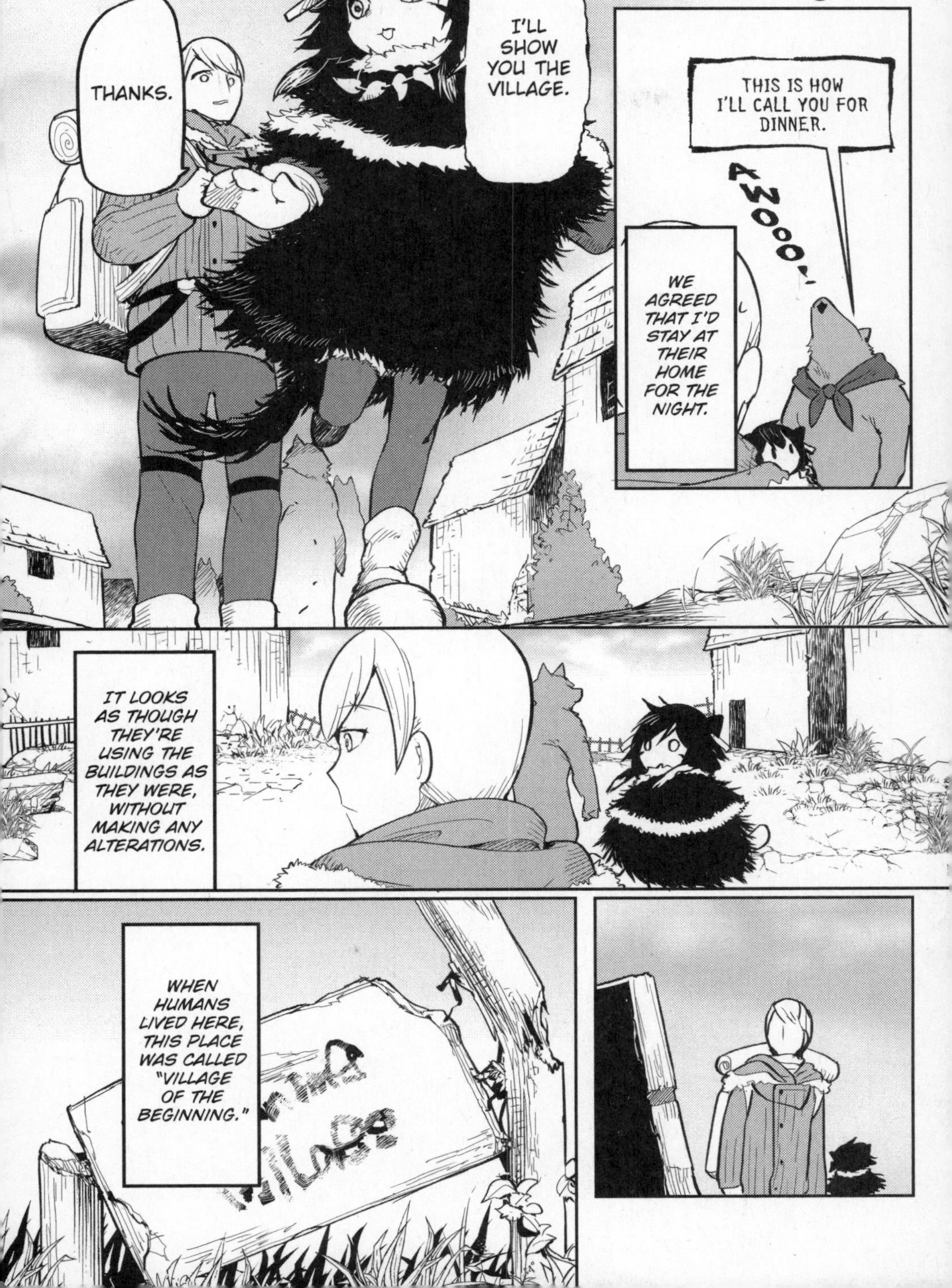
THIS IS HOW I'LL CALL YOU FOR DINNER.
AWOOO!
WE AGREED THAT I'D STAY AT THEIR HOME FOR THE NIGHT.
I'LL SHOW YOU THE VILLAGE.
THANKS.
IT LOOKS AS THOUGH THEY'RE USING THE BUILDINGS AS THEY WERE, WITHOUT MAKING ANY ALTERATIONS.
WHEN HUMANS LIVED HERE, THIS PLACE WAS CALLED "VILLAGE OF THE BEGINNING."

Greetings ①

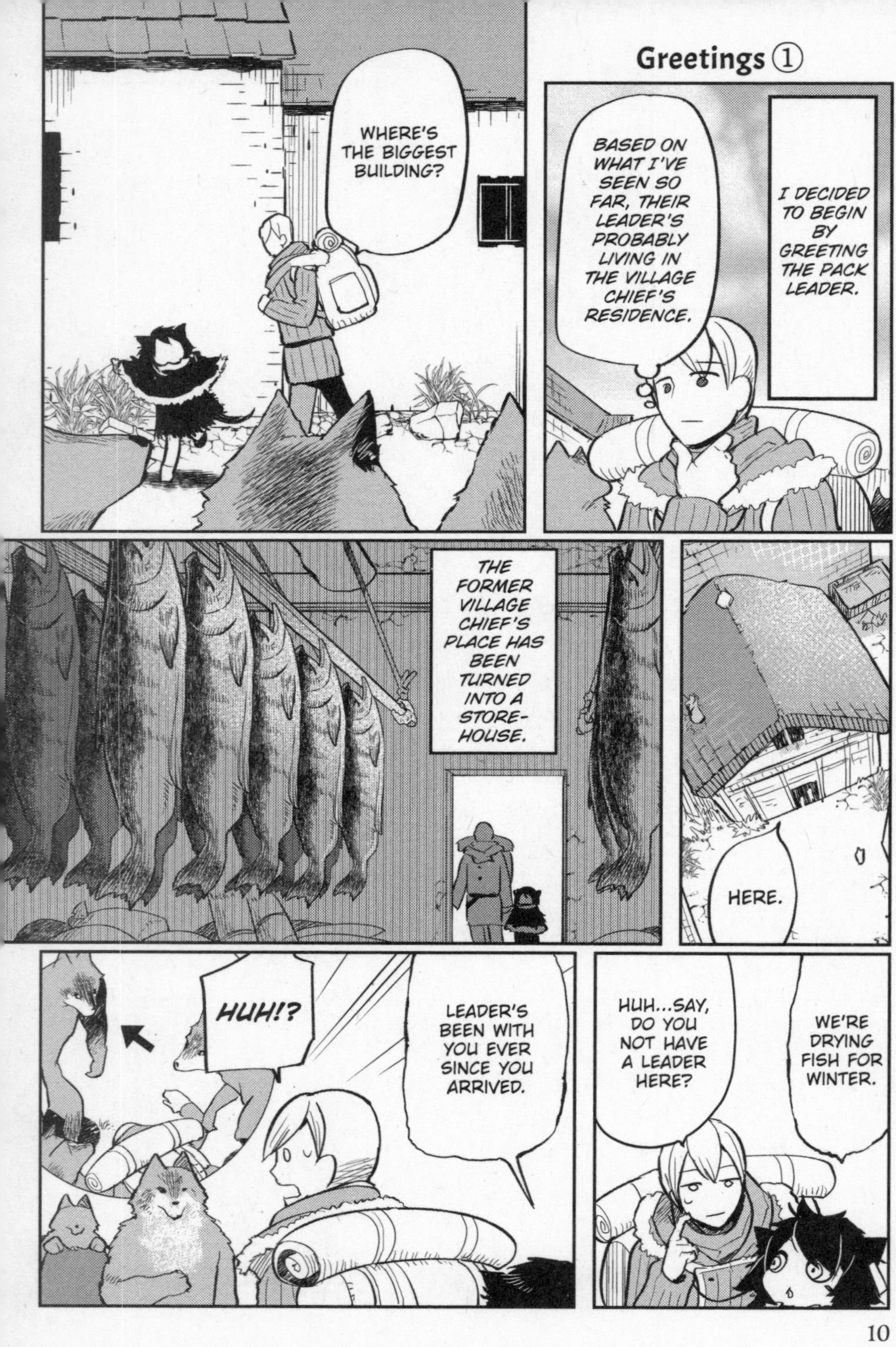
I DECIDED TO BEGIN BY GREETING THE PACK LEADER.
BASED ON WHAT I'VE SEEN SO FAR, THEIR LEADER'S PROBABLY LIVING IN THE VILLAGE CHIEF'S RESIDENCE.
WHERE'S THE BIGGEST BUILDING?
HERE.
THE FORMER VILLAGE CHIEF'S PLACE HAS BEEN TURNED INTO A STORE-HOUSE.
WE'RE DRYING FISH FOR WINTER.
HUH...SAY, DO YOU NOT HAVE A LEADER HERE?
LEADER'S BEEN WITH YOU EVER SINCE YOU ARRIVED.
HUH!?

Local Language

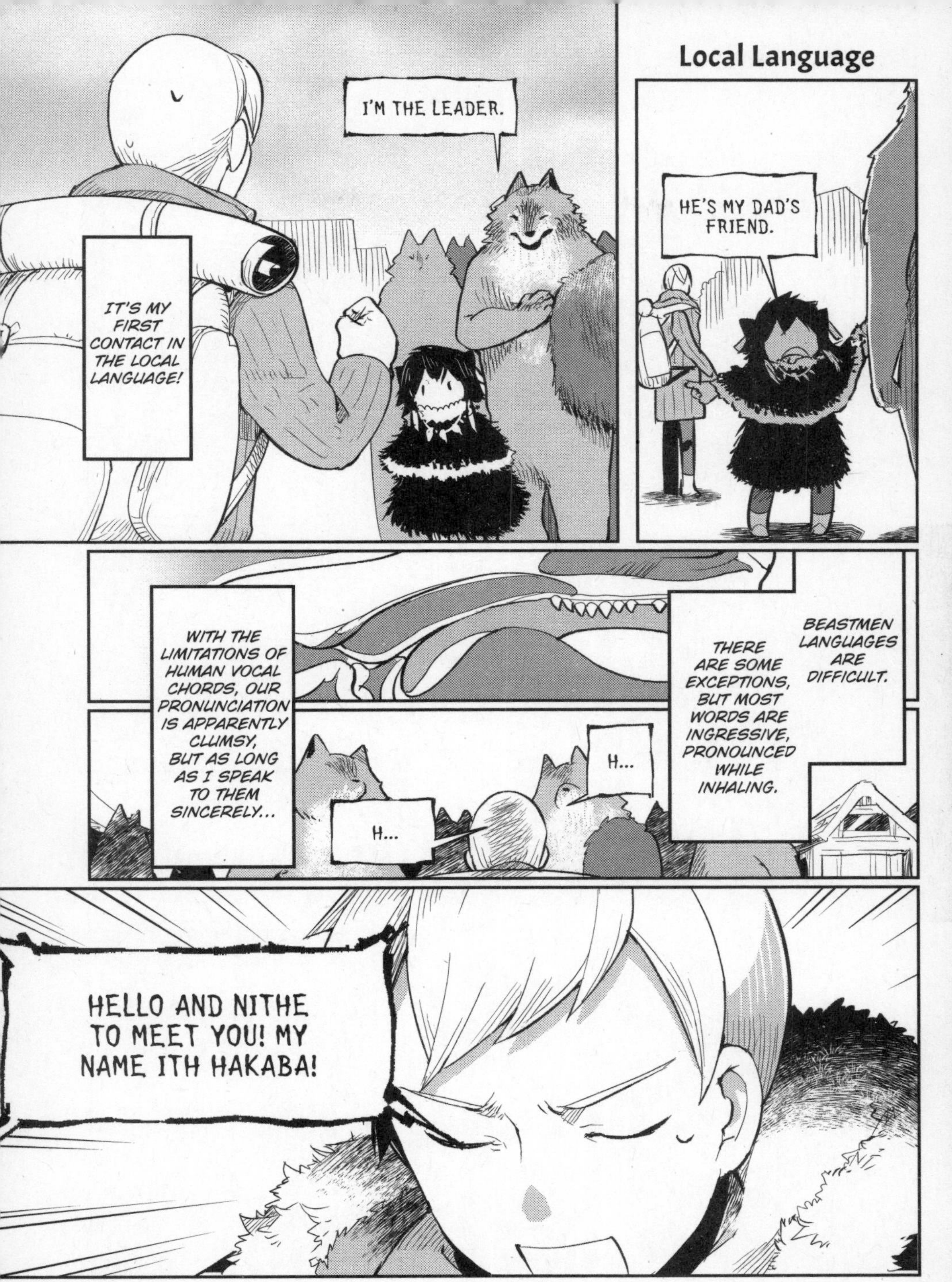

HE'S MY DAD'S FRIEND.
I'M THE LEADER.
IT'S MY FIRST CONTACT IN THE LOCAL LANGUAGE!
BEASTMEN LANGUAGES ARE DIFFICULT.
THERE ARE SOME EXCEPTIONS, BUT MOST WORDS ARE INGRESSIVE, PRONOUNCED WHILE INHALING.
WITH THE LIMITATIONS OF HUMAN VOCAL CHORDS, OUR PRONUNCIATION IS APPARENTLY CLUMSY, BUT AS LONG AS I SPEAK TO THEM SINCERELY...
H...
H...
HELLO AND NITHE TO MEET YOU! MY NAME ITH HAKABA!

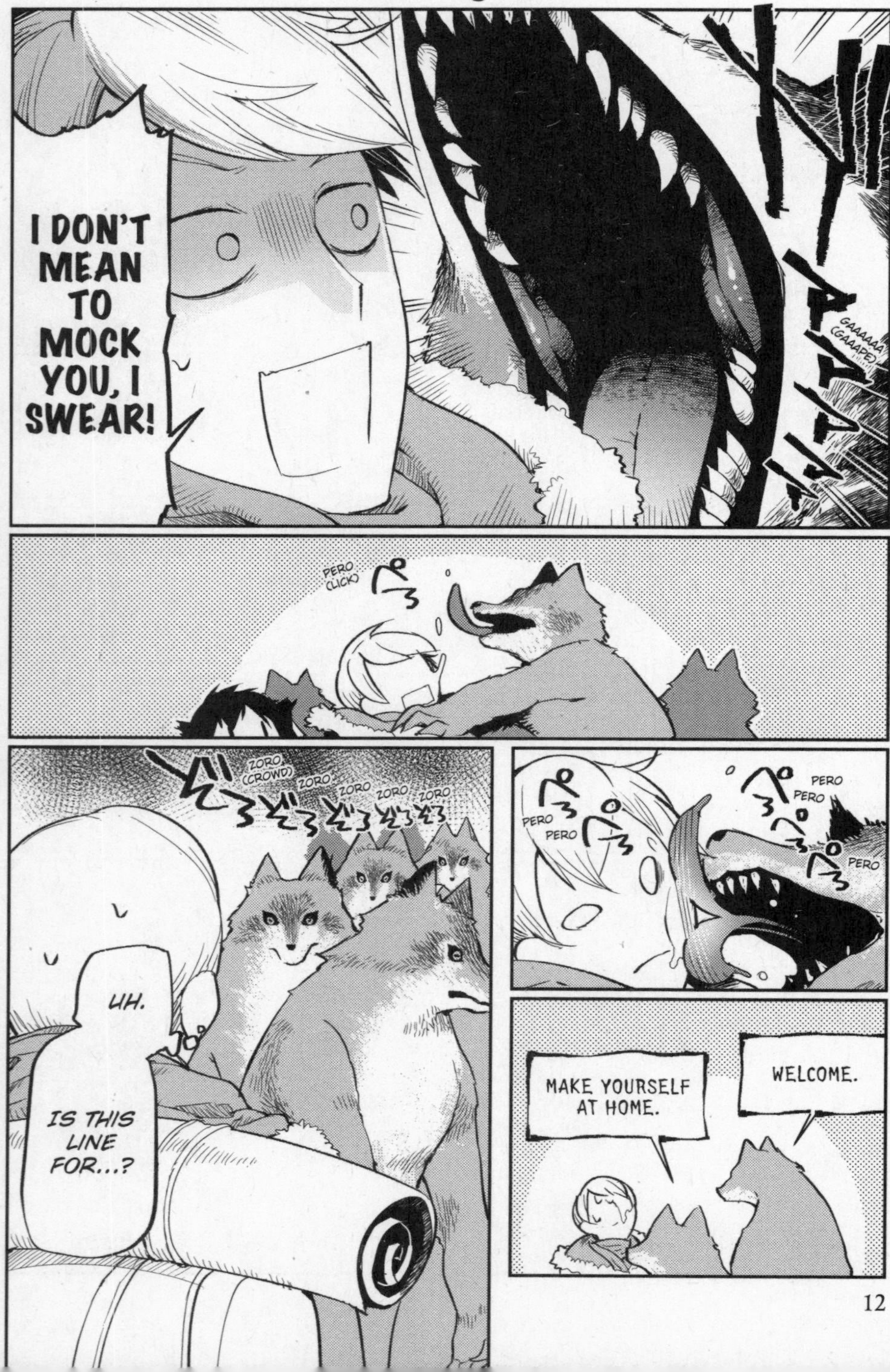
GAAAAAA (GAAAPE)
I DON'T MEAN TO MOCK YOU, I SWEAR!
PERO (LICK)
PERO PERO
PERO
PERO PERO
WELCOME.
MAKE YOURSELF AT HOME.
ZORO (CROWD)
ZORO
ZORO
ZORO
ZORO
UH.
IS THIS LINE FOR...?

Physical

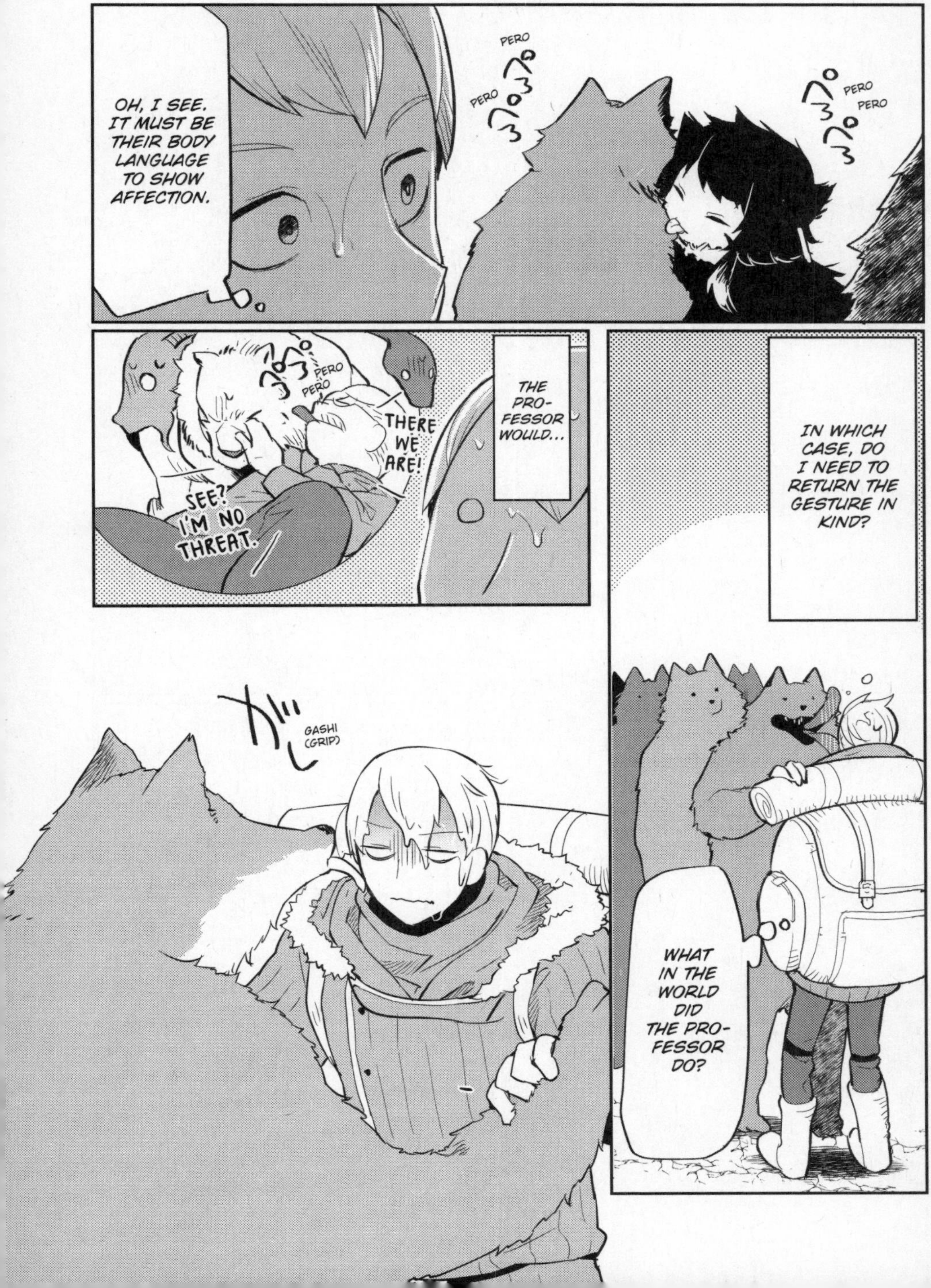
PERO
PERO
PERO
PERO
OH, I SEE. IT MUST BE THEIR BODY LANGUAGE TO SHOW AFFECTION.
IN WHICH CASE, DO I NEED TO RETURN THE GESTURE IN KIND?
WHAT IN THE WORLD DID THE PRO-FESSOR DO?
THE PRO-FESSOR WOULD...
PERO
PERO
THERE WE ARE!
SEE? I'M NO THREAT.
GASHI (GRIP)

Even Higher

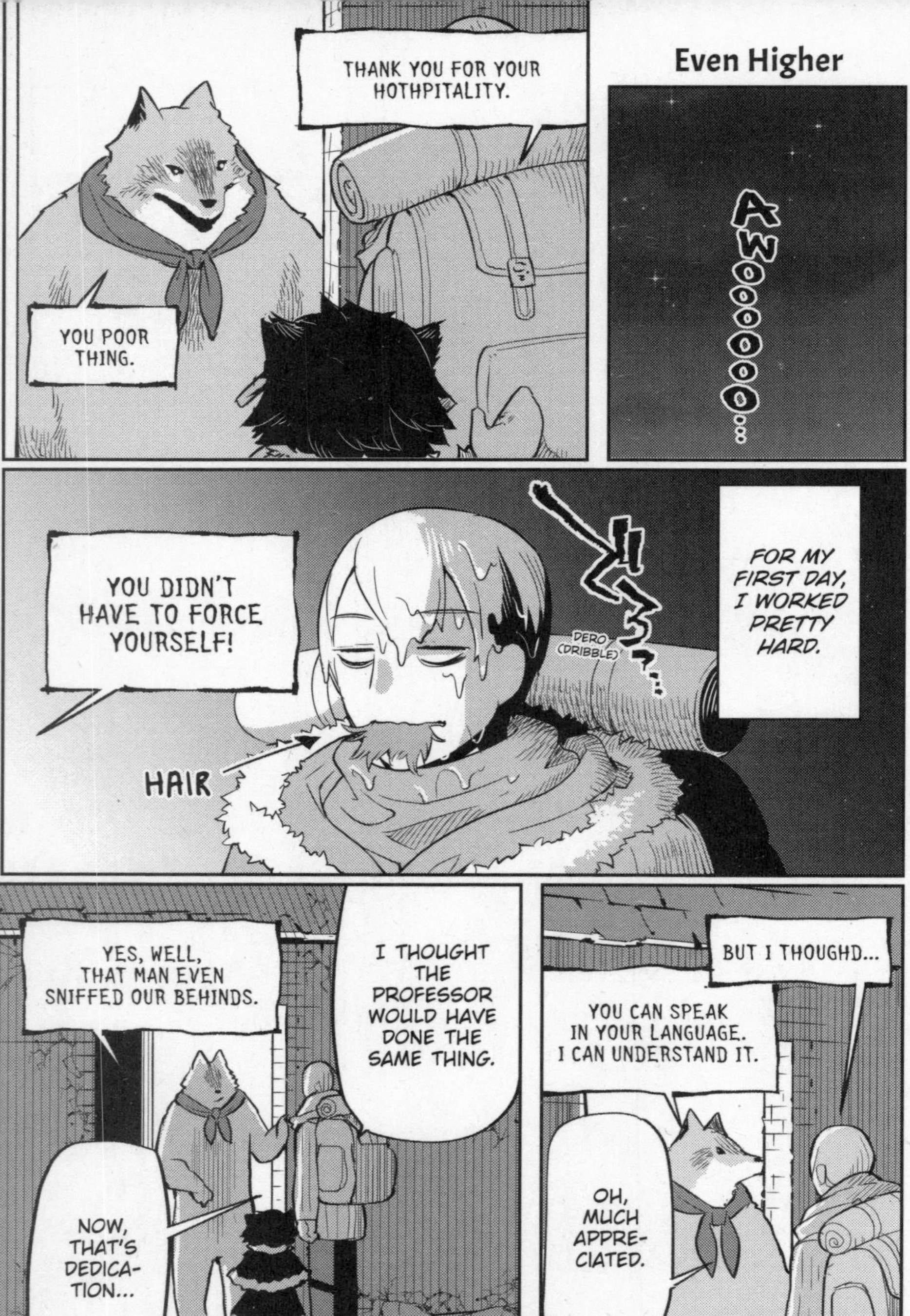
AWOOOOOOO...
THANK YOU FOR YOUR HOTHPITALITY.
YOU POOR THING.
FOR MY FIRST DAY, I WORKED PRETTY HARD.
DERO (DRIBBLE)
YOU DIDN'T HAVE TO FORCE YOURSELF!
HAIR
BUT I THOUGHD...
YOU CAN SPEAK IN YOUR LANGUAGE. I CAN UNDERSTAND IT.
OH, MUCH APPRECIATED.
I THOUGHT THE PROFESSOR WOULD HAVE DONE THE SAME THING.
YES, WELL, THAT MAN EVEN SNIFFED OUR BEHINDS.
NOW, THAT'S DEDICATION...

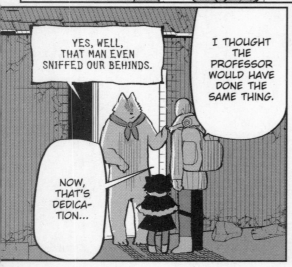

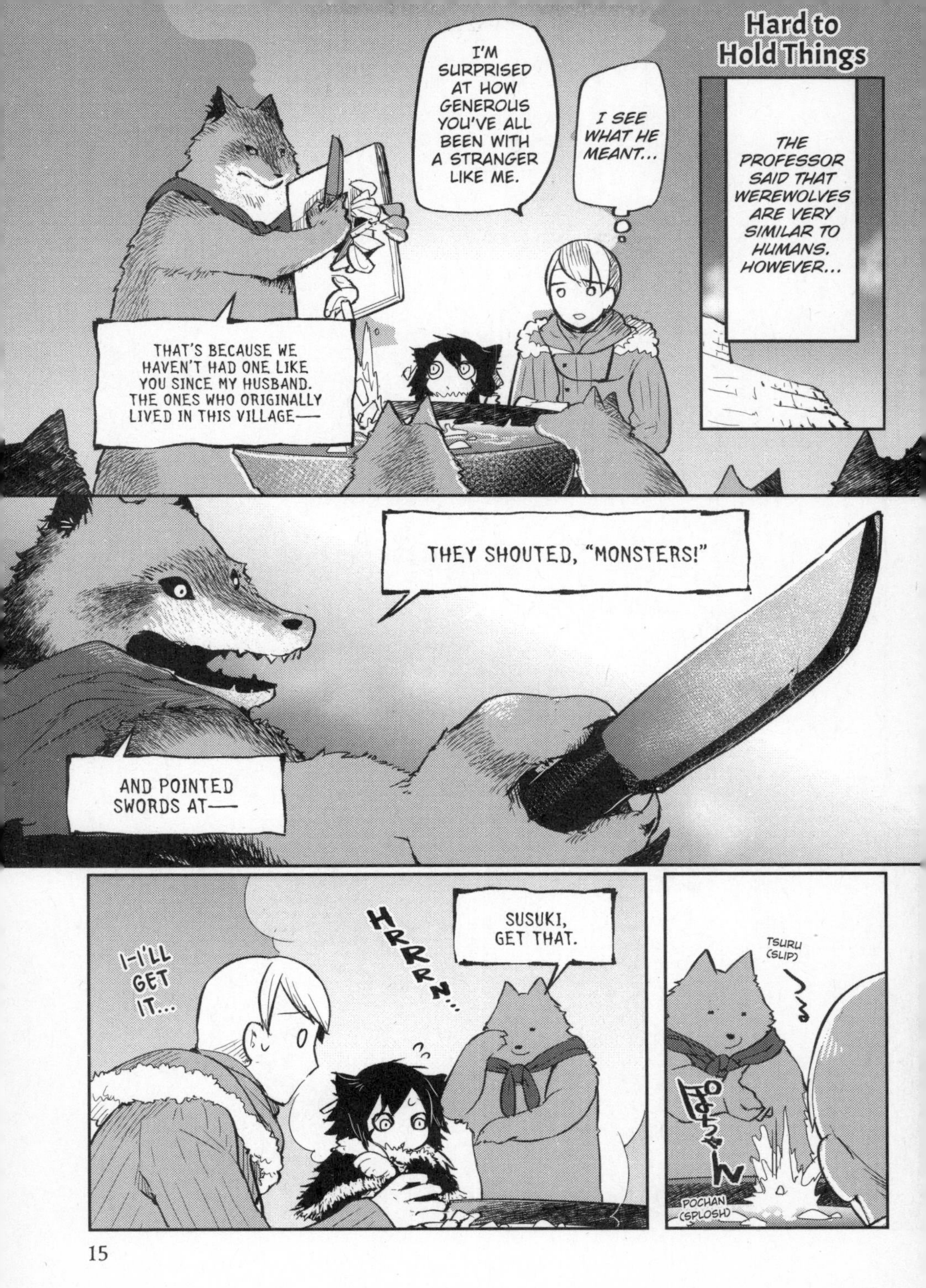
Hard to Hold Things
THE PROFESSOR SAID THAT WEREWOLVES ARE VERY SIMILAR TO HUMANS. HOWEVER...
I SEE WHAT HE MEANT...
I'M SURPRISED AT HOW GENEROUS YOU'VE ALL BEEN WITH A STRANGER LIKE ME.
THAT'S BECAUSE WE HAVEN'T HAD ONE LIKE YOU SINCE MY HUSBAND. THE ONES WHO ORIGINALLY LIVED IN THIS VILLAGE—
THEY SHOUTED, "MONSTERS!"
AND POINTED SWORDS AT—
TSURU (SLIP)
ぽちゃん
POCHAN (SPLOSH)
SUSUKI, GET THAT.
HRRRN...
I-I'LL GET IT...

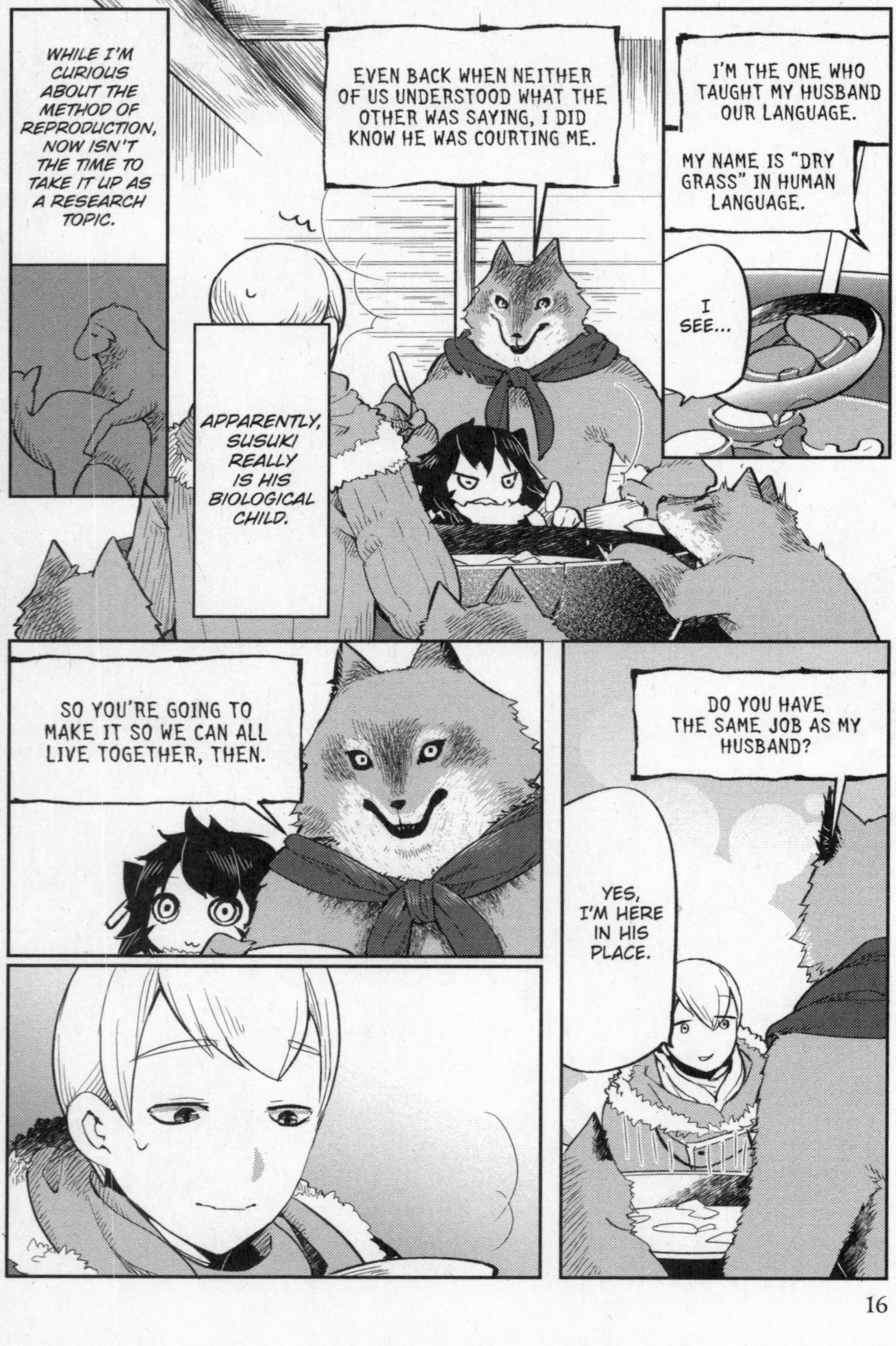
I'M THE ONE WHO TAUGHT MY HUSBAND OUR LANGUAGE.
MY NAME IS "DRY GRASS" IN HUMAN LANGUAGE.
I SEE...
EVEN BACK WHEN NEITHER OF US UNDERSTOOD WHAT THE OTHER WAS SAYING, I DID KNOW HE WAS COURTING ME.
APPARENTLY, SUSUKI REALLY IS HIS BIOLOGICAL CHILD.
WHILE I'M CURIOUS ABOUT THE METHOD OF REPRODUCTION, NOW ISN'T THE TIME TO TAKE IT UP AS A RESEARCH TOPIC.
DO YOU HAVE THE SAME JOB AS MY HUSBAND?
YES, I'M HERE IN HIS PLACE.
SO YOU'RE GOING TO MAKE IT SO WE CAN ALL LIVE TOGETHER, THEN.

Source of Fright

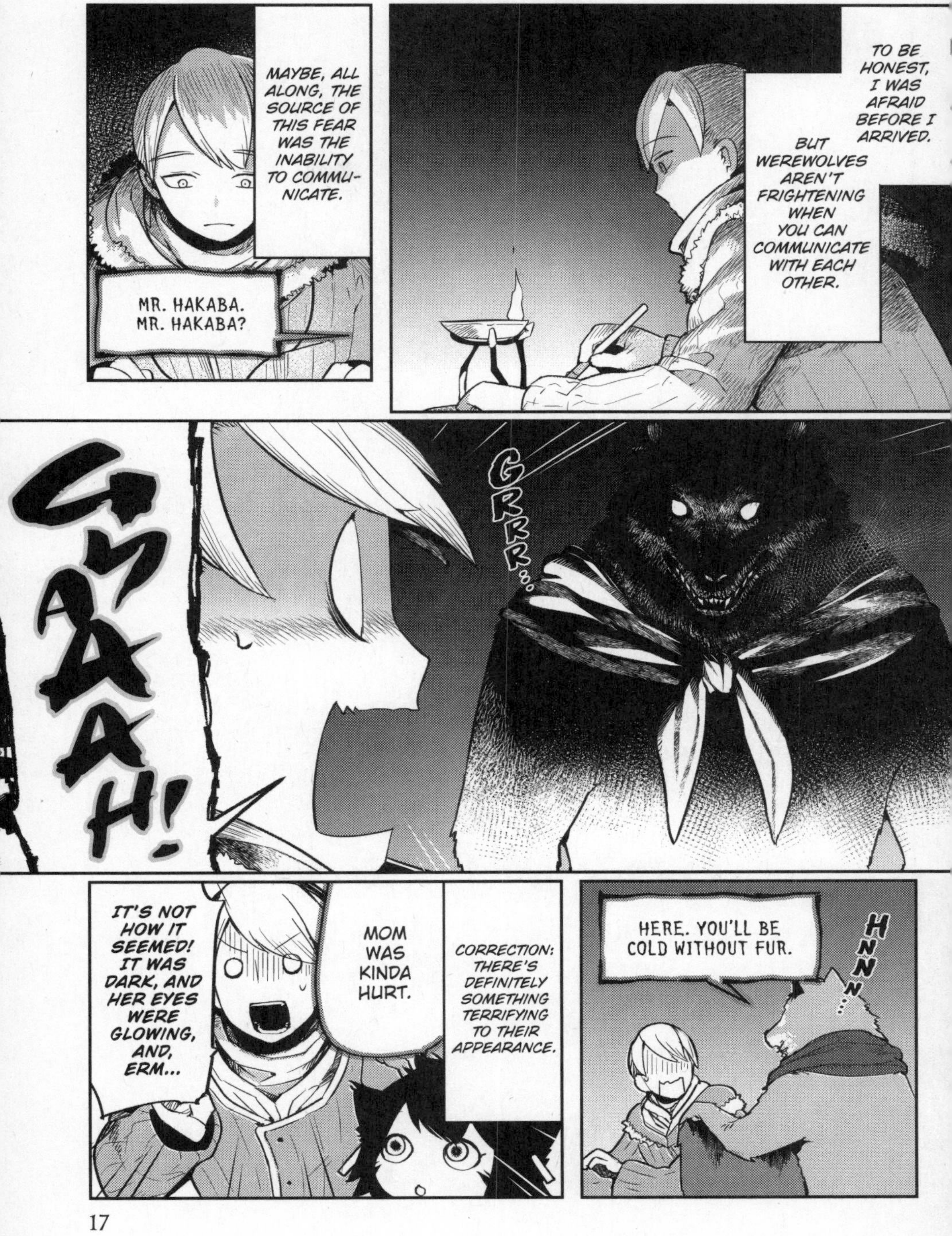
TO BE HONEST, I WAS AFRAID BEFORE I ARRIVED.
BUT WEREWOLVES AREN'T FRIGHTENING WHEN YOU CAN COMMUNICATE WITH EACH OTHER.
MAYBE, ALL ALONG, THE SOURCE OF THIS FEAR WAS THE INABILITY TO COMMUNICATE.
MR. HAKABA. MR. HAKABA?
GRRR..
GYAAAH!
HERE. YOU'LL BE COLD WITHOUT FUR.
HNNNN...
CORRECTION: THERE'S DEFINITELY SOMETHING TERRIFYING TO THEIR APPEARANCE.
MOM WAS KINDA HURT.
IT'S NOT HOW IT SEEMED! IT WAS DARK, AND HER EYES WERE GLOWING, AND, ERM...

Rules

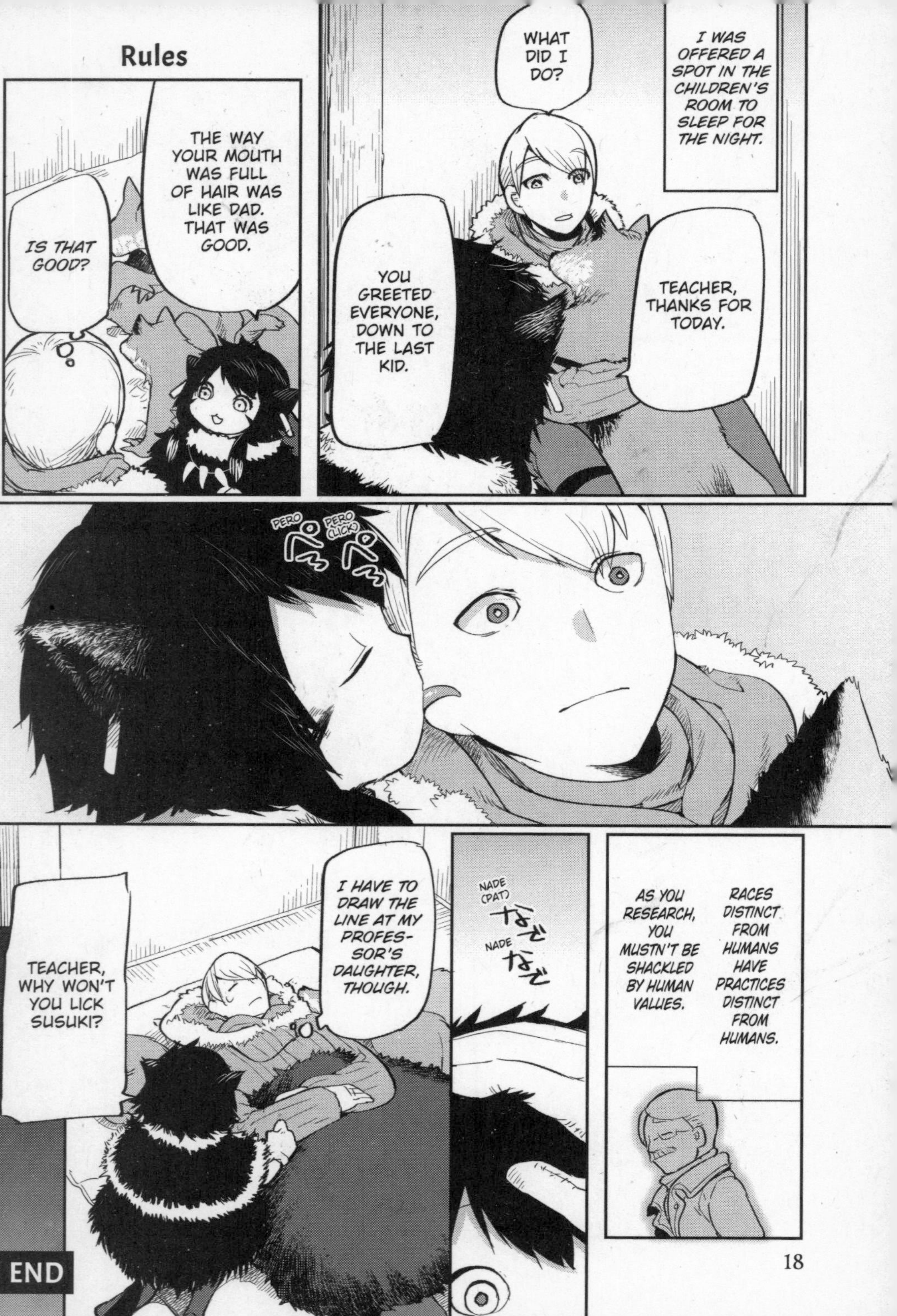
I WAS OFFERED A SPOT IN THE CHILDREN'S ROOM TO SLEEP FOR THE NIGHT.
WHAT DID I DO?
TEACHER, THANKS FOR TODAY.
YOU GREETED EVERYONE, DOWN TO THE LAST KID.
THE WAY YOUR MOUTH WAS FULL OF HAIR WAS LIKE DAD. THAT WAS GOOD.
IS THAT GOOD?
PERO PERO (LICK)
ぺろ ぺろ
RACES DISTINCT FROM HUMANS HAVE PRACTICES DISTINCT FROM HUMANS.
AS YOU RESEARCH, YOU MUSTN'T BE SHACKLED BY HUMAN VALUES.
NADE (PAT) NADE
なで なで
I HAVE TO DRAW THE LINE AT MY PROFES-SOR'S DAUGHTER, THOUGH.
TEACHER, WHY WON'T YOU LICK SUSUKI?
END

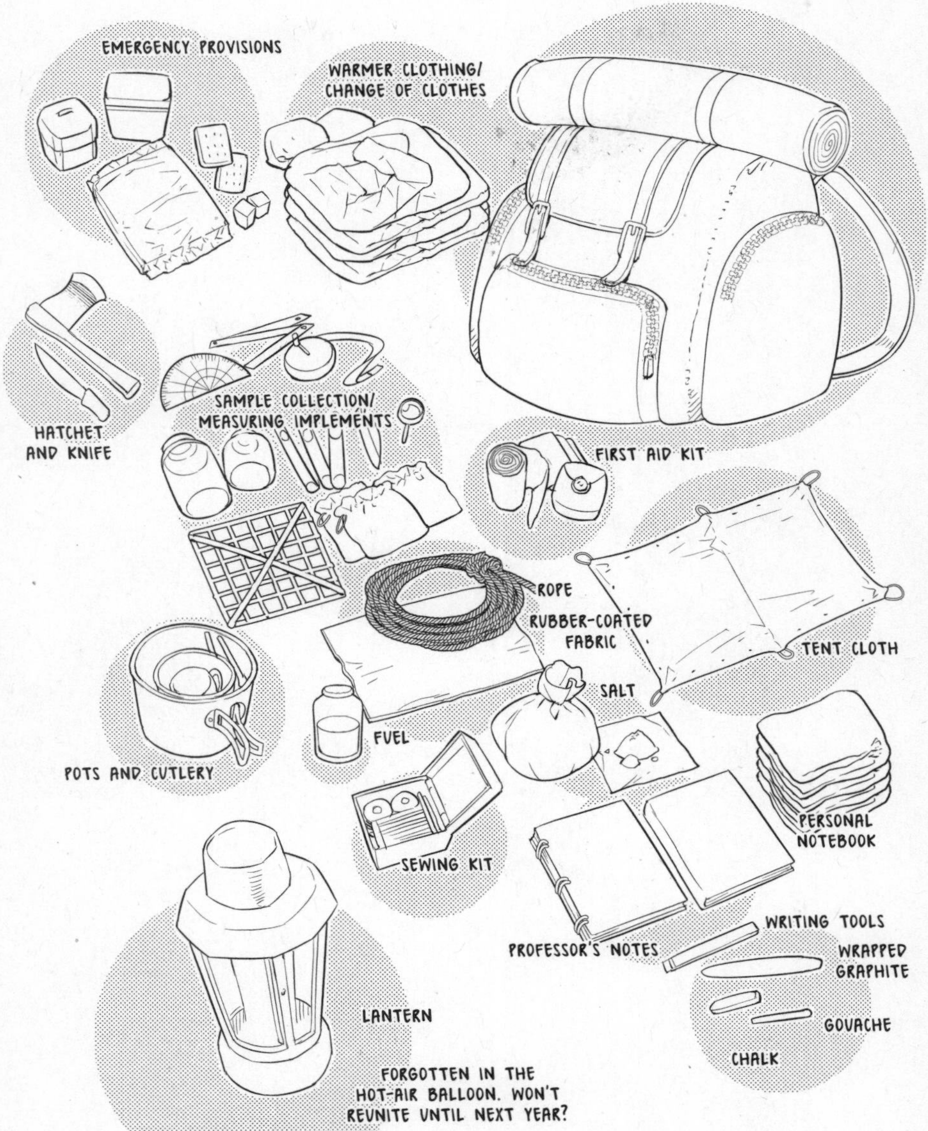
EMERGENCY PROVISIONS
WARMER CLOTHING/ CHANGE OF CLOTHES
HATCHET AND KNIFE
SAMPLE COLLECTION/ MEASURING IMPLEMENTS
FIRST AID KIT
ROPE
RUBBER-COATED FABRIC
TENT CLOTH
SALT
FUEL
POTS AND CUTLERY
SEWING KIT
PERSONAL NOTEBOOK
PROFESSOR'S NOTES
WRITING TOOLS
WRAPPED GRAPHITE
GOUACHE
CHALK
LANTERN
FORGOTTEN IN THE HOT-AIR BALLOON. WON'T REUNITE UNTIL NEXT YEAR?

WHAT WE ATE FOR DINNER—

A SOUP OF MUSHROOMS, DRIED FISH, AND AN UNFAMILIAR PLANT (SIMILAR TO SEAWEED).

THE NEXT DAY, THE WEREWOLVES, APART FROM SUSUKI, DRANK A SOUP THAT HAD BEEN COOKED SO LONG THAT ALL THE INGREDIENTS HAD LOST THEIR SHAPE.

CLUMP OF ROCK SALT ON A SHELF ON THE CENTRAL PILLAR

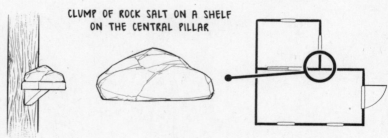

SHE MADE THEM LICK IT BEFORE BED.

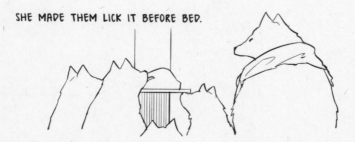

LOG 2

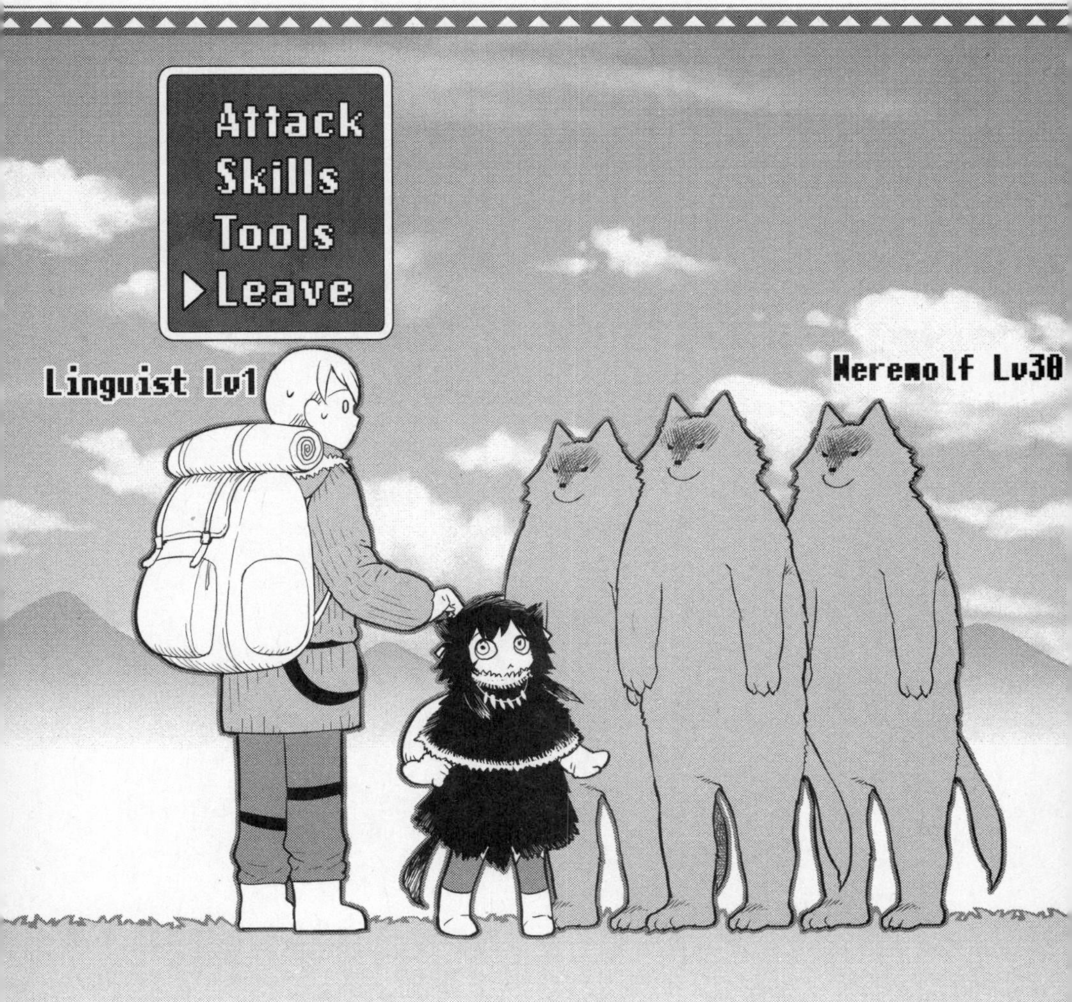
Attack
Skills
Tools
▶Leave
Werewolf Lv30
Linguist Lv1

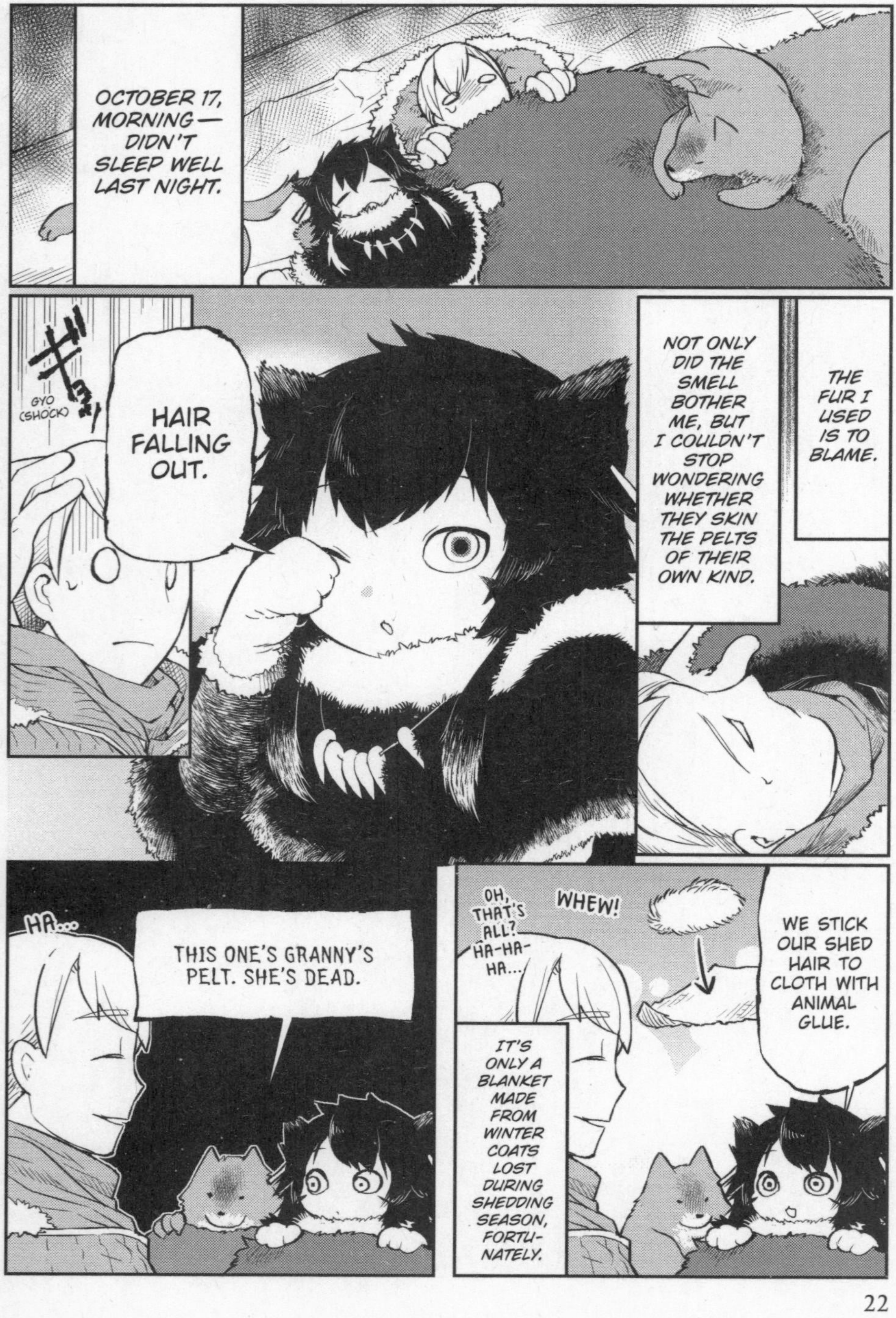
OCTOBER 17, MORNING— DIDN'T SLEEP WELL LAST NIGHT.
THE FUR I USED IS TO BLAME.
NOT ONLY DID THE SMELL BOTHER ME, BUT I COULDN'T STOP WONDERING WHETHER THEY SKIN THE PELTS OF THEIR OWN KIND.
GYO (SHOCK)
HAIR FALLING OUT.
WE STICK OUR SHED HAIR TO CLOTH WITH ANIMAL GLUE.
WHEW!
OH, THAT'S ALL? HA-HA-HA...
IT'S ONLY A BLANKET MADE FROM WINTER COATS LOST DURING SHEDDING SEASON, FORTUNATELY.
HA...
THIS ONE'S GRANNY'S PELT. SHE'S DEAD.

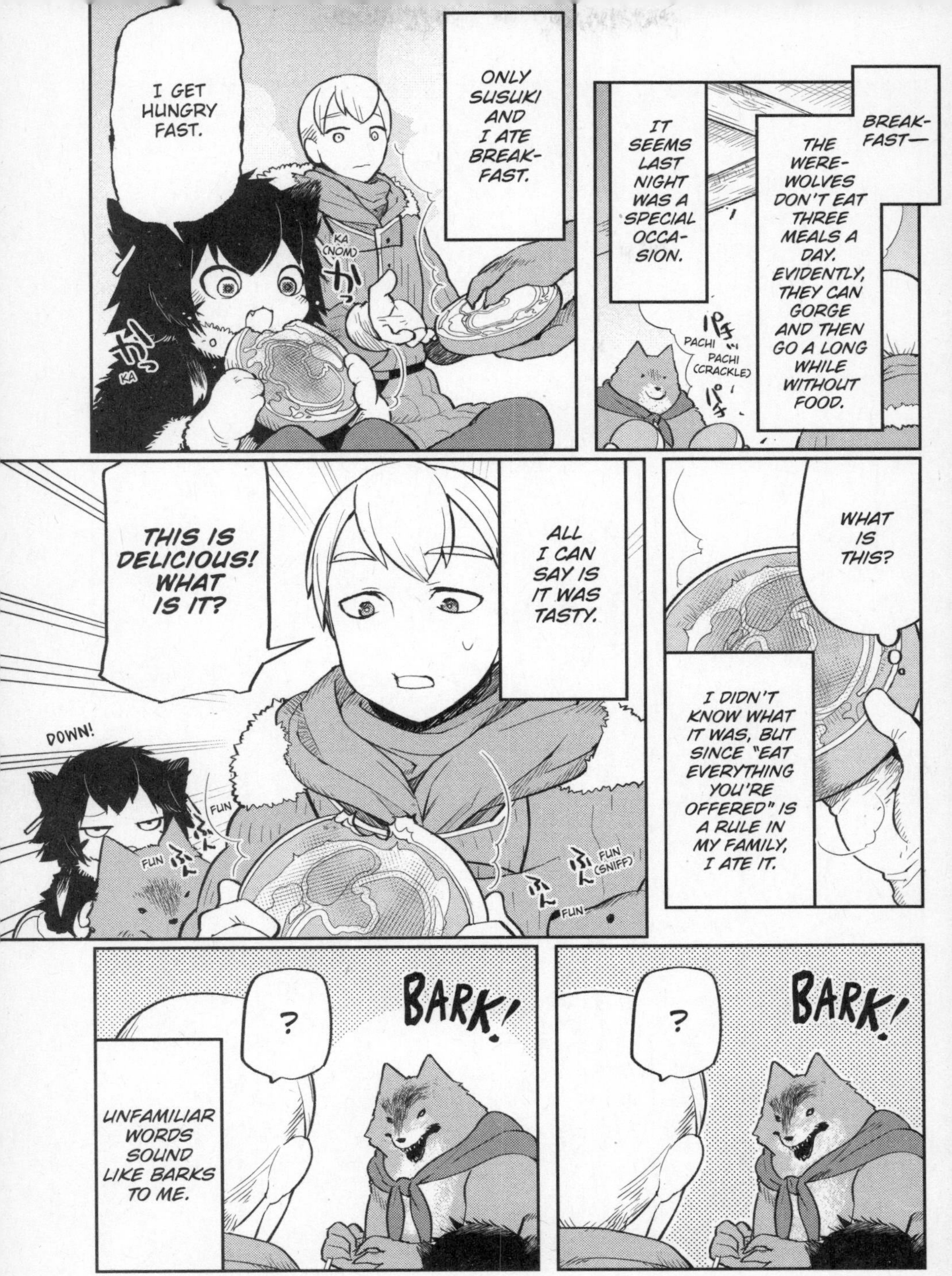
BREAKFAST—
THE WEREWOLVES DON'T EAT THREE MEALS A DAY. EVIDENTLY, THEY CAN GORGE AND THEN GO A LONG WHILE WITHOUT FOOD.
IT SEEMS LAST NIGHT WAS A SPECIAL OCCASION.
PACHI PACHI (CRACKLE)
ONLY SUSUKI AND I ATE BREAKFAST.
I GET HUNGRY FAST.
KA (NOM)
KA
WHAT IS THIS?
I DIDN'T KNOW WHAT IT WAS, BUT SINCE "EAT EVERYTHING YOU'RE OFFERED" IS A RULE IN MY FAMILY, I ATE IT.
ALL I CAN SAY IS IT WAS TASTY.
THIS IS DELICIOUS! WHAT IS IT?
FUN (SNIFF)
FUN
FUN
FUN
DOWN!
BARK!
?
BARK!
?
UNFAMILIAR WORDS SOUND LIKE BARKS TO ME.

Quiet

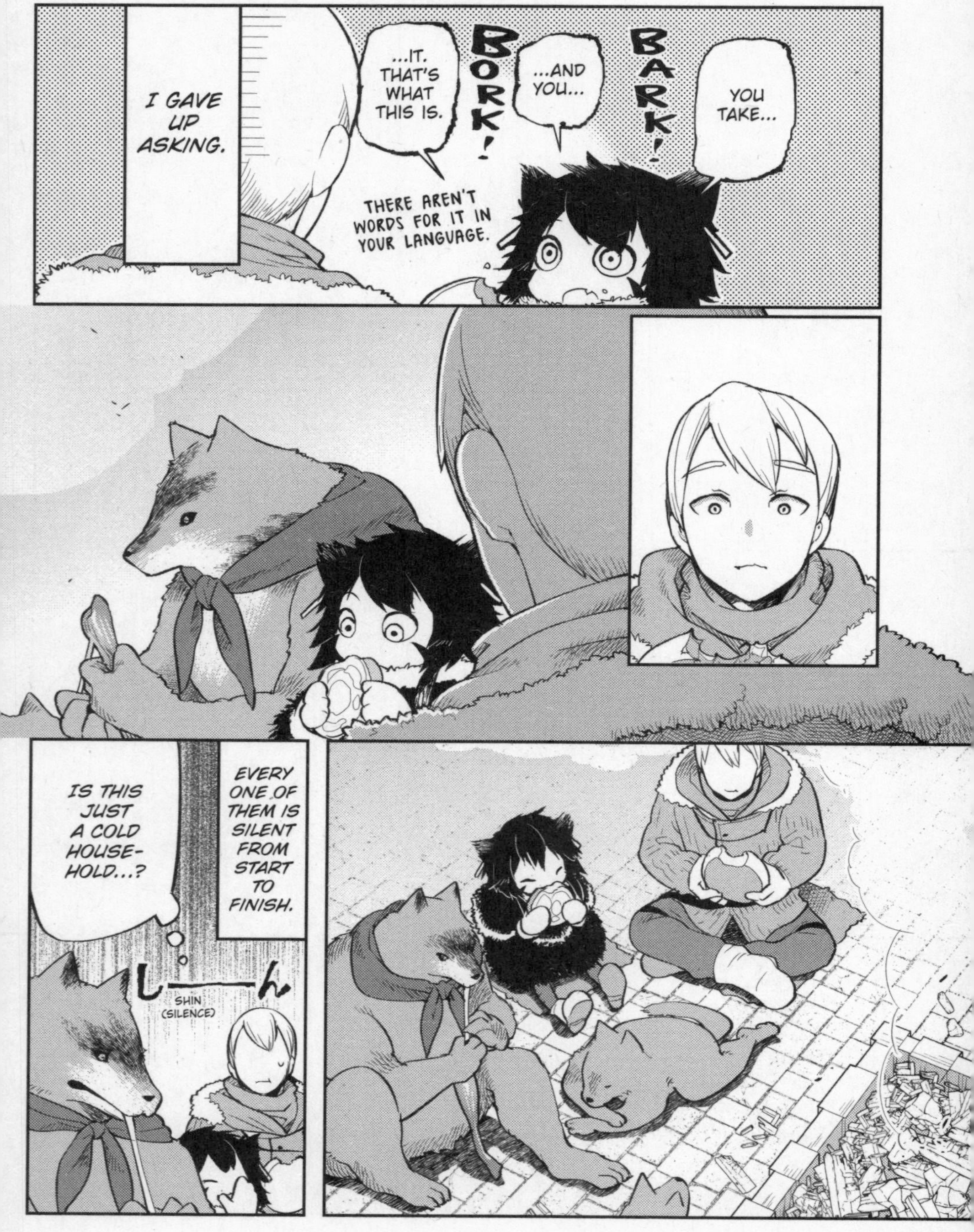
YOU TAKE...
BARK!
...AND YOU...
BORK!
...IT. THAT'S WHAT THIS IS.
THERE AREN'T WORDS FOR IT IN YOUR LANGUAGE.
I GAVE UP ASKING.
EVERY ONE OF THEM IS SILENT FROM START TO FINISH.
IS THIS JUST A COLD HOUSE-HOLD...?
しーん
SHIN (SILENCE)

Chilly Morning

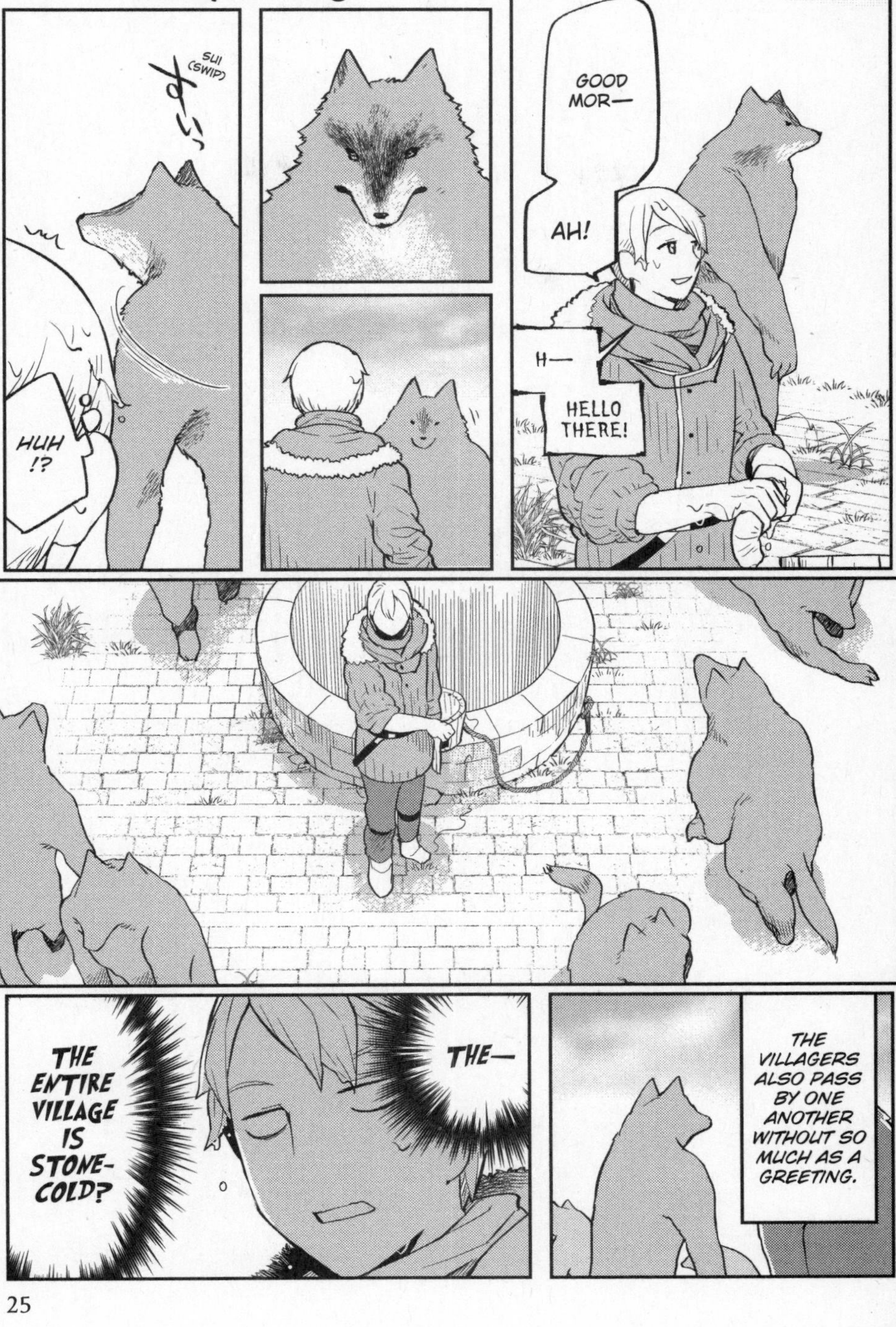
GOOD MOR—
AH!
H—
HELLO THERE!
すい
SUI (SWIP)
HUH !?
THE VILLAGERS ALSO PASS BY ONE ANOTHER WITHOUT SO MUCH AS A GREETING.
THE—
THE ENTIRE VILLAGE IS STONE-COLD?

Puzzling Approach

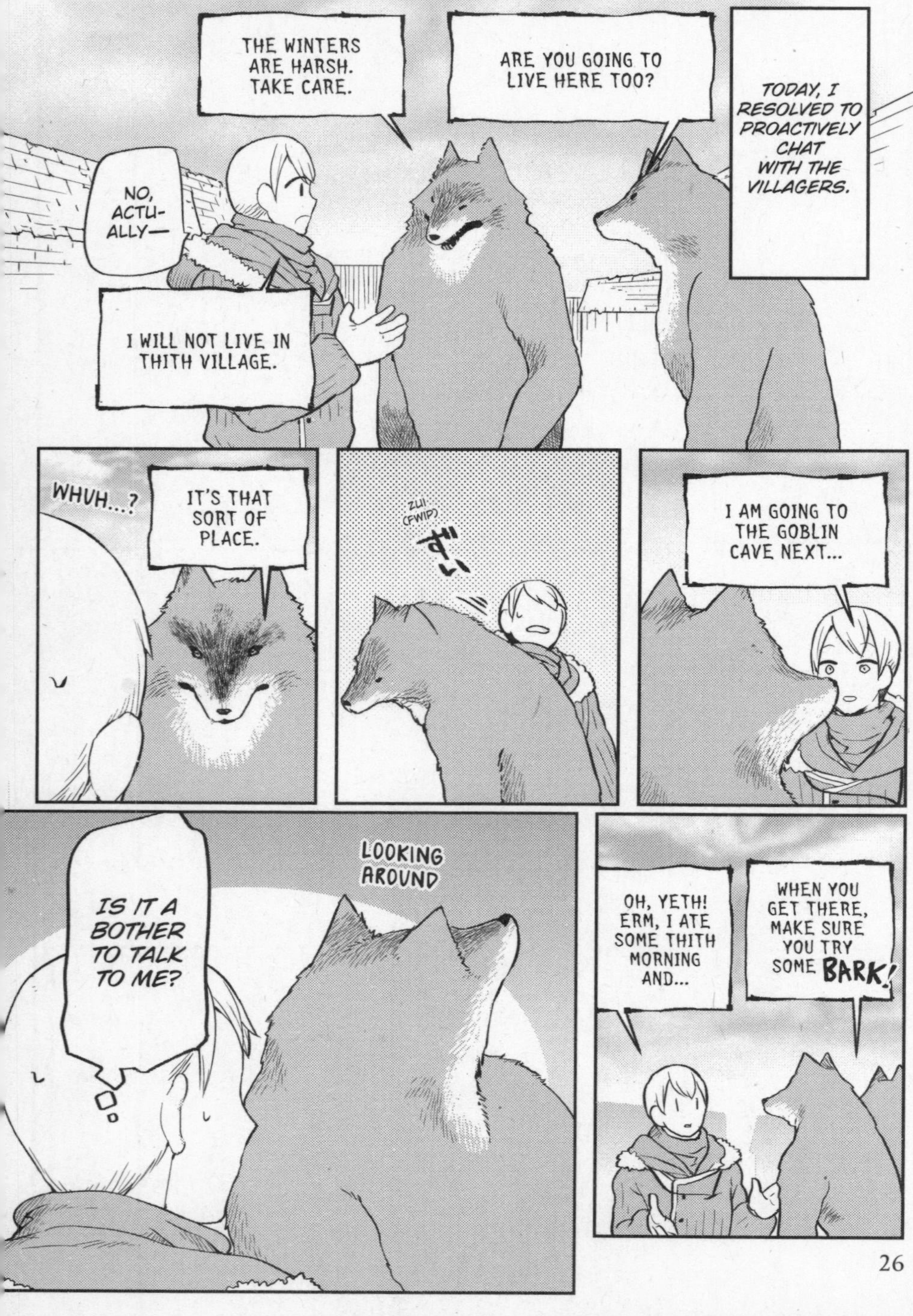
TODAY, I RESOLVED TO PROACTIVELY CHAT WITH THE VILLAGERS.
ARE YOU GOING TO LIVE HERE TOO?
THE WINTERS ARE HARSH. TAKE CARE.
NO, ACTU-ALLY—
I WILL NOT LIVE IN THITH VILLAGE.
I AM GOING TO THE GOBLIN CAVE NEXT...
ZUI (FWIP)
ずい
IT'S THAT SORT OF PLACE.
WHUH...?
WHEN YOU GET THERE, MAKE SURE YOU TRY SOME BARK!
OH, YETH! ERM, I ATE SOME THITH MORNING AND...
LOOKING AROUND
IS IT A BOTHER TO TALK TO ME?

Living Notes

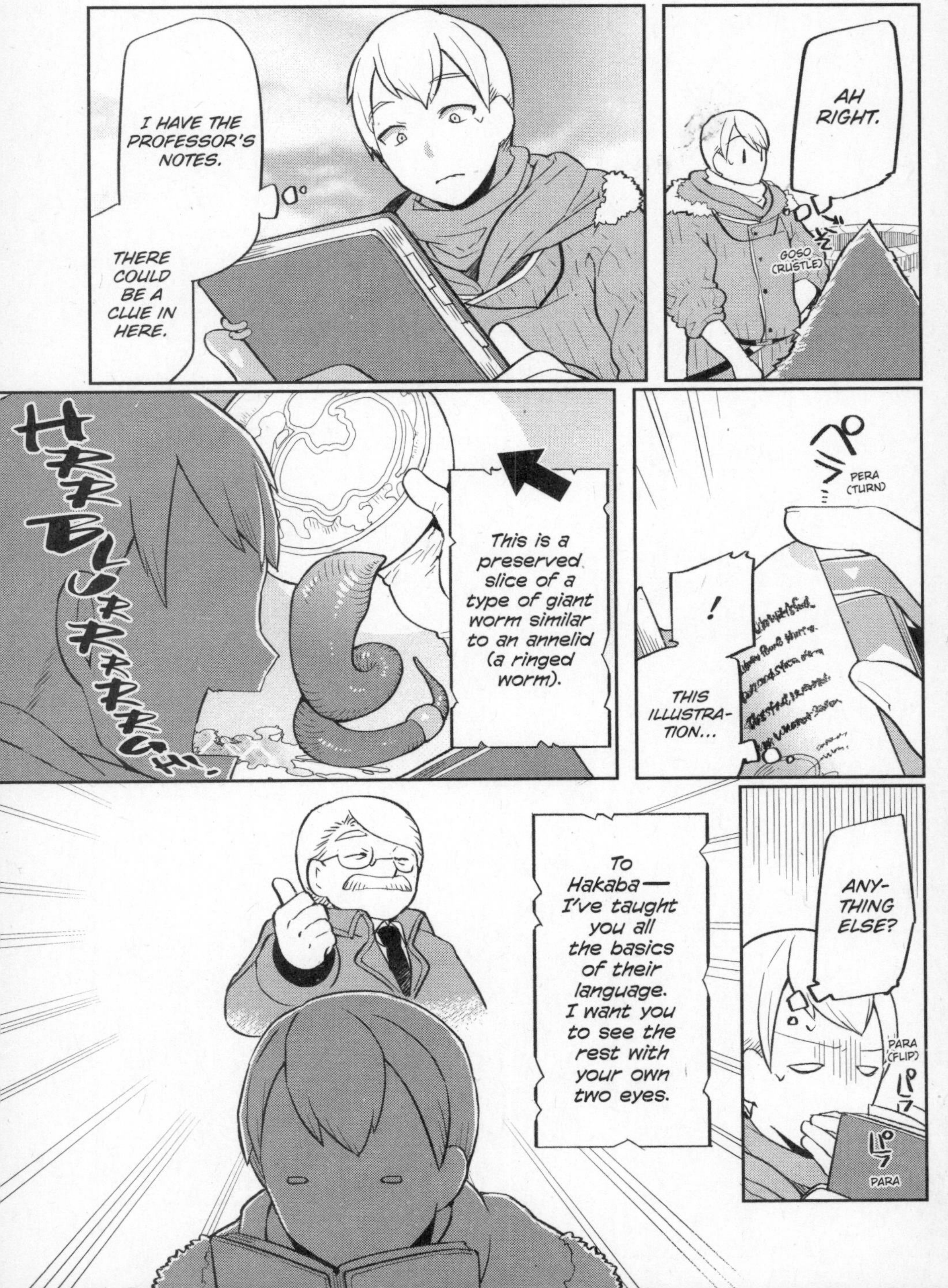
AH RIGHT.
GOSO (RUSTLE)
I HAVE THE PROFESSOR'S NOTES.
THERE COULD BE A CLUE IN HERE.
PERA (TURN)
!
THIS ILLUSTRATION...
This is a preserved slice of a type of giant worm similar to an annelid (a ringed worm).
HRRBLURRRRRRUGH!
ANYTHING ELSE?
PARA (FLIP)
PARA
To Hakaba— I've taught you all the basics of their language. I want you to see the rest with your own two eyes.

Inadequate

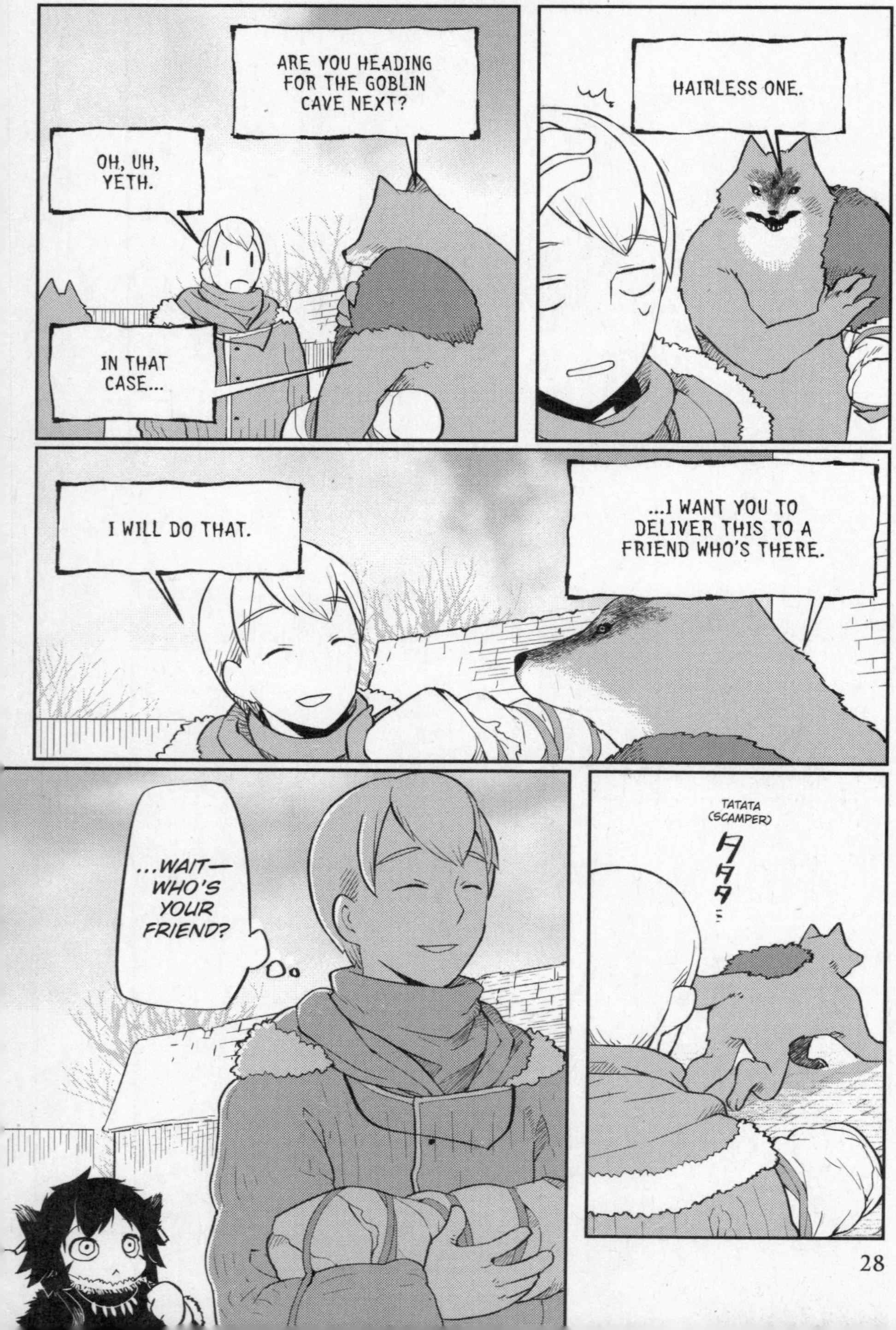
HAIRLESS ONE.
ARE YOU HEADING FOR THE GOBLIN CAVE NEXT?
OH, UH, YETH.
IN THAT CASE...
...I WANT YOU TO DELIVER THIS TO A FRIEND WHO'S THERE.
I WILL DO THAT.
TATATA (SCAMPER)
...WAIT— WHO'S YOUR FRIEND?

Do They Hate Talking?

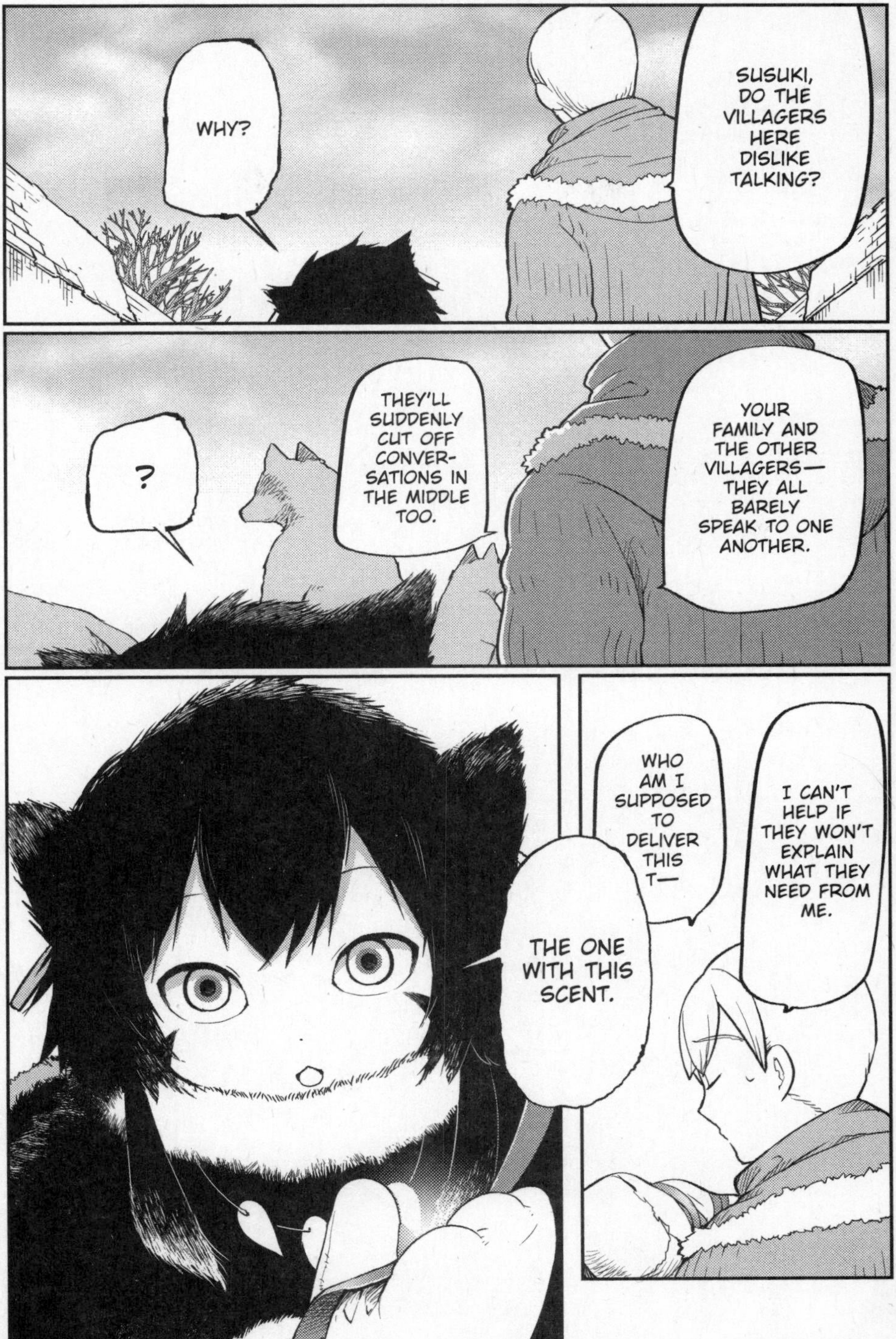
SUSUKI, DO THE VILLAGERS HERE DISLIKE TALKING?
WHY?
YOUR FAMILY AND THE OTHER VILLAGERS—THEY ALL BARELY SPEAK TO ONE ANOTHER.
THEY'LL SUDDENLY CUT OFF CONVER-SATIONS IN THE MIDDLE TOO.
?
I CAN'T HELP IF THEY WON'T EXPLAIN WHAT THEY NEED FROM ME.
WHO AM I SUPPOSED TO DELIVER THIS T—
THE ONE WITH THIS SCENT.

The Language of Smell

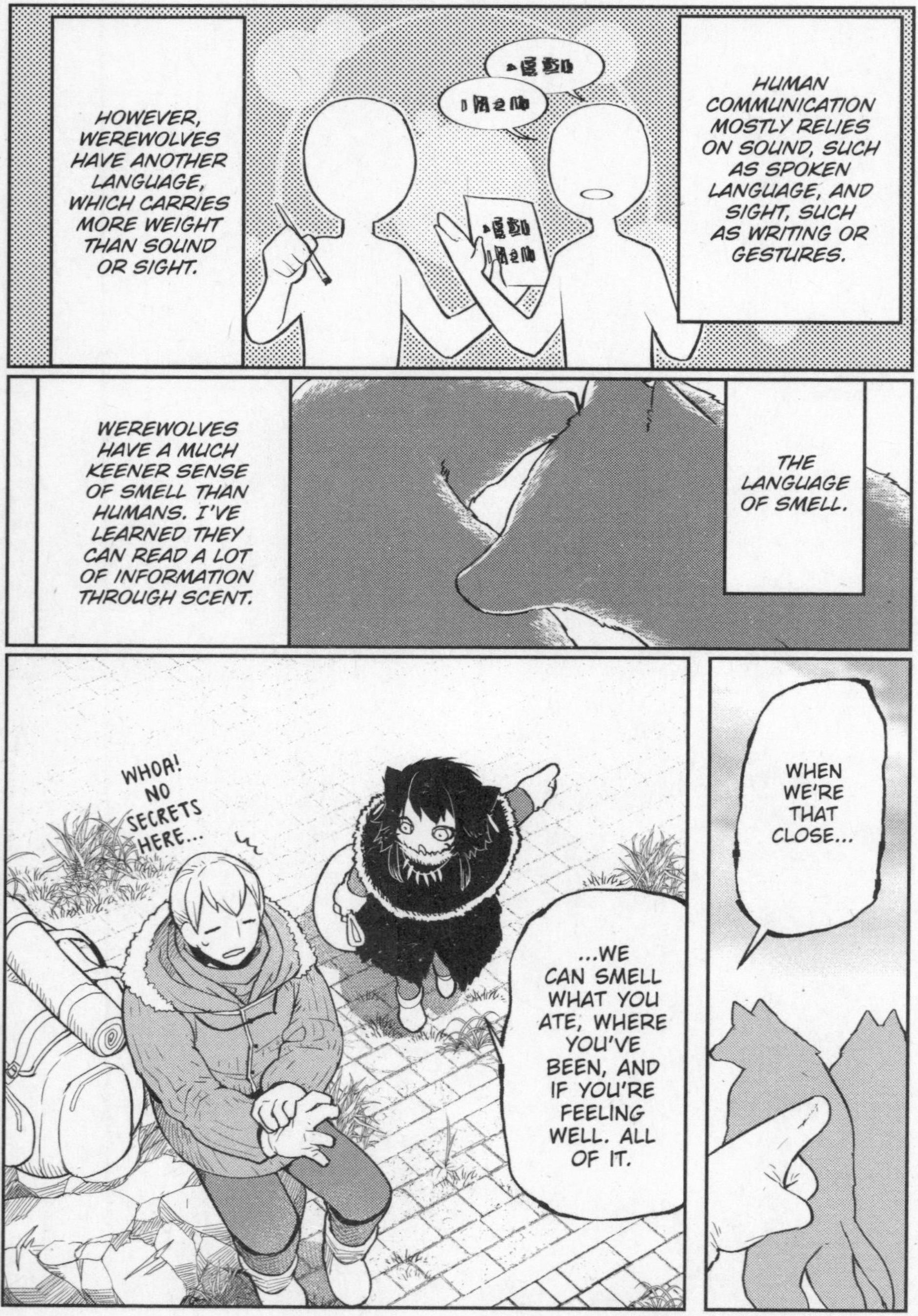
HUMAN COMMUNICATION MOSTLY RELIES ON SOUND, SUCH AS SPOKEN LANGUAGE, AND SIGHT, SUCH AS WRITING OR GESTURES.
HOWEVER, WEREWOLVES HAVE ANOTHER LANGUAGE, WHICH CARRIES MORE WEIGHT THAN SOUND OR SIGHT.
THE LANGUAGE OF SMELL.
WEREWOLVES HAVE A MUCH KEENER SENSE OF SMELL THAN HUMANS. I'VE LEARNED THEY CAN READ A LOT OF INFORMATION THROUGH SCENT.
WHEN WE'RE THAT CLOSE...
...WE CAN SMELL WHAT YOU ATE, WHERE YOU'VE BEEN, AND IF YOU'RE FEELING WELL. ALL OF IT.
WHOA! NO SECRETS HERE...

Lively Village

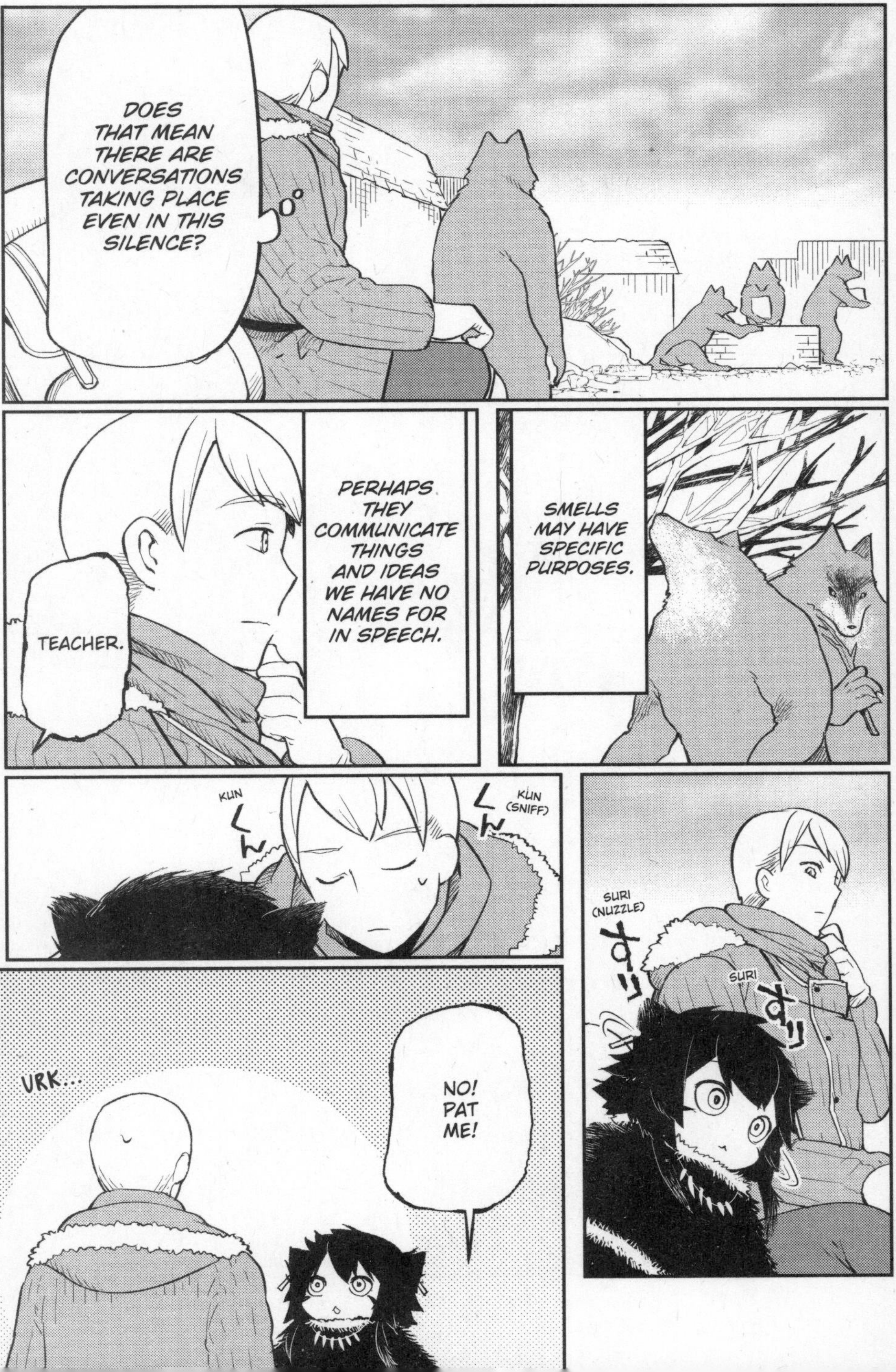
DOES THAT MEAN THERE ARE CONVERSATIONS TAKING PLACE EVEN IN THIS SILENCE?
SMELLS MAY HAVE SPECIFIC PURPOSES.
PERHAPS THEY COMMUNICATE THINGS AND IDEAS WE HAVE NO NAMES FOR IN SPEECH.
TEACHER.
SURI (NUZZLE)
SURI
KUN (SNIFF)
KUN
NO! PAT ME!
URK...

Send-Off

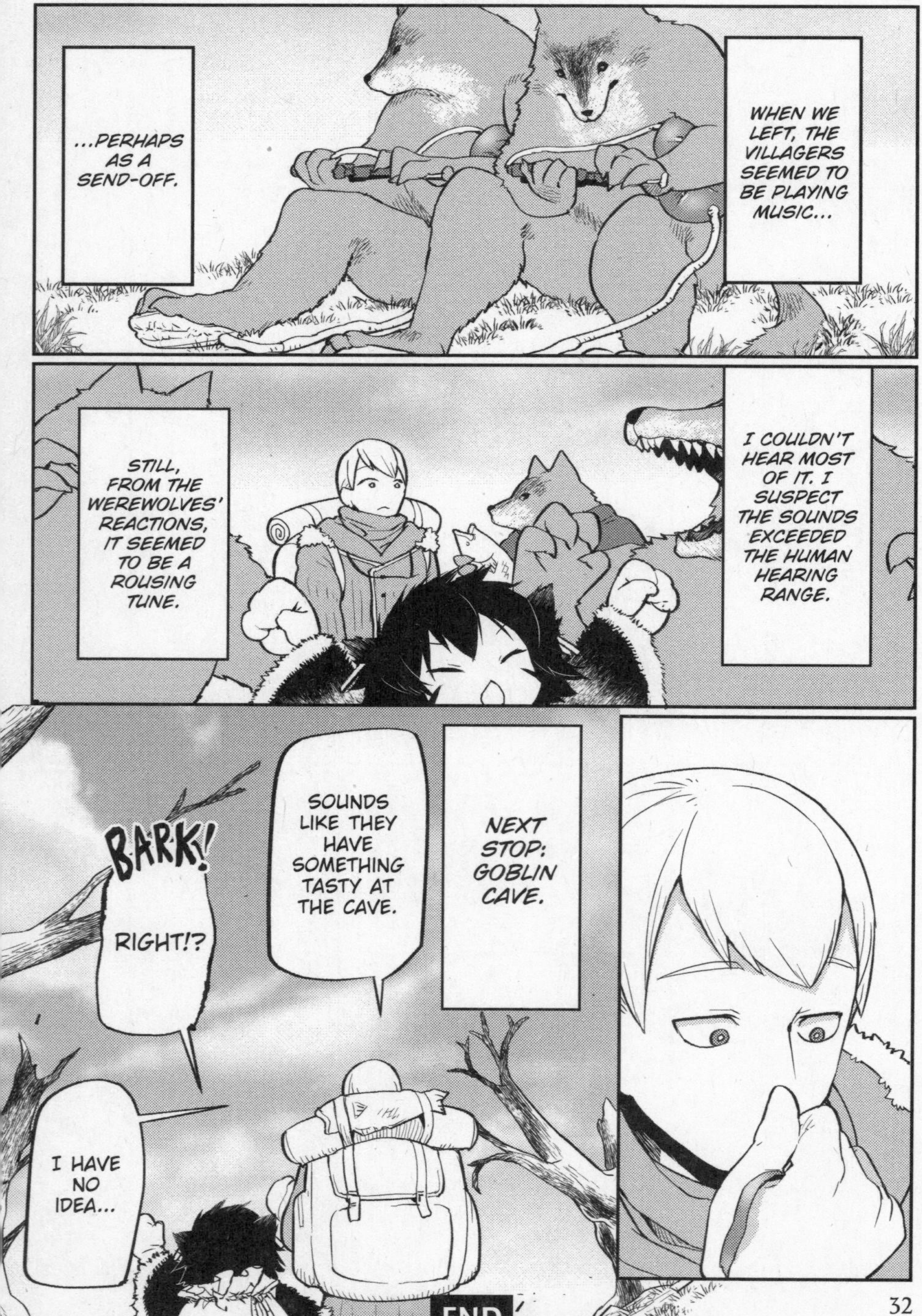
WHEN WE LEFT, THE VILLAGERS SEEMED TO BE PLAYING MUSIC...
...PERHAPS AS A SEND-OFF.
I COULDN'T HEAR MOST OF IT. I SUSPECT THE SOUNDS EXCEEDED THE HUMAN HEARING RANGE.
STILL, FROM THE WEREWOLVES' REACTIONS, IT SEEMED TO BE A ROUSING TUNE.
NEXT STOP: GOBLIN CAVE.
SOUNDS LIKE THEY HAVE SOMETHING TASTY AT THE CAVE.
BARK!
RIGHT!?
I HAVE NO IDEA...
END

THE WEREWOLVES' INSTRUMENTS (?)

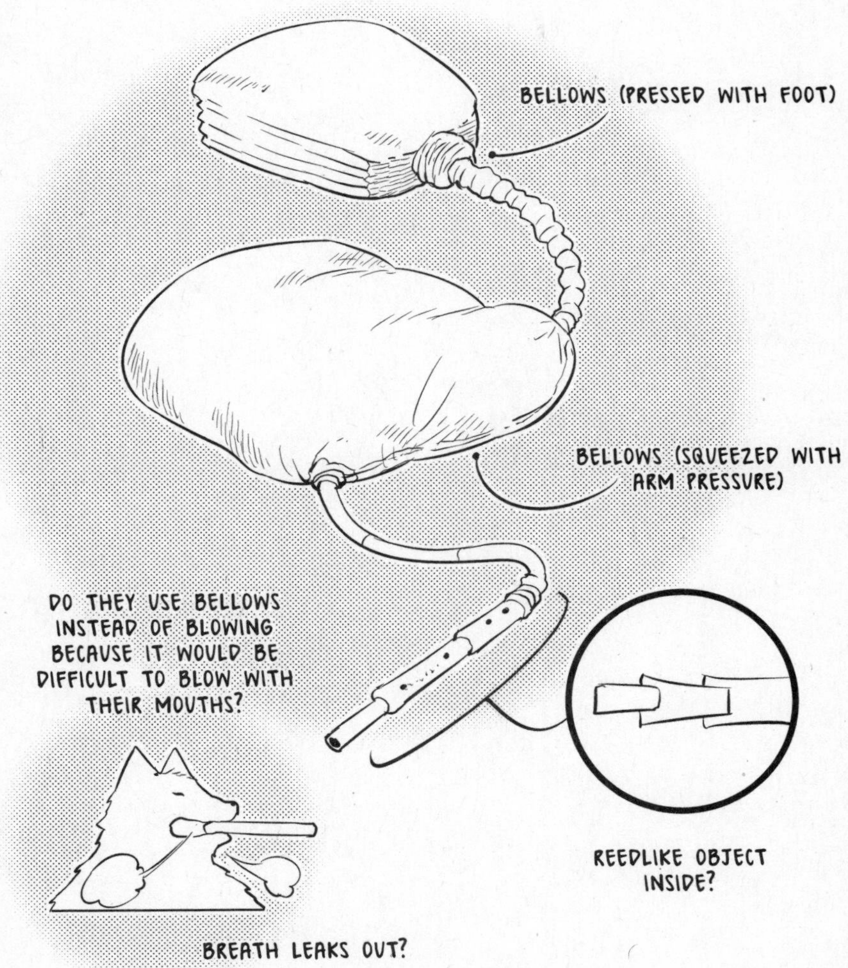
BELLOWS (PRESSED WITH FOOT)
BELLOWS (SQUEEZED WITH ARM PRESSURE)
DO THEY USE BELLOWS INSTEAD OF BLOWING BECAUSE IT WOULD BE DIFFICULT TO BLOW WITH THEIR MOUTHS?
REEDLIKE OBJECT INSIDE?
BREATH LEAKS OUT?

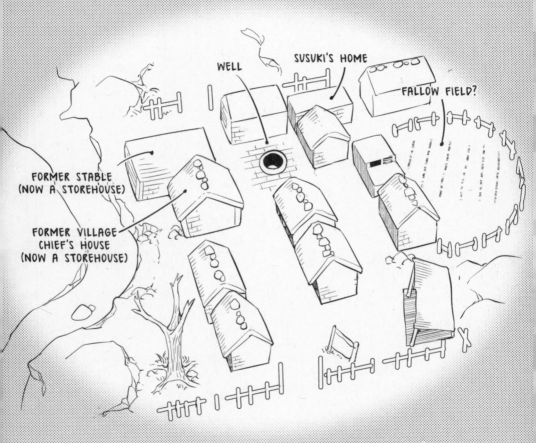

WELL

SUSUKI'S HOME

FALLOW FIELD?

FORMER STABLE
(NOW A STOREHOUSE)

FORMER VILLAGE
CHIEF'S HOUSE
(NOW A STOREHOUSE)

WEREWOLVES' VILLAGE

First Camp

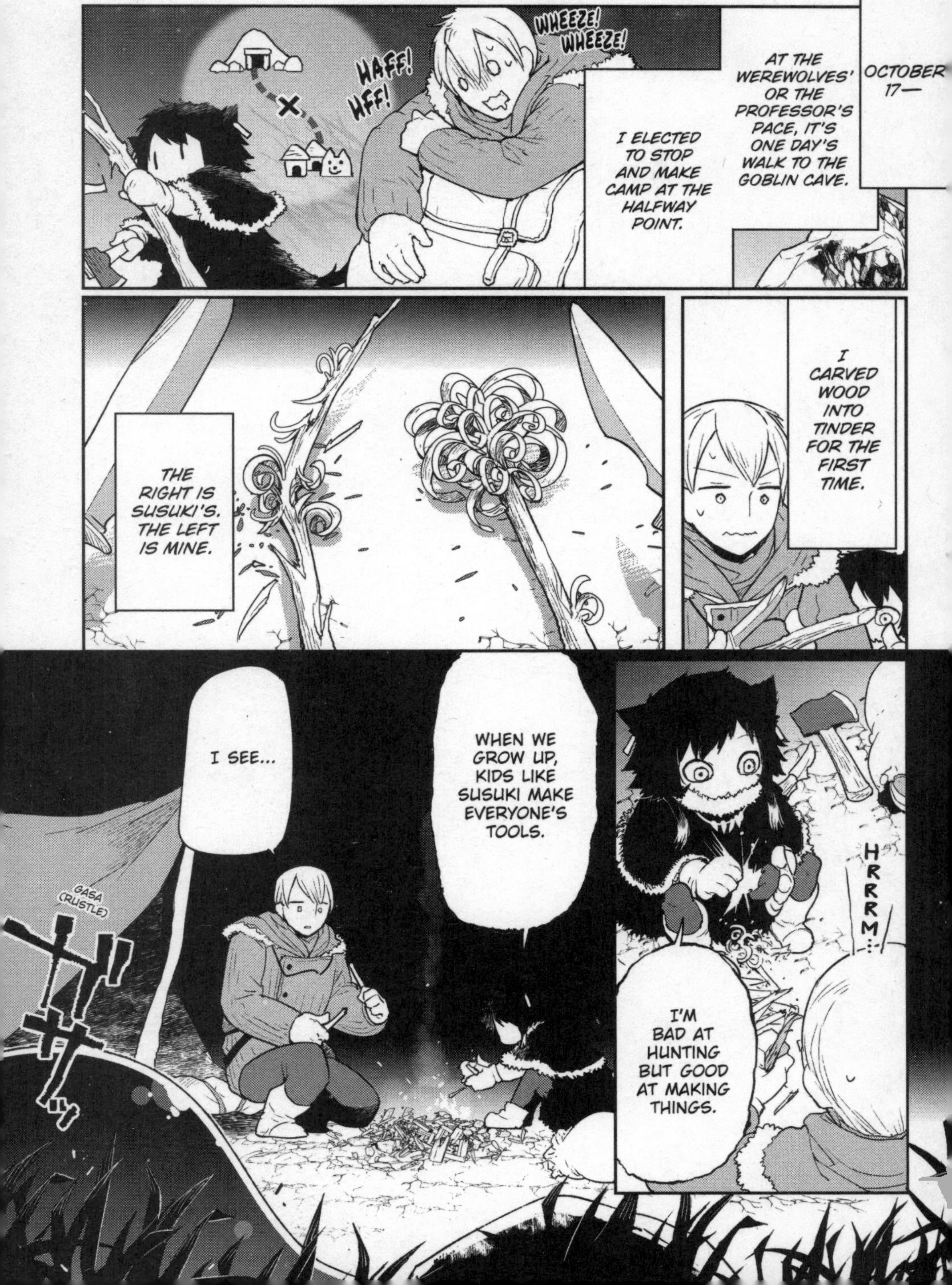
OCTOBER 17—
AT THE WEREWOLVES' OR THE PROFESSOR'S PACE, IT'S ONE DAY'S WALK TO THE GOBLIN CAVE.
I ELECTED TO STOP AND MAKE CAMP AT THE HALFWAY POINT.
WHEEZE! WHEEZE!
HAFF! HFF!
I CARVED WOOD INTO TINDER FOR THE FIRST TIME.
THE RIGHT IS SUSUKI'S. THE LEFT IS MINE.
HRRRM...
I'M BAD AT HUNTING BUT GOOD AT MAKING THINGS.
WHEN WE GROW UP, KIDS LIKE SUSUKI MAKE EVERYONE'S TOOLS.
I SEE...
GASA (RUSTLE)

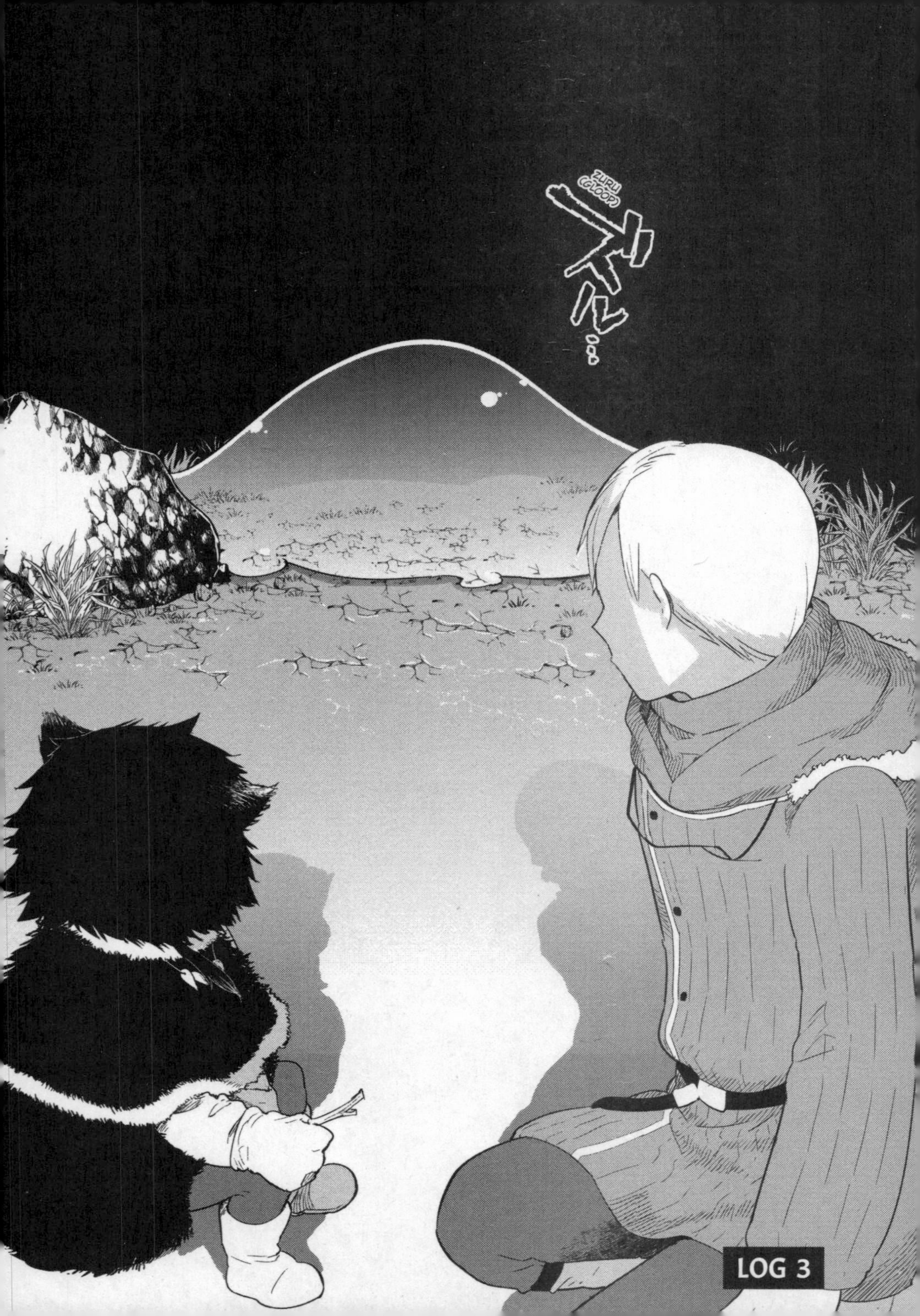
ズル…
ZURU (GLOOP)
LOG 3

Know-Water

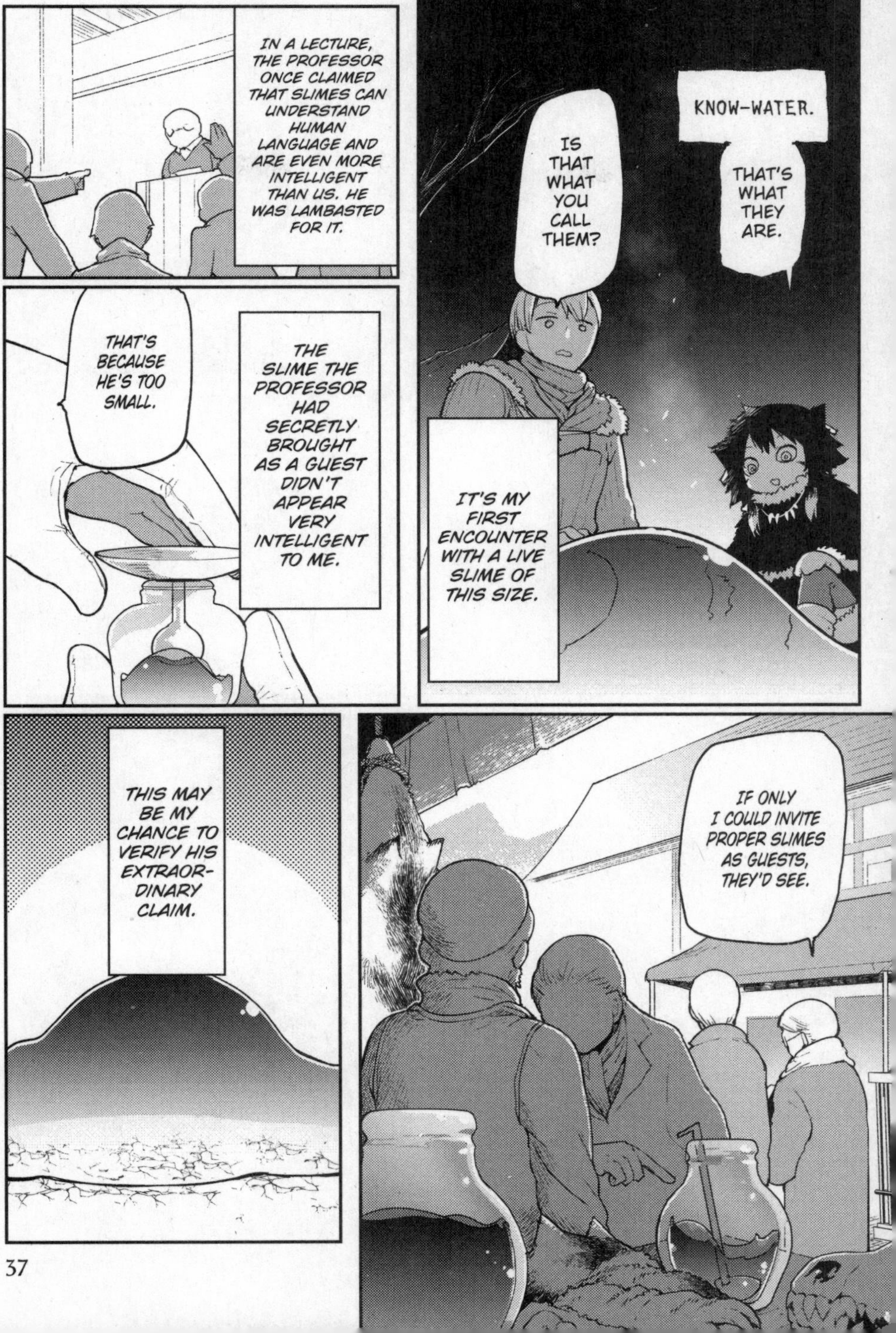
KNOW-WATER.
THAT'S WHAT THEY ARE.
IS THAT WHAT YOU CALL THEM?
IT'S MY FIRST ENCOUNTER WITH A LIVE SLIME OF THIS SIZE.
IN A LECTURE, THE PROFESSOR ONCE CLAIMED THAT SLIMES CAN UNDERSTAND HUMAN LANGUAGE AND ARE EVEN MORE INTELLIGENT THAN US. HE WAS LAMBASTED FOR IT.
THE SLIME THE PROFESSOR HAD SECRETLY BROUGHT AS A GUEST DIDN'T APPEAR VERY INTELLIGENT TO ME.
THAT'S BECAUSE HE'S TOO SMALL.
IF ONLY I COULD INVITE PROPER SLIMES AS GUESTS, THEY'D SEE.
THIS MAY BE MY CHANCE TO VERIFY HIS EXTRAOR-DINARY CLAIM.

Pleased to Meet You

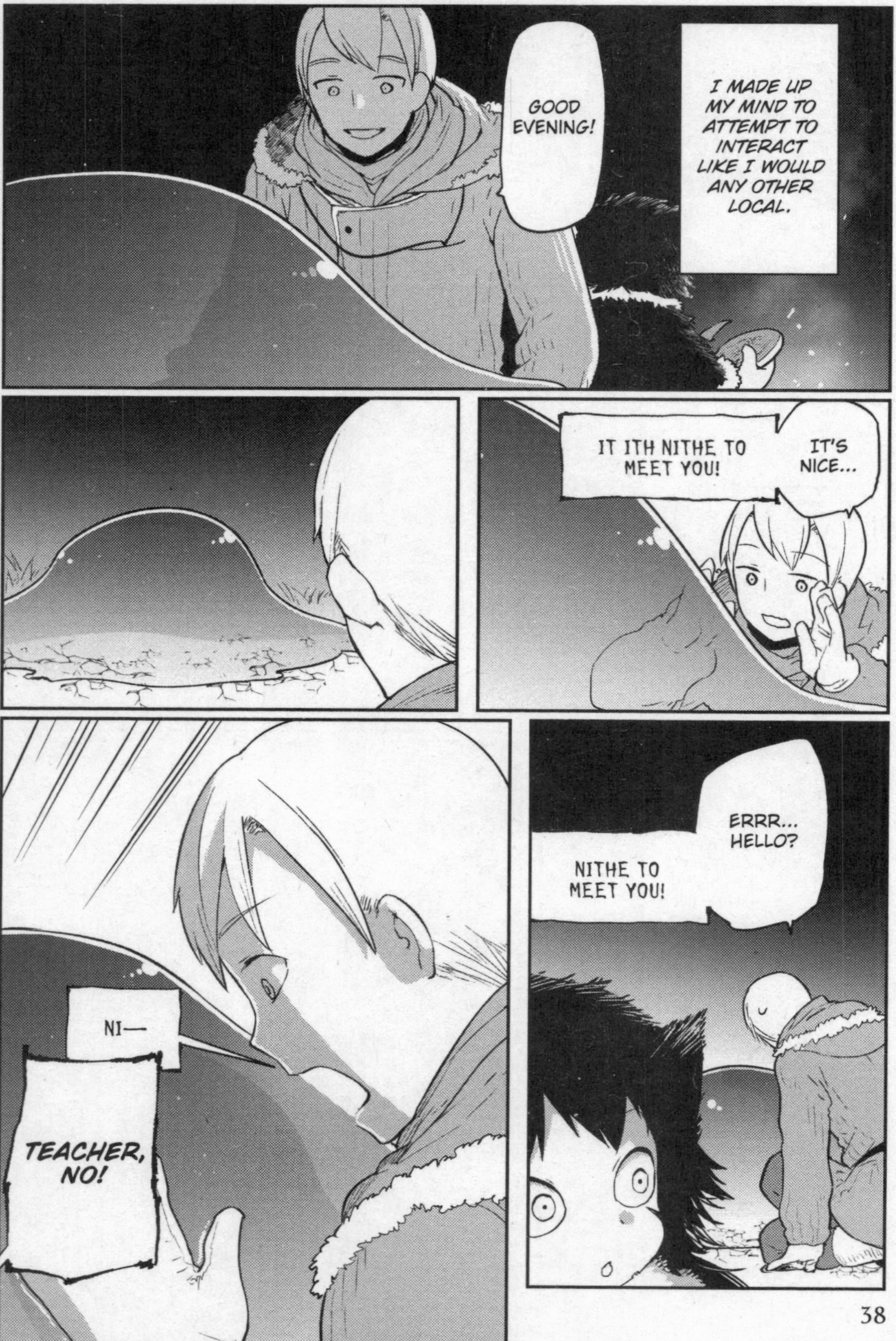
I MADE UP MY MIND TO ATTEMPT TO INTERACT LIKE I WOULD ANY OTHER LOCAL.
GOOD EVENING!
IT'S NICE...
IT ITH NITHE TO MEET YOU!
ERRR... HELLO?
NITHE TO MEET YOU!
NI—
TEACHER, NO!

By a Hair's Breadth

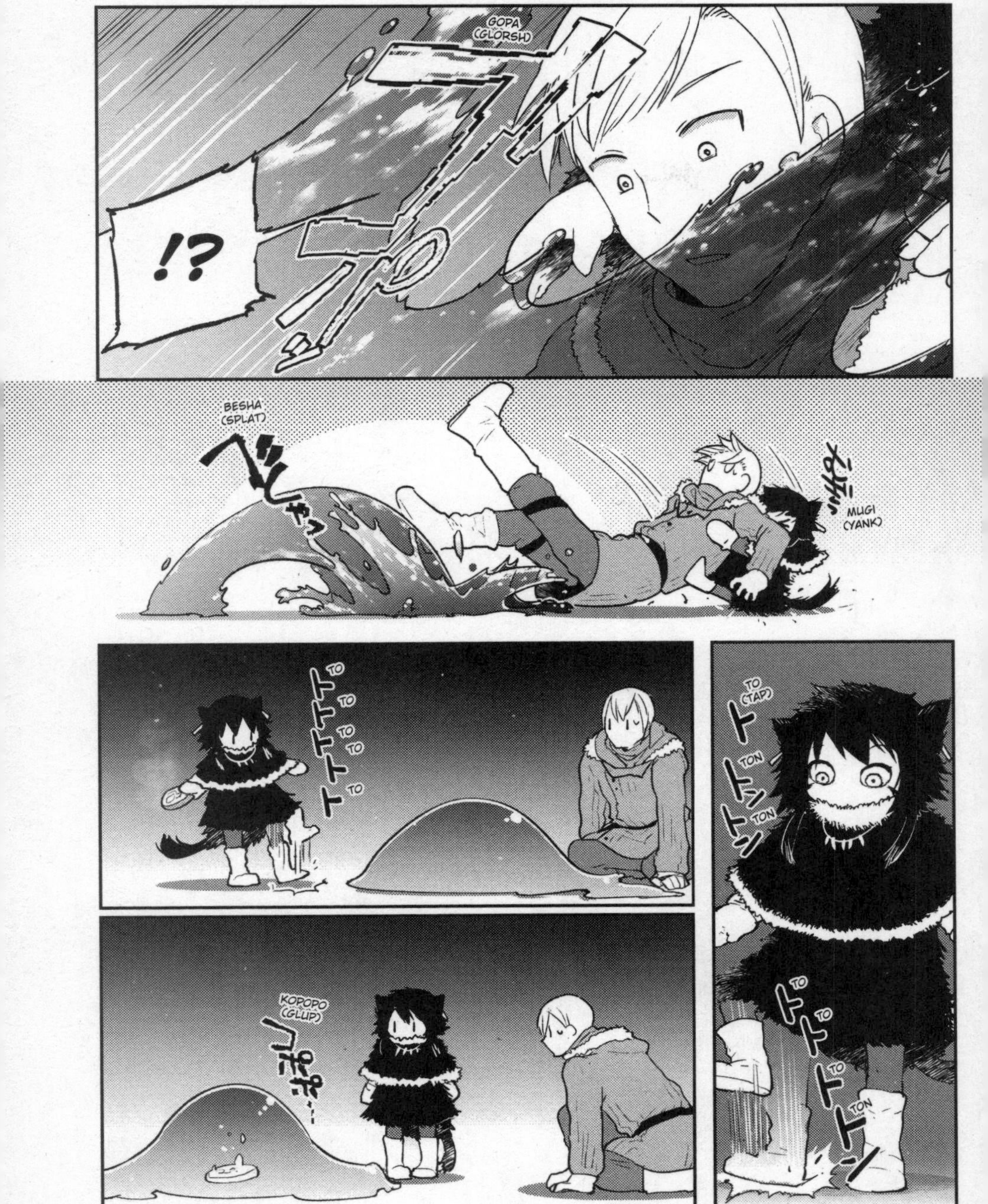

GOPA
(GLORSH)
!?
MUGI
(YANK)
BESHA
(SPLAT)
TO
(TAP)
TON
TON
TO
TO
TO
TON
TO
TO
TO
TO
TO
KOPOPO
(GLUP)

Vibrations

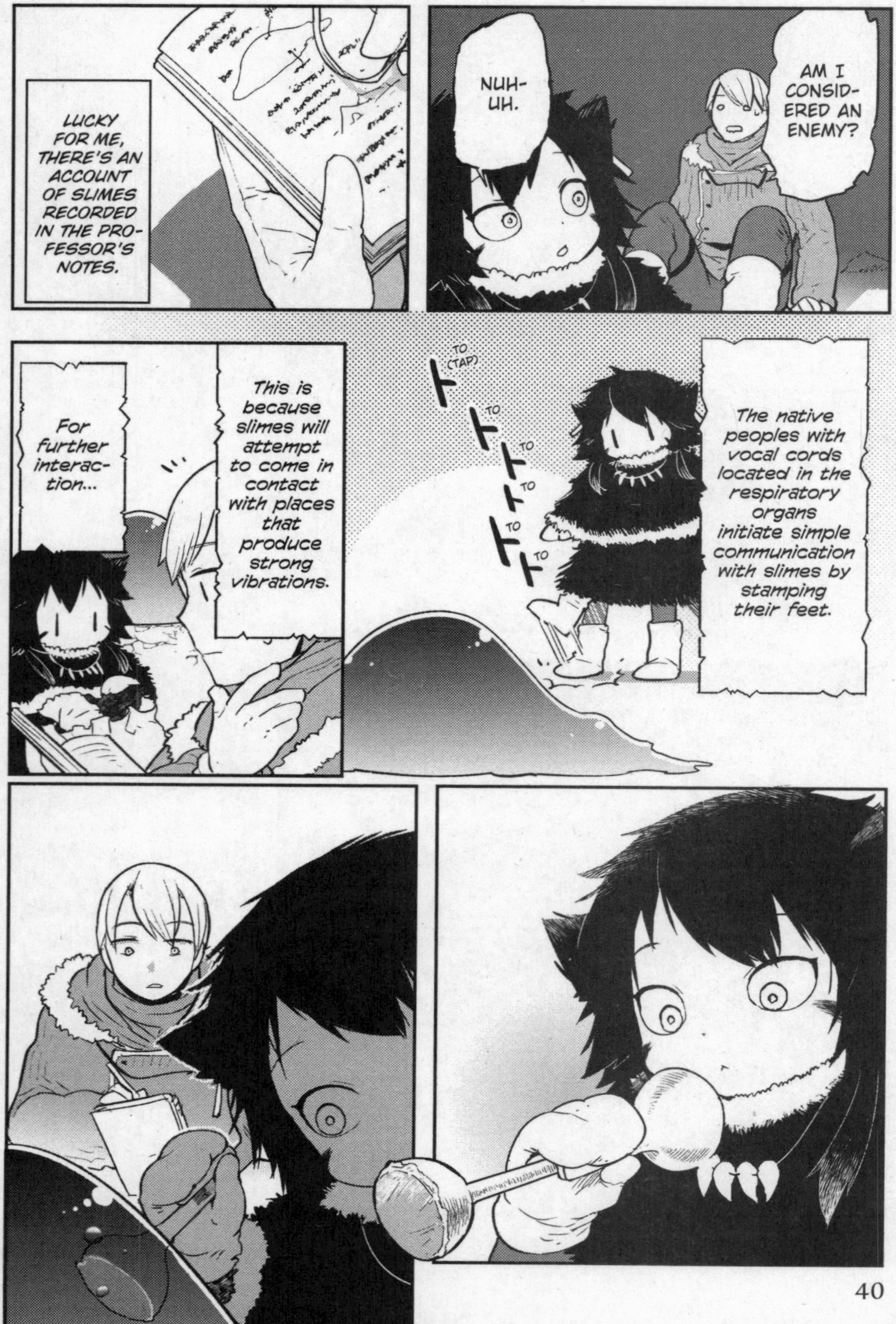

AM I CONSIDERED AN ENEMY?
NUH-UH.
LUCKY FOR ME, THERE'S AN ACCOUNT OF SLIMES RECORDED IN THE PROFESSOR'S NOTES.
The native peoples with vocal cords located in the respiratory organs initiate simple communication with slimes by stamping their feet.
TO (TAP)
TO
TO
TO
TO
TO
This is because slimes will attempt to come in contact with places that produce strong vibrations.
For further interaction...

Sound from Vibrations

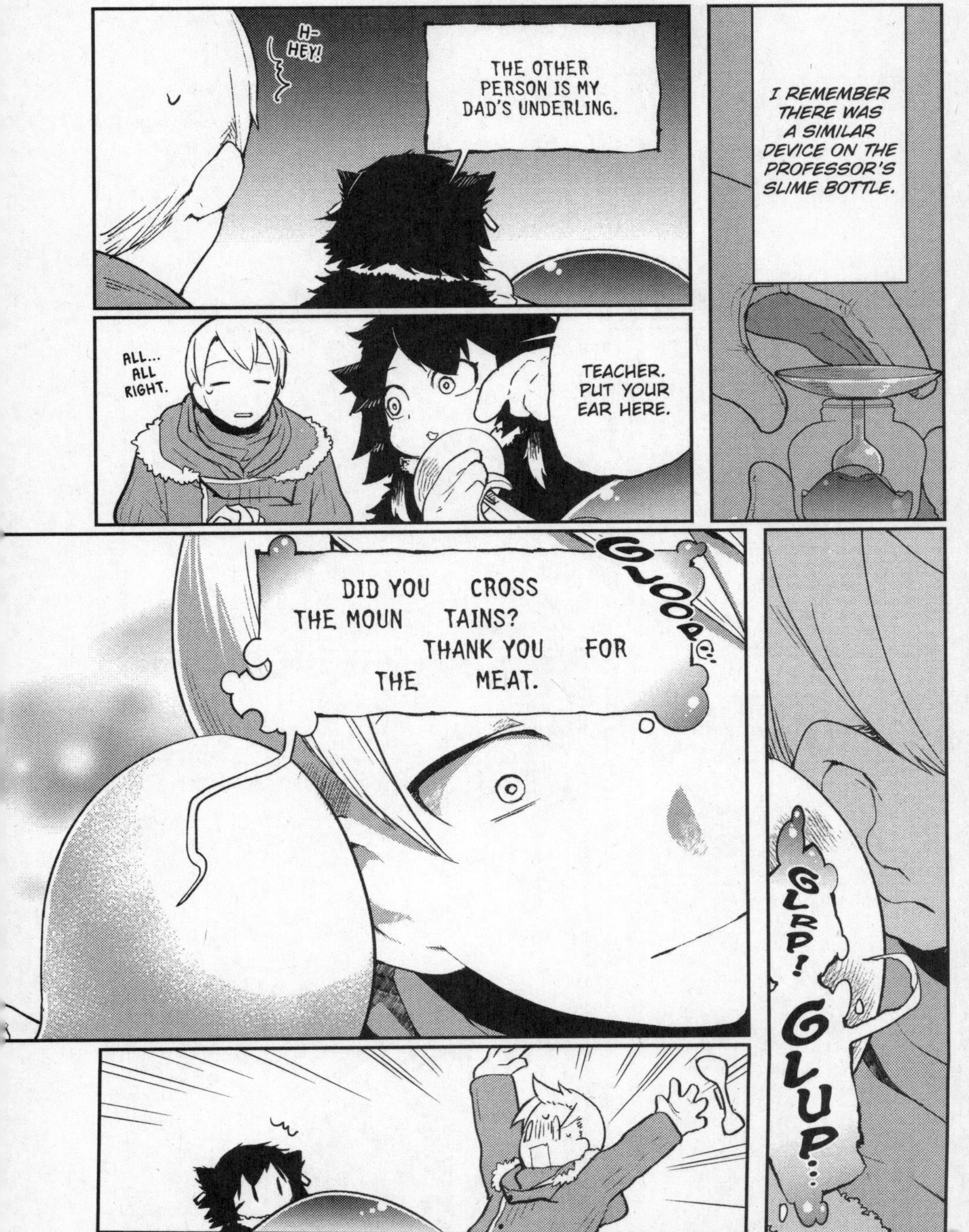
I REMEMBER THERE WAS A SIMILAR DEVICE ON THE PROFESSOR'S SLIME BOTTLE.
THE OTHER PERSON IS MY DAD'S UNDERLING.
H-HEY!
TEACHER. PUT YOUR EAR HERE.
ALL... ALL RIGHT.
GLRP! GLUP...
GLOOP
DID YOU CROSS THE MOUN TAINS? THANK YOU FOR THE MEAT.

All-Uses Tool

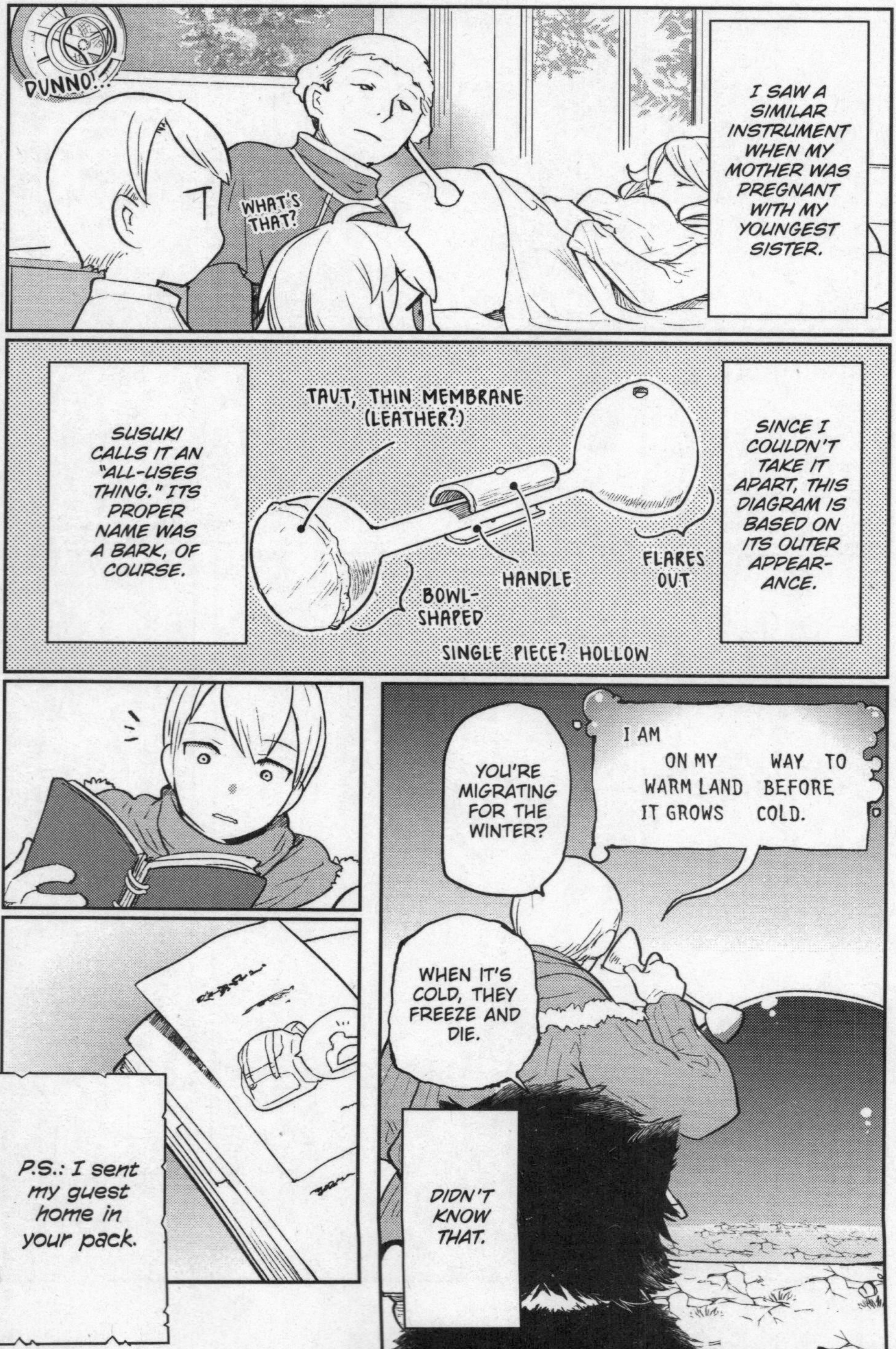
I SAW A SIMILAR INSTRUMENT WHEN MY MOTHER WAS PREGNANT WITH MY YOUNGEST SISTER.
DUNNO!...
WHAT'S THAT?
SINCE I COULDN'T TAKE IT APART, THIS DIAGRAM IS BASED ON ITS OUTER APPEARANCE.
TAUT, THIN MEMBRANE (LEATHER?)
FLARES OUT
HANDLE
BOWL-SHAPED
SINGLE PIECE? HOLLOW
SUSUKI CALLS IT AN "ALL-USES THING." ITS PROPER NAME WAS A BARK, OF COURSE.
I AM ON MY WAY TO WARM LAND BEFORE IT GROWS COLD.
YOU'RE MIGRATING FOR THE WINTER?
WHEN IT'S COLD, THEY FREEZE AND DIE.
DIDN'T KNOW THAT.
P.S.: I sent my guest home in your pack.

Slime-to-Slime Conversation

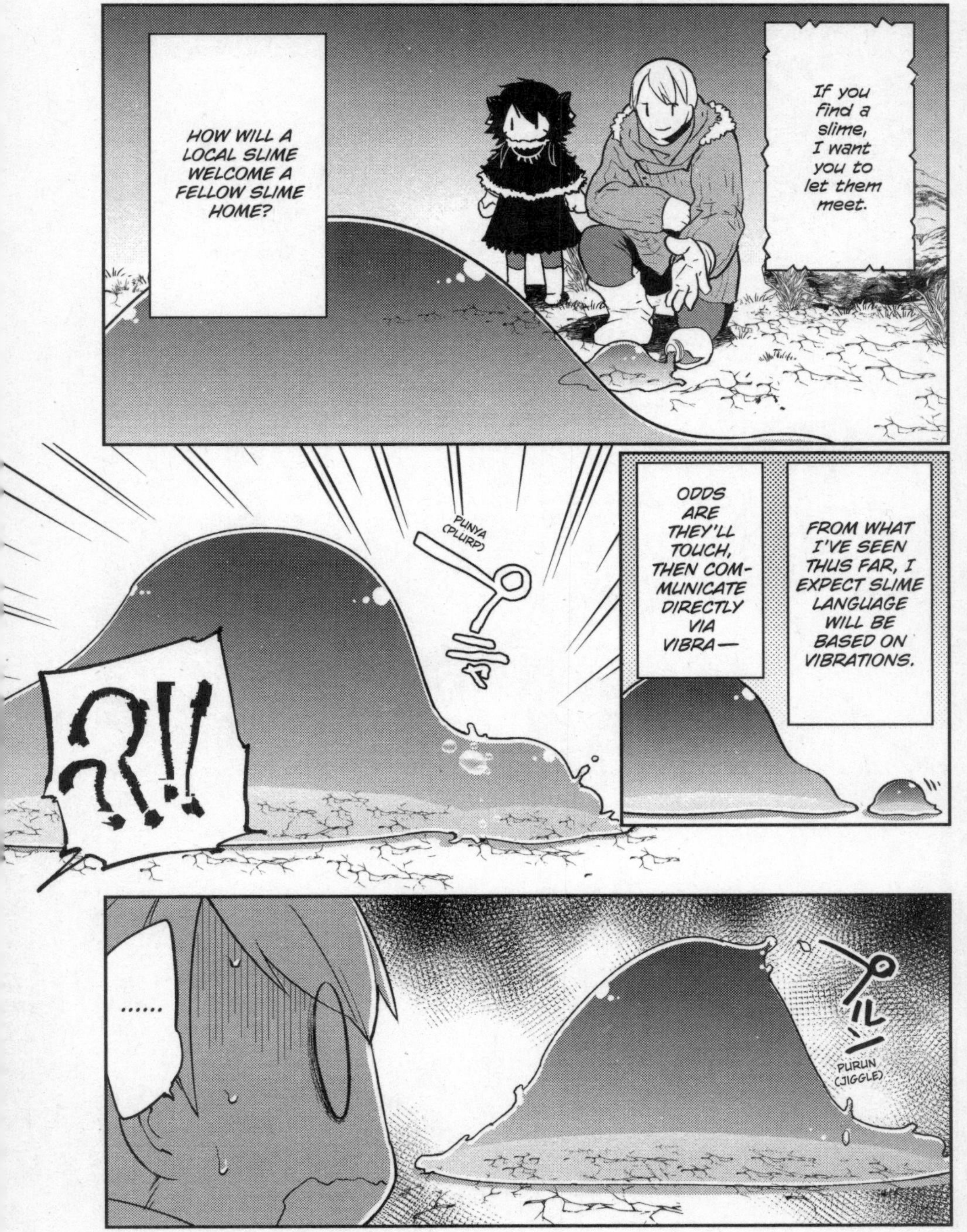
If you find a slime, I want you to let them meet.
HOW WILL A LOCAL SLIME WELCOME A FELLOW SLIME HOME?
FROM WHAT I'VE SEEN THUS FAR, I EXPECT SLIME LANGUAGE WILL BE BASED ON VIBRATIONS.
ODDS ARE THEY'LL TOUCH, THEN COM-MUNICATE DIRECTLY VIA VIBRA—
PUNYA (PLURP)
?!!
PURUN (JIGGLE)
......

Two Became One

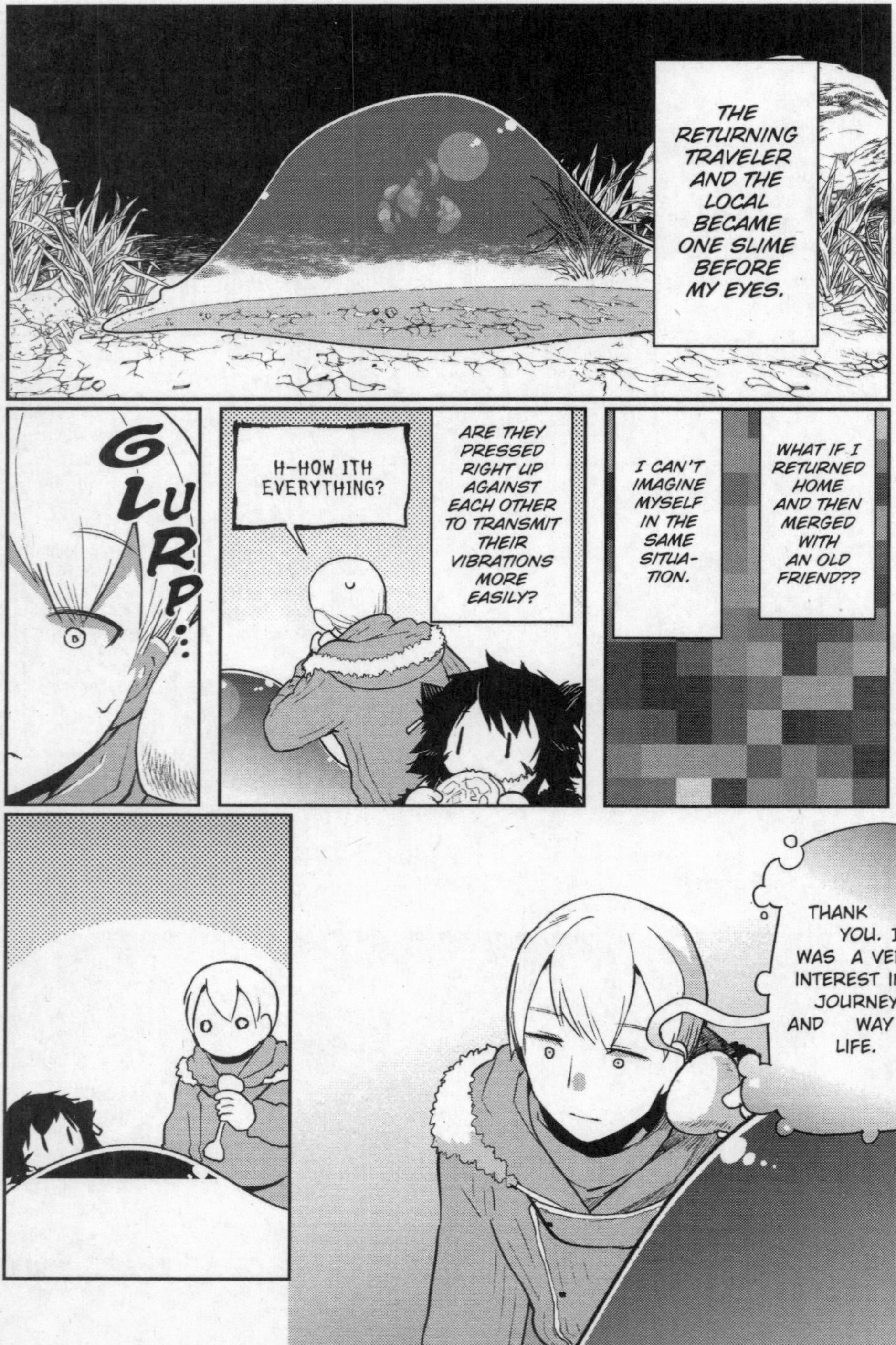
THE RETURNING TRAVELER AND THE LOCAL BECAME ONE SLIME BEFORE MY EYES.
WHAT IF I RETURNED HOME AND THEN MERGED WITH AN OLD FRIEND??
I CAN'T IMAGINE MYSELF IN THE SAME SITUATION.
ARE THEY PRESSED RIGHT UP AGAINST EACH OTHER TO TRANSMIT THEIR VIBRATIONS MORE EASILY?
H-HOW ITH EVERYTHING?
GLURP...
THANK YOU. IT WAS A VERY INTEREST ING JOURNEY AND WAY OF LIFE.

The Slime Advantage

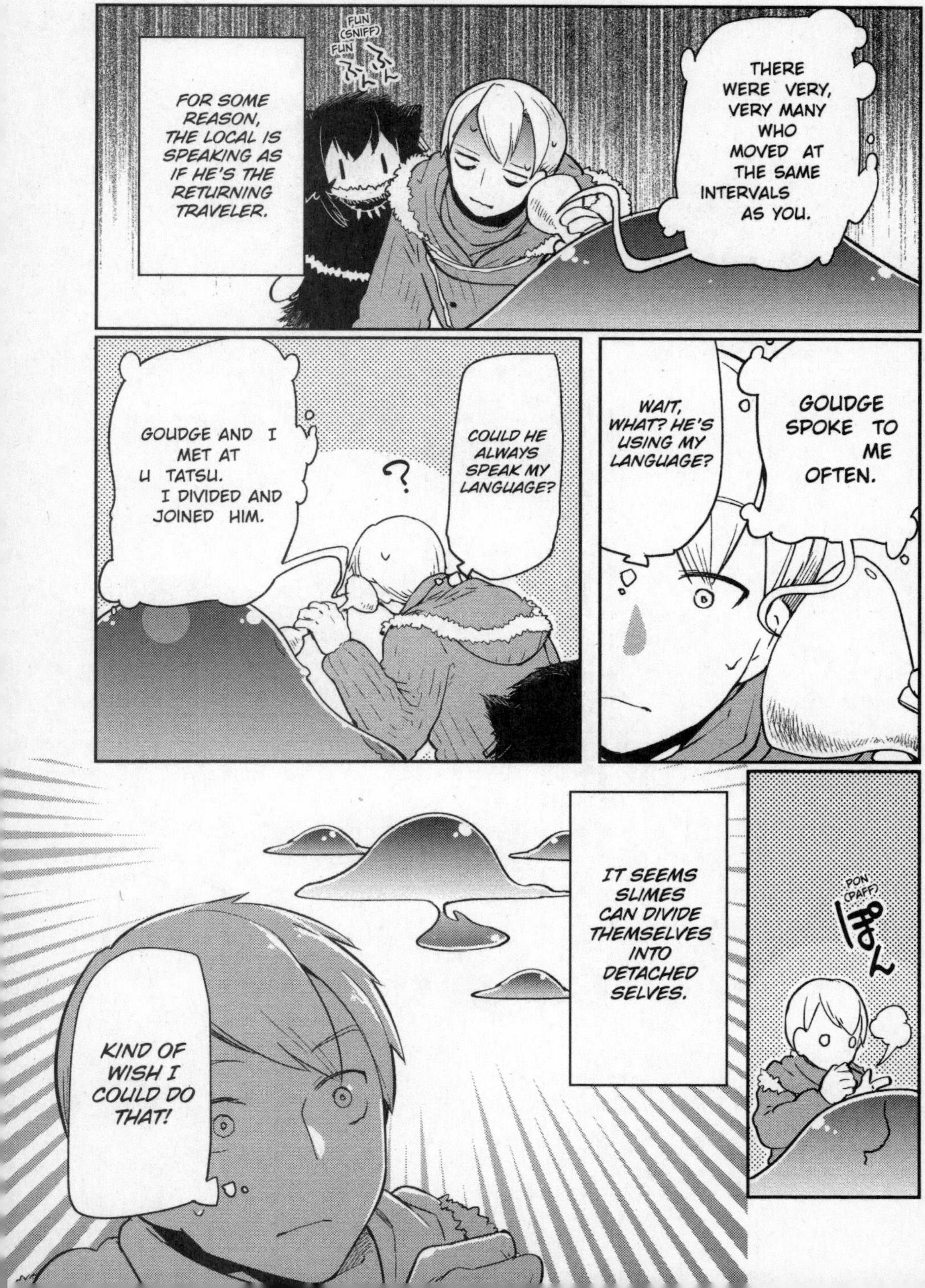
THERE WERE VERY, VERY MANY WHO MOVED AT THE SAME INTERVALS AS YOU.
FUN (SNIFF) FUN ふんふん
FOR SOME REASON, THE LOCAL IS SPEAKING AS IF HE'S THE RETURNING TRAVELER.
GOUDGE SPOKE TO ME OFTEN.
WAIT, WHAT? HE'S USING MY LANGUAGE?
COULD HE ALWAYS SPEAK MY LANGUAGE?
GOUDGE AND I MET AT U TATSU. I DIVIDED AND JOINED HIM.
PON (PAFF) ぽん
IT SEEMS SLIMES CAN DIVIDE THEMSELVES INTO DETACHED SELVES.
KIND OF WISH I COULD DO THAT!

A Race Without That

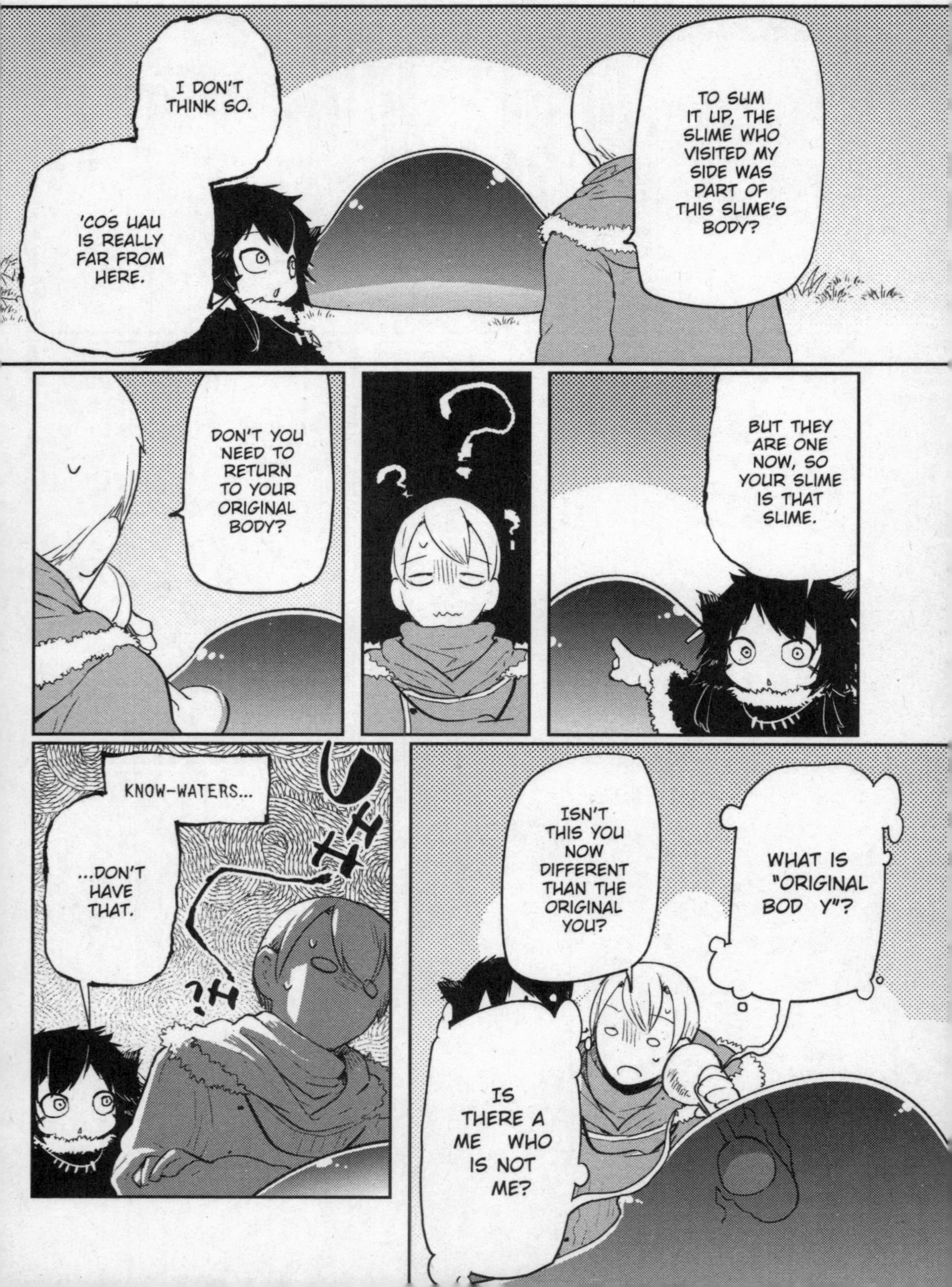
TO SUM IT UP, THE SLIME WHO VISITED MY SIDE WAS PART OF THIS SLIME'S BODY?
I DON'T THINK SO.
'COS UAU IS REALLY FAR FROM HERE.
BUT THEY ARE ONE NOW, SO YOUR SLIME IS THAT SLIME.
DON'T YOU NEED TO RETURN TO YOUR ORIGINAL BODY?
WHAT IS "ORIGINAL BOD Y"?
ISN'T THIS YOU NOW DIFFERENT THAN THE ORIGINAL YOU?
IS THERE A ME WHO IS NOT ME?
KNOW-WATERS...
...DON'T HAVE THAT.
?!

Partial Transportation

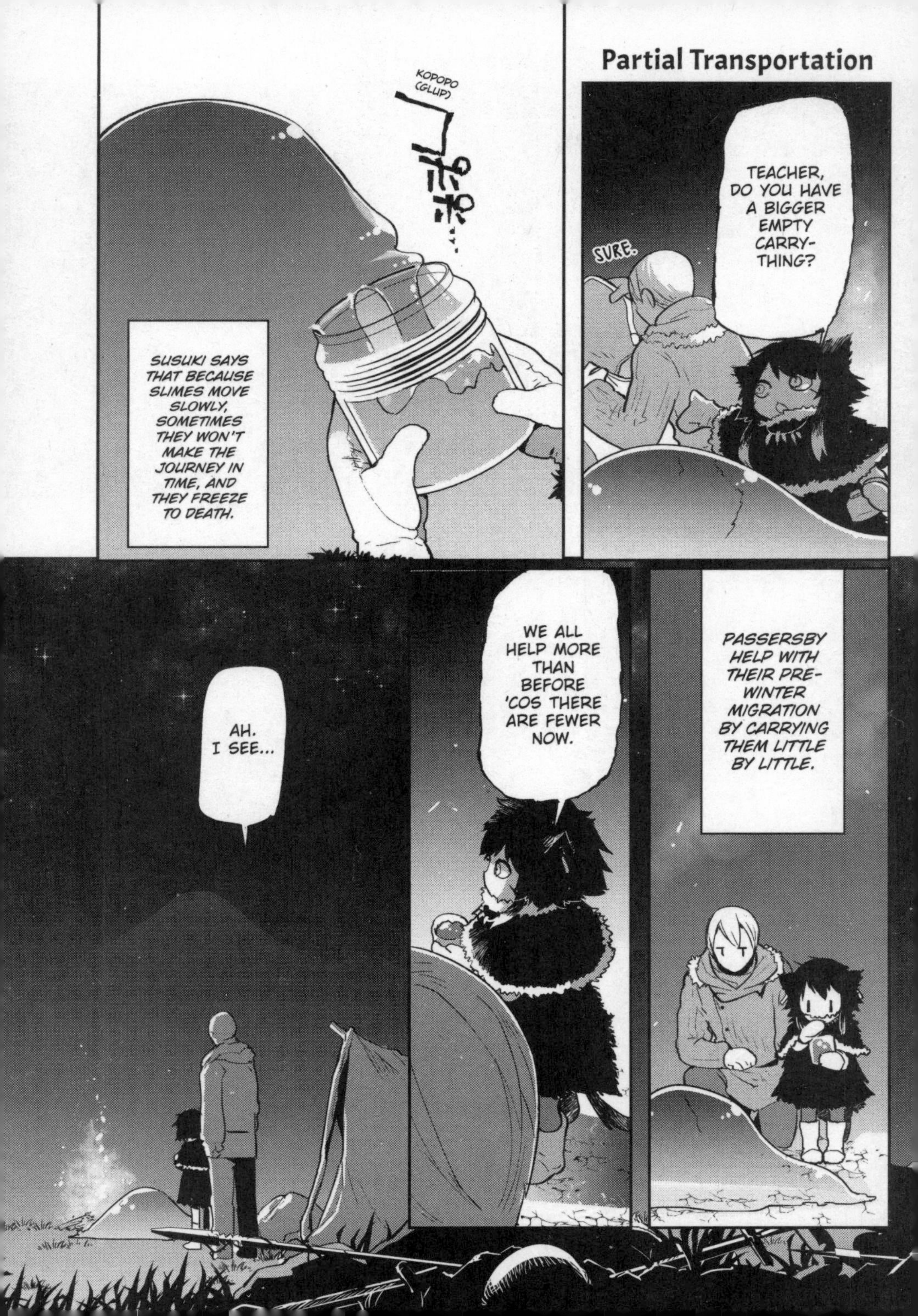

TEACHER, DO YOU HAVE A BIGGER EMPTY CARRYTHING?
SURE.
KOPOPO (GLUP)
コポポ…
SUSUKI SAYS THAT BECAUSE SLIMES MOVE SLOWLY, SOMETIMES THEY WON'T MAKE THE JOURNEY IN TIME, AND THEY FREEZE TO DEATH.
PASSERSBY HELP WITH THEIR PRE-WINTER MIGRATION BY CARRYING THEM LITTLE BY LITTLE.
WE ALL HELP MORE THAN BEFORE 'COS THERE ARE FEWER NOW.
AH. I SEE...

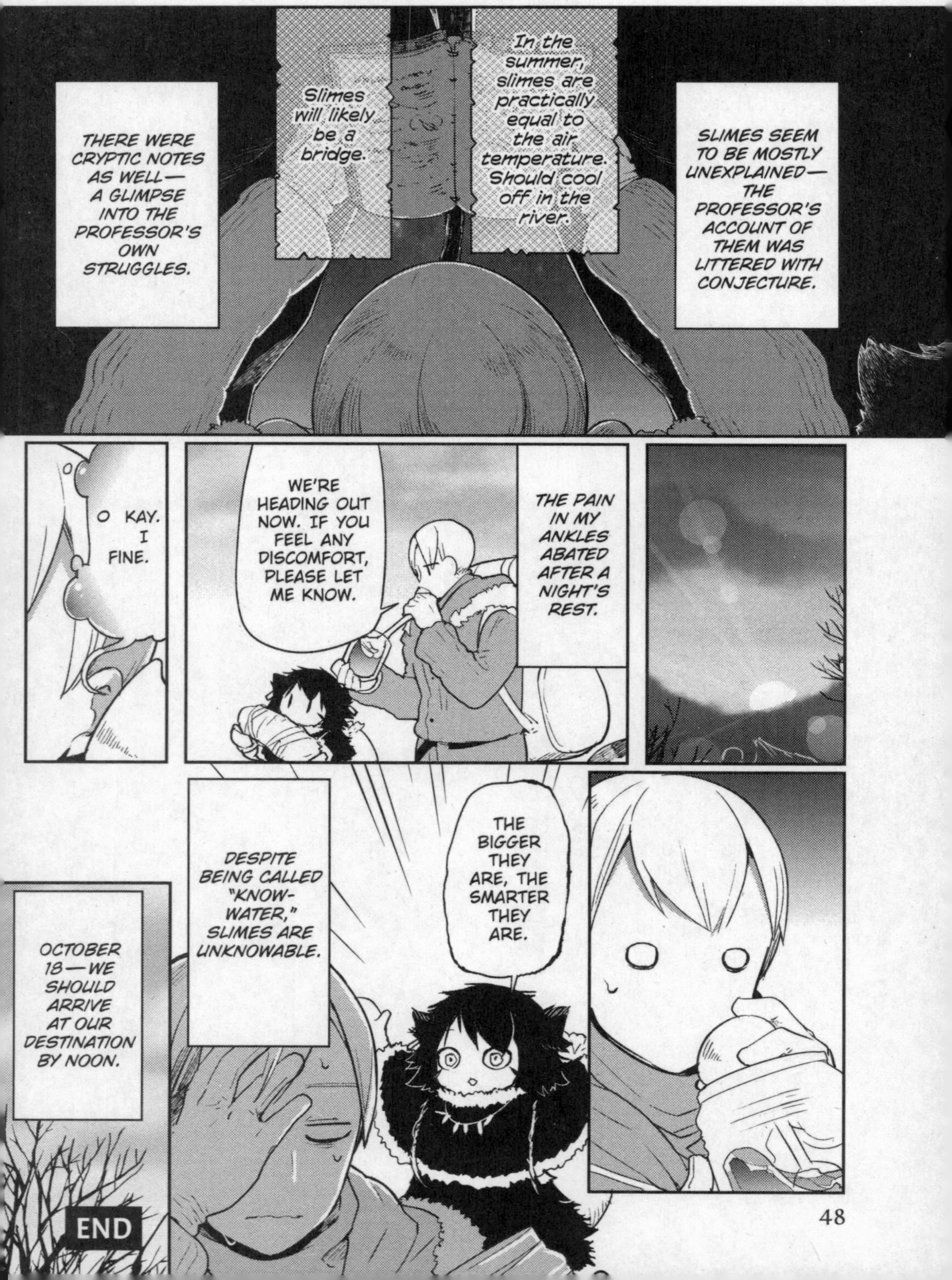
SLIMES SEEM TO BE MOSTLY UNEXPLAINED—THE PROFESSOR'S ACCOUNT OF THEM WAS LITTERED WITH CONJECTURE.
In the summer, slimes are practically equal to the air temperature. Should cool off in the river.
Slimes will likely be a bridge.
THERE WERE CRYPTIC NOTES AS WELL—A GLIMPSE INTO THE PROFESSOR'S OWN STRUGGLES.
THE PAIN IN MY ANKLES ABATED AFTER A NIGHT'S REST.
WE'RE HEADING OUT NOW. IF YOU FEEL ANY DISCOMFORT, PLEASE LET ME KNOW.
O KAY. I FINE.
THE BIGGER THEY ARE, THE SMARTER THEY ARE.
DESPITE BEING CALLED "KNOW-WATER," SLIMES ARE UNKNOWABLE.
OCTOBER 18—WE SHOULD ARRIVE AT OUR DESTINATION BY NOON.
END

CONVERSING WITH SUSUKI: PRAISE AND RESPONSES

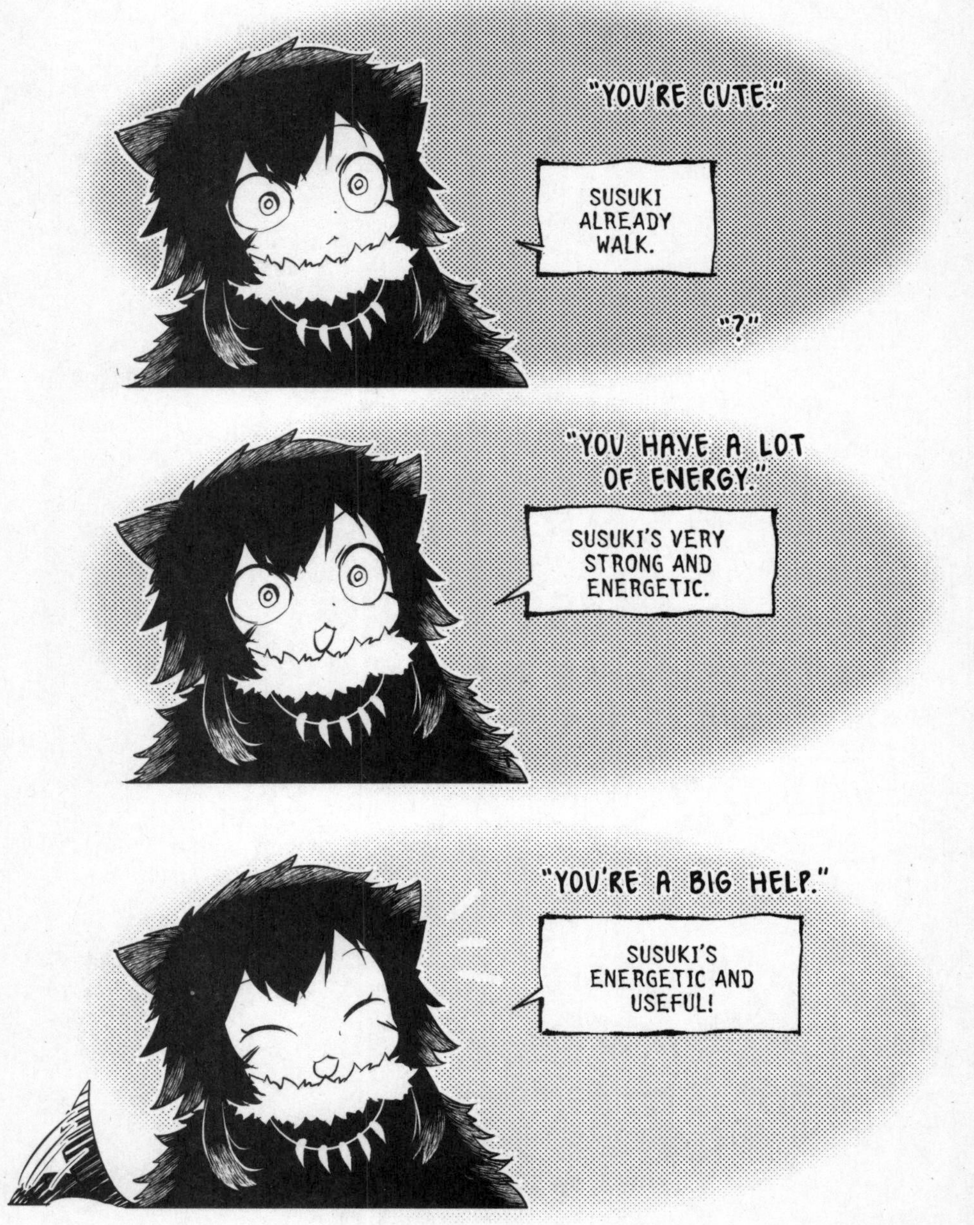
"YOU'RE CUTE."
SUSUKI ALREADY WALK.
"?"
"YOU HAVE A LOT OF ENERGY."
SUSUKI'S VERY STRONG AND ENERGETIC.
"YOU'RE A BIG HELP."
SUSUKI'S ENERGETIC AND USEFUL!

SUSUKI'S KNIFE

(GIVEN BY THE
PROFESSOR?)

MS. DRY-GRASS'S KNIFE

RUSTY

SHE SAYS SHE
DIDN'T GET IT FROM
THE PROFESSOR.

LOCALLY MADE?

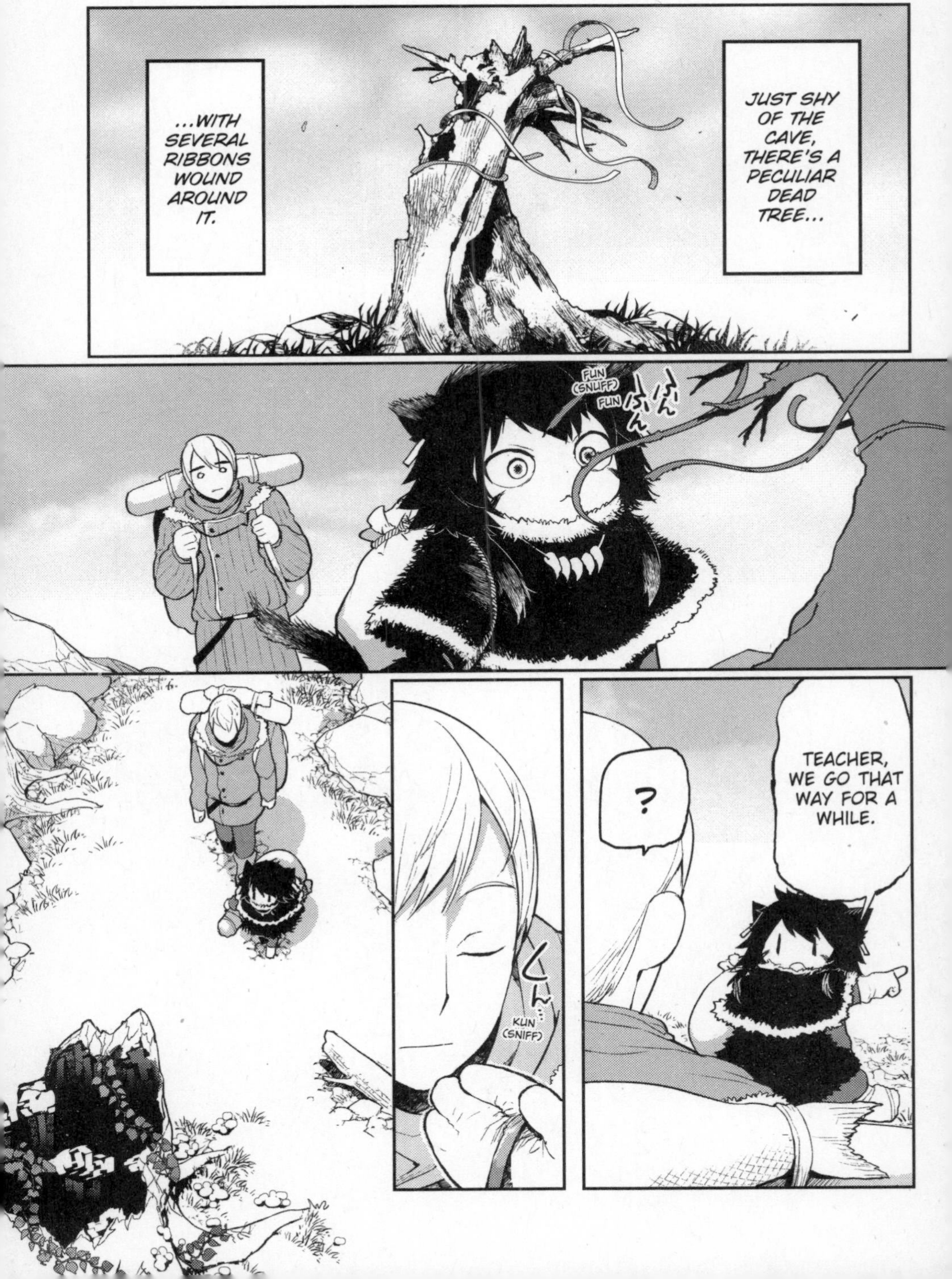
JUST SHY OF THE CAVE, THERE'S A PECULIAR DEAD TREE...
...WITH SEVERAL RIBBONS WOUND AROUND IT.
ふん ふん
FUN (SNUFF) FUN
TEACHER, WE GO THAT WAY FOR A WHILE.
?
くん…
KUN (SNIFF)

LOG 4

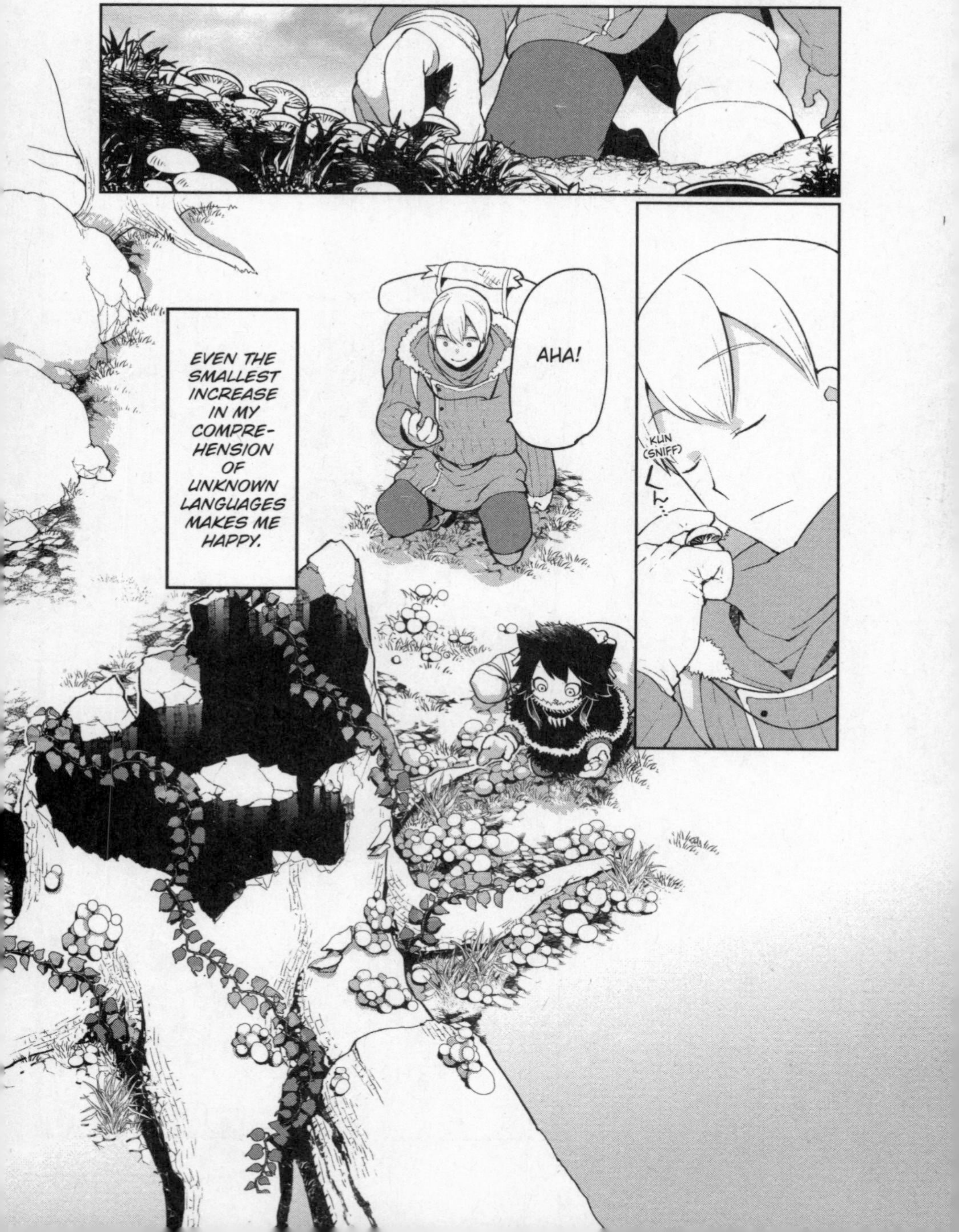
KUN (SNIFF)
AHA!
EVEN THE SMALLEST INCREASE IN MY COMPRE-HENSION OF UNKNOWN LANGUAGES MAKES ME HAPPY.

Arrival

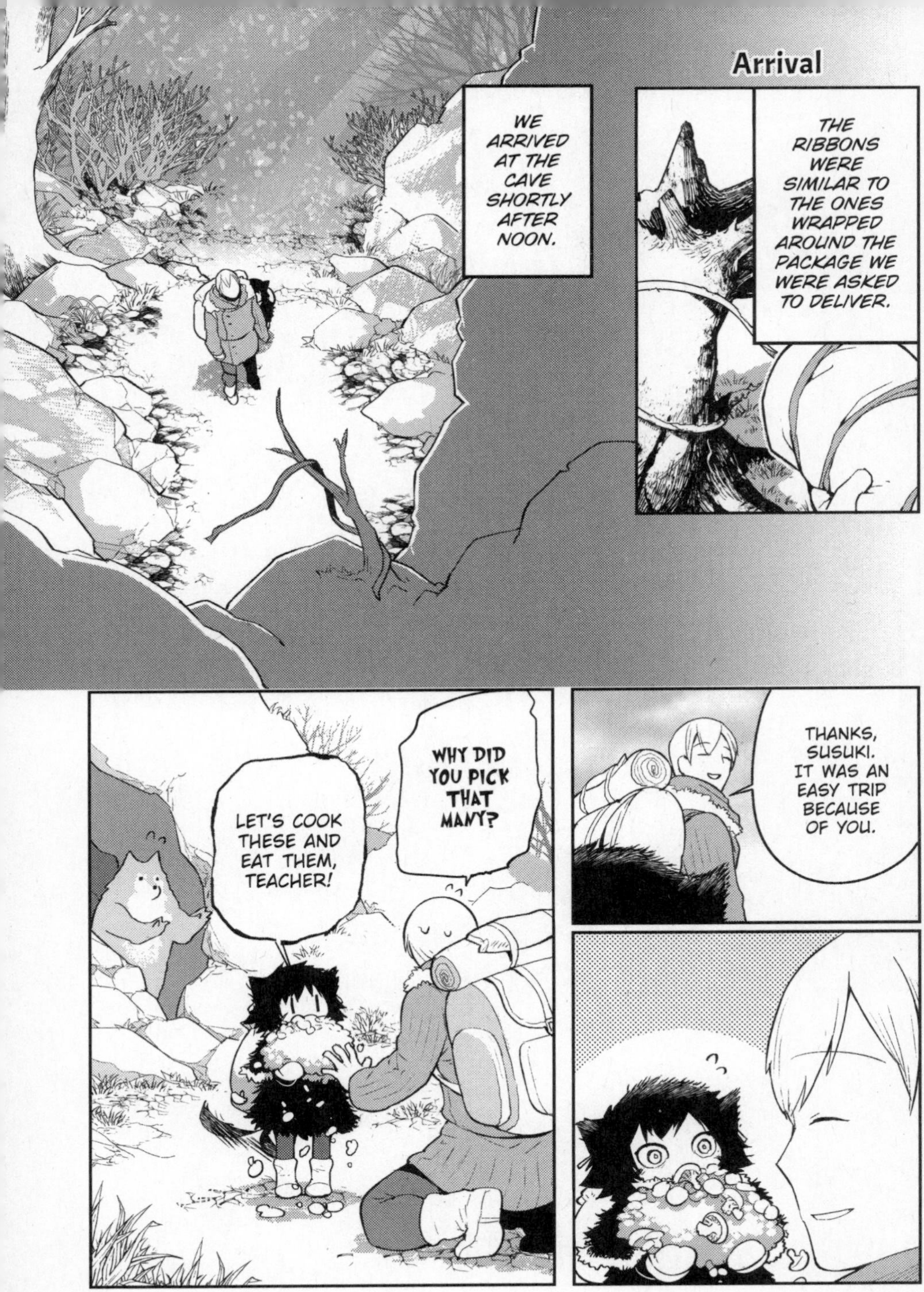

THE RIBBONS WERE SIMILAR TO THE ONES WRAPPED AROUND THE PACKAGE WE WERE ASKED TO DELIVER.
WE ARRIVED AT THE CAVE SHORTLY AFTER NOON.
THANKS, SUSUKI. IT WAS AN EASY TRIP BECAUSE OF YOU.
WHY DID YOU PICK THAT MANY?
LET'S COOK THESE AND EAT THEM, TEACHER!

The Cave Dwellers

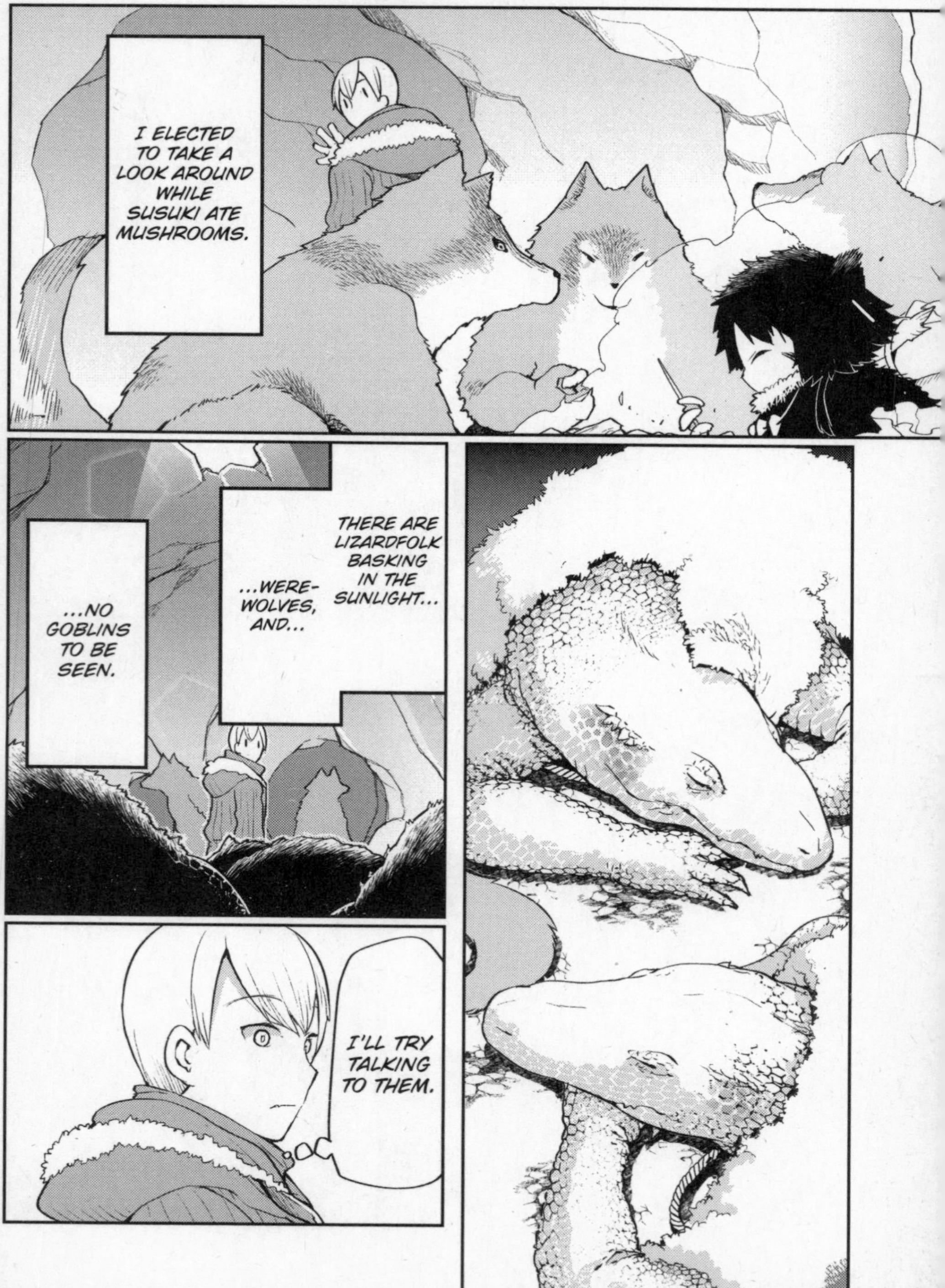
I ELECTED TO TAKE A LOOK AROUND WHILE SUSUKI ATE MUSHROOMS.
THERE ARE LIZARDFOLK BASKING IN THE SUNLIGHT...
...WERE-WOLVES, AND...
...NO GOBLINS TO BE SEEN.
I'LL TRY TALKING TO THEM.

Initiating Conversation

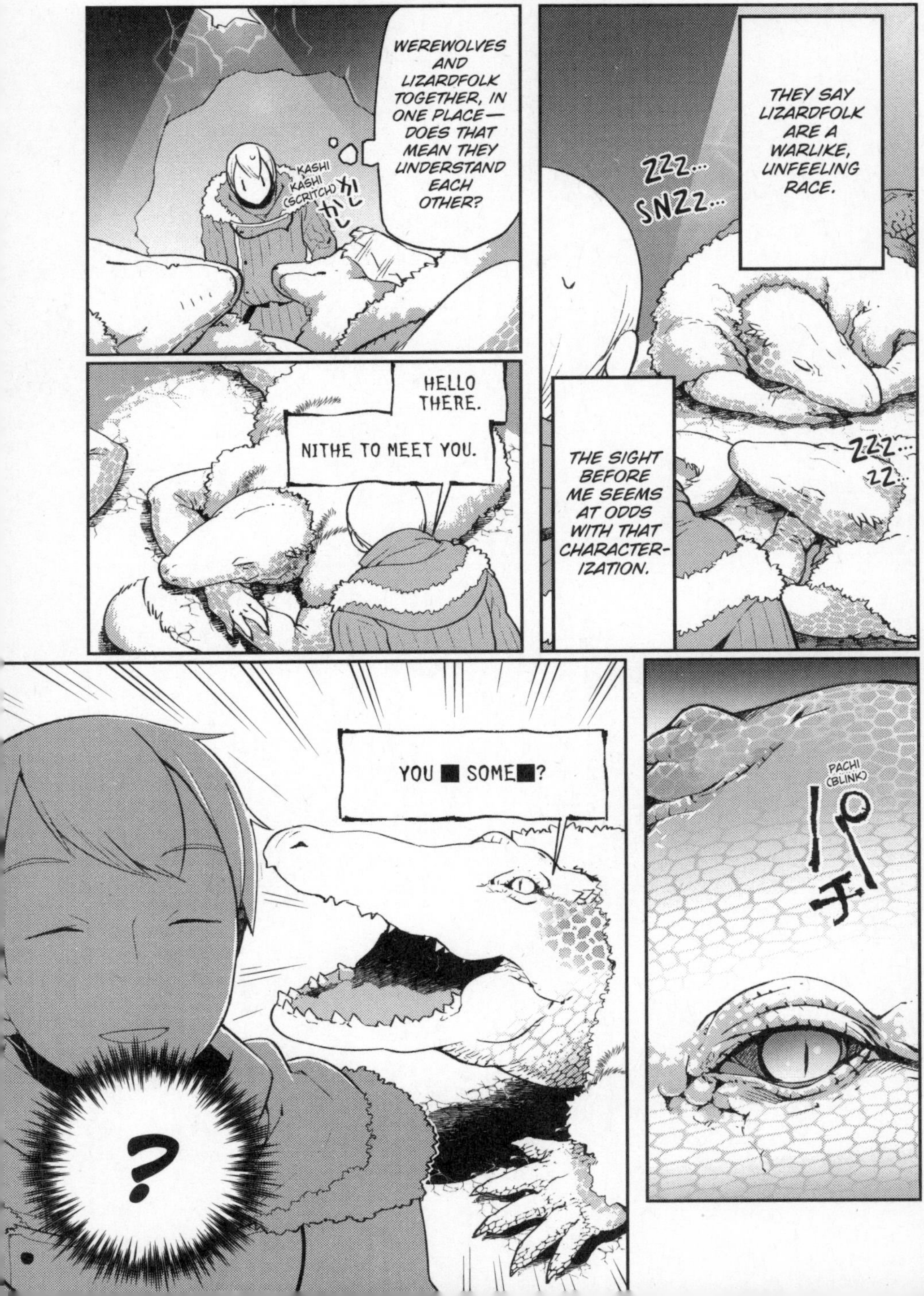
THEY SAY LIZARDFOLK ARE A WARLIKE, UNFEELING RACE.
ZZZ... SNZZ...
THE SIGHT BEFORE ME SEEMS AT ODDS WITH THAT CHARACTER-IZATION.
ZZZ... ZZ...
WEREWOLVES AND LIZARDFOLK TOGETHER, IN ONE PLACE—DOES THAT MEAN THEY UNDERSTAND EACH OTHER?
KASHI KASHI (SCRITCH)
かしかし
HELLO THERE.
NITHE TO MEET YOU.
PACHI (BLINK)
パチ
YOU ■ SOME■?
?

Pronunciation Differences

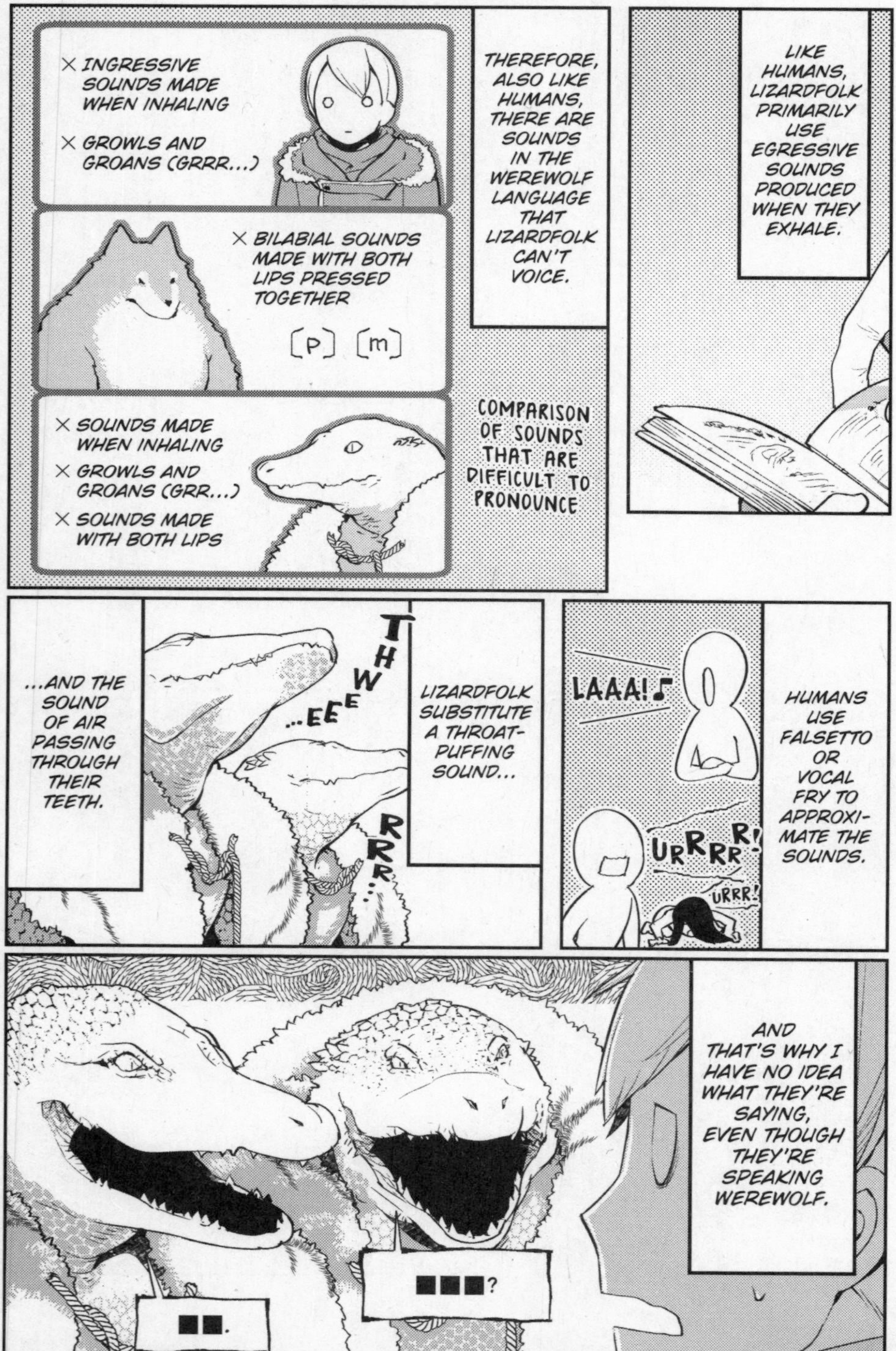
LIKE HUMANS, LIZARDFOLK PRIMARILY USE EGRESSIVE SOUNDS PRODUCED WHEN THEY EXHALE.
THEREFORE, ALSO LIKE HUMANS, THERE ARE SOUNDS IN THE WEREWOLF LANGUAGE THAT LIZARDFOLK CAN'T VOICE.
COMPARISON OF SOUNDS THAT ARE DIFFICULT TO PRONOUNCE
× INGRESSIVE SOUNDS MADE WHEN INHALING
× GROWLS AND GROANS (GRRR...)
× BILABIAL SOUNDS MADE WITH BOTH LIPS PRESSED TOGETHER
[p] [m]
× SOUNDS MADE WHEN INHALING
× GROWLS AND GROANS (GRR...)
× SOUNDS MADE WITH BOTH LIPS
HUMANS USE FALSETTO OR VOCAL FRY TO APPROXIMATE THE SOUNDS.
LAAA!♪
URRRR!
URRR!
LIZARDFOLK SUBSTITUTE A THROAT-PUFFING SOUND...
RRR...
THWEEE...
...AND THE SOUND OF AIR PASSING THROUGH THEIR TEETH.
AND THAT'S WHY I HAVE NO IDEA WHAT THEY'RE SAYING, EVEN THOUGH THEY'RE SPEAKING WEREWOLF.
■■■?
■■.

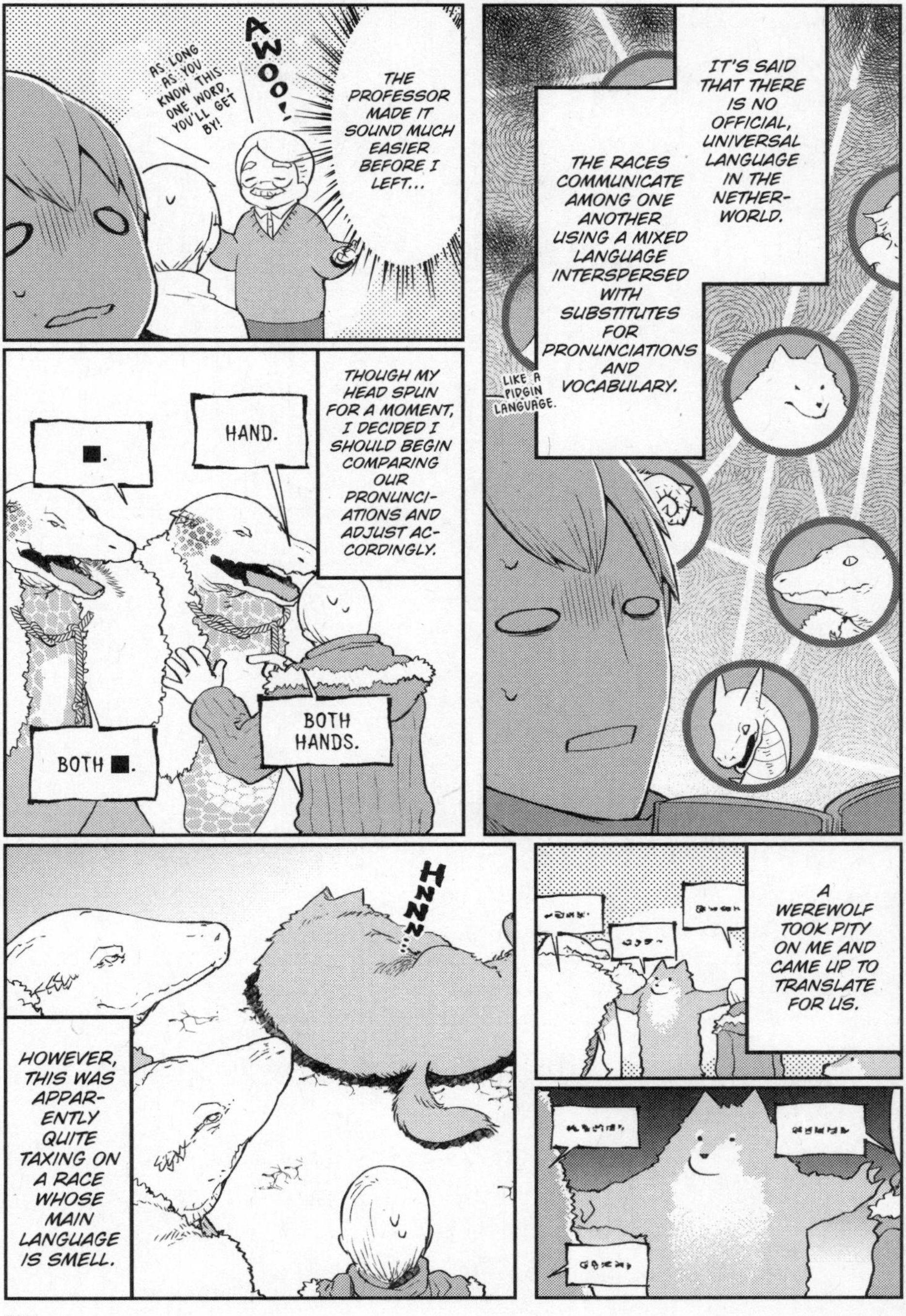
IT'S SAID THAT THERE IS NO OFFICIAL, UNIVERSAL LANGUAGE IN THE NETHER-WORLD.
THE RACES COMMUNICATE AMONG ONE ANOTHER USING A MIXED LANGUAGE INTERSPERSED WITH SUBSTITUTES FOR PRONUNCIATIONS AND VOCABULARY.
LIKE A PIDGIN LANGUAGE.
THE PROFESSOR MADE IT SOUND MUCH EASIER BEFORE I LEFT...
AWOO!
AS LONG AS YOU KNOW THIS ONE WORD, YOU'LL GET BY!
THOUGH MY HEAD SPUN FOR A MOMENT, I DECIDED I SHOULD BEGIN COMPARING OUR PRONUNCI-ATIONS AND ADJUST AC-CORDINGLY.
HAND.
■.
BOTH HANDS.
BOTH ■.
A WEREWOLF TOOK PITY ON ME AND CAME UP TO TRANSLATE FOR US.
HNNN...
HOWEVER, THIS WAS APPAR-ENTLY QUITE TAXING ON A RACE WHOSE MAIN LANGUAGE IS SMELL.

Beyond Words Too

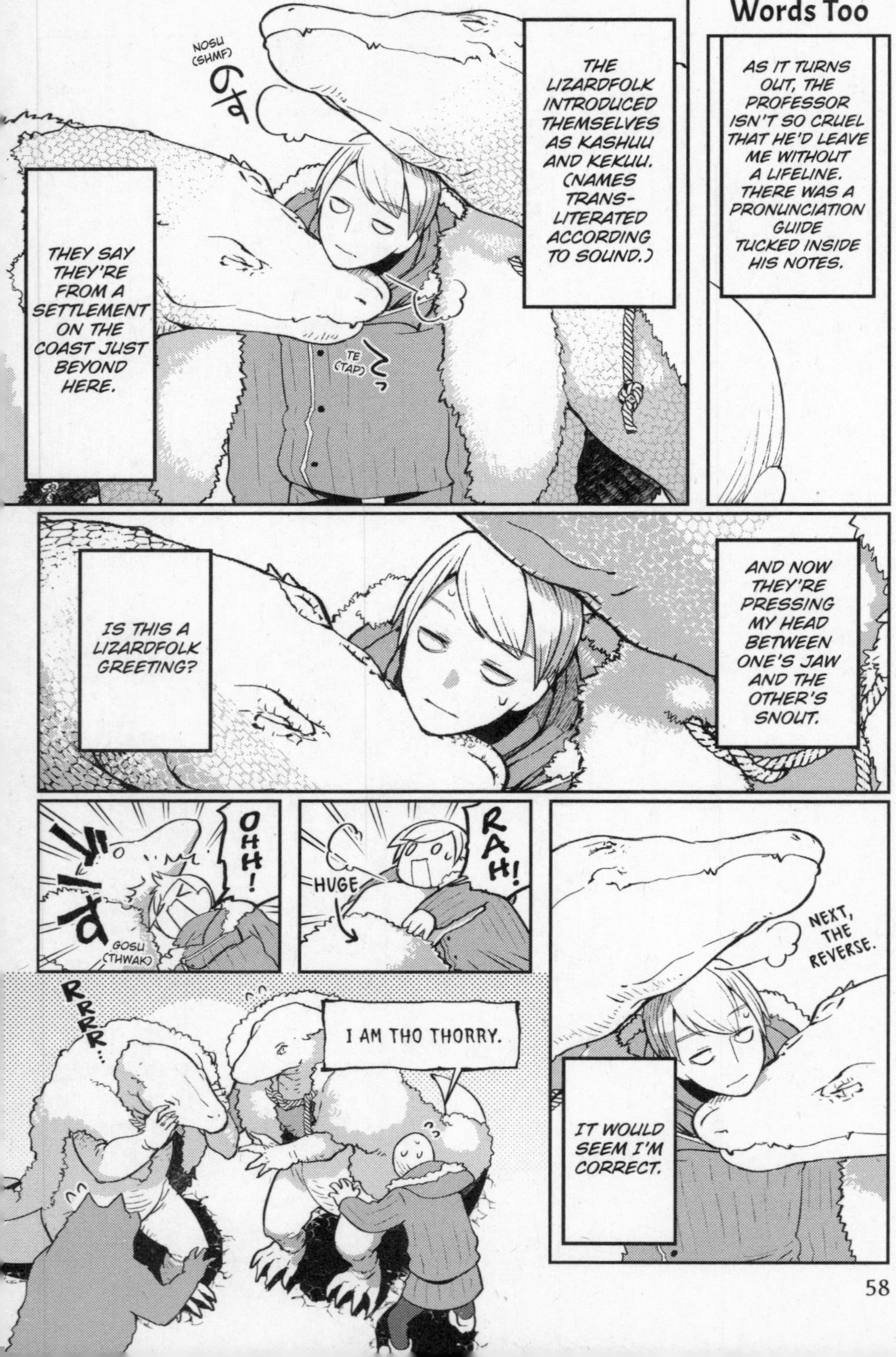

AS IT TURNS OUT, THE PROFESSOR ISN'T SO CRUEL THAT HE'D LEAVE ME WITHOUT A LIFELINE. THERE WAS A PRONUNCIATION GUIDE TUCKED INSIDE HIS NOTES.
THE LIZARDFOLK INTRODUCED THEMSELVES AS KASHUU AND KEKUU. (NAMES TRANS-LITERATED ACCORDING TO SOUND.)
NOSU (SHMF)
THEY SAY THEY'RE FROM A SETTLEMENT ON THE COAST JUST BEYOND HERE.
TE (TAP)
AND NOW THEY'RE PRESSING MY HEAD BETWEEN ONE'S JAW AND THE OTHER'S SNOUT.
IS THIS A LIZARDFOLK GREETING?
NEXT, THE REVERSE.
IT WOULD SEEM I'M CORRECT.
RAH!
HUGE
OHH!
GOSU (THWAK)
I AM THO THORRY.
RRRR...

Not So Much "Possessions" As...

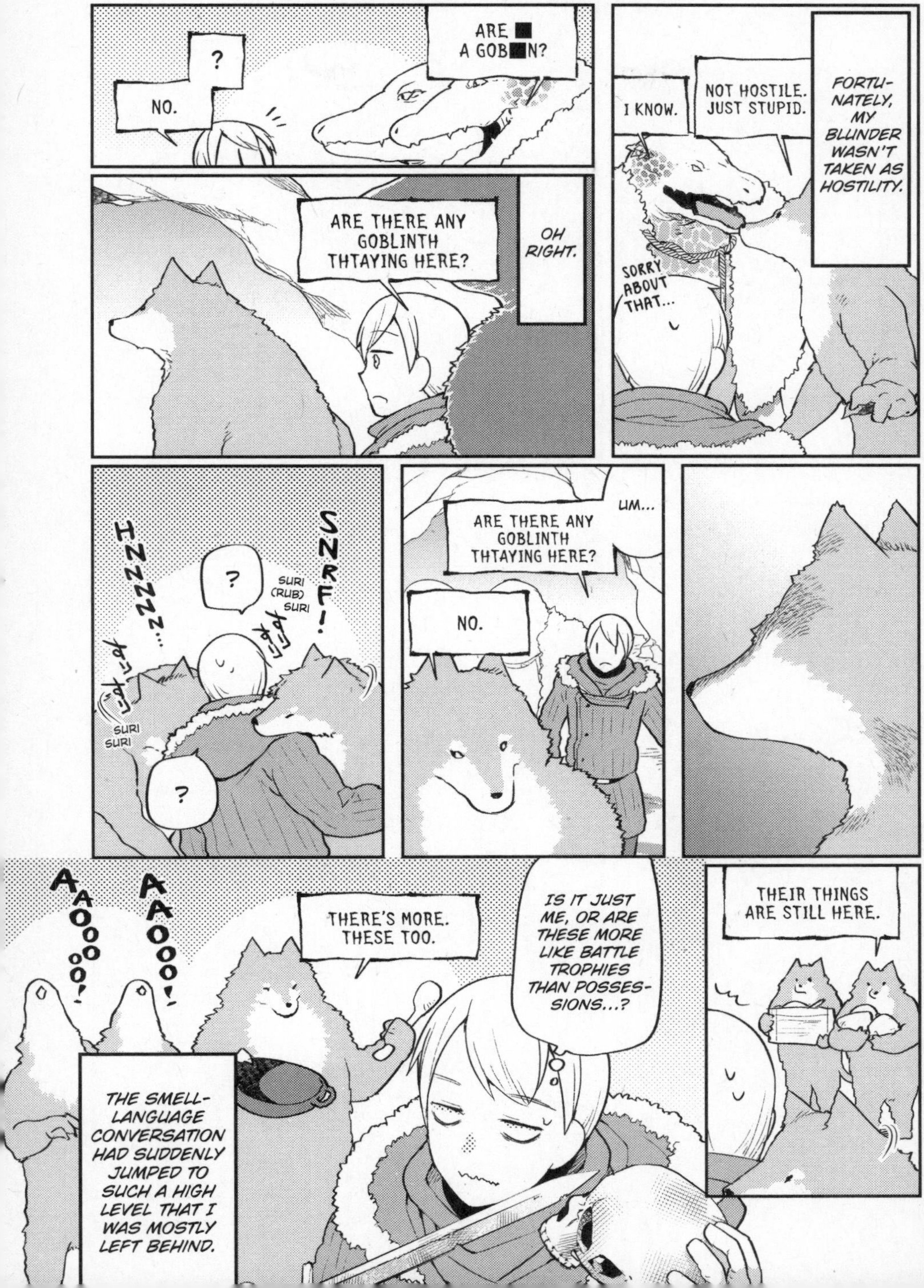
FORTUNATELY, MY BLUNDER WASN'T TAKEN AS HOSTILITY.
NOT HOSTILE. JUST STUPID.
I KNOW.
SORRY ABOUT THAT...
ARE [redacted] A GOB[redacted]N?
?
NO.
OH RIGHT.
ARE THERE ANY GOBLINTH THTAYING HERE?
UM...
ARE THERE ANY GOBLINTH THTAYING HERE?
NO.
SNRF!
SURI (RUB) SURI
?
HNNNNN...
SURI SURI
?
THEIR THINGS ARE STILL HERE.
IS IT JUST ME, OR ARE THESE MORE LIKE BATTLE TROPHIES THAN POSSESSIONS...?
THERE'S MORE. THESE TOO.
AAOOOO!
AAOOOOO!
THE SMELL-LANGUAGE CONVERSATION HAD SUDDENLY JUMPED TO SUCH A HIGH LEVEL THAT I WAS MOSTLY LEFT BEHIND.

The Cave Currently

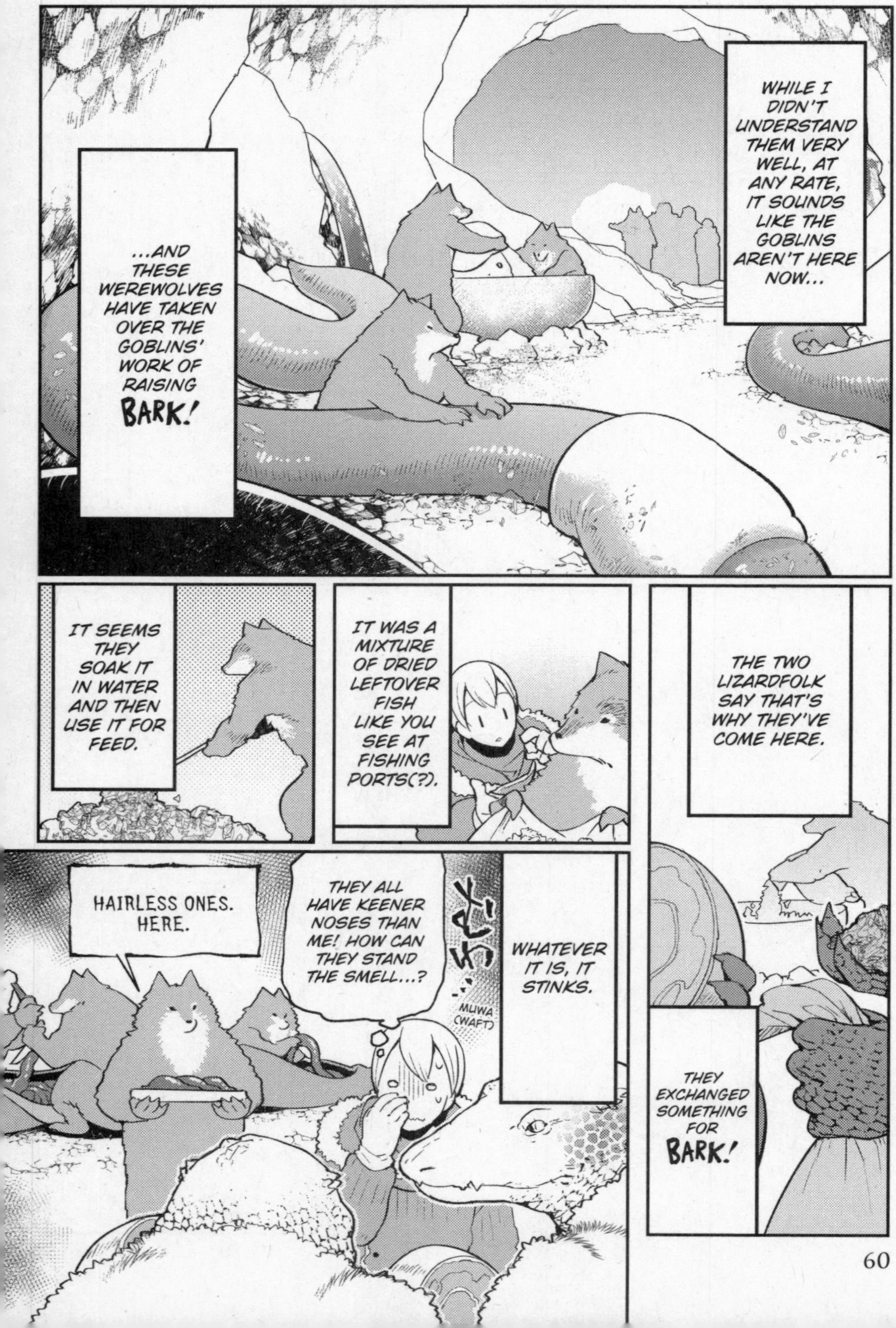
WHILE I DIDN'T UNDERSTAND THEM VERY WELL, AT ANY RATE, IT SOUNDS LIKE THE GOBLINS AREN'T HERE NOW...
...AND THESE WEREWOLVES HAVE TAKEN OVER THE GOBLINS' WORK OF RAISING BARK!
THE TWO LIZARDFOLK SAY THAT'S WHY THEY'VE COME HERE.
THEY EXCHANGED SOMETHING FOR BARK!
IT WAS A MIXTURE OF DRIED LEFTOVER FISH LIKE YOU SEE AT FISHING PORTS(?).
IT SEEMS THEY SOAK IT IN WATER AND THEN USE IT FOR FEED.
WHATEVER IT IS, IT STINKS.
MUWA (WAFT)
THEY ALL HAVE KEENER NOSES THAN ME! HOW CAN THEY STAND THE SMELL...?
HAIRLESS ONES. HERE.

Hospitality

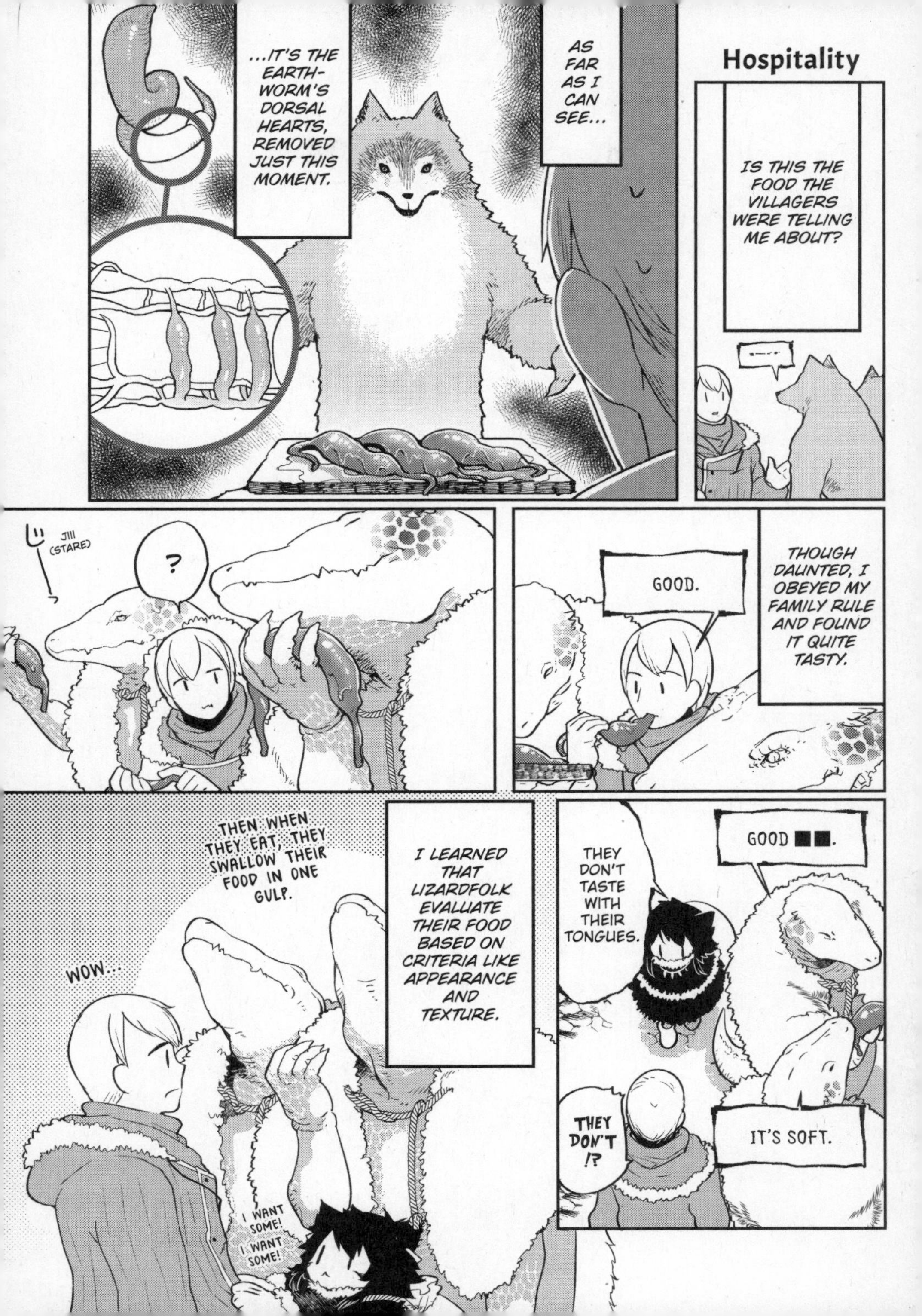

IS THIS THE FOOD THE VILLAGERS WERE TELLING ME ABOUT?
....
AS FAR AS I CAN SEE...
...IT'S THE EARTH-WORM'S DORSAL HEARTS, REMOVED JUST THIS MOMENT.
THOUGH DAUNTED, I OBEYED MY FAMILY RULE AND FOUND IT QUITE TASTY.
GOOD.
?
じ JIII (STARE)
GOOD [redacted].
THEY DON'T TASTE WITH THEIR TONGUES.
IT'S SOFT.
THEY DON'T!?
I LEARNED THAT LIZARDFOLK EVALUATE THEIR FOOD BASED ON CRITERIA LIKE APPEARANCE AND TEXTURE.
THEN WHEN THEY EAT, THEY SWALLOW THEIR FOOD IN ONE GULP.
WOW...
I WANT SOME! I WANT SOME!

Do It Myself

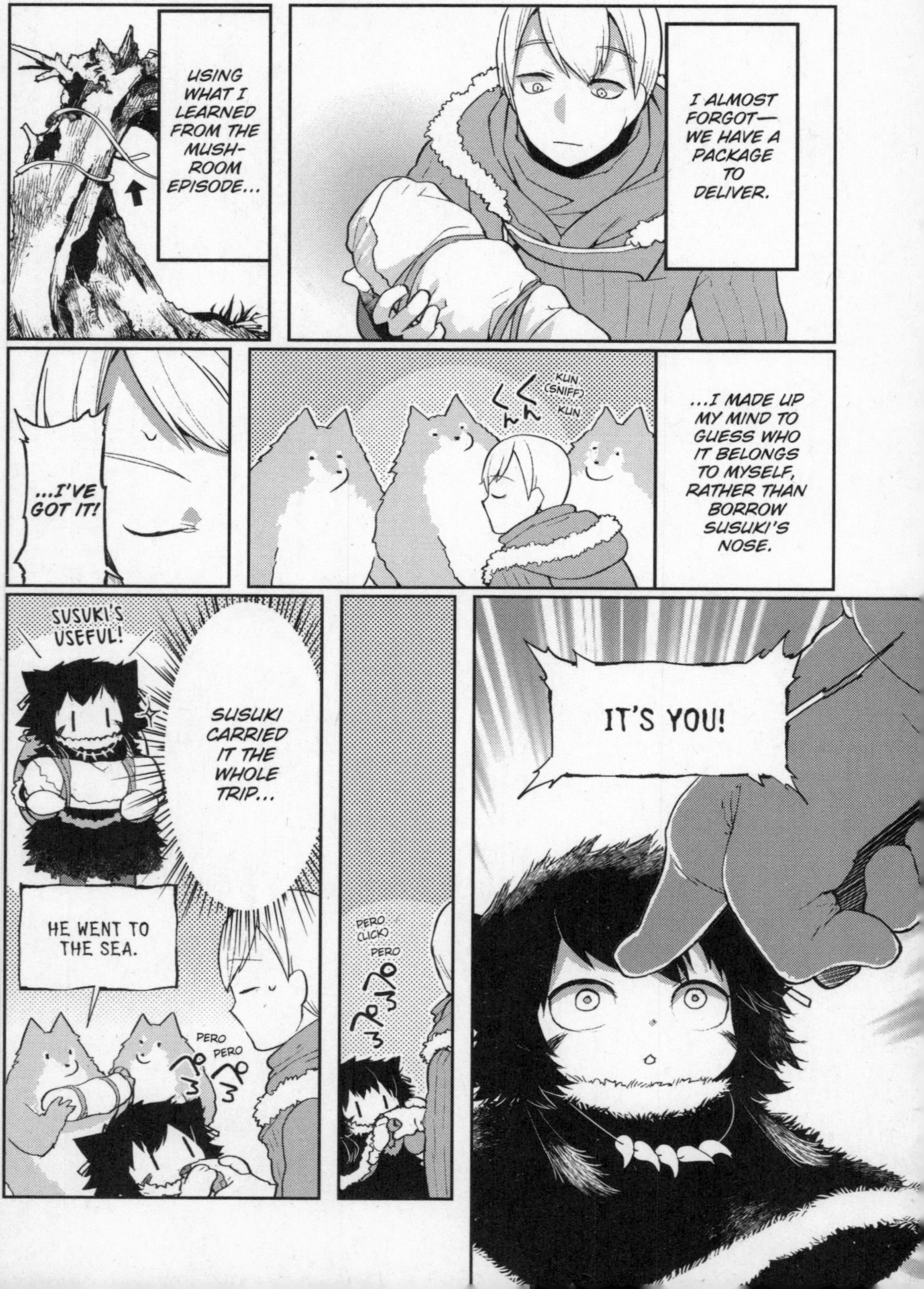
I ALMOST FORGOT—WE HAVE A PACKAGE TO DELIVER.
USING WHAT I LEARNED FROM THE MUSH-ROOM EPISODE...
...I MADE UP MY MIND TO GUESS WHO IT BELONGS TO MYSELF, RATHER THAN BORROW SUSUKI'S NOSE.
くんくん
KUN (SNIFF) KUN
...I'VE GOT IT!
IT'S YOU!
ぺろぺろ
PERO (LICK) PERO
SUSUKI CARRIED IT THE WHOLE TRIP...
SUSUKI'S USEFUL!
HE WENT TO THE SEA.
ぺろぺろ
PERO PERO

No Road Is Long with Good Company

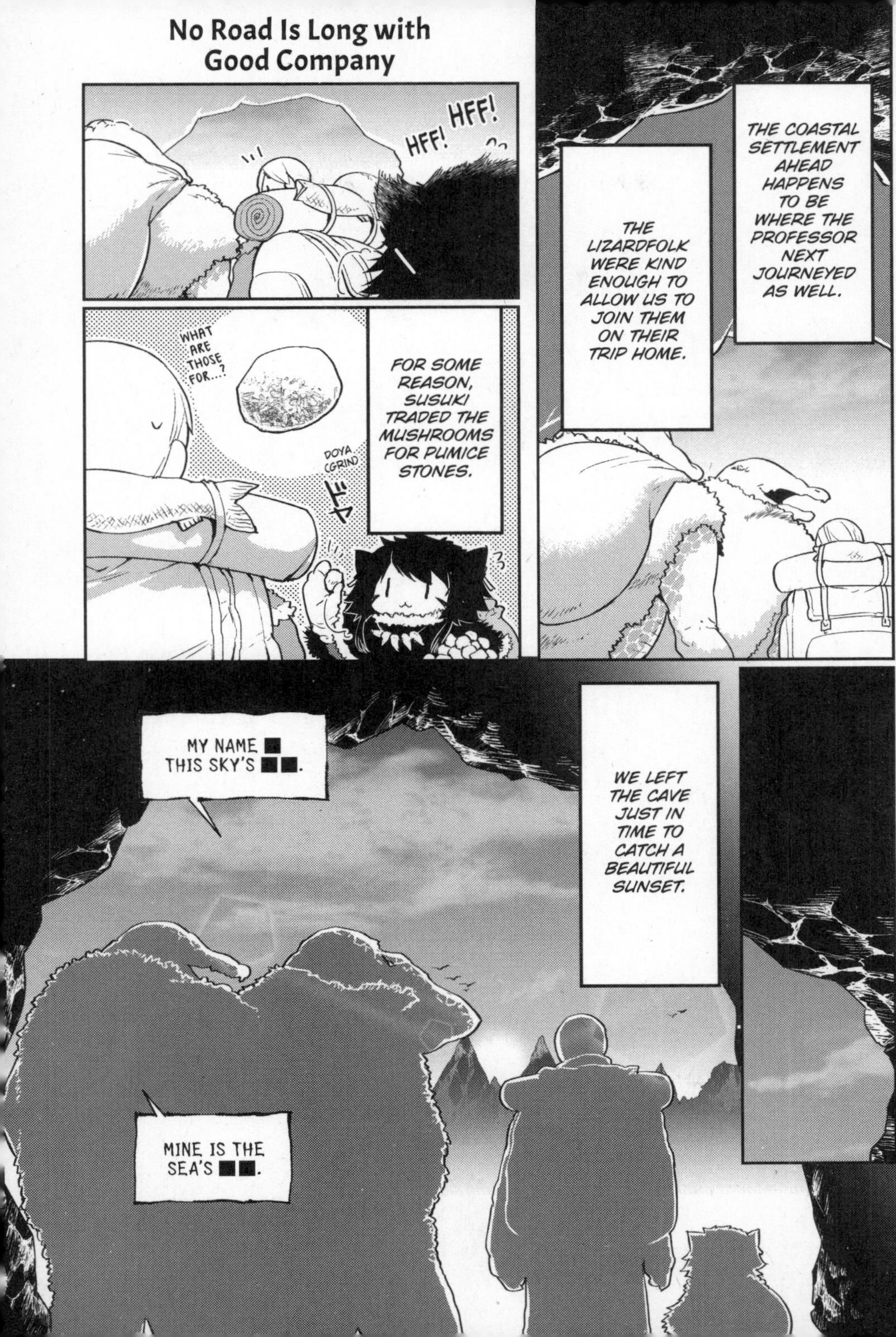
THE COASTAL SETTLEMENT AHEAD HAPPENS TO BE WHERE THE PROFESSOR NEXT JOURNEYED AS WELL.
THE LIZARDFOLK WERE KIND ENOUGH TO ALLOW US TO JOIN THEM ON THEIR TRIP HOME.
HFF! HFF!
FOR SOME REASON, SUSUKI TRADED THE MUSHROOMS FOR PUMICE STONES.
WHAT ARE THOSE FOR...?
DOYA (GRIND)
WE LEFT THE CAVE JUST IN TIME TO CATCH A BEAUTIFUL SUNSET.
MY NAME [redacted] THIS SKY'S [redacted].
MINE IS THE SEA'S [redacted].

Information Overload

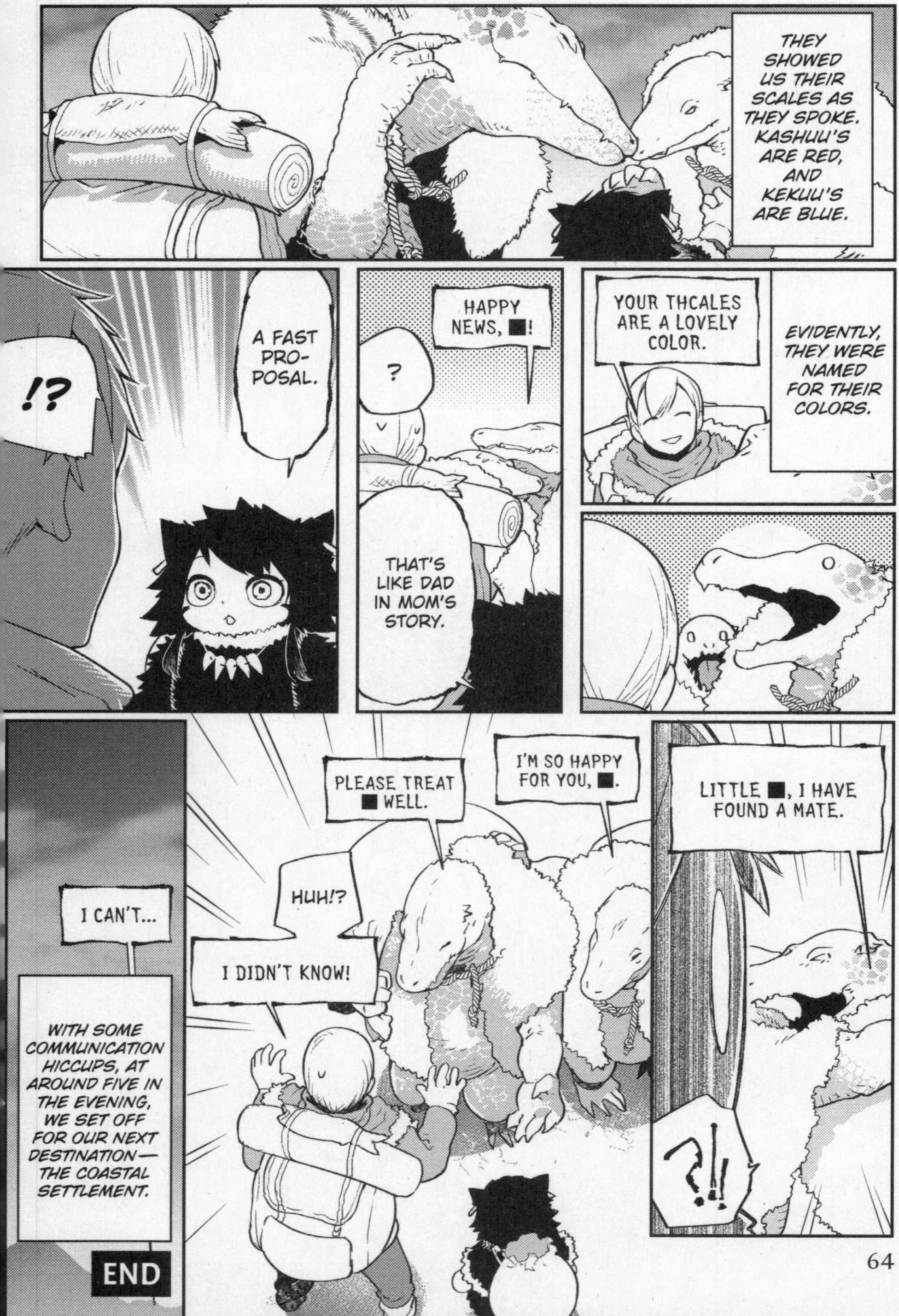

THEY SHOWED US THEIR SCALES AS THEY SPOKE. KASHUU'S ARE RED, AND KEKUU'S ARE BLUE.
EVIDENTLY, THEY WERE NAMED FOR THEIR COLORS.
YOUR THCALES ARE A LOVELY COLOR.
HAPPY NEWS, [redacted]!
?
THAT'S LIKE DAD IN MOM'S STORY.
A FAST PRO-POSAL.
!?
LITTLE [redacted], I HAVE FOUND A MATE.
?!!
I'M SO HAPPY FOR YOU, [redacted].
PLEASE TREAT [redacted] WELL.
HUH!?
I DIDN'T KNOW!
I CAN'T...
WITH SOME COMMUNICATION HICCUPS, AT AROUND FIVE IN THE EVENING, WE SET OFF FOR OUR NEXT DESTINATION—THE COASTAL SETTLEMENT.
END

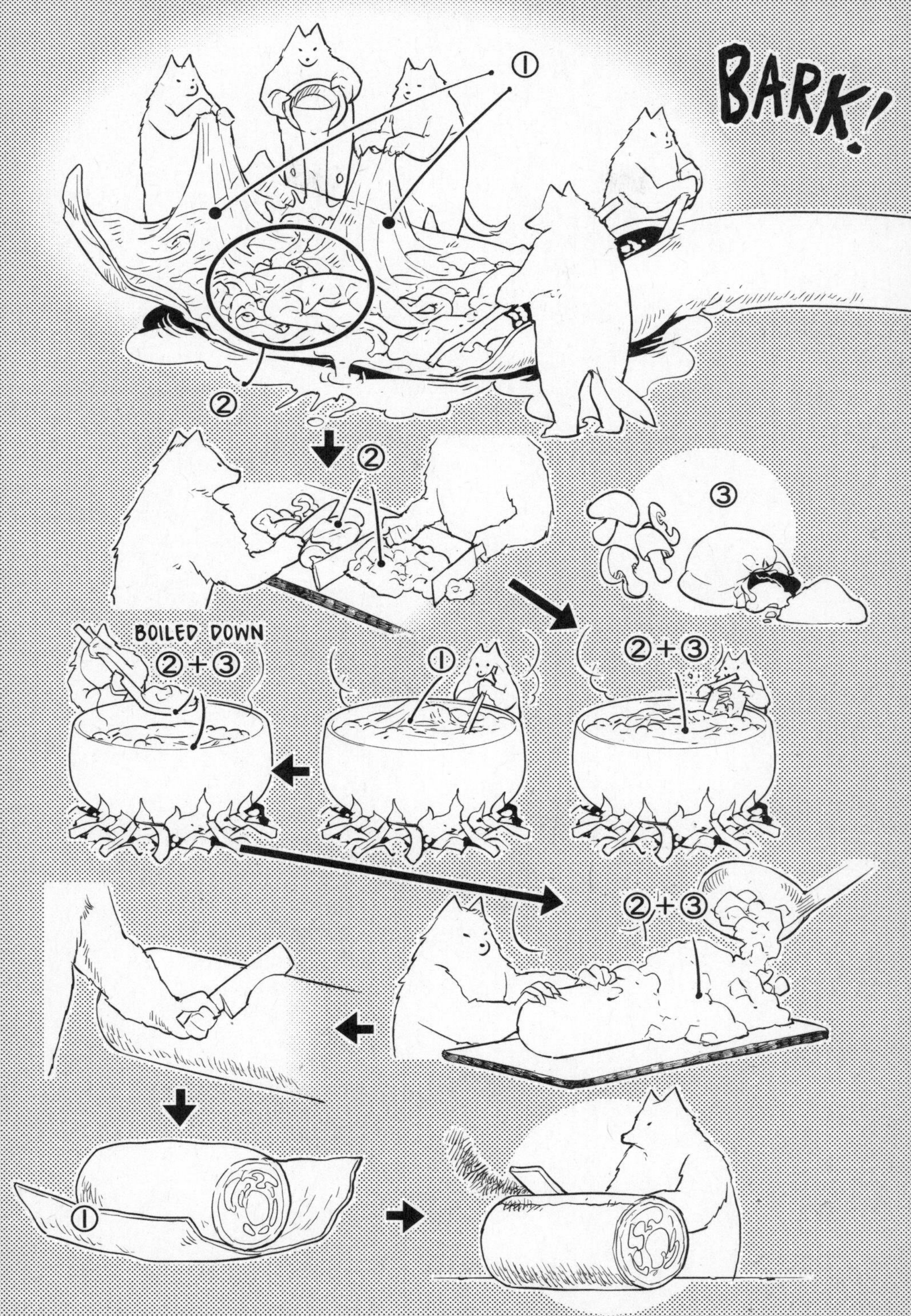
BARK!
①
②
②
③
②+③
①
BOILED DOWN
②+③
②+③
①

WHEN CONVERSING,
THEY SOMETIMES STOP WITH
THEIR MOUTHS OPEN.

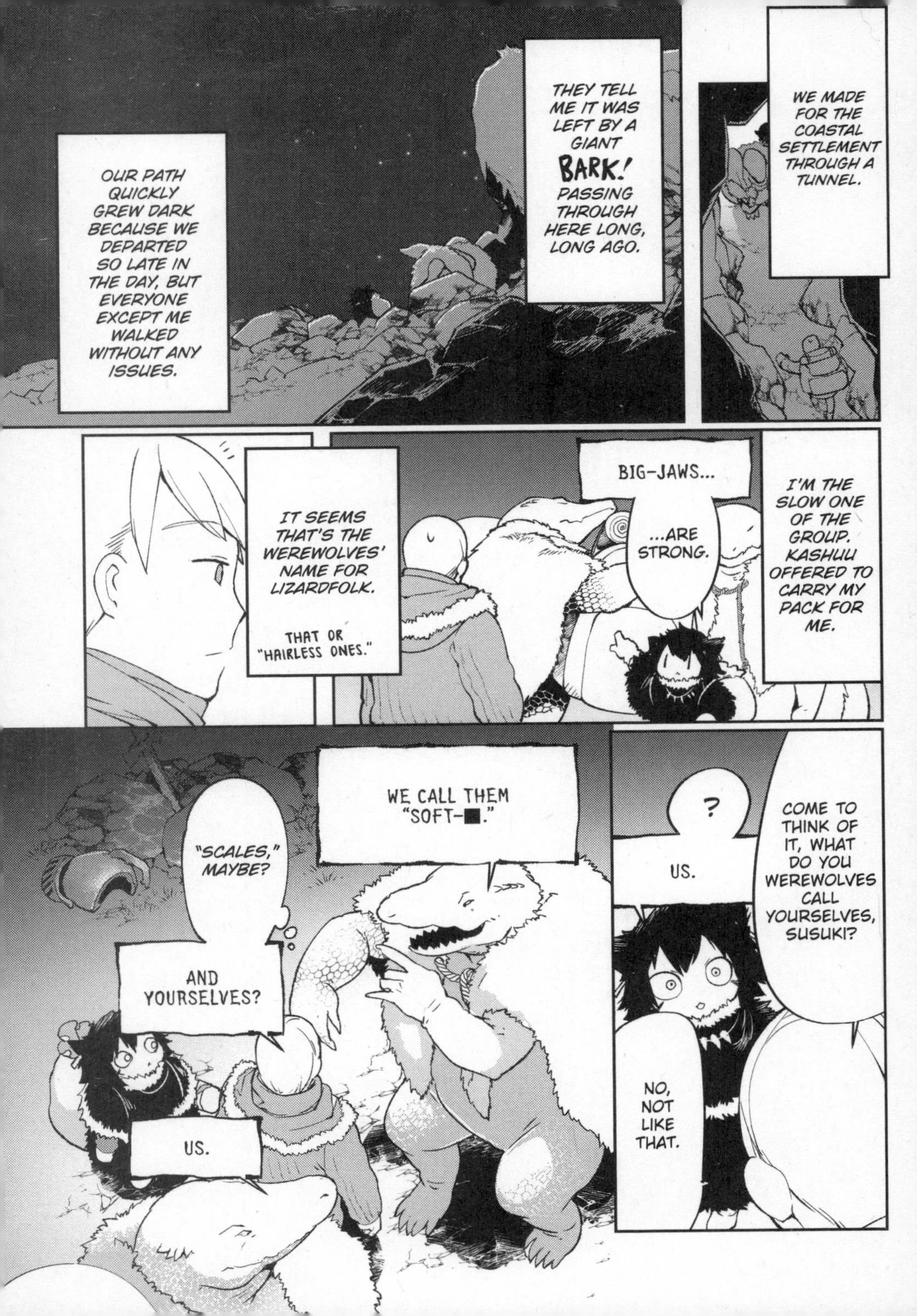
WE MADE FOR THE COASTAL SETTLEMENT THROUGH A TUNNEL.
THEY TELL ME IT WAS LEFT BY A GIANT BARK! PASSING THROUGH HERE LONG, LONG AGO.
OUR PATH QUICKLY GREW DARK BECAUSE WE DEPARTED SO LATE IN THE DAY, BUT EVERYONE EXCEPT ME WALKED WITHOUT ANY ISSUES.
I'M THE SLOW ONE OF THE GROUP. KASHUU OFFERED TO CARRY MY PACK FOR ME.
BIG-JAWS...
...ARE STRONG.
IT SEEMS THAT'S THE WEREWOLVES' NAME FOR LIZARDFOLK.
THAT OR "HAIRLESS ONES."
COME TO THINK OF IT, WHAT DO YOU WEREWOLVES CALL YOURSELVES, SUSUKI?
?
US.
NO, NOT LIKE THAT.
WE CALL THEM "SOFT-■."
"SCALES," MAYBE?
AND YOURSELVES?
US.

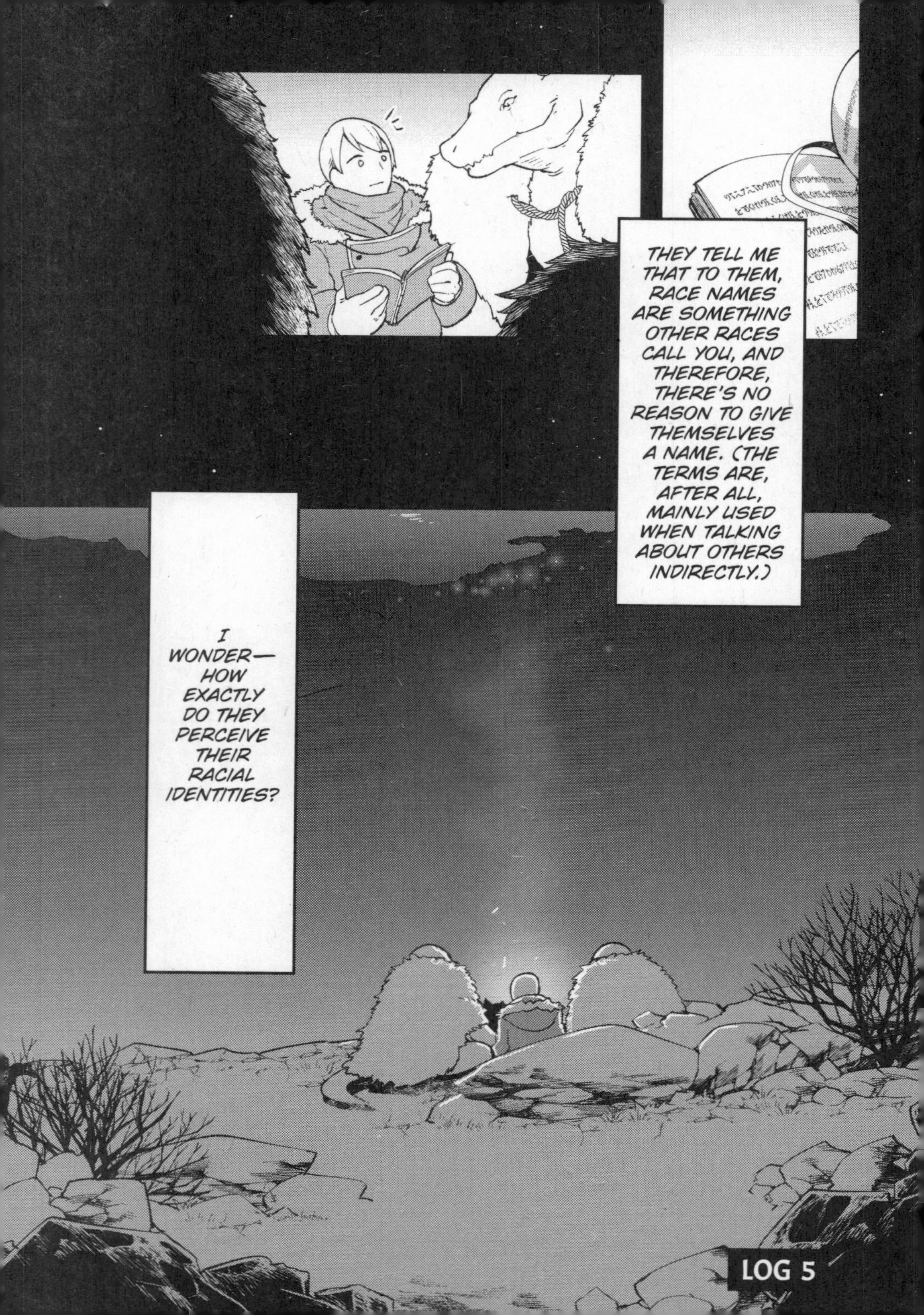
THEY TELL ME THAT TO THEM, RACE NAMES ARE SOMETHING OTHER RACES CALL YOU, AND THEREFORE, THERE'S NO REASON TO GIVE THEMSELVES A NAME. (THE TERMS ARE, AFTER ALL, MAINLY USED WHEN TALKING ABOUT OTHERS INDIRECTLY.)
I WONDER—HOW EXACTLY DO THEY PERCEIVE THEIR RACIAL IDENTITIES?

Object of Interest

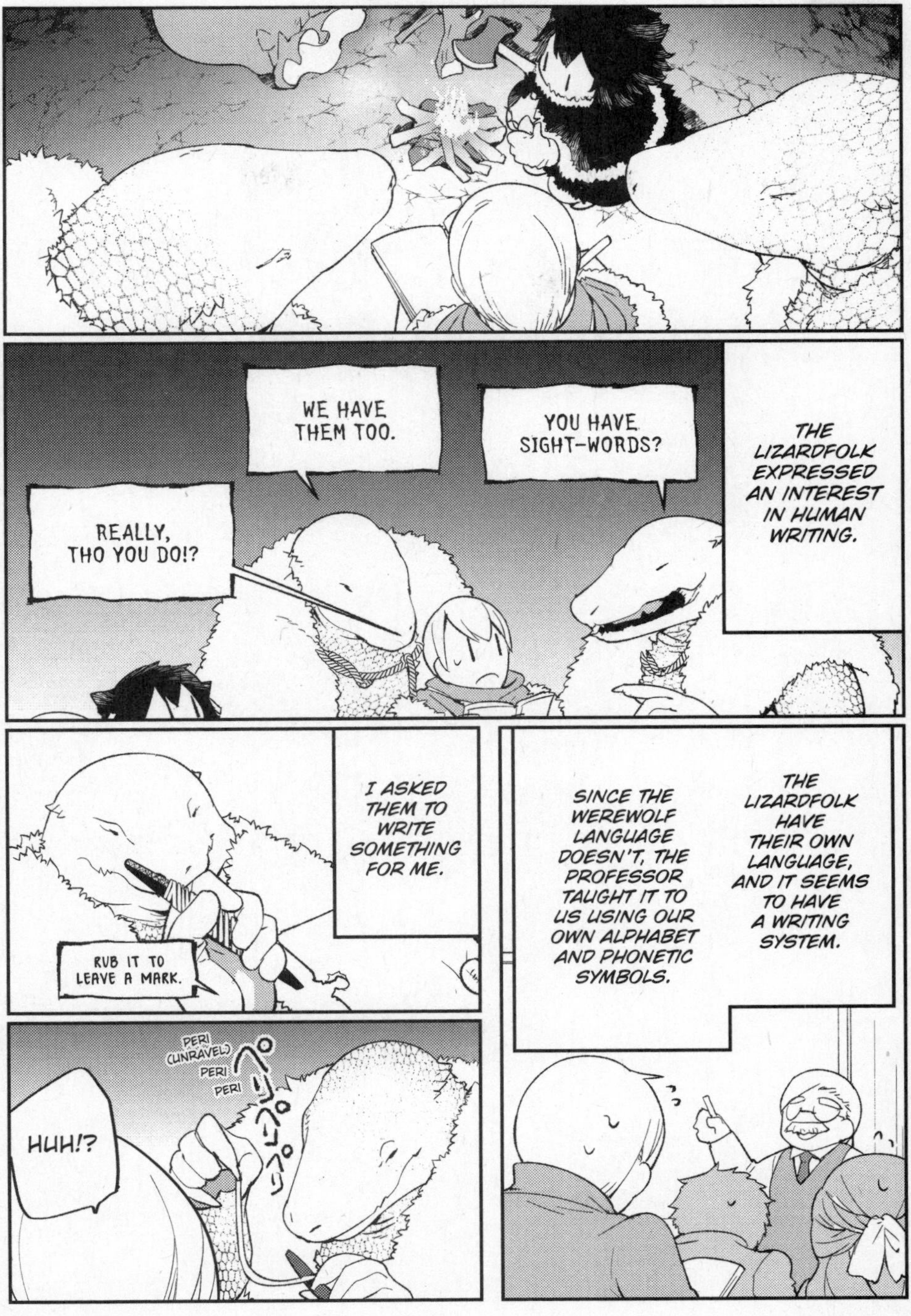
THE LIZARDFOLK EXPRESSED AN INTEREST IN HUMAN WRITING.
YOU HAVE SIGHT-WORDS?
WE HAVE THEM TOO.
REALLY, THO YOU DO!?
THE LIZARDFOLK HAVE THEIR OWN LANGUAGE, AND IT SEEMS TO HAVE A WRITING SYSTEM.
SINCE THE WEREWOLF LANGUAGE DOESN'T, THE PROFESSOR TAUGHT IT TO US USING OUR OWN ALPHABET AND PHONETIC SYMBOLS.
I ASKED THEM TO WRITE SOMETHING FOR ME.
RUB IT TO LEAVE A MARK.
PERI (UNRAVEL) PERI PERI
HUH!?

Lizardfolk Writing

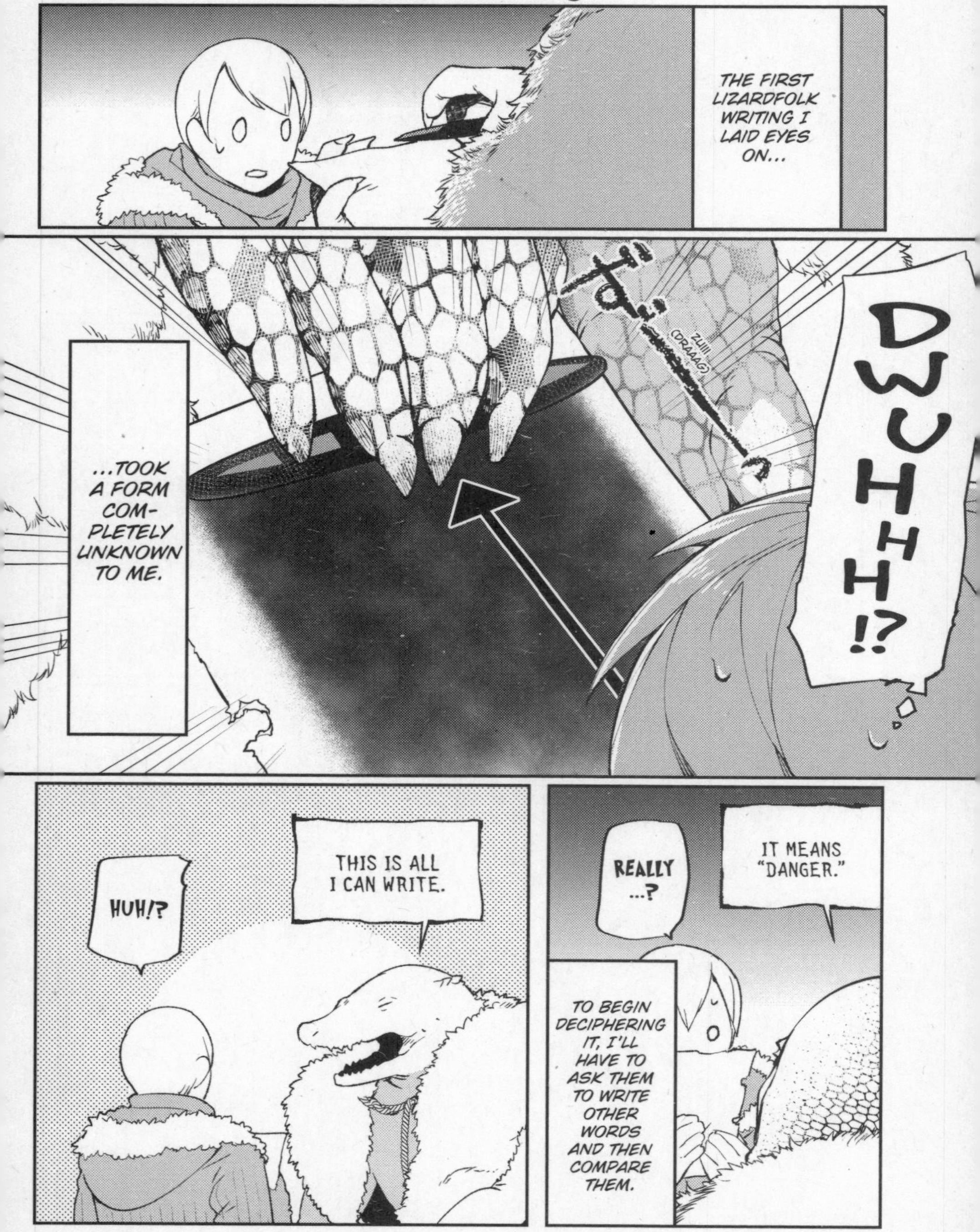
THE FIRST LIZARDFOLK WRITING I LAID EYES ON...
DWUHHH!?
ZUIII (DRAAAG)
...TOOK A FORM COMPLETELY UNKNOWN TO ME.
IT MEANS "DANGER."
REALLY ...?
TO BEGIN DECIPHERING IT, I'LL HAVE TO ASK THEM TO WRITE OTHER WORDS AND THEN COMPARE THEM.
THIS IS ALL I CAN WRITE.
HUH!?

The Mystery Deepens

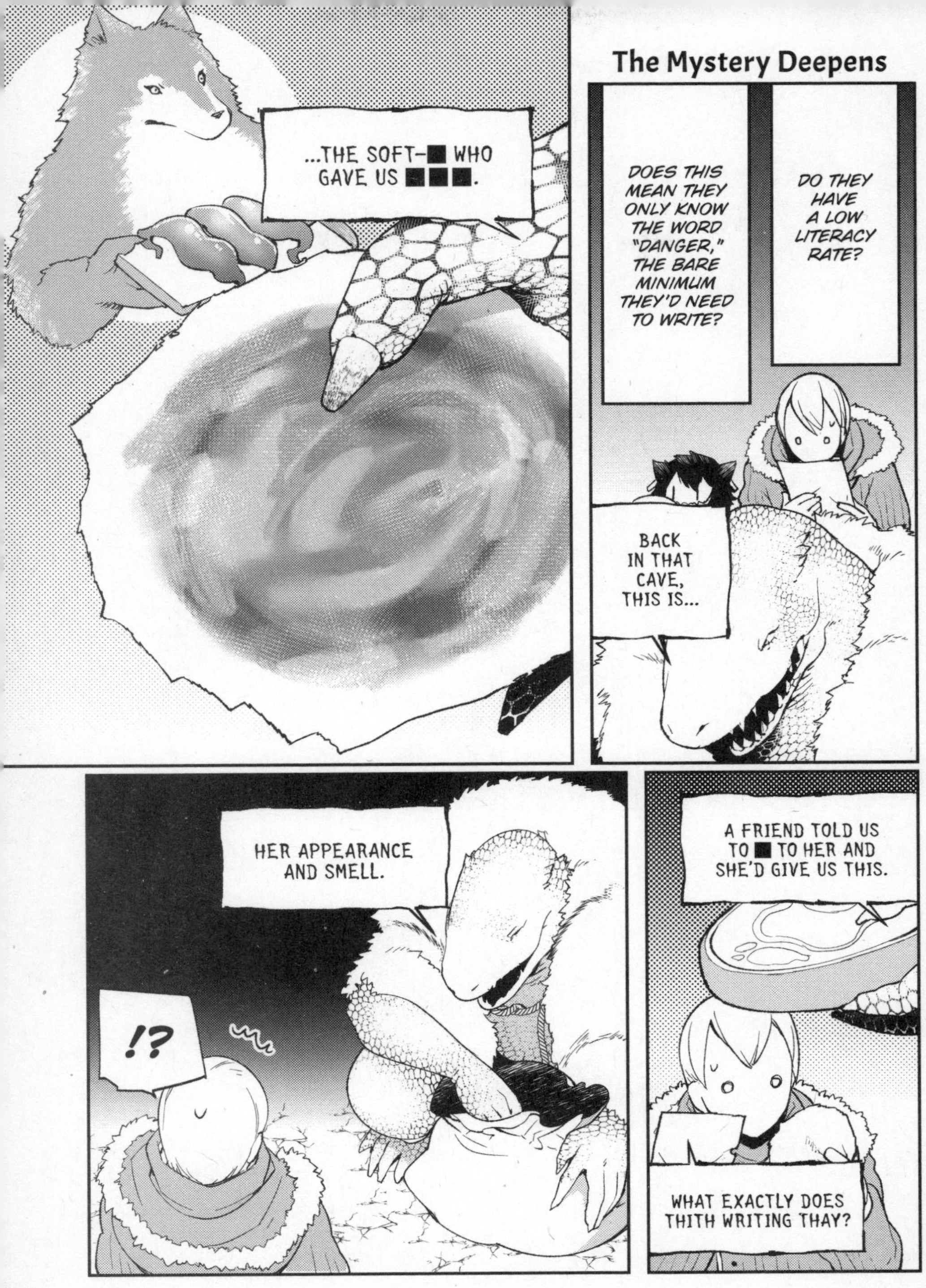
DO THEY HAVE A LOW LITERACY RATE?
DOES THIS MEAN THEY ONLY KNOW THE WORD "DANGER," THE BARE MINIMUM THEY'D NEED TO WRITE?
BACK IN THAT CAVE, THIS IS...
...THE SOFT-[redacted] WHO GAVE US [redacted].
A FRIEND TOLD US TO [redacted] TO HER AND SHE'D GIVE US THIS.
WHAT EXACTLY DOES THITH WRITING THAY?
HER APPEARANCE AND SMELL.
!?

Commence Puzzle-Solving

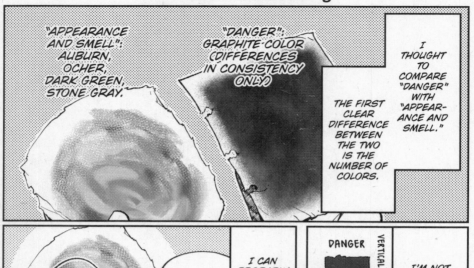

"APPEARANCE AND SMELL": AUBURN, OCHER, DARK GREEN, STONE GRAY.

"DANGER": GRAPHITE COLOR (DIFFERENCES IN CONSISTENCY ONLY.)

THE FIRST CLEAR DIFFERENCE BETWEEN THE TWO IS THE NUMBER OF COLORS.

I THOUGHT TO COMPARE "DANGER" WITH "APPEARANCE AND SMELL."

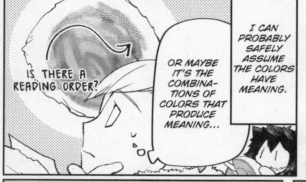

IS THERE A READING ORDER?

OR MAYBE IT'S THE COMBINATIONS OF COLORS THAT PRODUCE MEANING...

I CAN PROBABLY SAFELY ASSUME THE COLORS HAVE MEANING.

DANGER

VERTICAL STROKE ↓

APPEARANCE/SMELL

I'M NOT SURE I UNDERSTAND THE DIFFERENCE IN SHAPE, BUT I'LL WRITE IT DOWN IN A SIMPLIFIED FORM.

THAT MEANS "THIS IS ALL I CAN WRITE" ACTUALLY MEANT "THIS IS ALL I CAN WRITE WITH THIS COLOR"!?

I CAN WRITE MORE WITH THIS.

Their Writing Tools

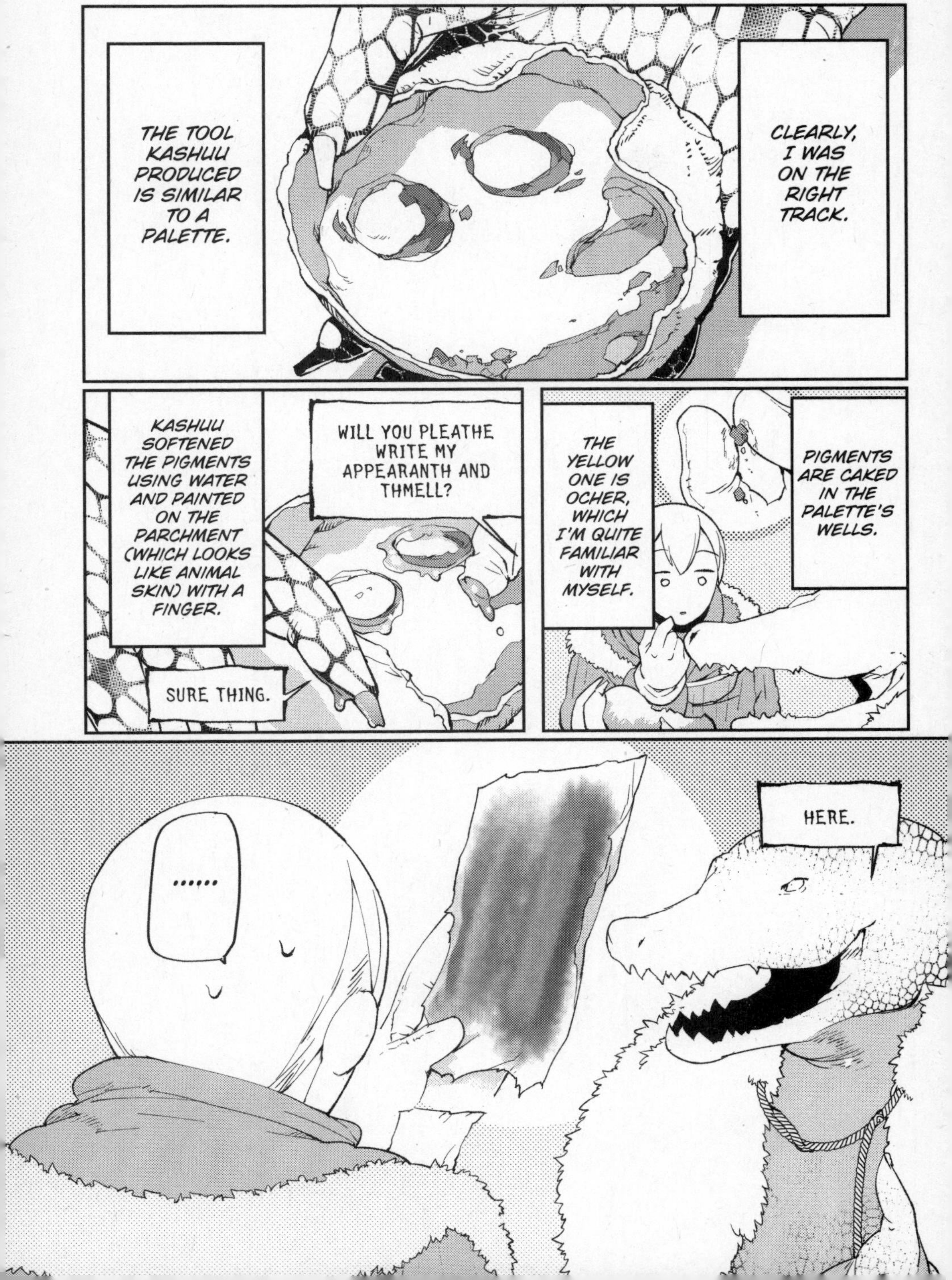
CLEARLY, I WAS ON THE RIGHT TRACK.
THE TOOL KASHUU PRODUCED IS SIMILAR TO A PALETTE.
PIGMENTS ARE CAKED IN THE PALETTE'S WELLS.
THE YELLOW ONE IS OCHER, WHICH I'M QUITE FAMILIAR WITH MYSELF.
WILL YOU PLEATHE WRITE MY APPEARANTH AND THMELL?
KASHUU SOFTENED THE PIGMENTS USING WATER AND PAINTED ON THE PARCHMENT (WHICH LOOKS LIKE ANIMAL SKIN) WITH A FINGER.
SURE THING.
HERE.
......

On My Own

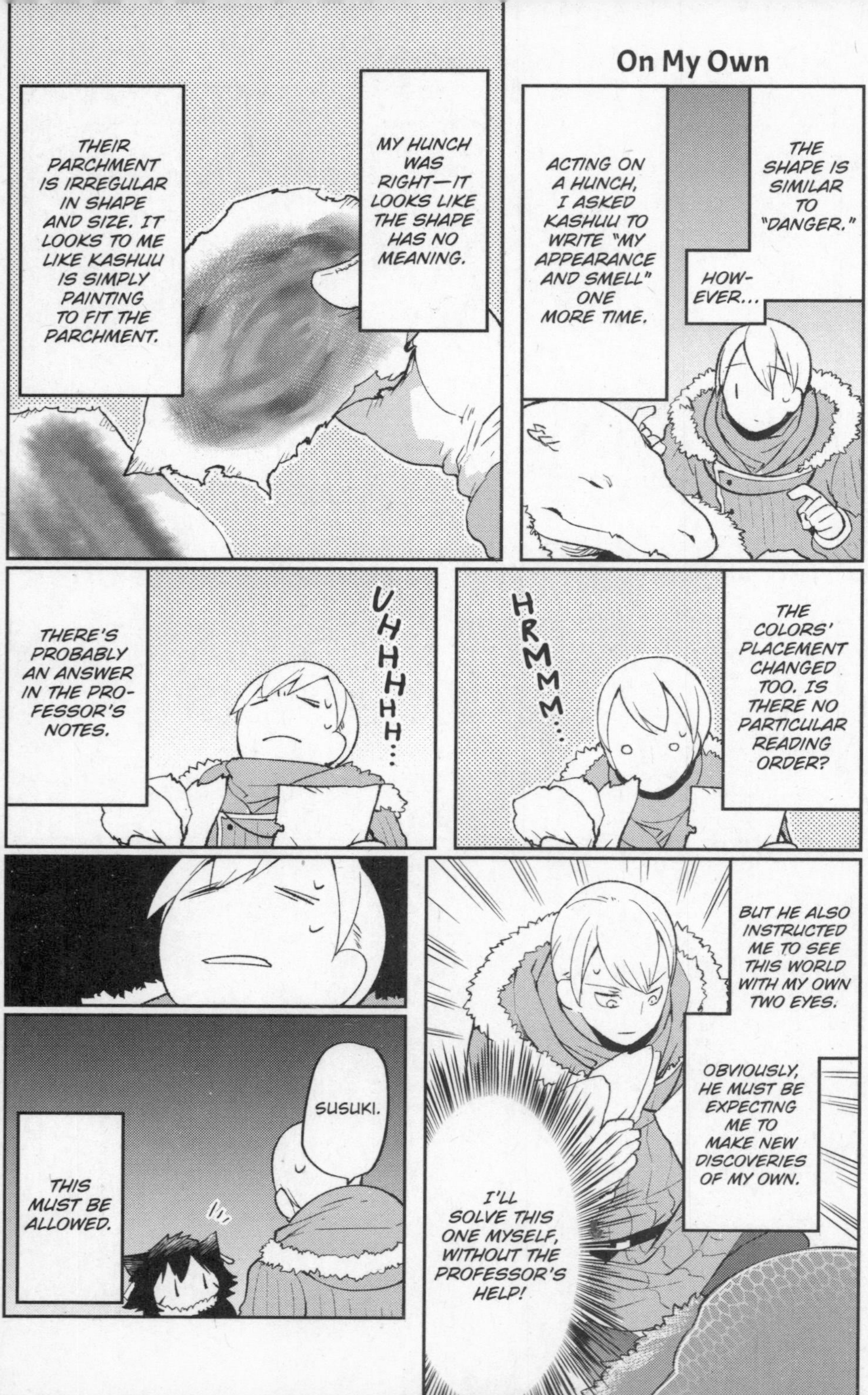
THE SHAPE IS SIMILAR TO "DANGER."
ACTING ON A HUNCH, I ASKED KASHUU TO WRITE "MY APPEARANCE AND SMELL" ONE MORE TIME.
HOW-EVER...
MY HUNCH WAS RIGHT—IT LOOKS LIKE THE SHAPE HAS NO MEANING.
THEIR PARCHMENT IS IRREGULAR IN SHAPE AND SIZE. IT LOOKS TO ME LIKE KASHUU IS SIMPLY PAINTING TO FIT THE PARCHMENT.
THE COLORS' PLACEMENT CHANGED TOO. IS THERE NO PARTICULAR READING ORDER?
HRMMM...
UHHHHH...
THERE'S PROBABLY AN ANSWER IN THE PRO-FESSOR'S NOTES.
BUT HE ALSO INSTRUCTED ME TO SEE THIS WORLD WITH MY OWN TWO EYES.
OBVIOUSLY, HE MUST BE EXPECTING ME TO MAKE NEW DISCOVERIES OF MY OWN.
I'LL SOLVE THIS ONE MYSELF, WITHOUT THE PROFESSOR'S HELP!
SUSUKI.
THIS MUST BE ALLOWED.

Strange Reaction

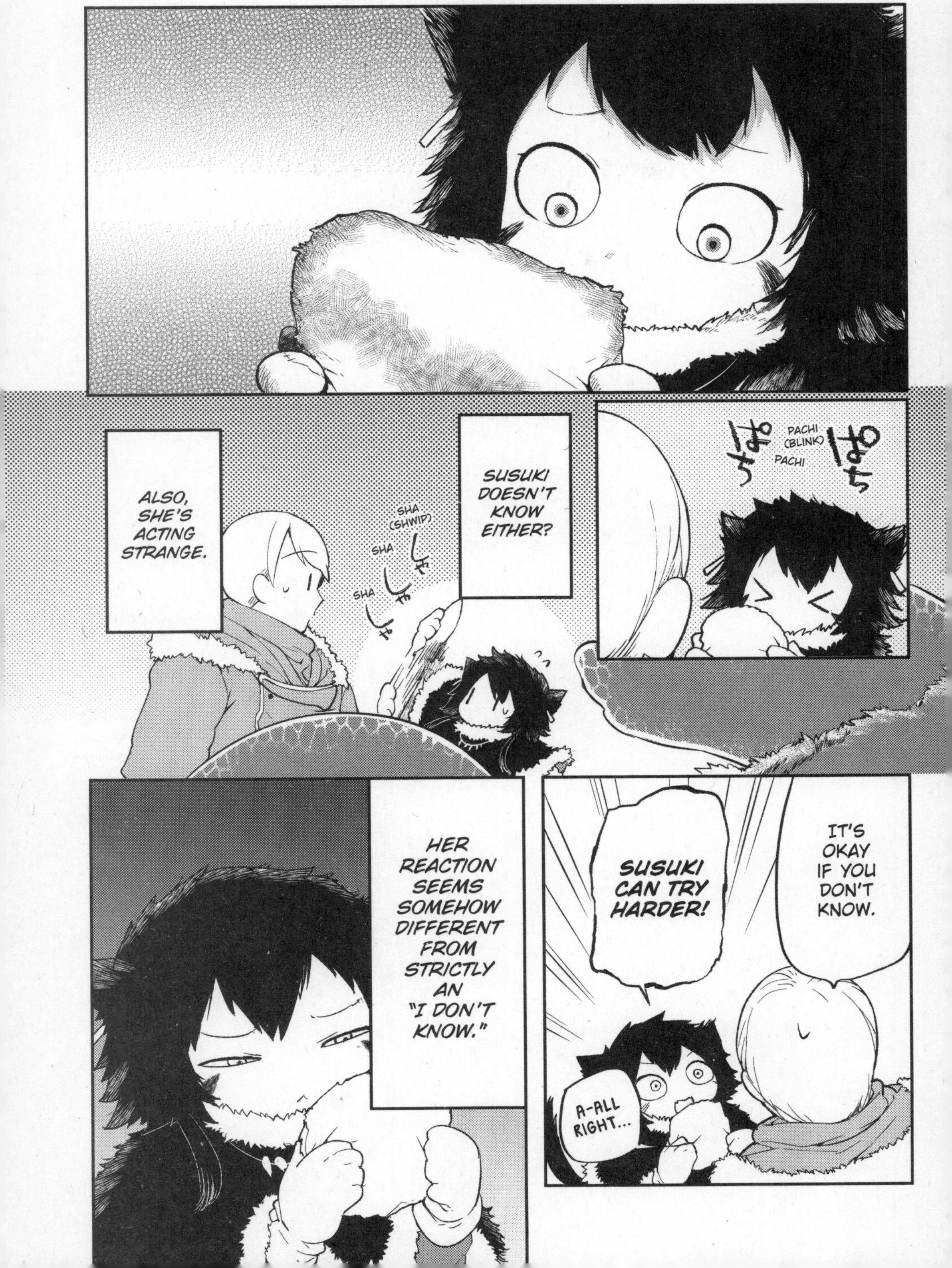
ぱち ぱち
PACHI (BLINK) PACHI
SUSUKI DOESN'T KNOW EITHER?
しゃ しゃ しゃ
SHA (SHWIP) SHA SHA
ALSO, SHE'S ACTING STRANGE.
IT'S OKAY IF YOU DON'T KNOW.
SUSUKI CAN TRY HARDER!
A-ALL RIGHT...
HER REACTION SEEMS SOMEHOW DIFFERENT FROM STRICTLY AN "I DON'T KNOW."

Synesthetic

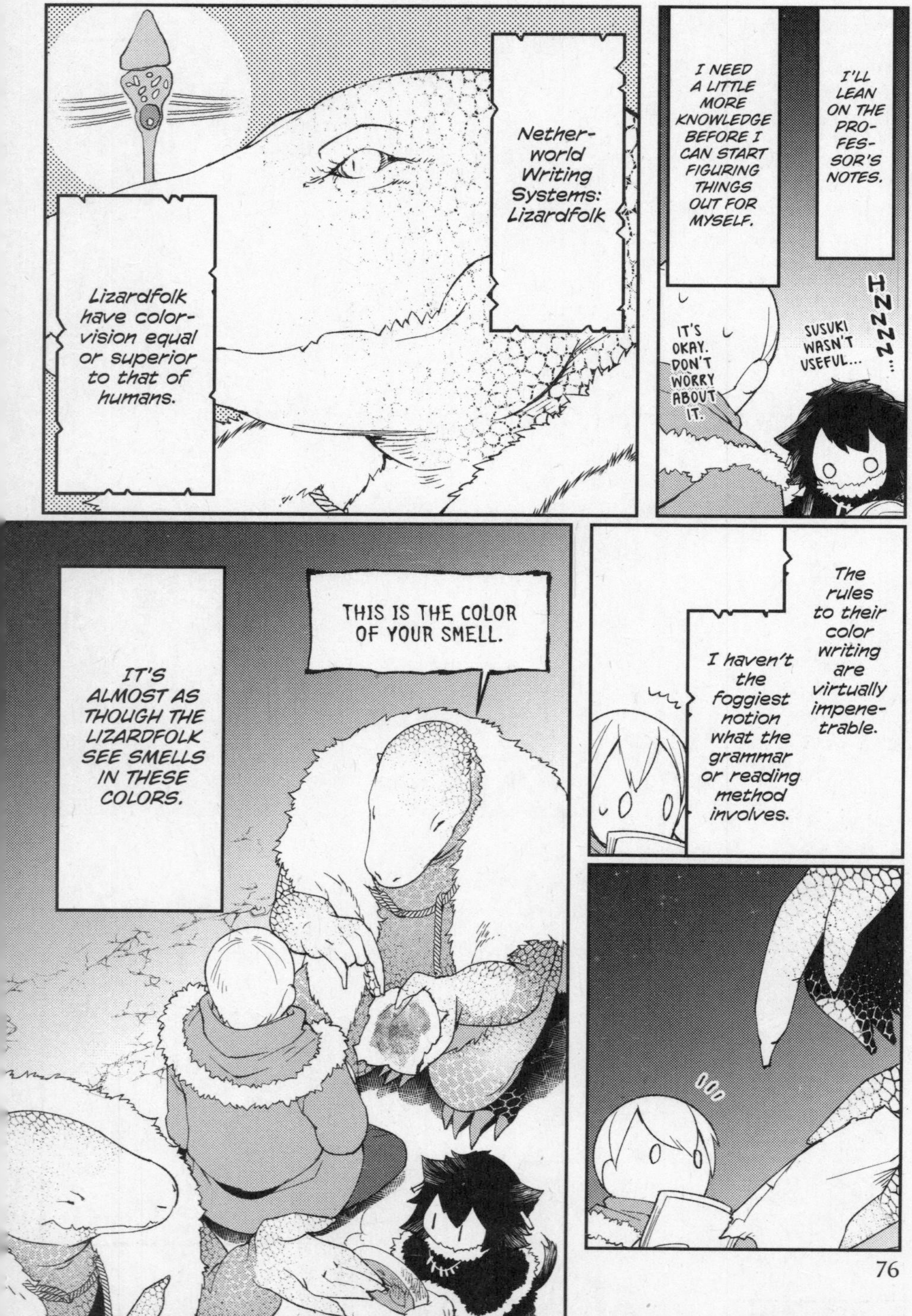

I'LL LEAN ON THE PROFESSOR'S NOTES.
I NEED A LITTLE MORE KNOWLEDGE BEFORE I CAN START FIGURING THINGS OUT FOR MYSELF.
HNNNN...
SUSUKI WASN'T USEFUL...
IT'S OKAY. DON'T WORRY ABOUT IT.
Netherworld Writing Systems: Lizardfolk
Lizardfolk have color-vision equal or superior to that of humans.
The rules to their color writing are virtually impenetrable.
I haven't the foggiest notion what the grammar or reading method involves.
THIS IS THE COLOR OF YOUR SMELL.
IT'S ALMOST AS THOUGH THE LIZARDFOLK SEE SMELLS IN THESE COLORS.

Theory Overturned

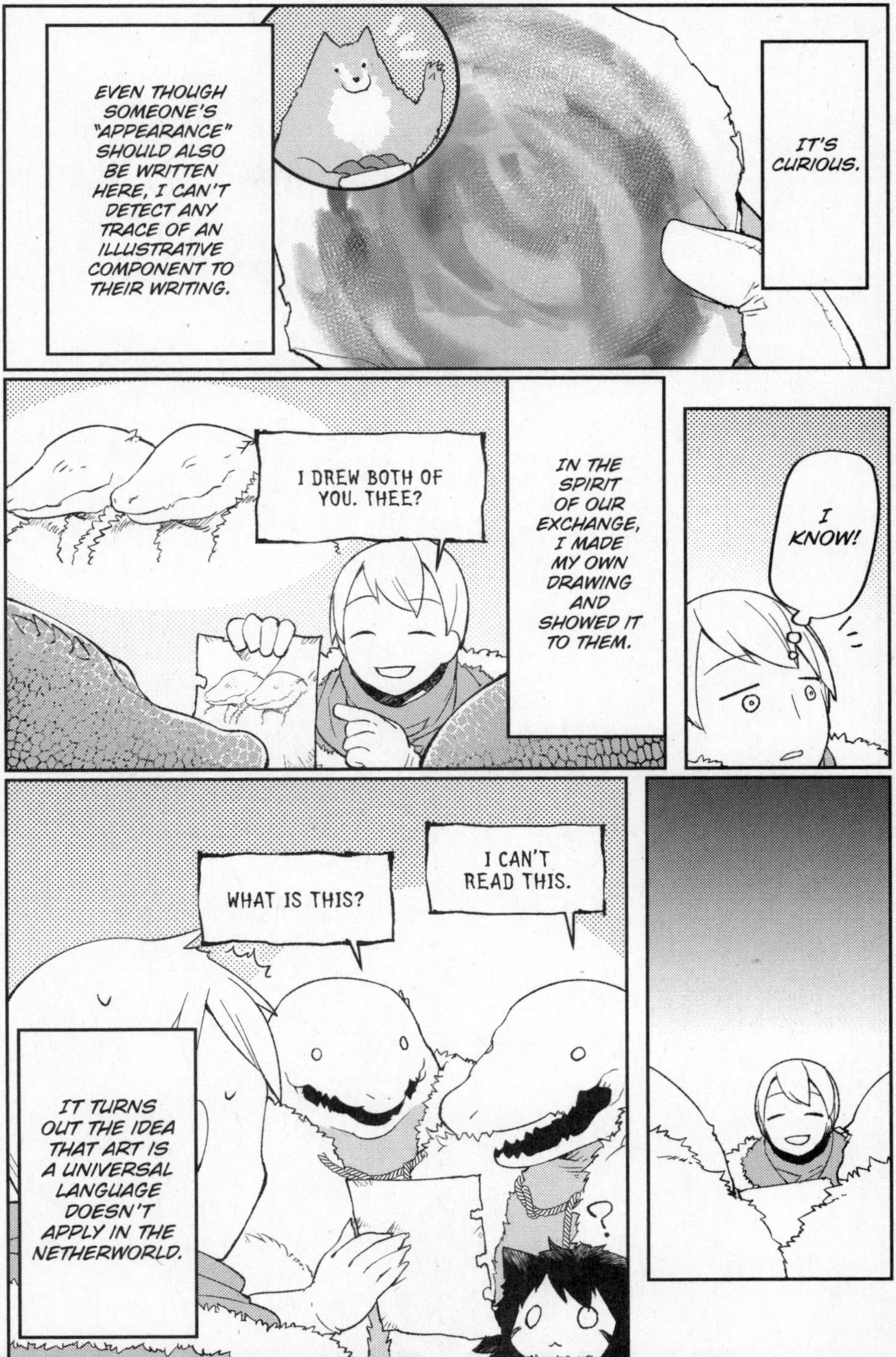
IT'S CURIOUS.
EVEN THOUGH SOMEONE'S "APPEARANCE" SHOULD ALSO BE WRITTEN HERE, I CAN'T DETECT ANY TRACE OF AN ILLUSTRATIVE COMPONENT TO THEIR WRITING.
I KNOW!
IN THE SPIRIT OF OUR EXCHANGE, I MADE MY OWN DRAWING AND SHOWED IT TO THEM.
I DREW BOTH OF YOU. THEE?
I CAN'T READ THIS.
WHAT IS THIS?
IT TURNS OUT THE IDEA THAT ART IS A UNIVERSAL LANGUAGE DOESN'T APPLY IN THE NETHERWORLD.

What Do You Want?

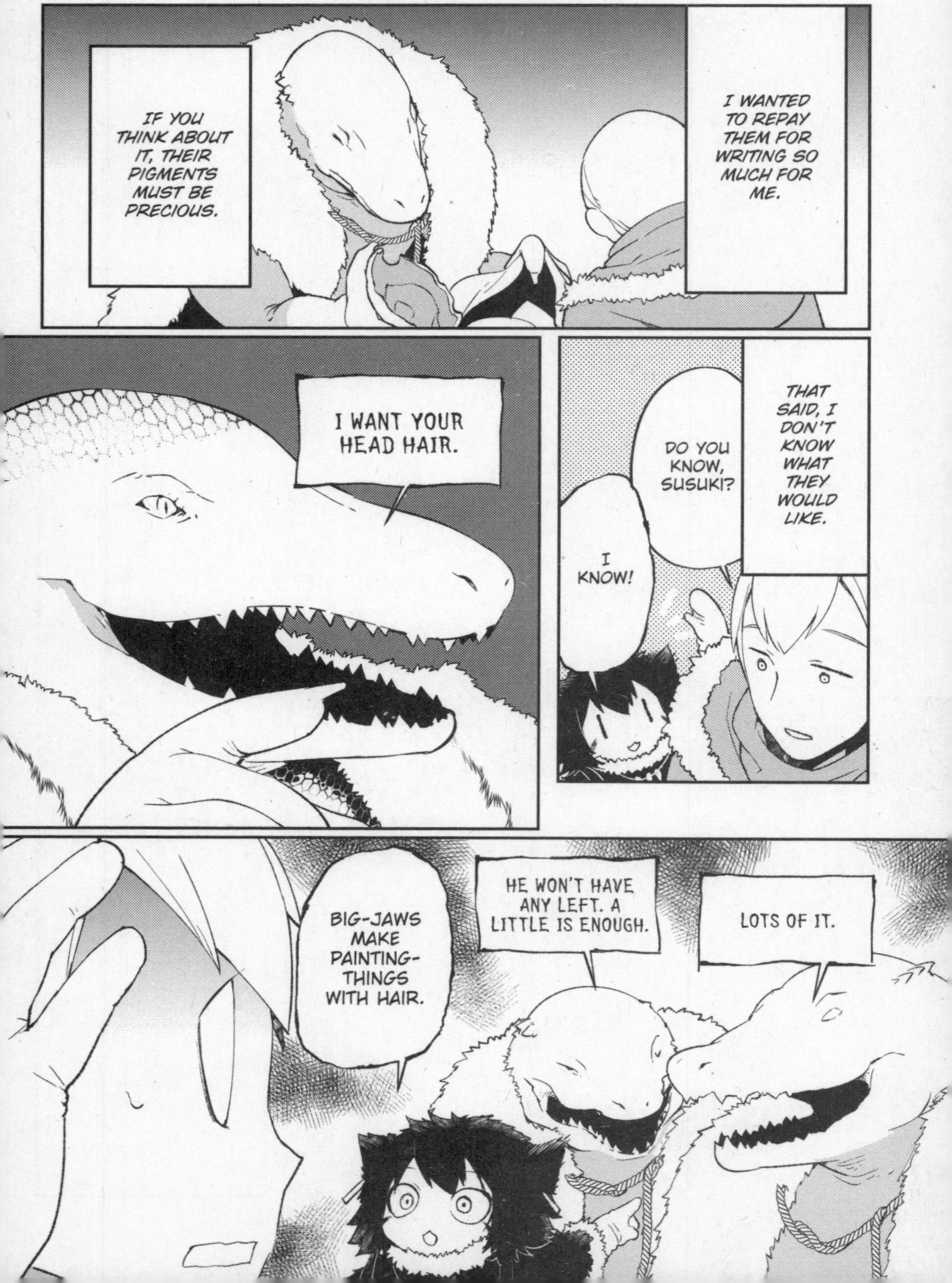
I WANTED TO REPAY THEM FOR WRITING SO MUCH FOR ME.
IF YOU THINK ABOUT IT, THEIR PIGMENTS MUST BE PRECIOUS.
THAT SAID, I DON'T KNOW WHAT THEY WOULD LIKE.
DO YOU KNOW, SUSUKI?
I KNOW!
I WANT YOUR HEAD HAIR.
LOTS OF IT.
HE WON'T HAVE ANY LEFT. A LITTLE IS ENOUGH.
BIG-JAWS MAKE PAINTING-THINGS WITH HAIR.

Token of Gratitude and Words of Praise

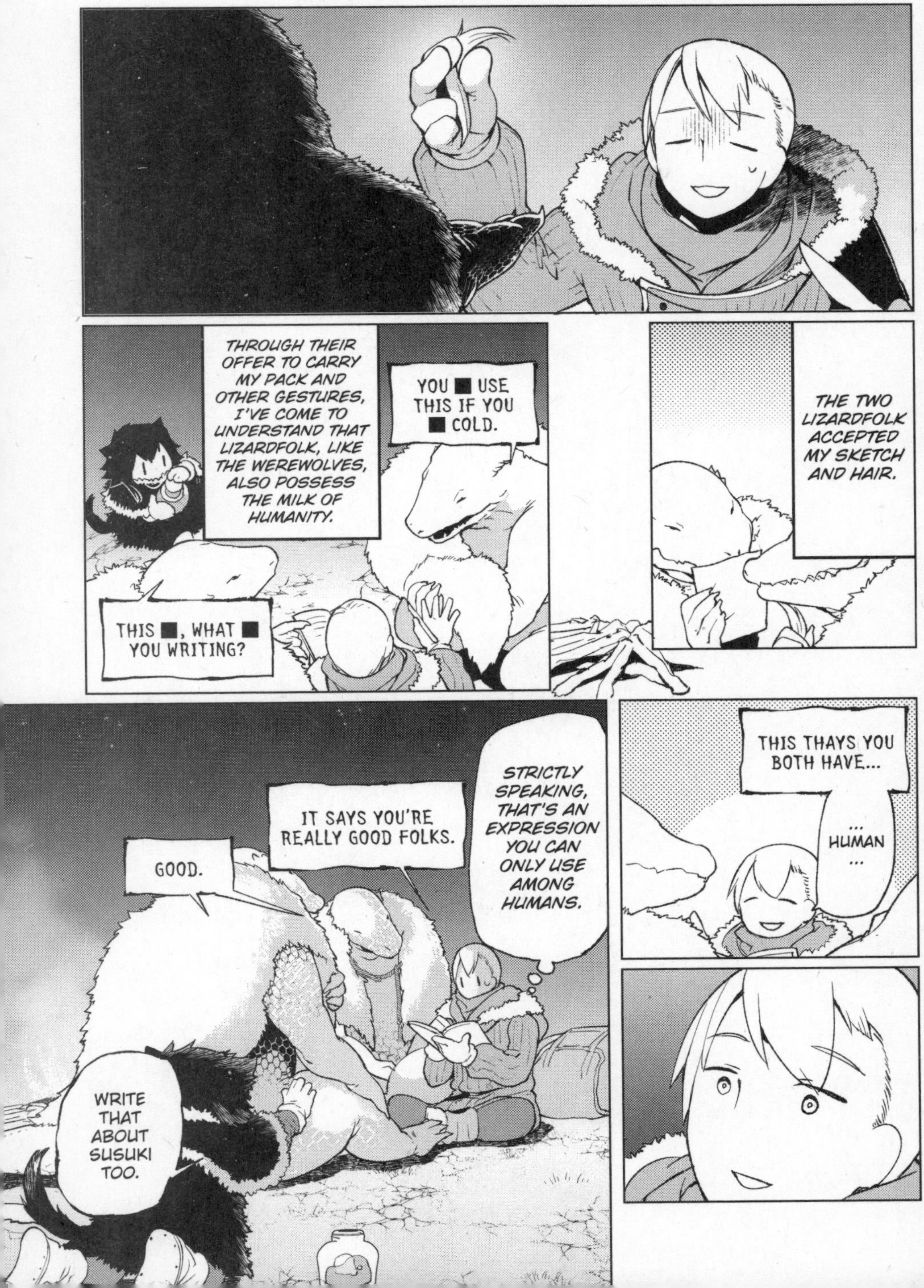
THE TWO LIZARDFOLK ACCEPTED MY SKETCH AND HAIR.
YOU ■ USE THIS IF YOU ■ COLD.
THROUGH THEIR OFFER TO CARRY MY PACK AND OTHER GESTURES, I'VE COME TO UNDERSTAND THAT LIZARDFOLK, LIKE THE WEREWOLVES, ALSO POSSESS THE MILK OF HUMANITY.
THIS ■, WHAT ■ YOU WRITING?
THIS THAYS YOU BOTH HAVE...
...HUMAN...
STRICTLY SPEAKING, THAT'S AN EXPRESSION YOU CAN ONLY USE AMONG HUMANS.
IT SAYS YOU'RE REALLY GOOD FOLKS.
GOOD.
WRITE THAT ABOUT SUSUKI TOO.

Thank-Yous

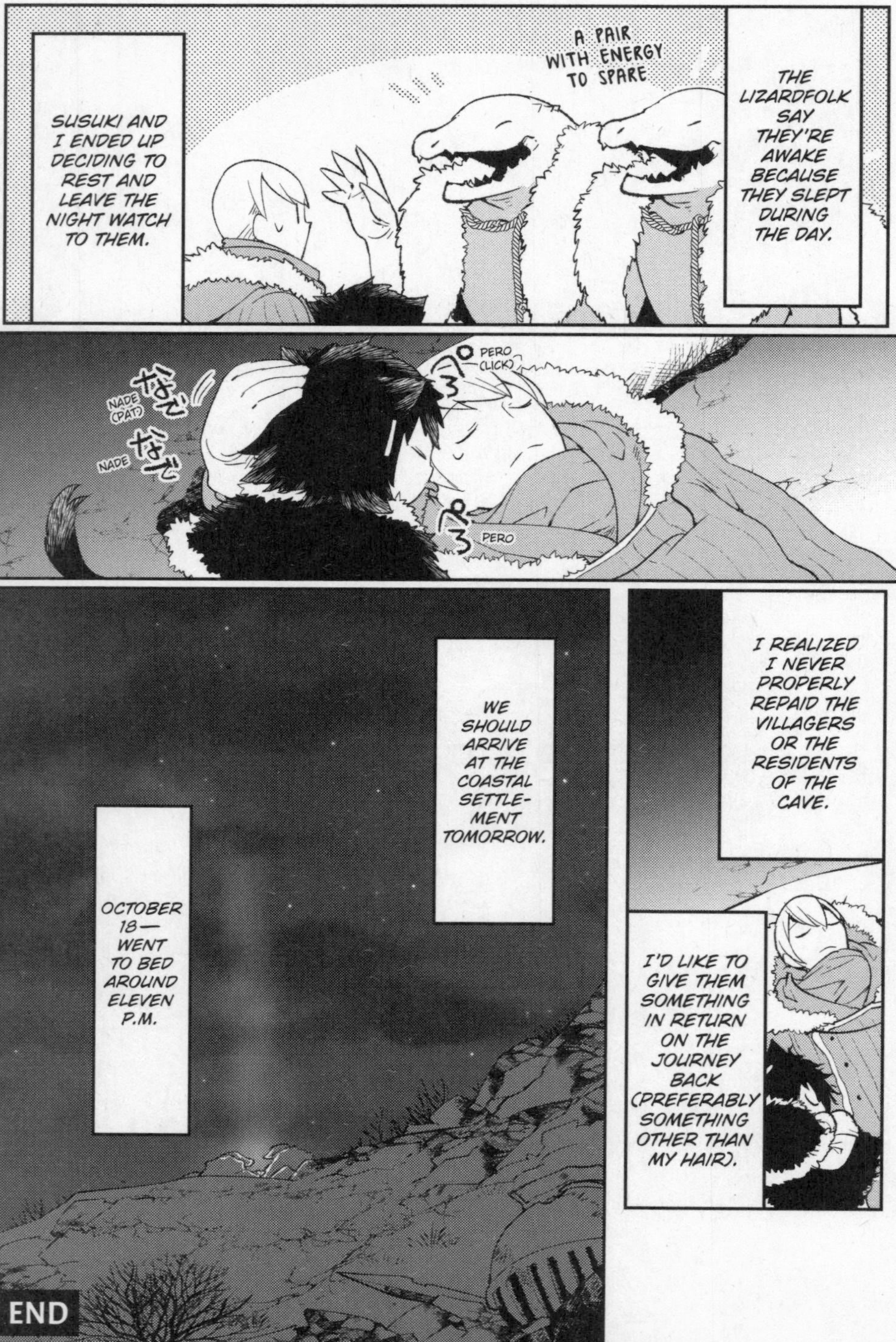
THE LIZARDFOLK SAY THEY'RE AWAKE BECAUSE THEY SLEPT DURING THE DAY.
A PAIR WITH ENERGY TO SPARE
SUSUKI AND I ENDED UP DECIDING TO REST AND LEAVE THE NIGHT WATCH TO THEM.
ぺろ
PERO (LICK)
なで
NADE (PAT)
なで
NADE
ぺろ
PERO
I REALIZED I NEVER PROPERLY REPAID THE VILLAGERS OR THE RESIDENTS OF THE CAVE.
I'D LIKE TO GIVE THEM SOMETHING IN RETURN ON THE JOURNEY BACK (PREFERABLY SOMETHING OTHER THAN MY HAIR).
WE SHOULD ARRIVE AT THE COASTAL SETTLE-MENT TOMORROW.
OCTOBER 18— WENT TO BED AROUND ELEVEN P.M.
END

AT NIGHT, THEY PUT THEIR JAWS ON THE GROUND SEVERAL TIMES.
NOT SLEEPING

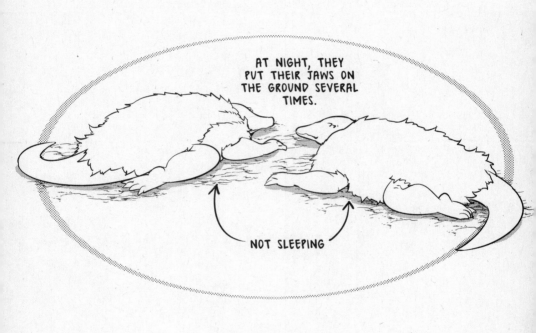

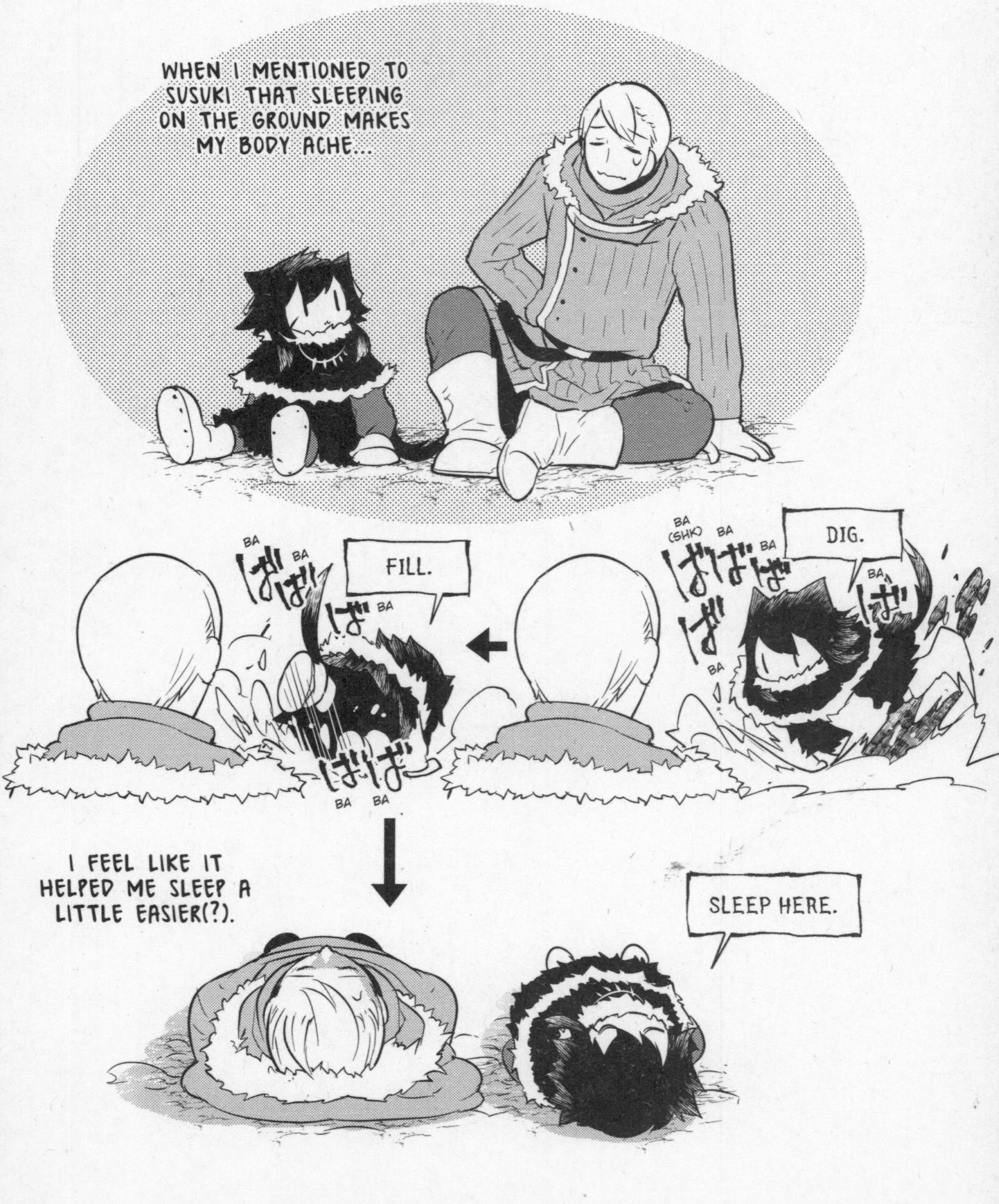
WHEN I MENTIONED TO SUSUKI THAT SLEEPING ON THE GROUND MAKES MY BODY ACHE...
DIG.
BA (SHK) BA BA BA BA
FILL.
BA BA BA BA BA
SLEEP HERE.
I FEEL LIKE IT HELPED ME SLEEP A LITTLE EASIER(?).

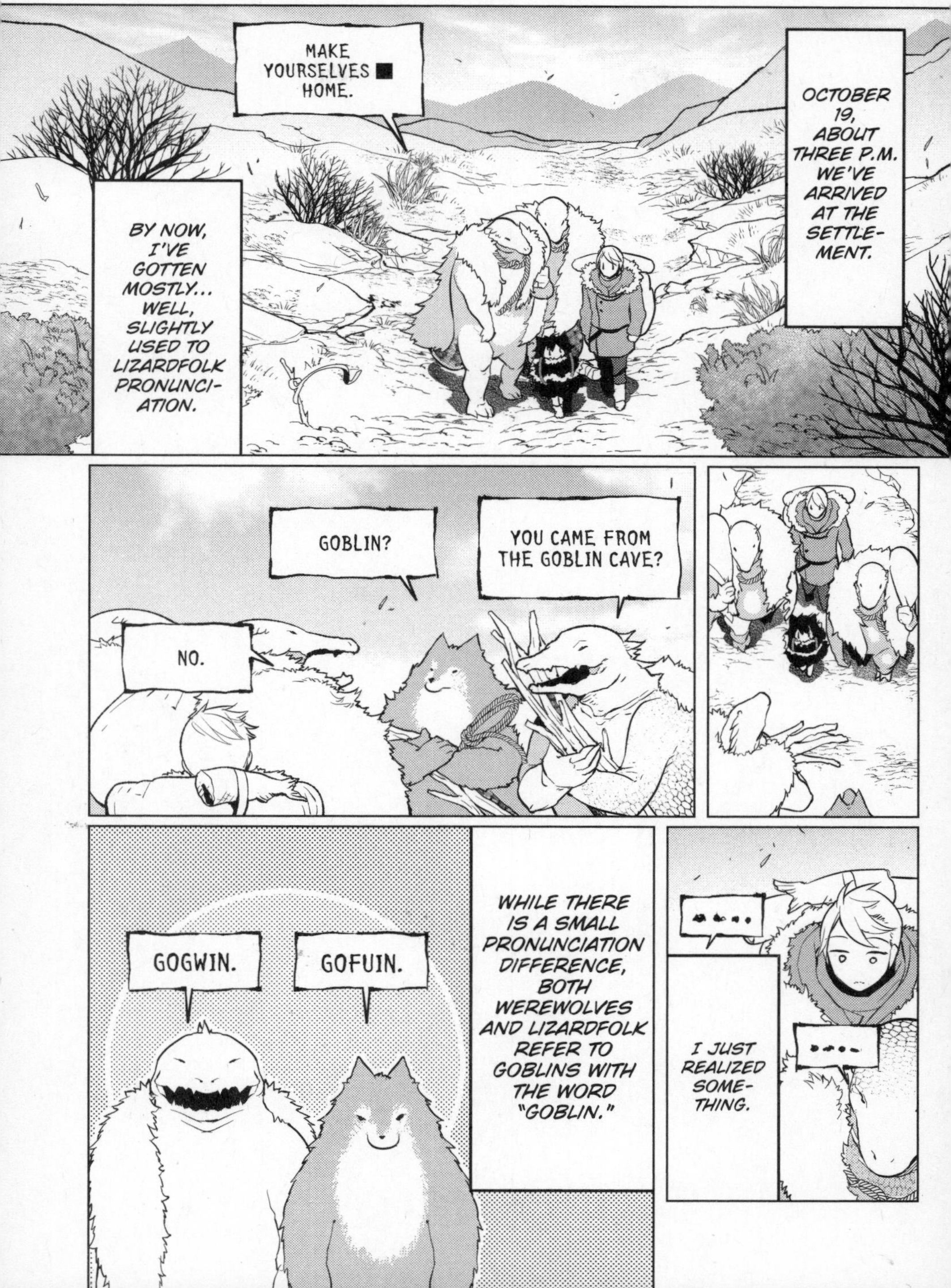
OCTOBER 19, ABOUT THREE P.M. WE'VE ARRIVED AT THE SETTLEMENT.
MAKE YOURSELVES ■ HOME.
BY NOW, I'VE GOTTEN MOSTLY... WELL, SLIGHTLY USED TO LIZARDFOLK PRONUNCIATION.
YOU CAME FROM THE GOBLIN CAVE?
GOBLIN?
NO.
.....
I JUST REALIZED SOMETHING.
.....
WHILE THERE IS A SMALL PRONUNCIATION DIFFERENCE, BOTH WEREWOLVES AND LIZARDFOLK REFER TO GOBLINS WITH THE WORD "GOBLIN."
GOFUIN.
GOGWIN.

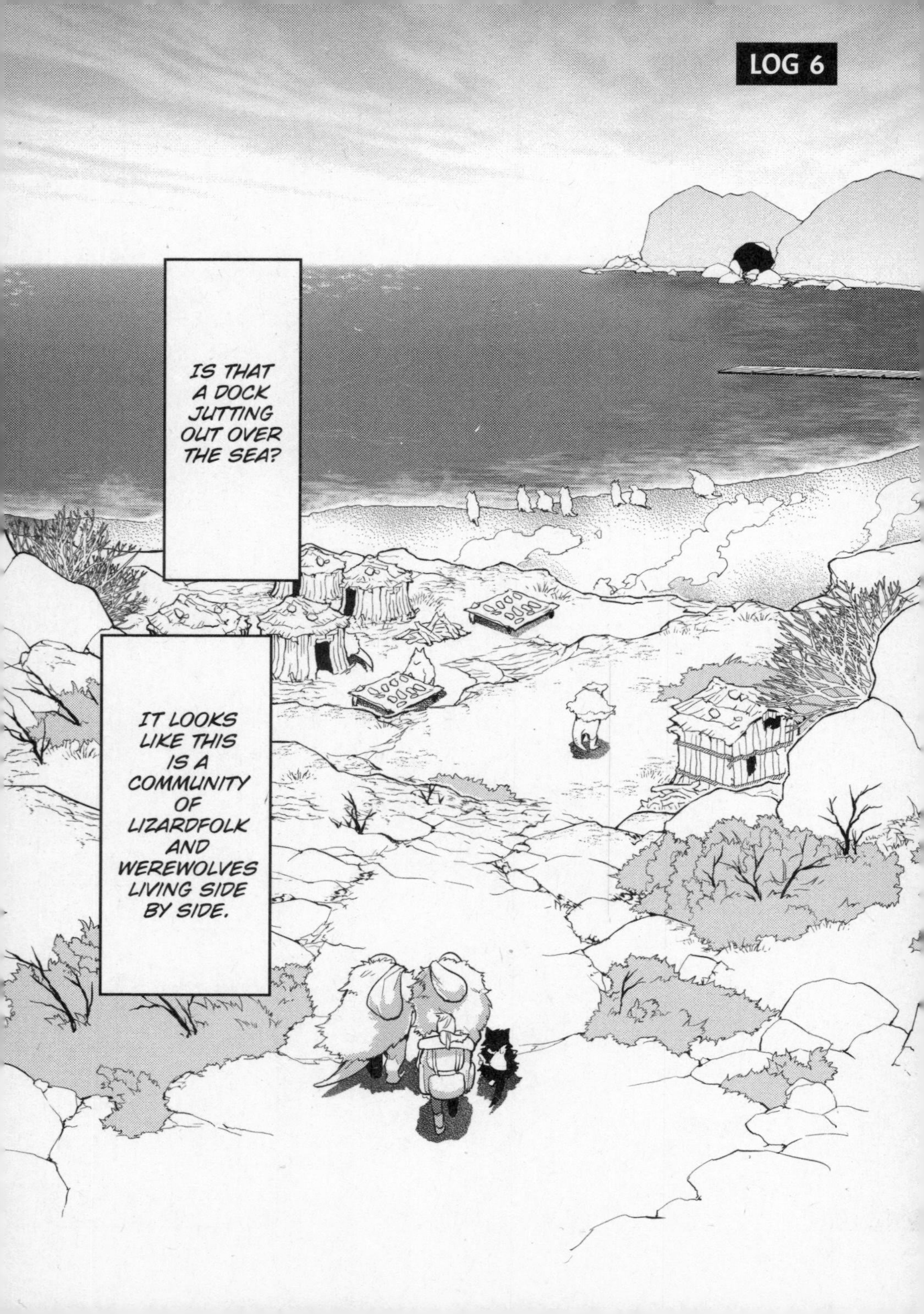
LOG 6
IS THAT A DOCK JUTTING OUT OVER THE SEA?
IT LOOKS LIKE THIS IS A COMMUNITY OF LIZARDFOLK AND WEREWOLVES LIVING SIDE BY SIDE.

Their House

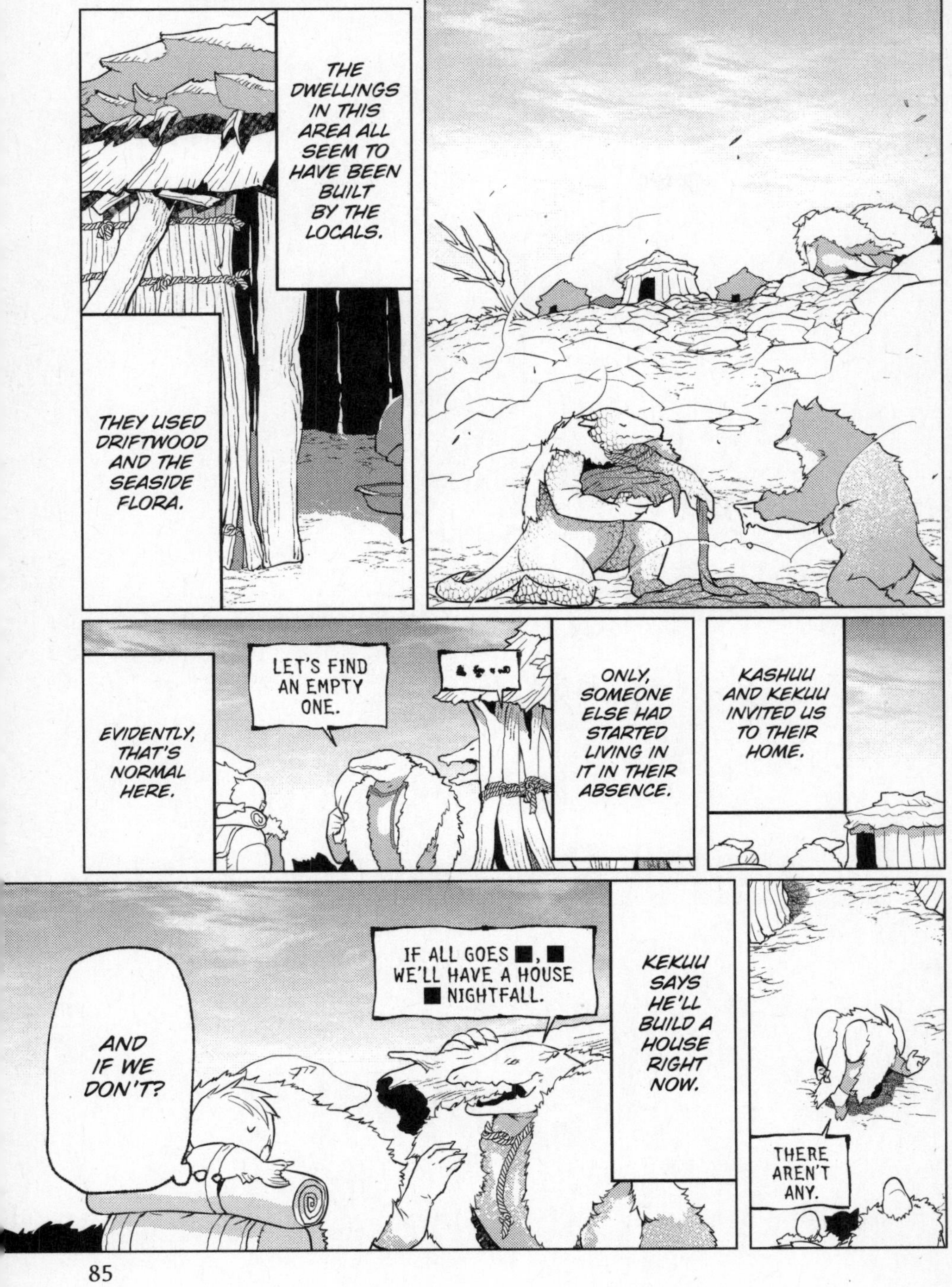
THE DWELLINGS IN THIS AREA ALL SEEM TO HAVE BEEN BUILT BY THE LOCALS.
THEY USED DRIFTWOOD AND THE SEASIDE FLORA.
KASHUU AND KEKUU INVITED US TO THEIR HOME.
ONLY, SOMEONE ELSE HAD STARTED LIVING IN IT IN THEIR ABSENCE.
LET'S FIND AN EMPTY ONE.
EVIDENTLY, THAT'S NORMAL HERE.
THERE AREN'T ANY.
KEKUU SAYS HE'LL BUILD A HOUSE RIGHT NOW.
IF ALL GOES ■, ■ WE'LL HAVE A HOUSE ■ NIGHTFALL.
AND IF WE DON'T?

Seaside Settlement

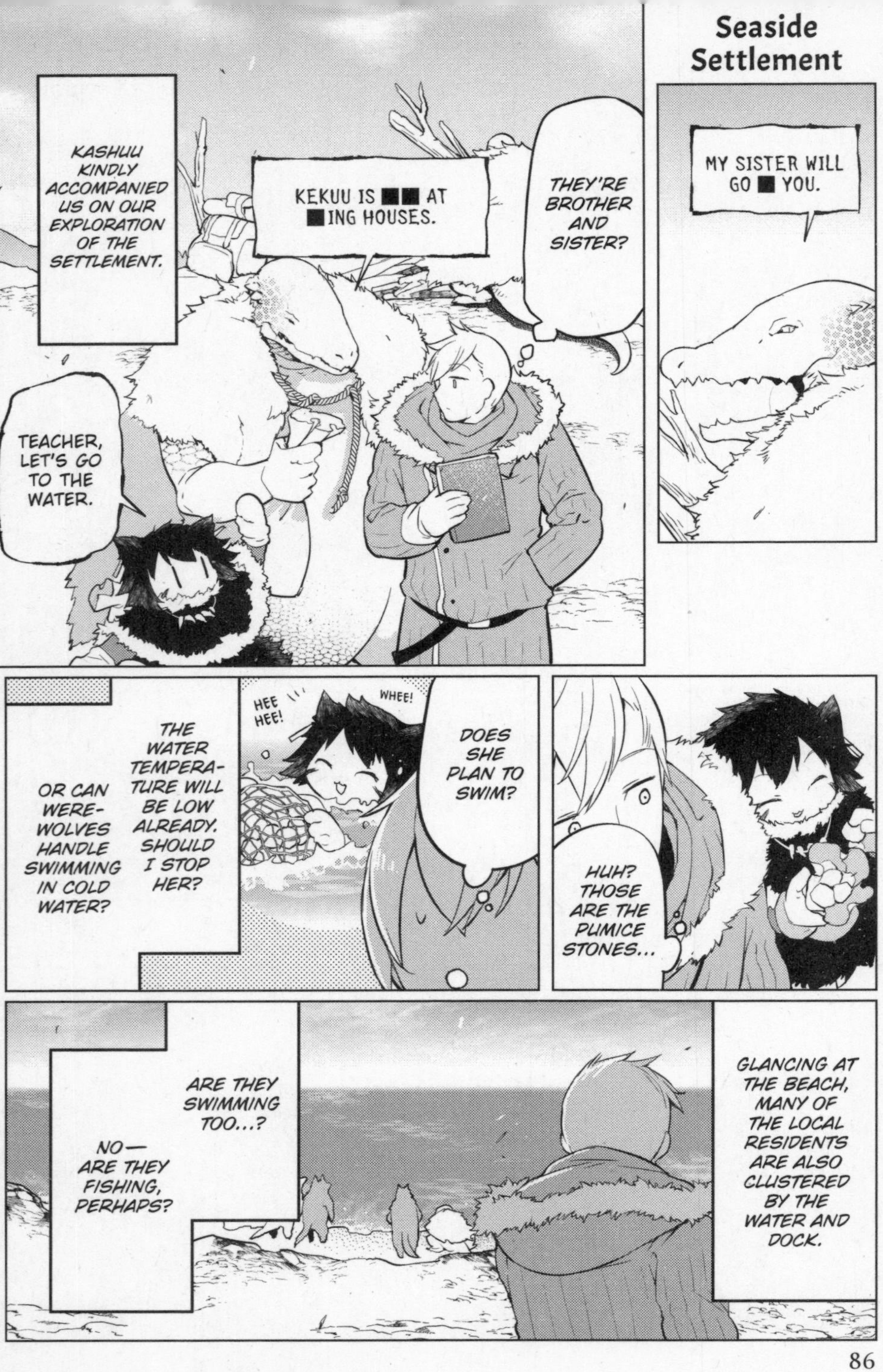

MY SISTER WILL GO [redacted] YOU.
THEY'RE BROTHER AND SISTER?
KEKUU IS [redacted] AT [redacted]ING HOUSES.
KASHUU KINDLY ACCOMPANIED US ON OUR EXPLORATION OF THE SETTLEMENT.
TEACHER, LET'S GO TO THE WATER.
HUH? THOSE ARE THE PUMICE STONES...
WHEE!
DOES SHE PLAN TO SWIM?
HEE HEE!
THE WATER TEMPERATURE WILL BE LOW ALREADY. SHOULD I STOP HER?
OR CAN WEREWOLVES HANDLE SWIMMING IN COLD WATER?
GLANCING AT THE BEACH, MANY OF THE LOCAL RESIDENTS ARE ALSO CLUSTERED BY THE WATER AND DOCK.
ARE THEY SWIMMING TOO...?
NO— ARE THEY FISHING, PERHAPS?

The People at the Beach

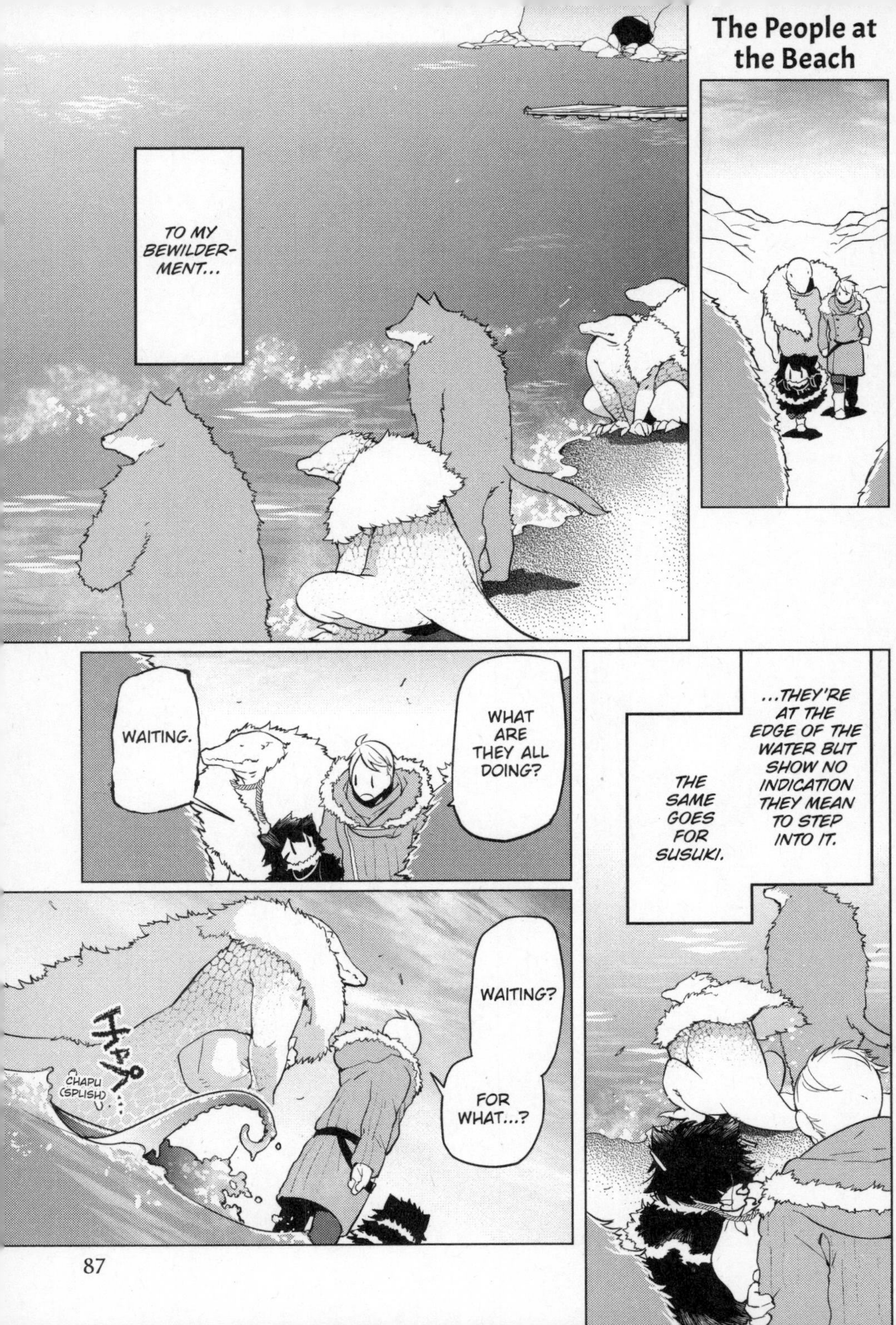
TO MY BEWILDERMENT...
...THEY'RE AT THE EDGE OF THE WATER BUT SHOW NO INDICATION THEY MEAN TO STEP INTO IT.
THE SAME GOES FOR SUSUKI.
WHAT ARE THEY ALL DOING?
WAITING.
WAITING?
FOR WHAT...?
CHAPU (SPLISH)

Small Kraken

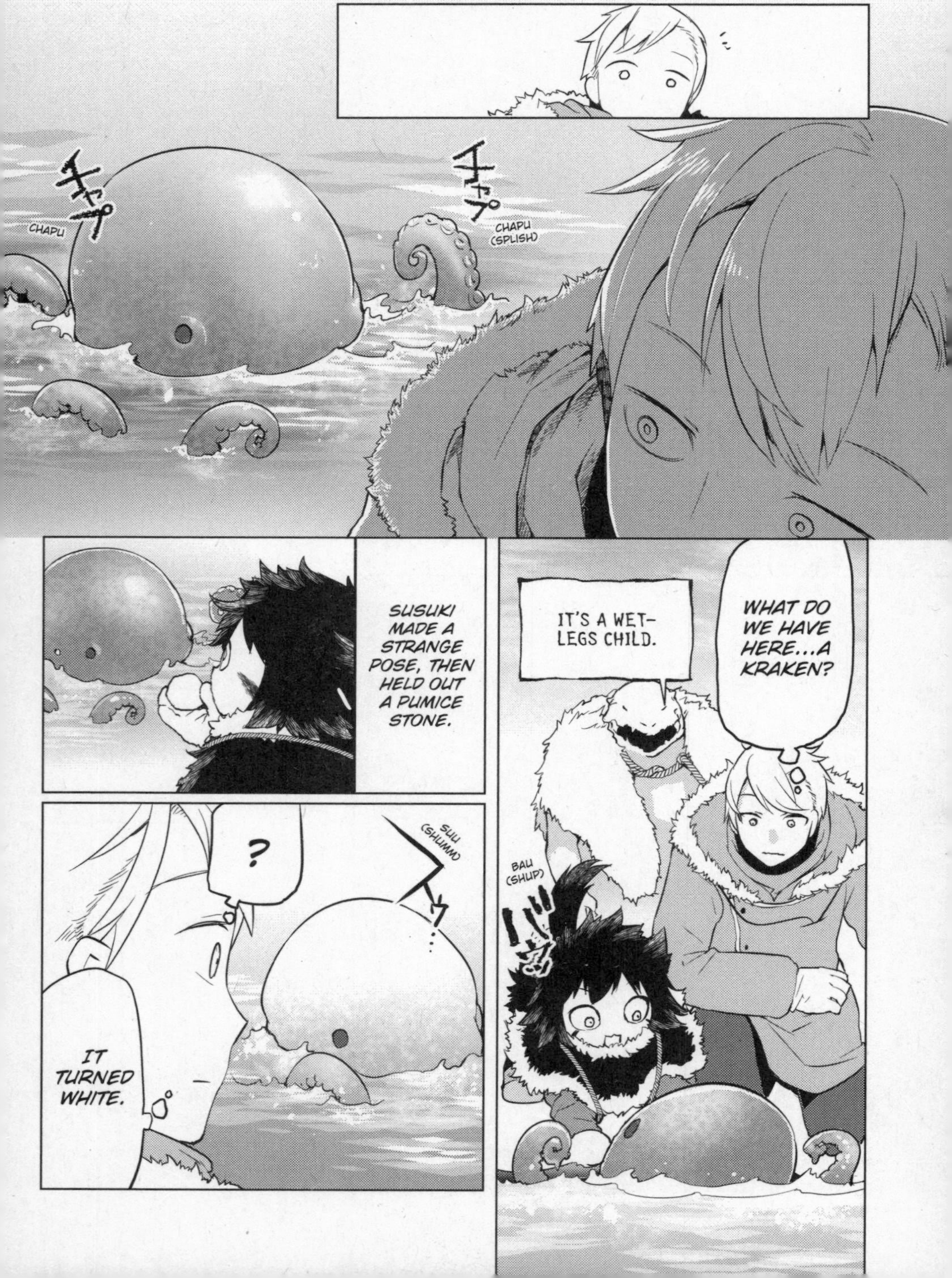

CHAPU (SPLISH)
CHAPU
WHAT DO WE HAVE HERE...A KRAKEN?
IT'S A WET-LEGS CHILD.
BAU (SHUP)
SUSUKI MADE A STRANGE POSE, THEN HELD OUT A PUMICE STONE.
?
SUU (SHUMM)
IT TURNED WHITE.

Gimme

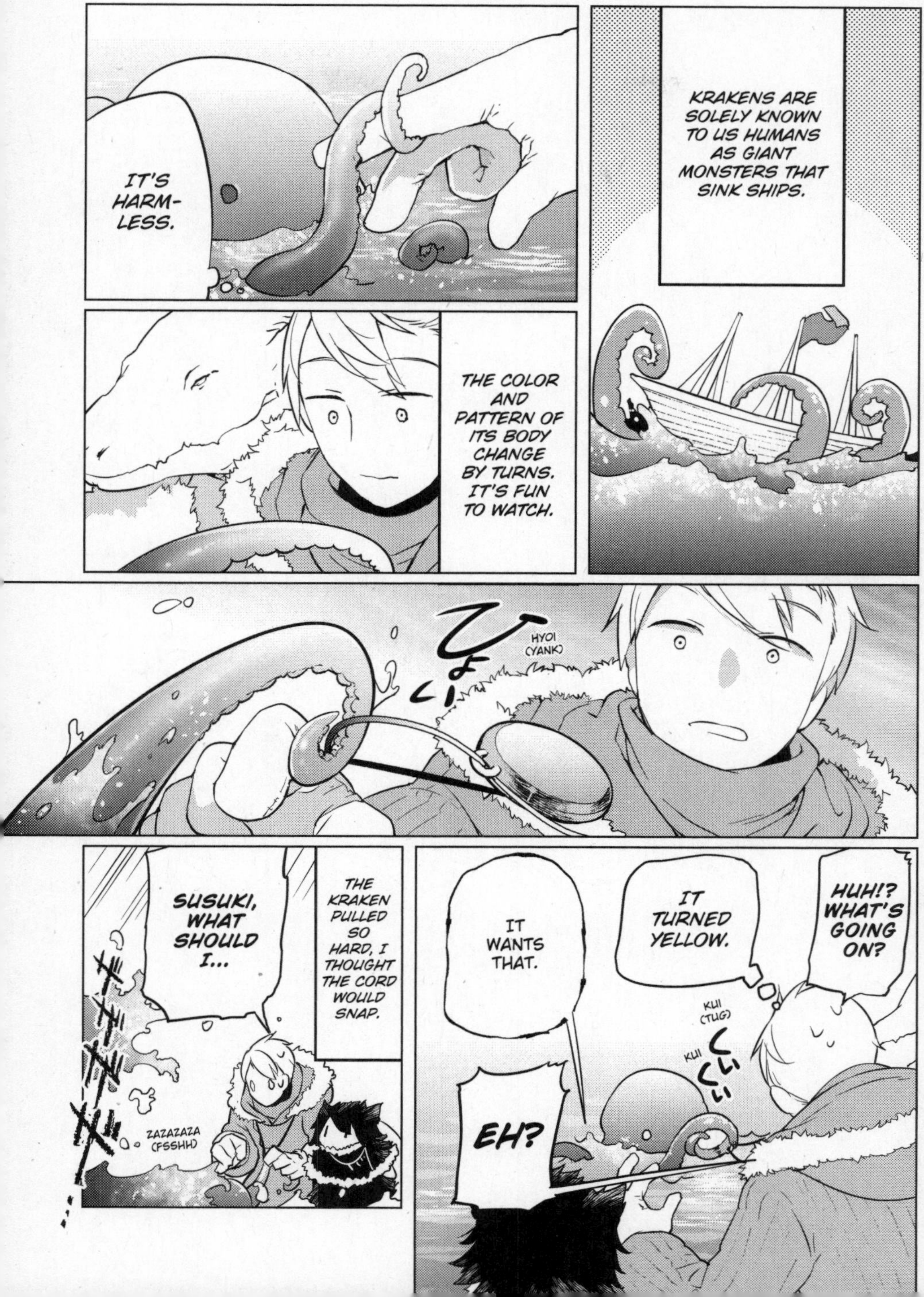
KRAKENS ARE SOLELY KNOWN TO US HUMANS AS GIANT MONSTERS THAT SINK SHIPS.
IT'S HARM-LESS.
THE COLOR AND PATTERN OF ITS BODY CHANGE BY TURNS. IT'S FUN TO WATCH.
ひょい
HYOI (YANK)
HUH!? WHAT'S GOING ON?
IT TURNED YELLOW.
IT WANTS THAT.
KUI (TUG)
くい くい
KUI
EH?
THE KRAKEN PULLED SO HARD, I THOUGHT THE CORD WOULD SNAP.
SUSUKI, WHAT SHOULD I...
ZAZAZAZA (FSSHH)

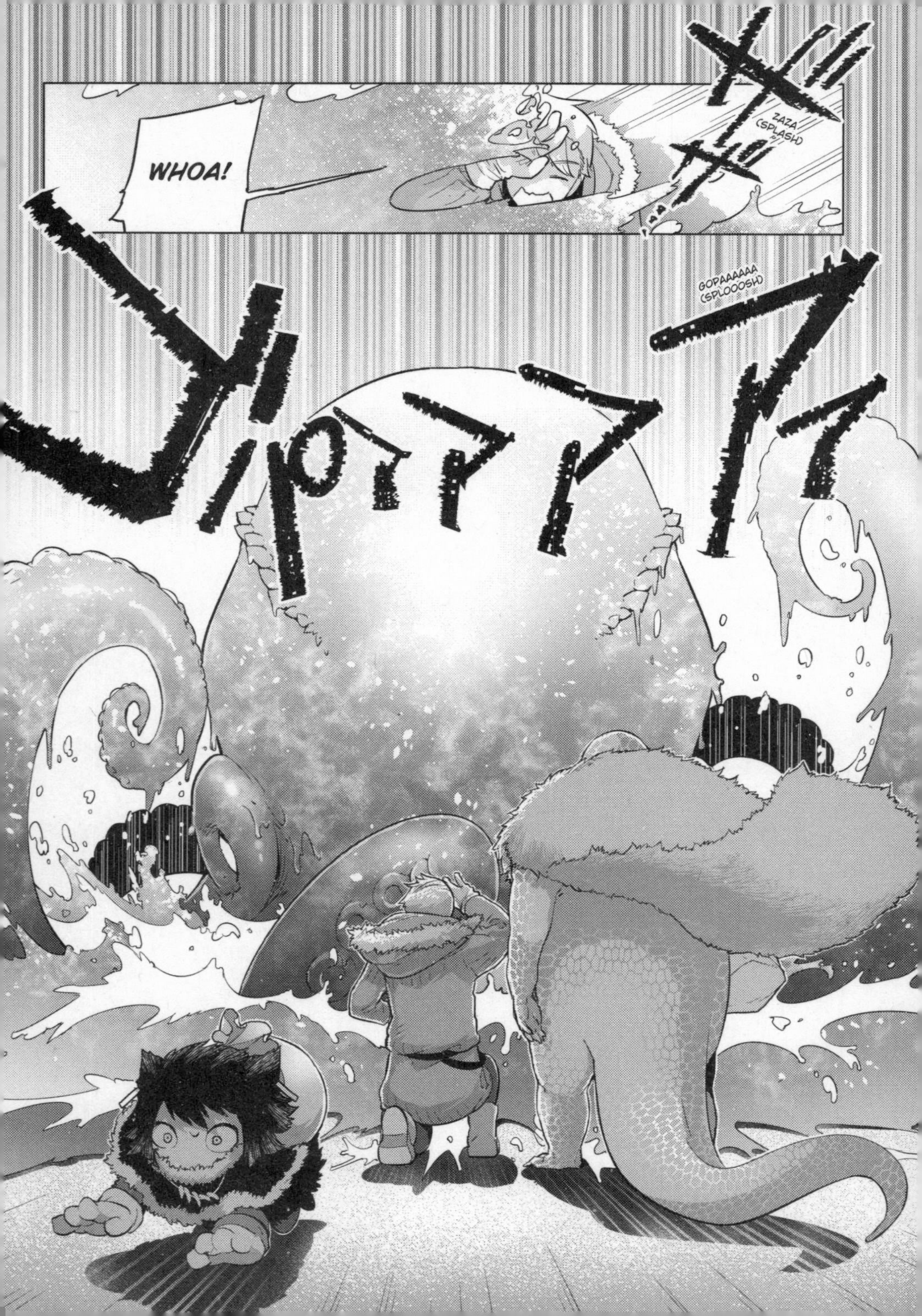
ZAZA (SPLASH)
WHOA!
GOPAAAAAA (SPLOOOSH)

Big Kraken

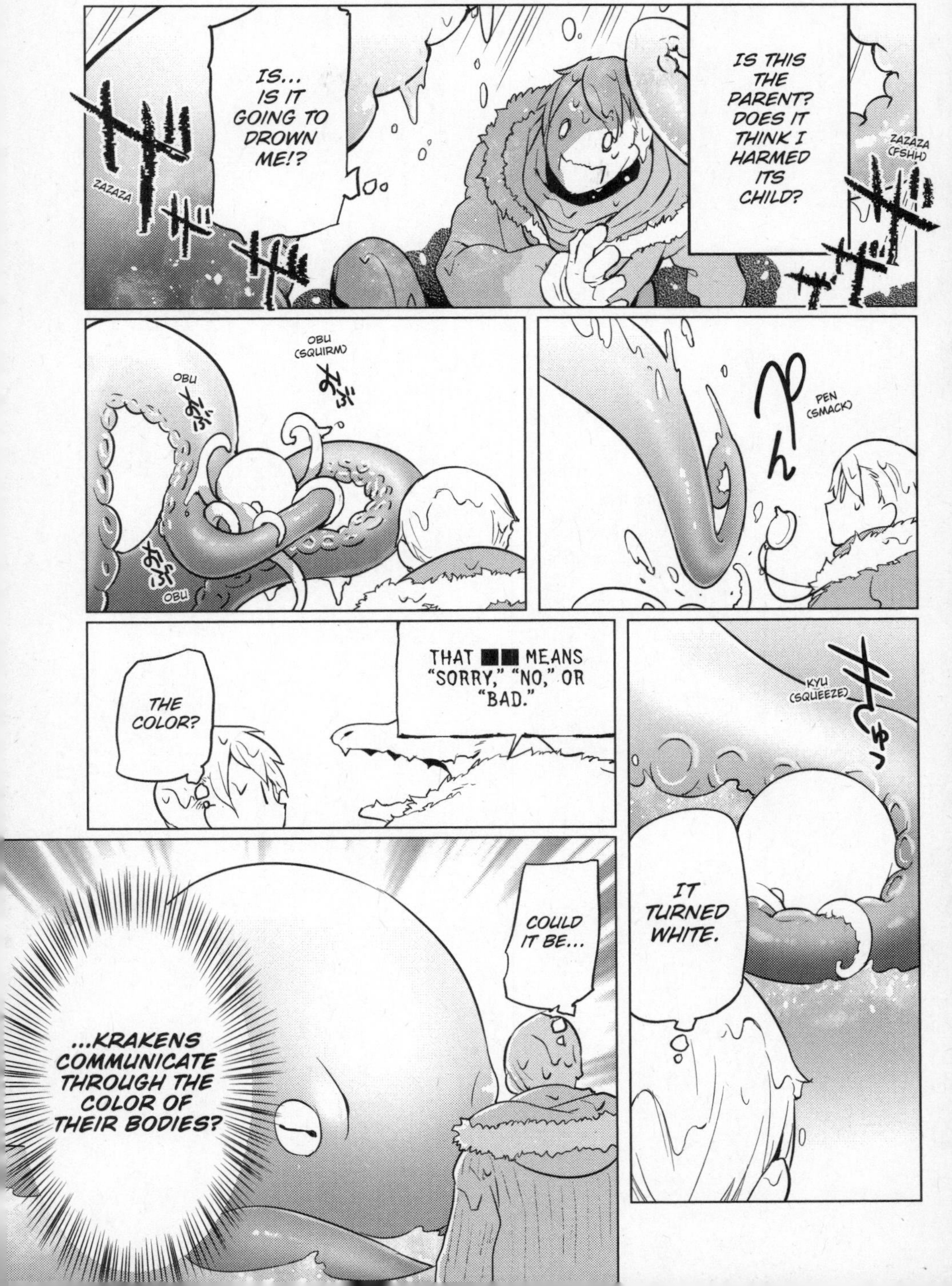
IS THIS THE PARENT? DOES IT THINK I HARMED ITS CHILD?
ZAZAZA (FSHH)
IS... IS IT GOING TO DROWN ME!?
ZAZAZA
ぺん
PEN (SMACK)
おぶ
OBU (SQUIRM)
おぶ
OBU
おぶ
OBU
KYU (SQUEEZE)
IT TURNED WHITE.
THAT [redacted] MEANS "SORRY," "NO," OR "BAD."
THE COLOR?
COULD IT BE...
...KRAKENS COMMUNICATE THROUGH THE COLOR OF THEIR BODIES?

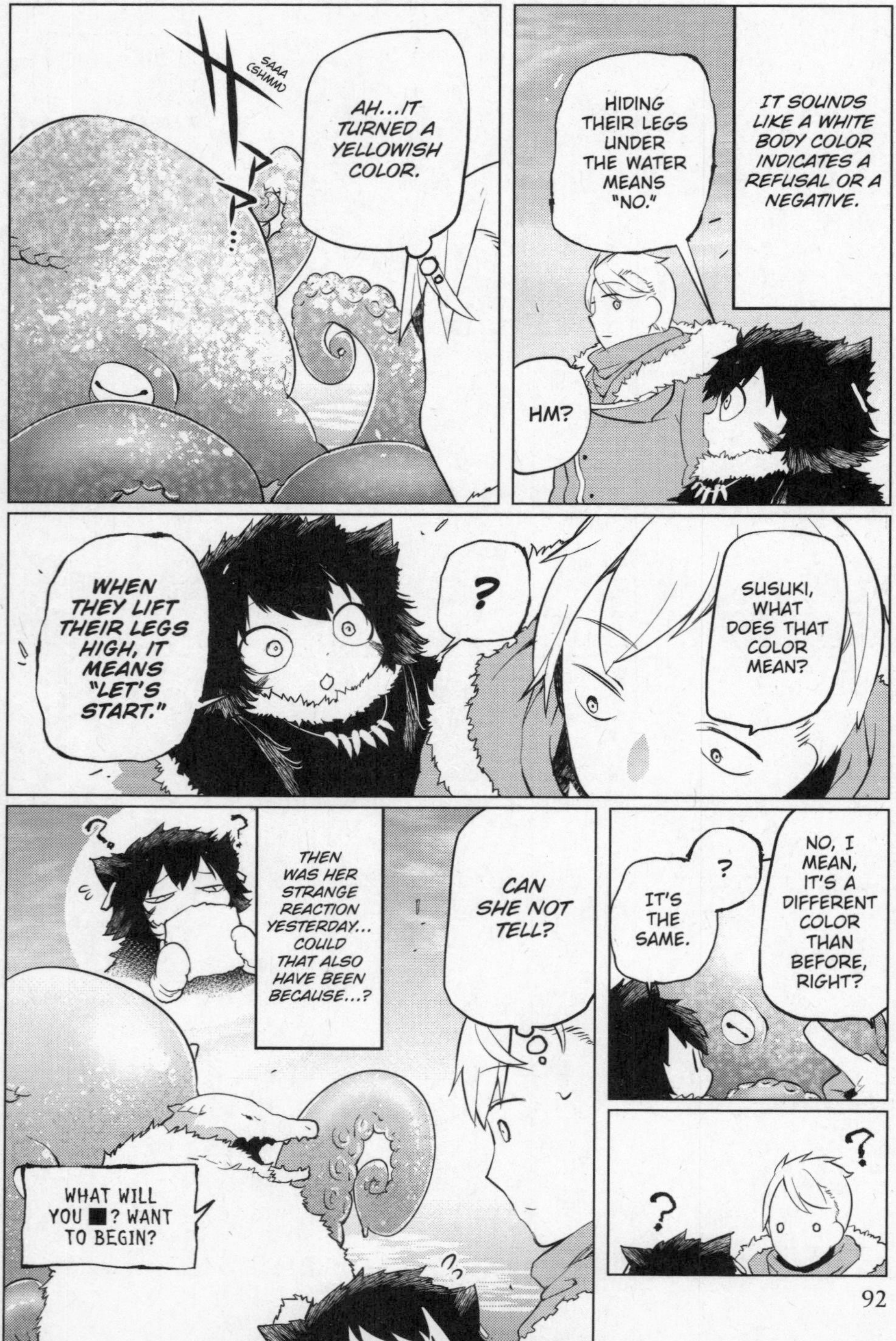
IT SOUNDS LIKE A WHITE BODY COLOR INDICATES A REFUSAL OR A NEGATIVE.
HIDING THEIR LEGS UNDER THE WATER MEANS "NO."
HM?
AH...IT TURNED A YELLOWISH COLOR.
SAAA (SHMM)
SUSUKI, WHAT DOES THAT COLOR MEAN?
?
WHEN THEY LIFT THEIR LEGS HIGH, IT MEANS "LET'S START."
NO, I MEAN, IT'S A DIFFERENT COLOR THAN BEFORE, RIGHT?
?
IT'S THE SAME.
?
?
CAN SHE NOT TELL?
THEN WAS HER STRANGE REACTION YESTERDAY... COULD THAT ALSO HAVE BEEN BECAUSE...?
WHAT WILL YOU ■? WANT TO BEGIN?

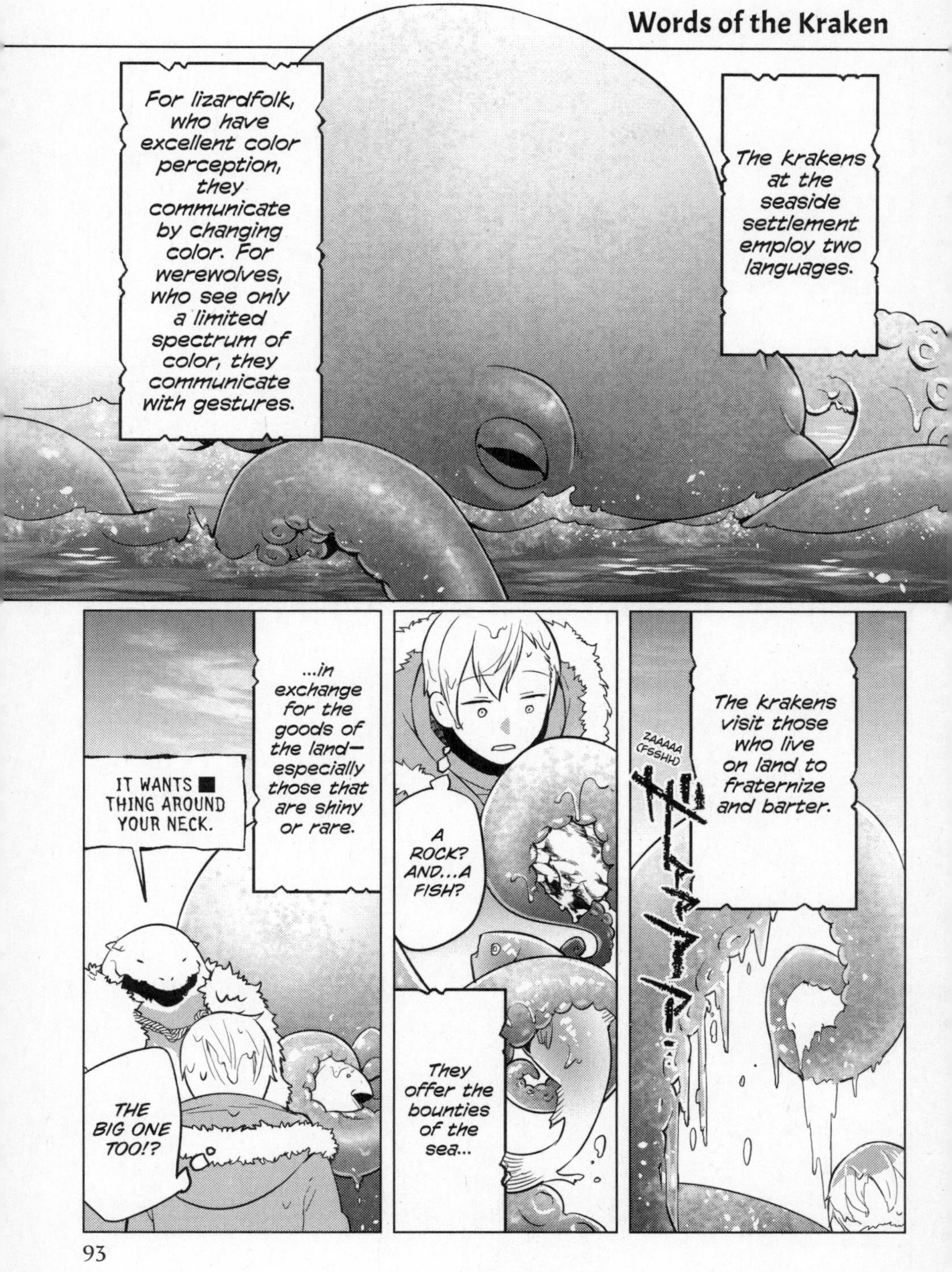
The krakens at the seaside settlement employ two languages.
For lizardfolk, who have excellent color perception, they communicate by changing color. For werewolves, who see only a limited spectrum of color, they communicate with gestures.
The krakens visit those who live on land to fraternize and barter.
ZAAAAA (FSSHH)
A ROCK? AND...A FISH?
They offer the bounties of the sea...
...in exchange for the goods of the land—especially those that are shiny or rare.
IT WANTS [redacted] THING AROUND YOUR NECK.
THE BIG ONE TOO!?

Body-Color Language

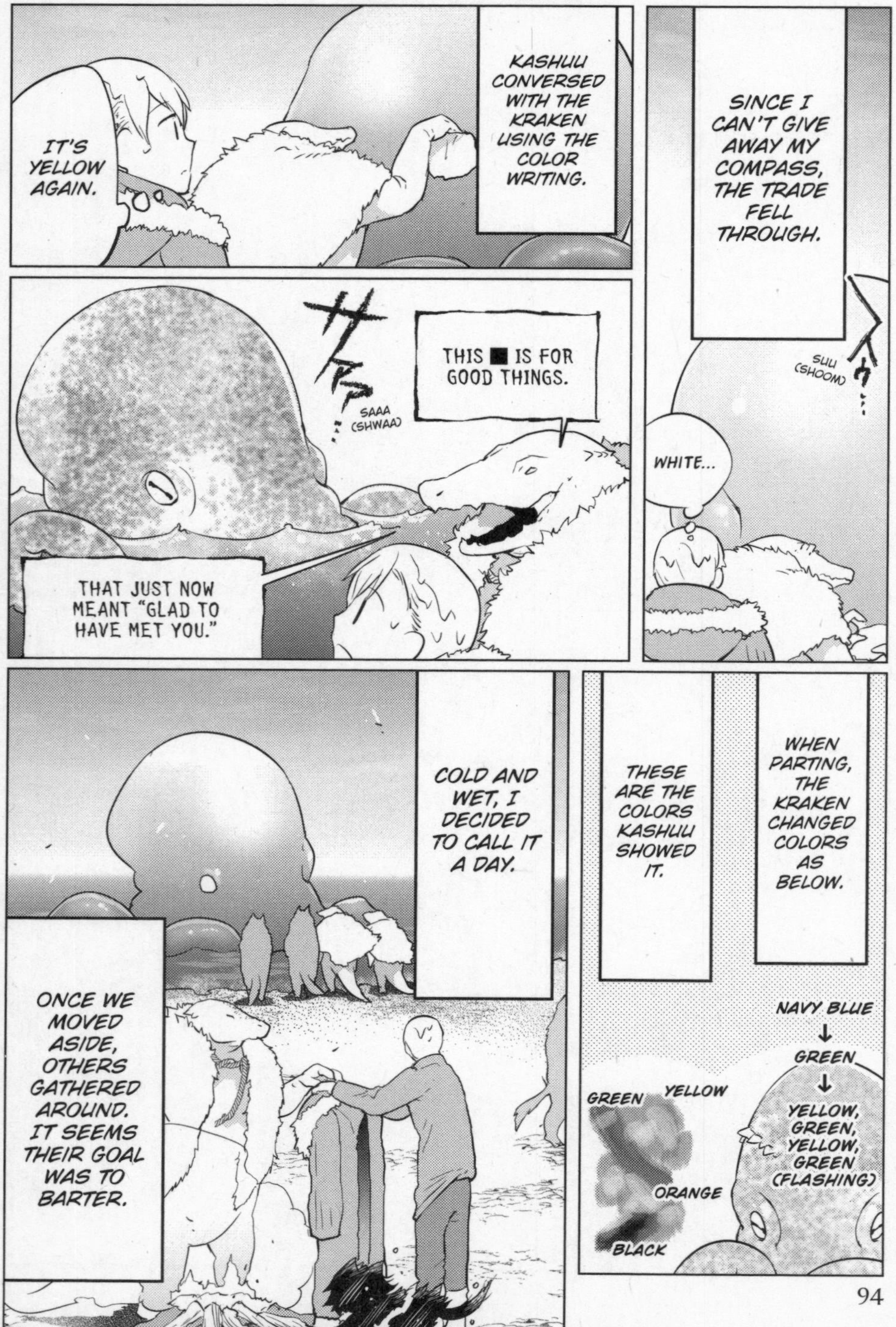
SINCE I CAN'T GIVE AWAY MY COMPASS, THE TRADE FELL THROUGH.
SUU (SHOOM)
WHITE...
KASHUU CONVERSED WITH THE KRAKEN USING THE COLOR WRITING.
IT'S YELLOW AGAIN.
SAAA (SHWAA)
THIS ■ IS FOR GOOD THINGS.
THAT JUST NOW MEANT "GLAD TO HAVE MET YOU."
WHEN PARTING, THE KRAKEN CHANGED COLORS AS BELOW.
THESE ARE THE COLORS KASHUU SHOWED IT.
NAVY BLUE
↓
GREEN
↓
YELLOW, GREEN, YELLOW, GREEN (FLASHING)
GREEN
YELLOW
ORANGE
BLACK
COLD AND WET, I DECIDED TO CALL IT A DAY.
ONCE WE MOVED ASIDE, OTHERS GATHERED AROUND. IT SEEMS THEIR GOAL WAS TO BARTER.

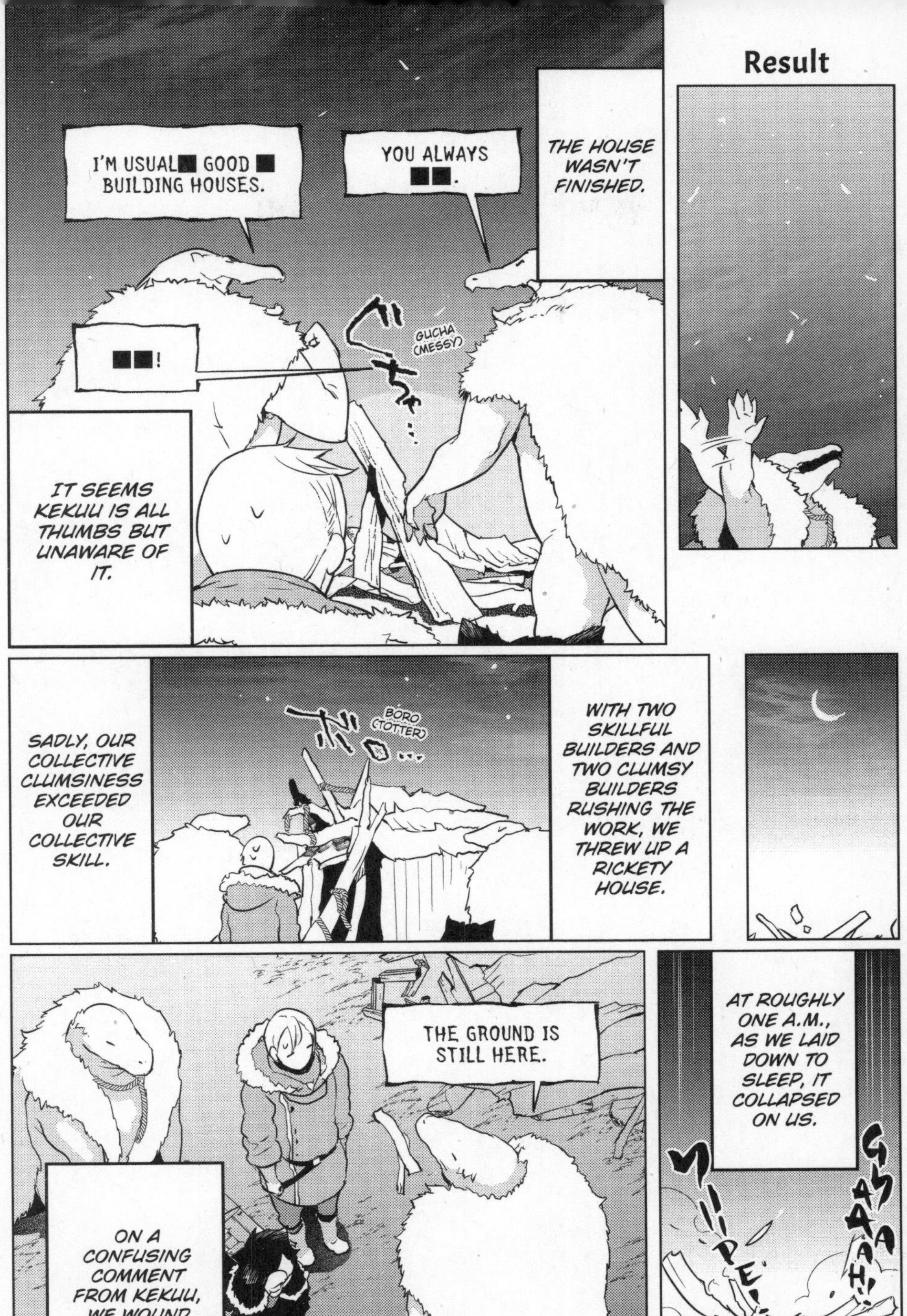
Result
THE HOUSE WASN'T FINISHED.
YOU ALWAYS [redacted].
I'M USUAL[redacted] GOOD [redacted] BUILDING HOUSES.
GUCHA (MESSY)
[redacted]!
IT SEEMS KEKUU IS ALL THUMBS BUT UNAWARE OF IT.
WITH TWO SKILLFUL BUILDERS AND TWO CLUMSY BUILDERS RUSHING THE WORK, WE THREW UP A RICKETY HOUSE.
BORO (TOTTER)
SADLY, OUR COLLECTIVE CLUMSINESS EXCEEDED OUR COLLECTIVE SKILL.
AT ROUGHLY ONE A.M., AS WE LAID DOWN TO SLEEP, IT COLLAPSED ON US.
GYAAAAH!
MIIPE!
THE GROUND IS STILL HERE.
ON A CONFUSING COMMENT FROM KEKUU, WE WOUND UP CAMPING INSIDE THE SETTLEMENT.

From Two-Way Communication

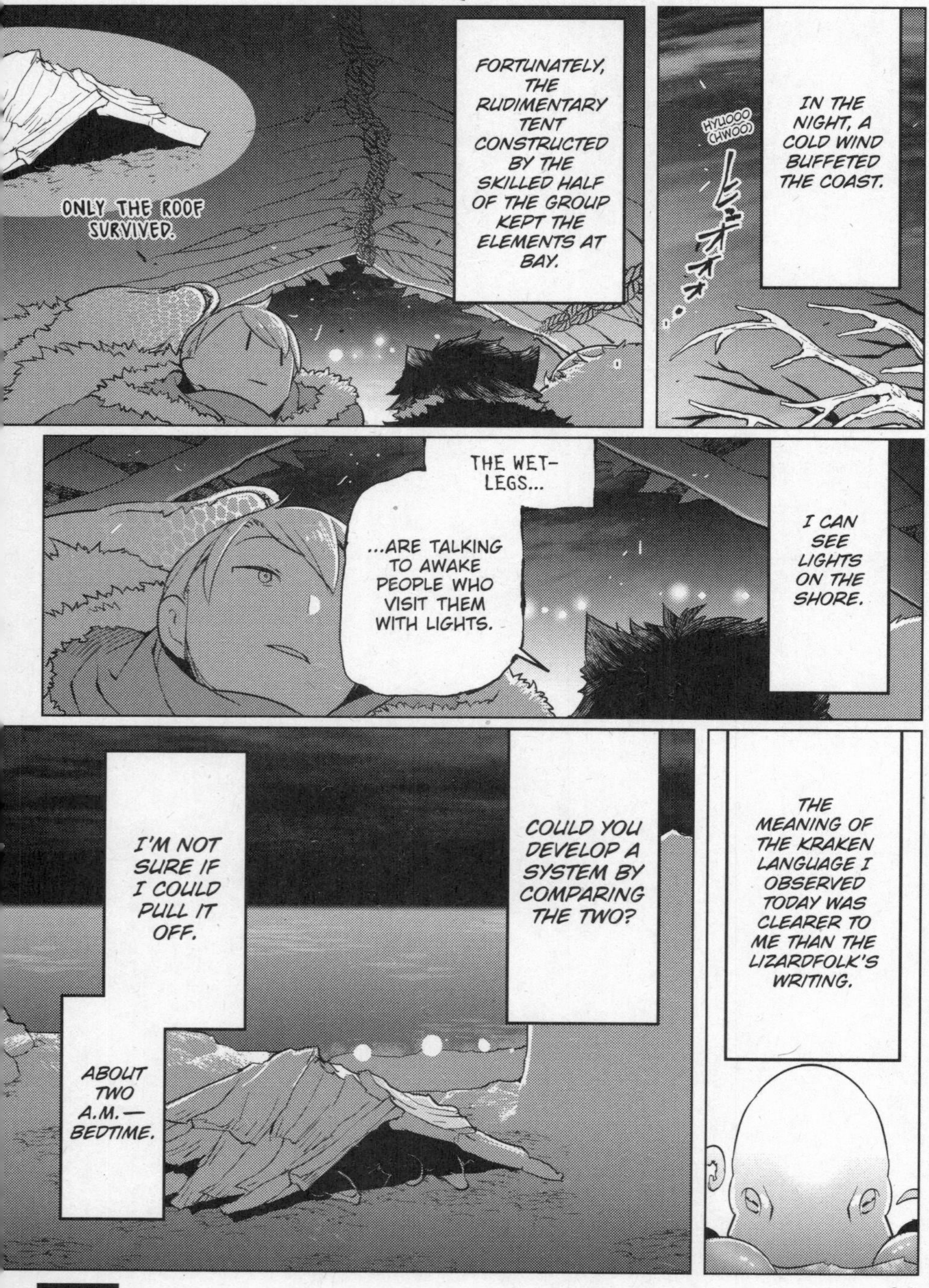

IN THE NIGHT, A COLD WIND BUFFETED THE COAST.
HYUOOO (HWOO)
FORTUNATELY, THE RUDIMENTARY TENT CONSTRUCTED BY THE SKILLED HALF OF THE GROUP KEPT THE ELEMENTS AT BAY.
ONLY THE ROOF SURVIVED.
I CAN SEE LIGHTS ON THE SHORE.
THE WET-LEGS...
...ARE TALKING TO AWAKE PEOPLE WHO VISIT THEM WITH LIGHTS.
THE MEANING OF THE KRAKEN LANGUAGE I OBSERVED TODAY WAS CLEARER TO ME THAN THE LIZARDFOLK'S WRITING.
COULD YOU DEVELOP A SYSTEM BY COMPARING THE TWO?
I'M NOT SURE IF I COULD PULL IT OFF.
ABOUT TWO A.M.— BEDTIME.

END

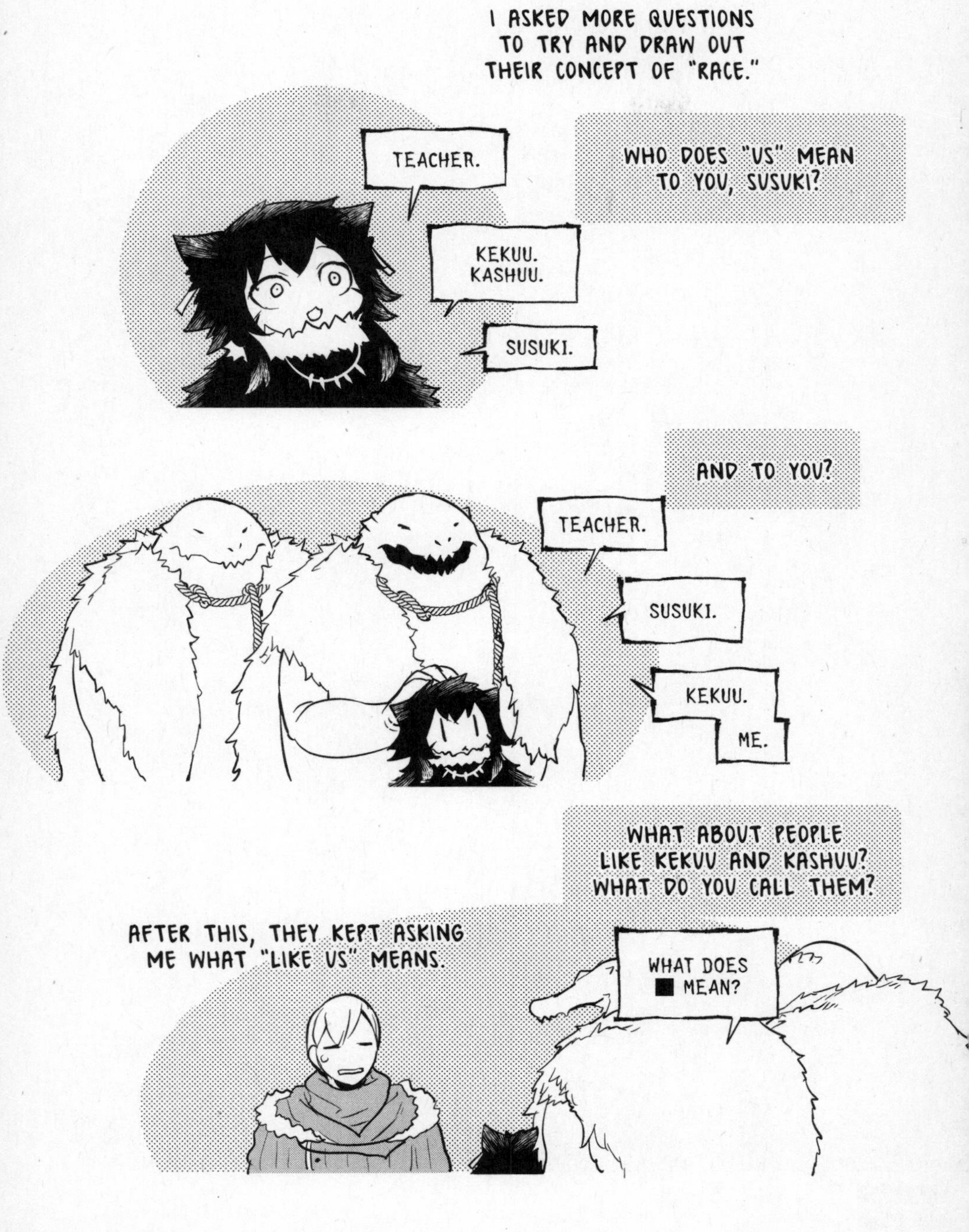
I ASKED MORE QUESTIONS TO TRY AND DRAW OUT THEIR CONCEPT OF "RACE."
WHO DOES "US" MEAN TO YOU, SUSUKI?
TEACHER.
KEKUU. KASHUU.
SUSUKI.
AND TO YOU?
TEACHER.
SUSUKI.
KEKUU.
ME.
WHAT ABOUT PEOPLE LIKE KEKUU AND KASHUU? WHAT DO YOU CALL THEM?
WHAT DOES ■ MEAN?
AFTER THIS, THEY KEPT ASKING ME WHAT "LIKE US" MEANS.

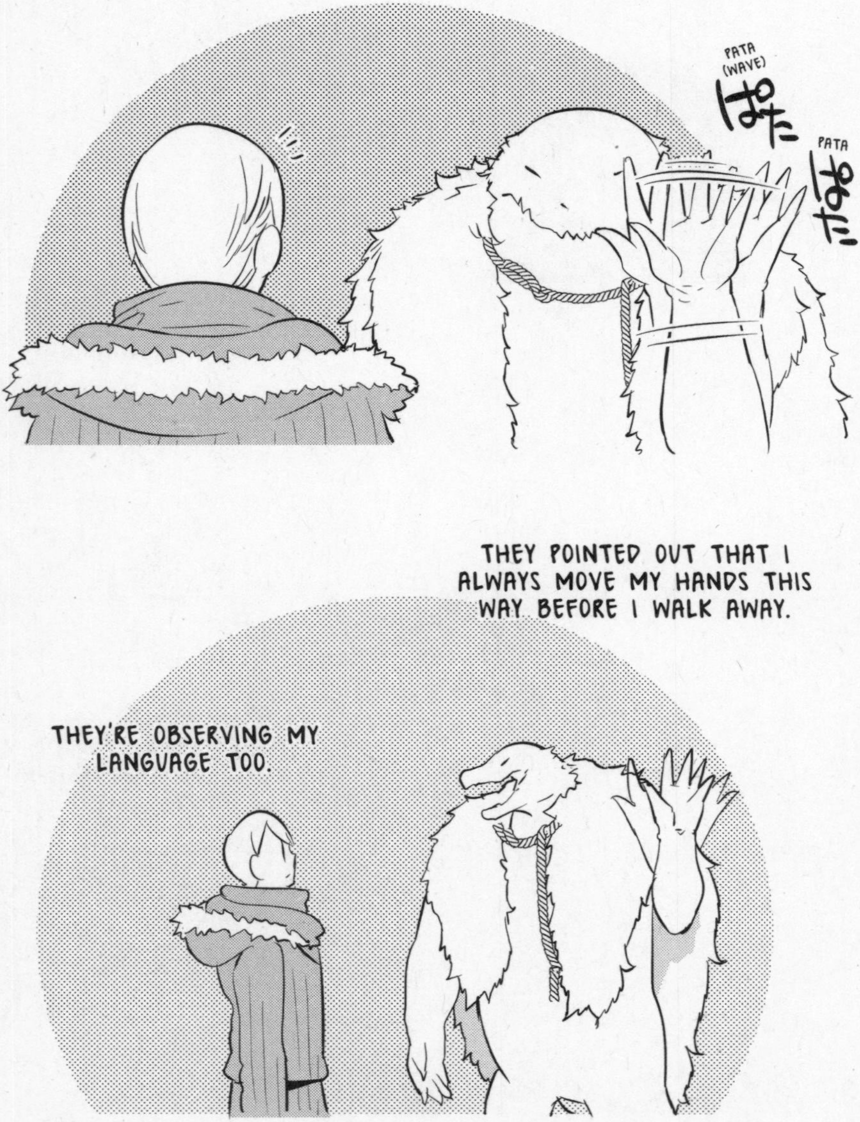
PATA (WAVE)
ぱた
PATA
ぱた
THEY POINTED OUT THAT I ALWAYS MOVE MY HANDS THIS WAY BEFORE I WALK AWAY.
THEY'RE OBSERVING MY LANGUAGE TOO.

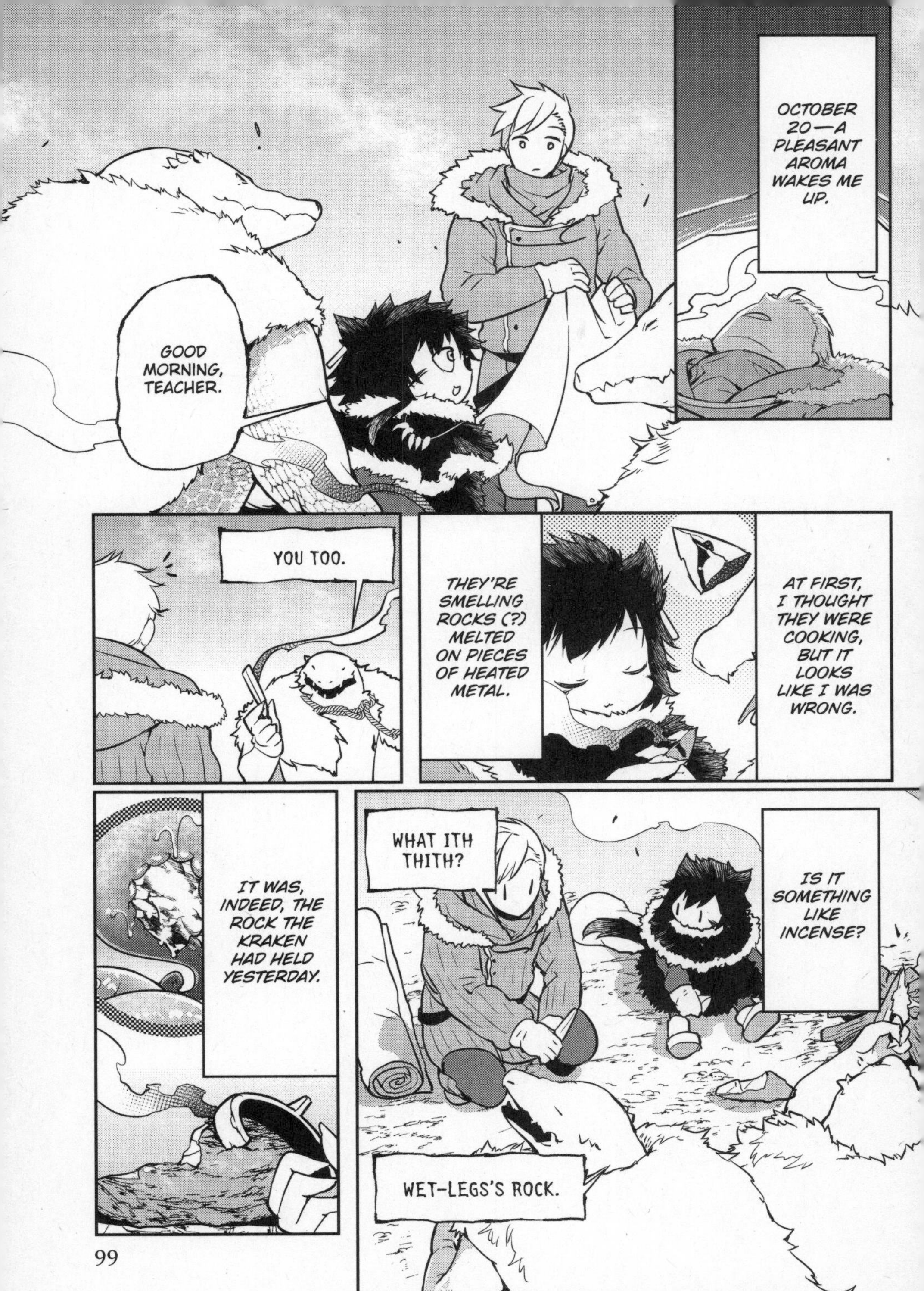
OCTOBER 20—A PLEASANT AROMA WAKES ME UP.
GOOD MORNING, TEACHER.
AT FIRST, I THOUGHT THEY WERE COOKING, BUT IT LOOKS LIKE I WAS WRONG.
THEY'RE SMELLING ROCKS (?) MELTED ON PIECES OF HEATED METAL.
YOU TOO.
IS IT SOMETHING LIKE INCENSE?
WHAT ITH THITH?
WET-LEGS'S ROCK.
IT WAS, INDEED, THE ROCK THE KRAKEN HAD HELD YESTERDAY.

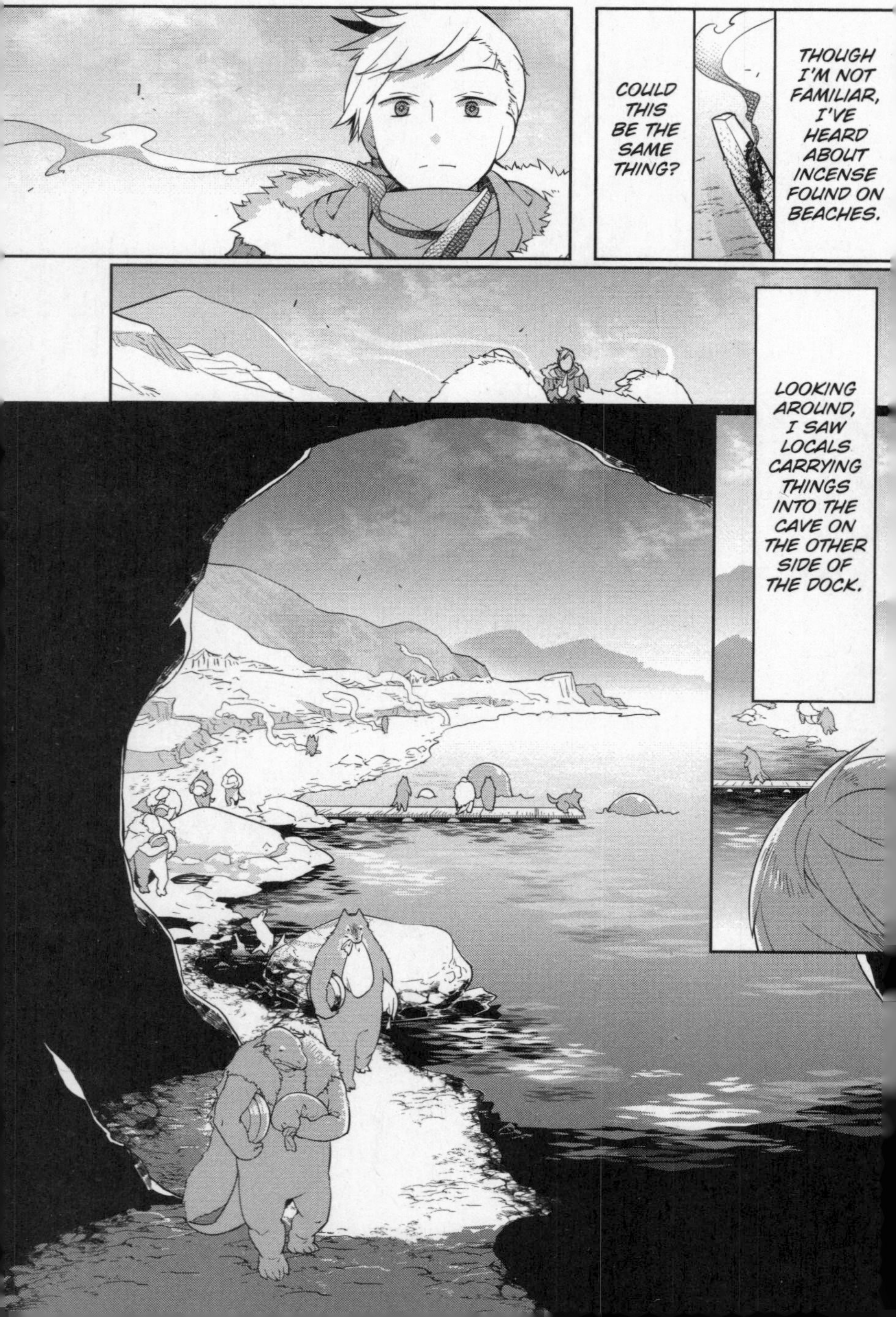
THOUGH I'M NOT FAMILIAR, I'VE HEARD ABOUT INCENSE FOUND ON BEACHES.
COULD THIS BE THE SAME THING?
LOOKING AROUND, I SAW LOCALS CARRYING THINGS INTO THE CAVE ON THE OTHER SIDE OF THE DOCK.

Errand

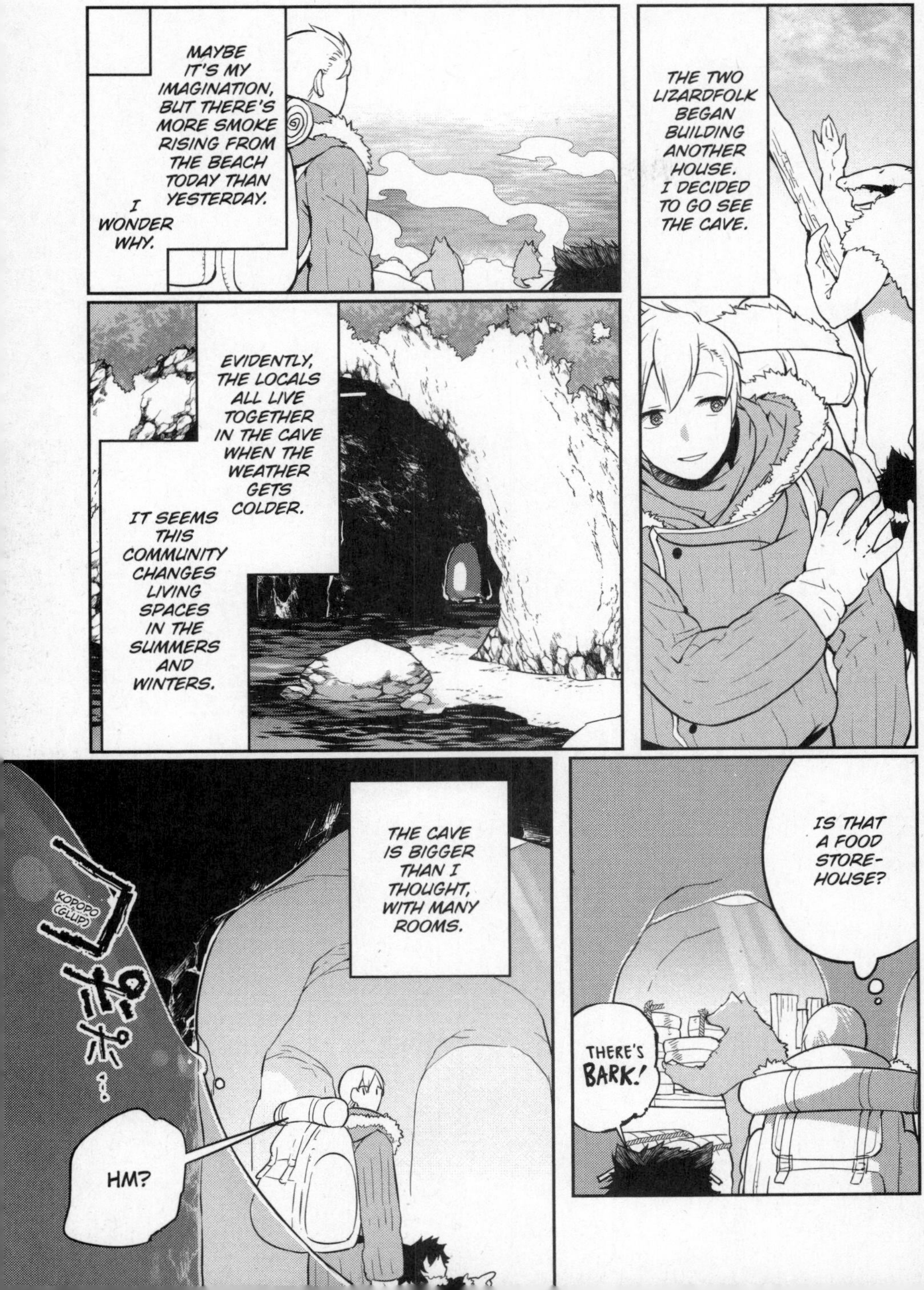
THE TWO LIZARDFOLK BEGAN BUILDING ANOTHER HOUSE. I DECIDED TO GO SEE THE CAVE.
MAYBE IT'S MY IMAGINATION, BUT THERE'S MORE SMOKE RISING FROM THE BEACH TODAY THAN YESTERDAY.
I WONDER WHY.
EVIDENTLY, THE LOCALS ALL LIVE TOGETHER IN THE CAVE WHEN THE WEATHER GETS COLDER.
IT SEEMS THIS COMMUNITY CHANGES LIVING SPACES IN THE SUMMERS AND WINTERS.
IS THAT A FOOD STORE-HOUSE?
THERE'S BARK!
THE CAVE IS BIGGER THAN I THOUGHT, WITH MANY ROOMS.
KOPOPO (GLUP)
HM?

Slime in a Warm Place

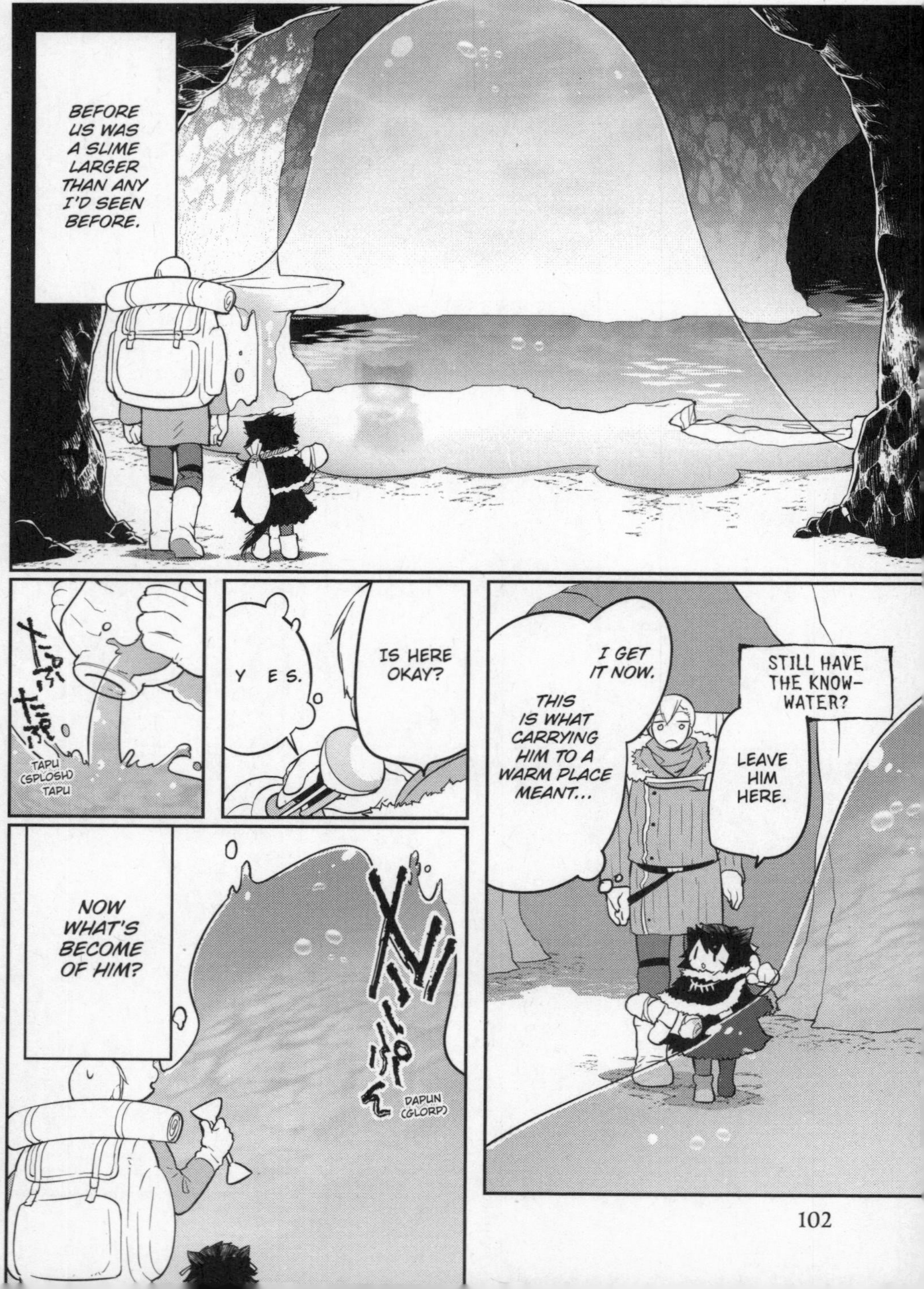
BEFORE US WAS A SLIME LARGER THAN ANY I'D SEEN BEFORE.
STILL HAVE THE KNOW-WATER?
LEAVE HIM HERE.
I GET IT NOW.
THIS IS WHAT CARRYING HIM TO A WARM PLACE MEANT...
IS HERE OKAY?
Y E S.
TAPU (SPLOSH) TAPU
NOW WHAT'S BECOME OF HIM?
DAPUN (GLORP)

Lost Nuance

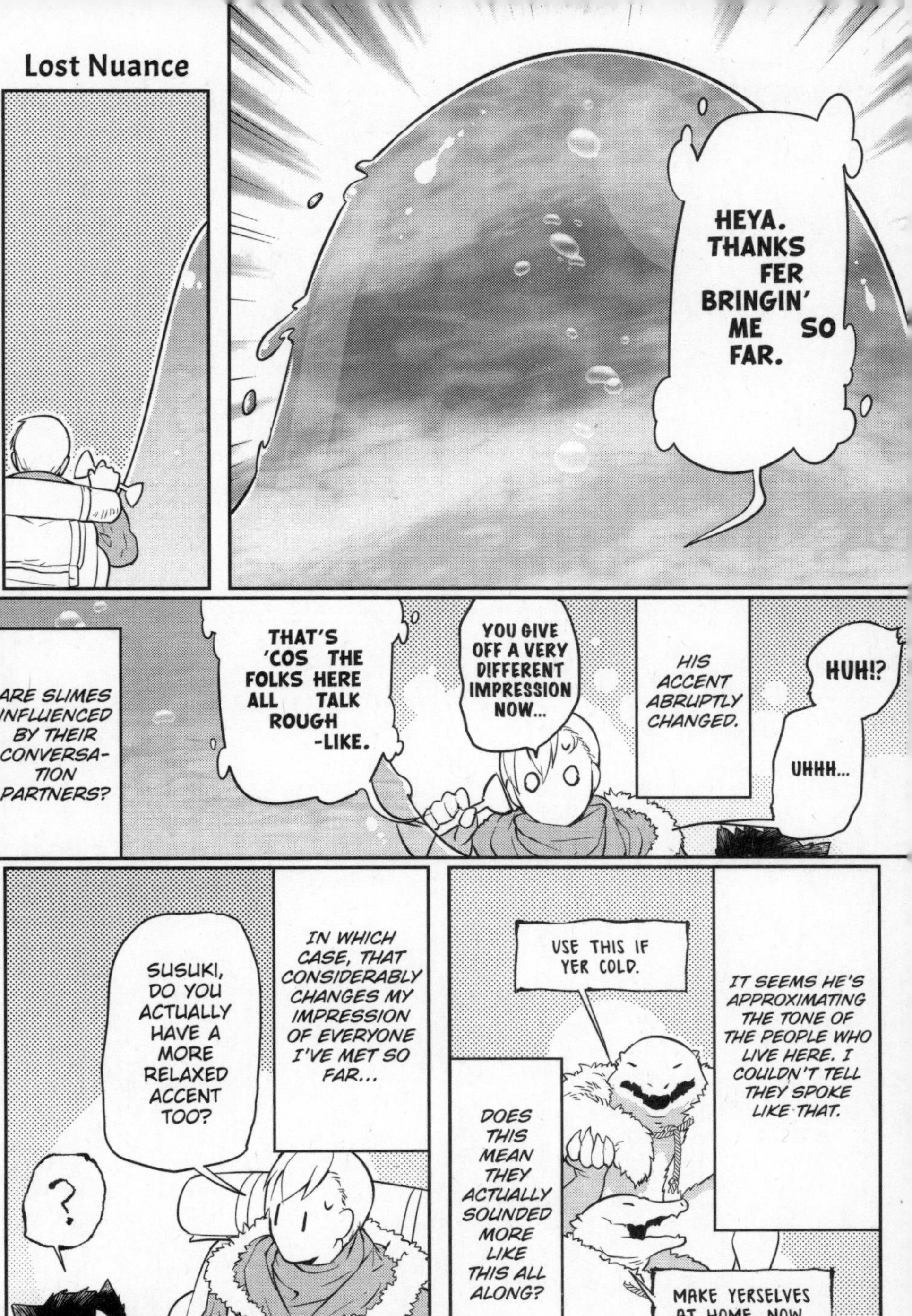
HEYA. THANKS FER BRINGIN' ME SO FAR.
HUH!?
UHHH...
HIS ACCENT ABRUPTLY CHANGED.
YOU GIVE OFF A VERY DIFFERENT IMPRESSION NOW...
THAT'S 'COS THE FOLKS HERE ALL TALK ROUGH-LIKE.
ARE SLIMES INFLUENCED BY THEIR CONVERSATION PARTNERS?
USE THIS IF YER COLD.
IT SEEMS HE'S APPROXIMATING THE TONE OF THE PEOPLE WHO LIVE HERE. I COULDN'T TELL THEY SPOKE LIKE THAT.
DOES THIS MEAN THEY ACTUALLY SOUNDED MORE LIKE THIS ALL ALONG?
MAKE YERSELVES AT HOME, NOW.
IN WHICH CASE, THAT CONSIDERABLY CHANGES MY IMPRESSION OF EVERYONE I'VE MET SO FAR...
SUSUKI, DO YOU ACTUALLY HAVE A MORE RELAXED ACCENT TOO?
?

A Second Departure and an Empty Stomach

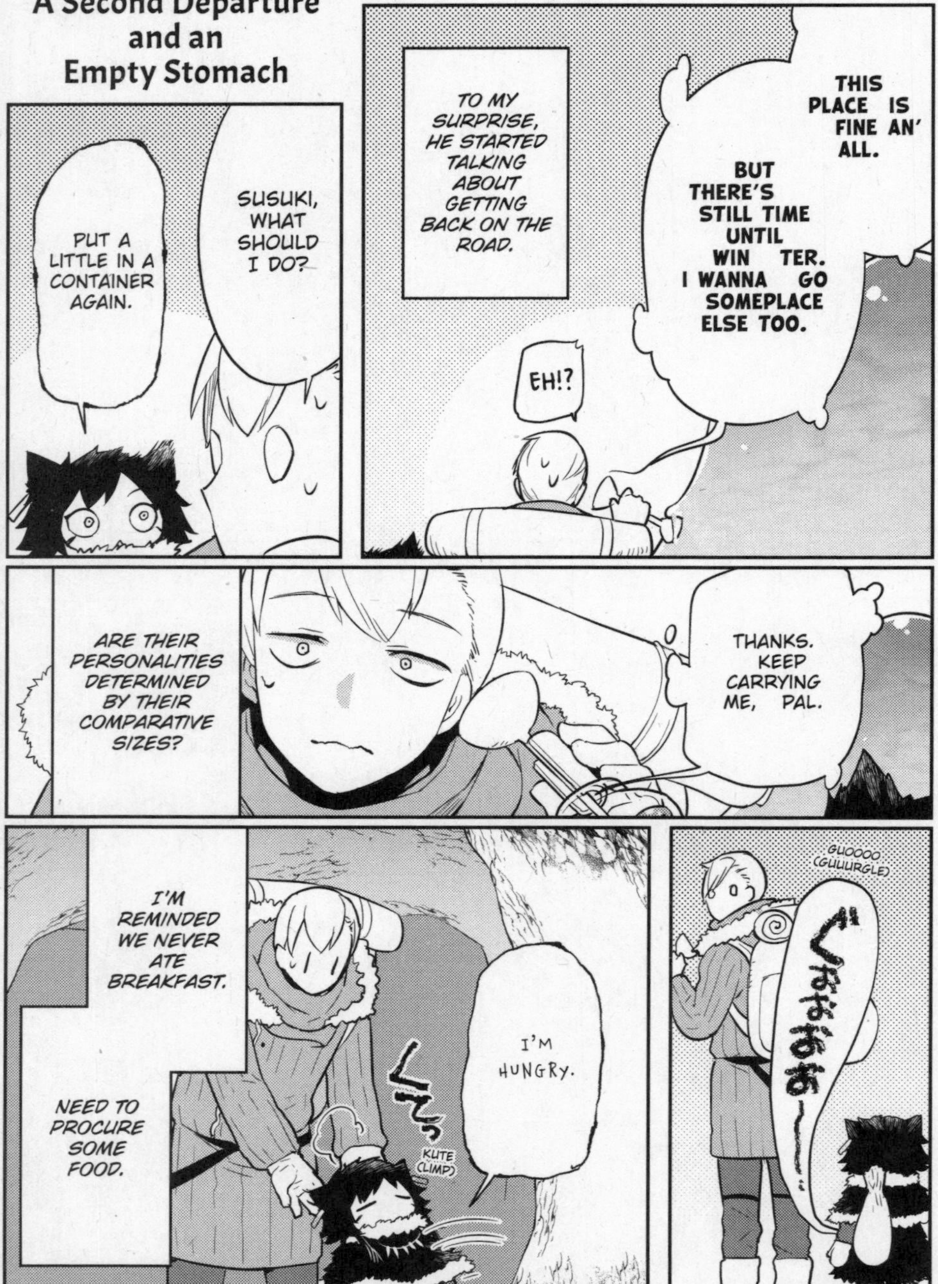
THIS PLACE IS FINE AN' ALL.
BUT THERE'S STILL TIME UNTIL WIN TER. I WANNA GO SOMEPLACE ELSE TOO.
TO MY SURPRISE, HE STARTED TALKING ABOUT GETTING BACK ON THE ROAD.
EH!?
SUSUKI, WHAT SHOULD I DO?
PUT A LITTLE IN A CONTAINER AGAIN.
THANKS. KEEP CARRYING ME, PAL.
ARE THEIR PERSONALITIES DETERMINED BY THEIR COMPARATIVE SIZES?
GUOOOO (GUUURGLE)
ぐおおおお～…
I'M REMINDED WE NEVER ATE BREAKFAST.
I'M HUNGRY.
くてっ
KUTE (LIMP)
NEED TO PROCURE SOME FOOD.

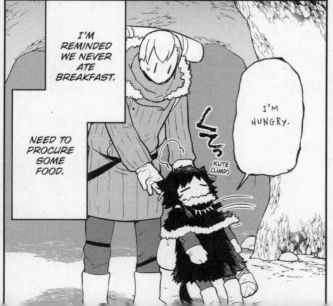

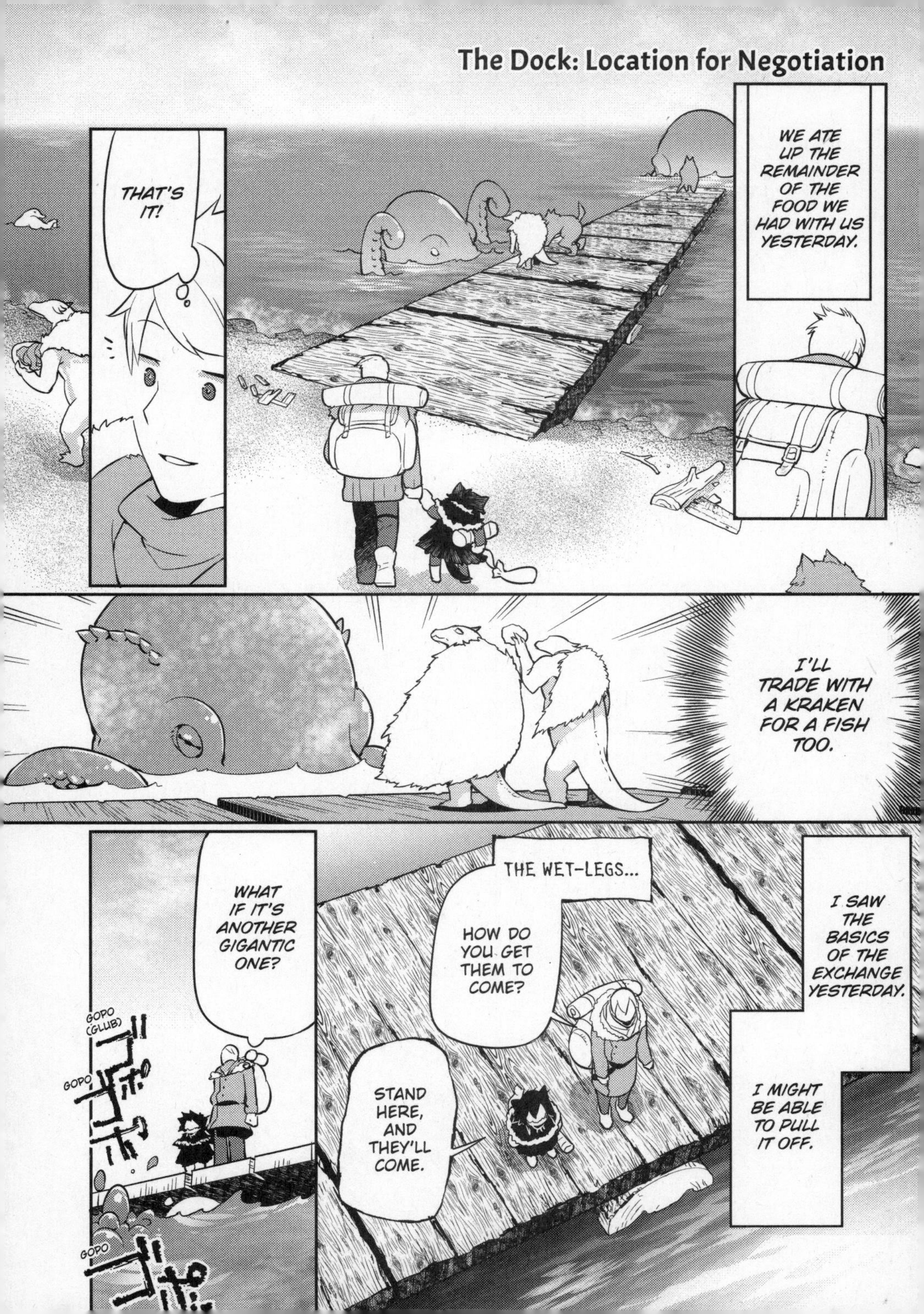
The Dock: Location for Negotiation
WE ATE UP THE REMAINDER OF THE FOOD WE HAD WITH US YESTERDAY.
THAT'S IT!
I'LL TRADE WITH A KRAKEN FOR A FISH TOO.
I SAW THE BASICS OF THE EXCHANGE YESTERDAY.
I MIGHT BE ABLE TO PULL IT OFF.
THE WET-LEGS...
HOW DO YOU GET THEM TO COME?
STAND HERE, AND THEY'LL COME.
WHAT IF IT'S ANOTHER GIGANTIC ONE?
GOPO (GLUB)
GOPO
GOPO

Challenge

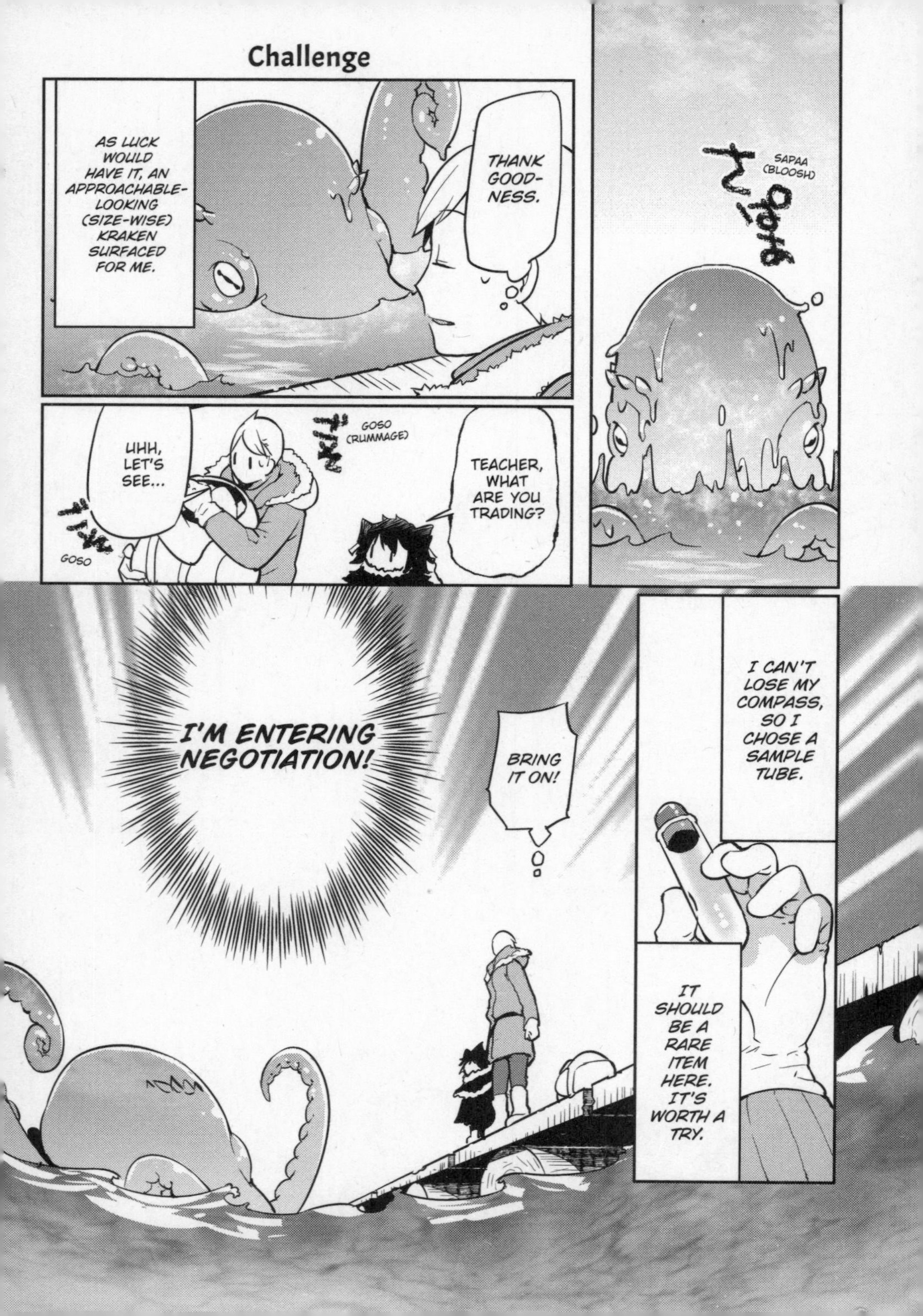
SAPAA (BLOOSH)
THANK GOODNESS.
AS LUCK WOULD HAVE IT, AN APPROACHABLE-LOOKING (SIZE-WISE) KRAKEN SURFACED FOR ME.
TEACHER, WHAT ARE YOU TRADING?
GOSO (RUMMAGE)
UHH, LET'S SEE...
GOSO
I CAN'T LOSE MY COMPASS, SO I CHOSE A SAMPLE TUBE.
IT SHOULD BE A RARE ITEM HERE. IT'S WORTH A TRY.
BRING IT ON!
I'M ENTERING NEGOTIATION!

Unexpected Situation

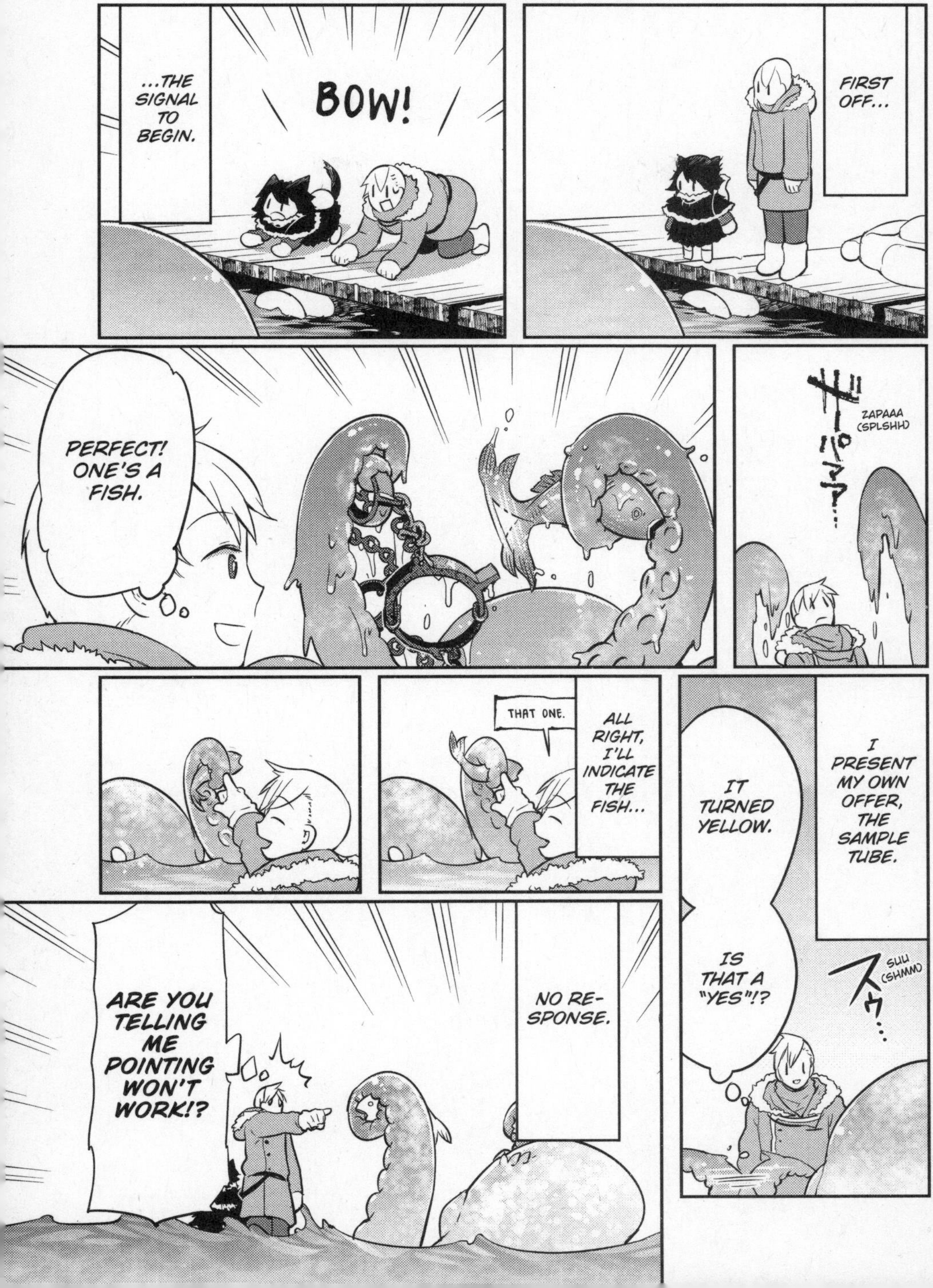
FIRST OFF...
...THE SIGNAL TO BEGIN.
BOW!
ザパァァ…
ZAPAAA (SPLSHH)
PERFECT! ONE'S A FISH.
I PRESENT MY OWN OFFER, THE SAMPLE TUBE.
IT TURNED YELLOW.
IS THAT A "YES"!?
スゥ…
SUU (SHMM)
ALL RIGHT, I'LL INDICATE THE FISH...
THAT ONE.
NO RE-SPONSE.
ARE YOU TELLING ME POINTING WON'T WORK!?

Primitive

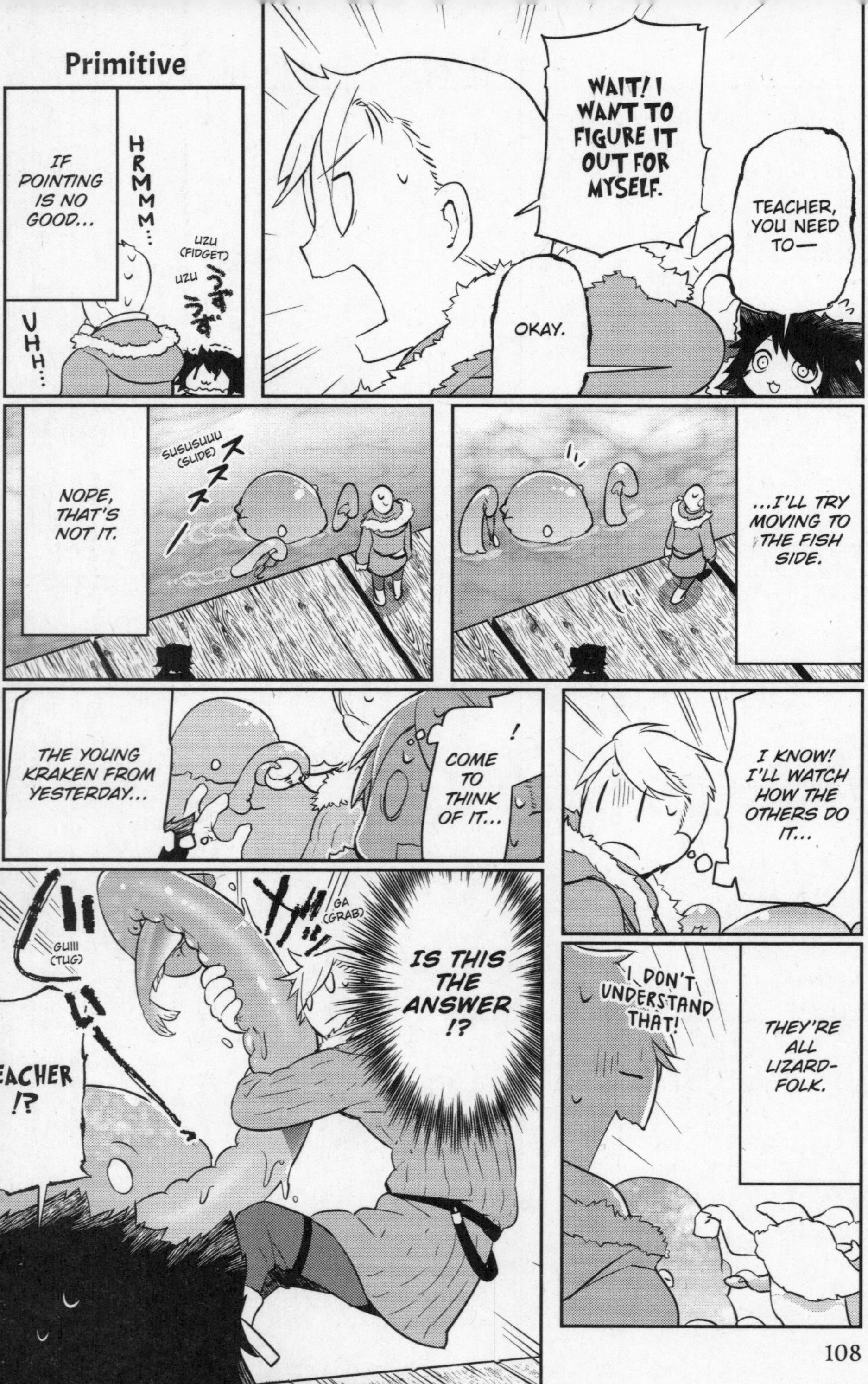
TEACHER, YOU NEED TO—
WAIT! I WANT TO FIGURE IT OUT FOR MYSELF.
OKAY.
HRMMM...
UZU (FIDGET)
UZU
IF POINTING IS NO GOOD...
UHH...
...I'LL TRY MOVING TO THE FISH SIDE.
SUSUSUUU (SLIDE)
NOPE, THAT'S NOT IT.
I KNOW! I'LL WATCH HOW THE OTHERS DO IT...
!
COME TO THINK OF IT...
THE YOUNG KRAKEN FROM YESTERDAY...
THEY'RE ALL LIZARD-FOLK.
I DON'T UNDERSTAND THAT!
IS THIS THE ANSWER!?
GA (GRAB)
GUIII (TUG)
TEACHER!?

The Correct Answer

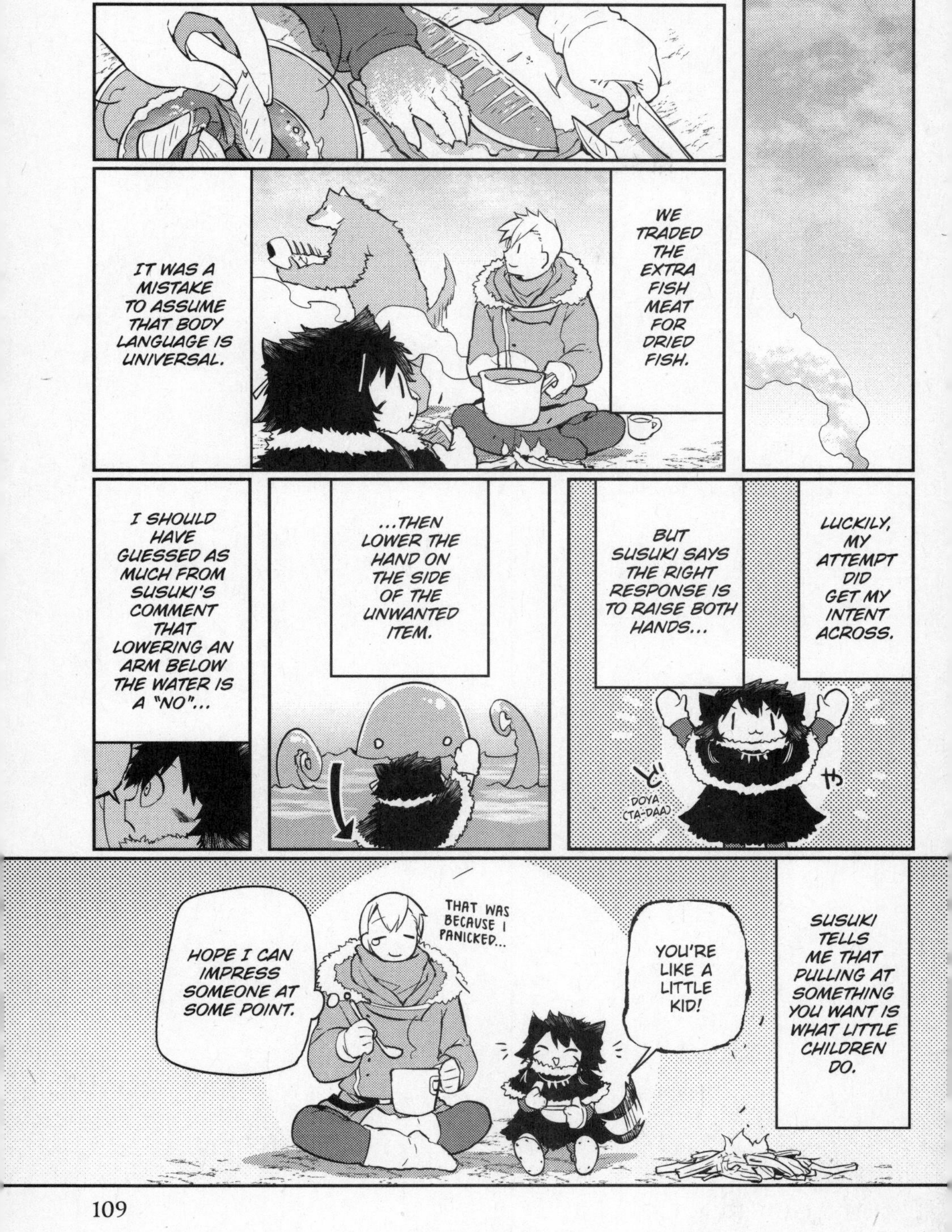

WE TRADED THE EXTRA FISH MEAT FOR DRIED FISH.
IT WAS A MISTAKE TO ASSUME THAT BODY LANGUAGE IS UNIVERSAL.
LUCKILY, MY ATTEMPT DID GET MY INTENT ACROSS.
BUT SUSUKI SAYS THE RIGHT RESPONSE IS TO RAISE BOTH HANDS...
DOYA (TA-DAA)
...THEN LOWER THE HAND ON THE SIDE OF THE UNWANTED ITEM.
I SHOULD HAVE GUESSED AS MUCH FROM SUSUKI'S COMMENT THAT LOWERING AN ARM BELOW THE WATER IS A "NO"...
SUSUKI TELLS ME THAT PULLING AT SOMETHING YOU WANT IS WHAT LITTLE CHILDREN DO.
YOU'RE LIKE A LITTLE KID!
THAT WAS BECAUSE I PANICKED...
HOPE I CAN IMPRESS SOMEONE AT SOME POINT.

Delivery

SUSUKI?

SUKU
(HOP)

HEY, SUSUKI.

TOTOTO
(PATTER)

WE FOUND THE PACKAGE'S RECIPIENT.

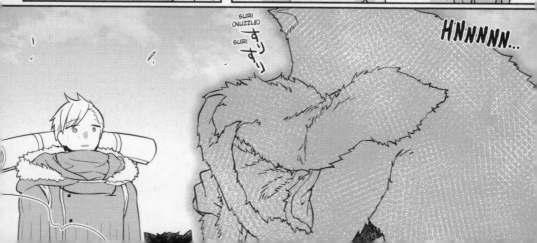

SURI
(NUZZLE)
SURI

HNNNNN...

The Smoke

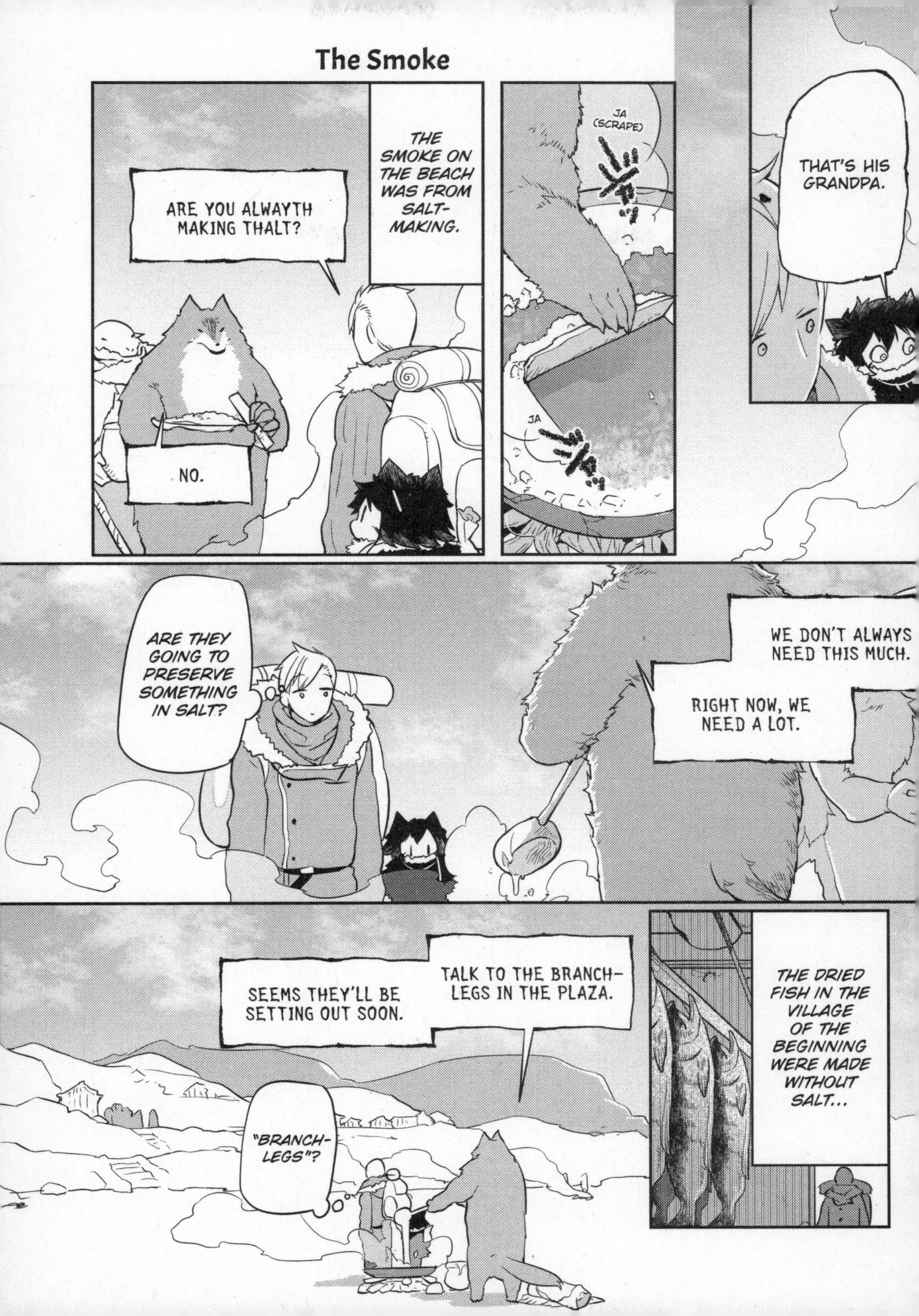
THAT'S HIS GRANDPA.
JA (SCRAPE)
JA
THE SMOKE ON THE BEACH WAS FROM SALT-MAKING.
ARE YOU ALWAYTH MAKING THALT?
NO.
WE DON'T ALWAYS NEED THIS MUCH.
RIGHT NOW, WE NEED A LOT.
ARE THEY GOING TO PRESERVE SOMETHING IN SALT?
THE DRIED FISH IN THE VILLAGE OF THE BEGINNING WERE MADE WITHOUT SALT...
TALK TO THE BRANCH-LEGS IN THE PLAZA.
SEEMS THEY'LL BE SETTING OUT SOON.
"BRANCH-LEGS"?

Celebration?

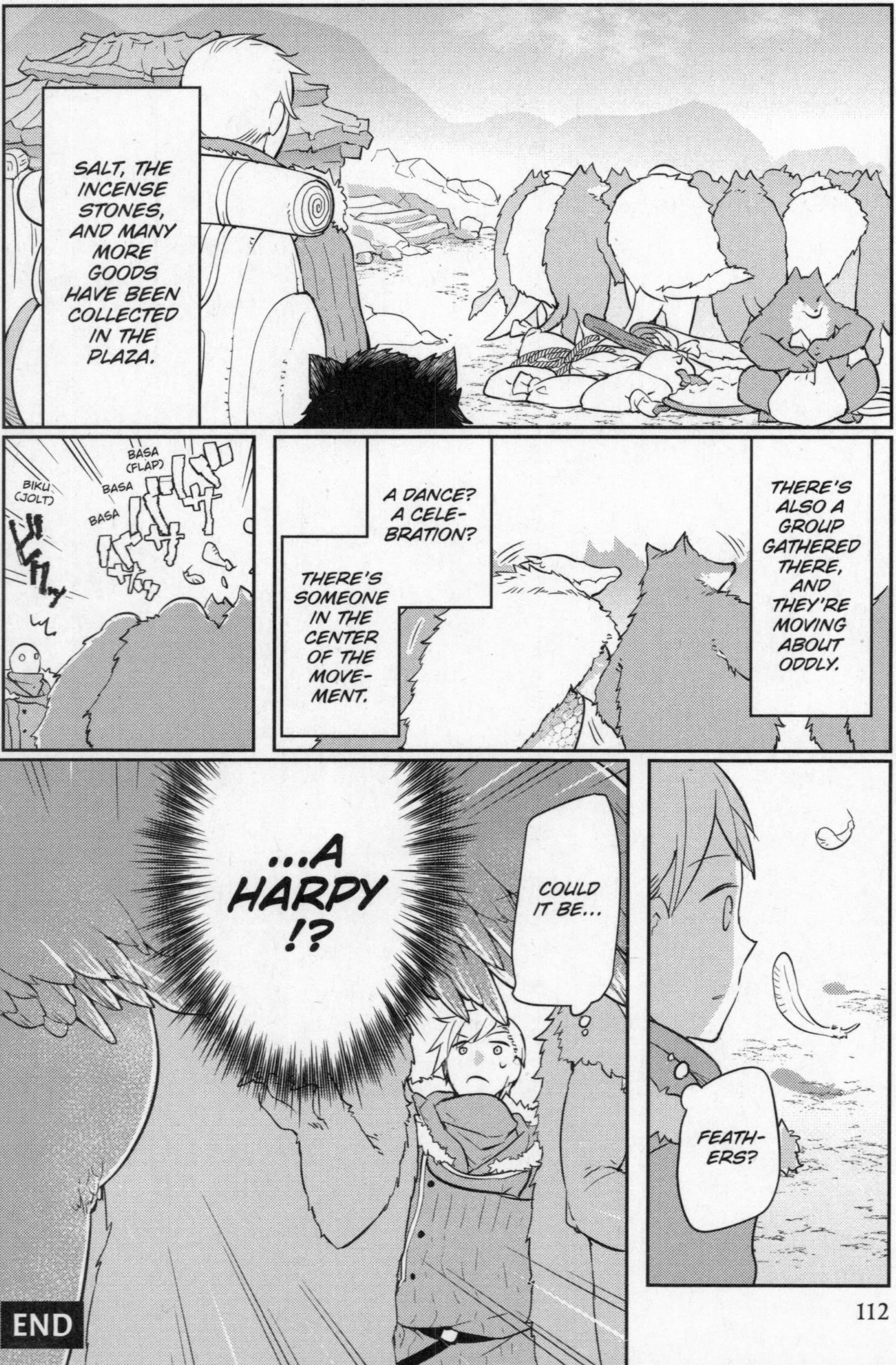
SALT, THE INCENSE STONES, AND MANY MORE GOODS HAVE BEEN COLLECTED IN THE PLAZA.
THERE'S ALSO A GROUP GATHERED THERE, AND THEY'RE MOVING ABOUT ODDLY.
A DANCE? A CELEBRATION?
THERE'S SOMEONE IN THE CENTER OF THE MOVEMENT.
BASA (FLAP)
BASA
BASA
BIKU (JOLT)
FEATHERS?
COULD IT BE...
...A HARPY!?
END

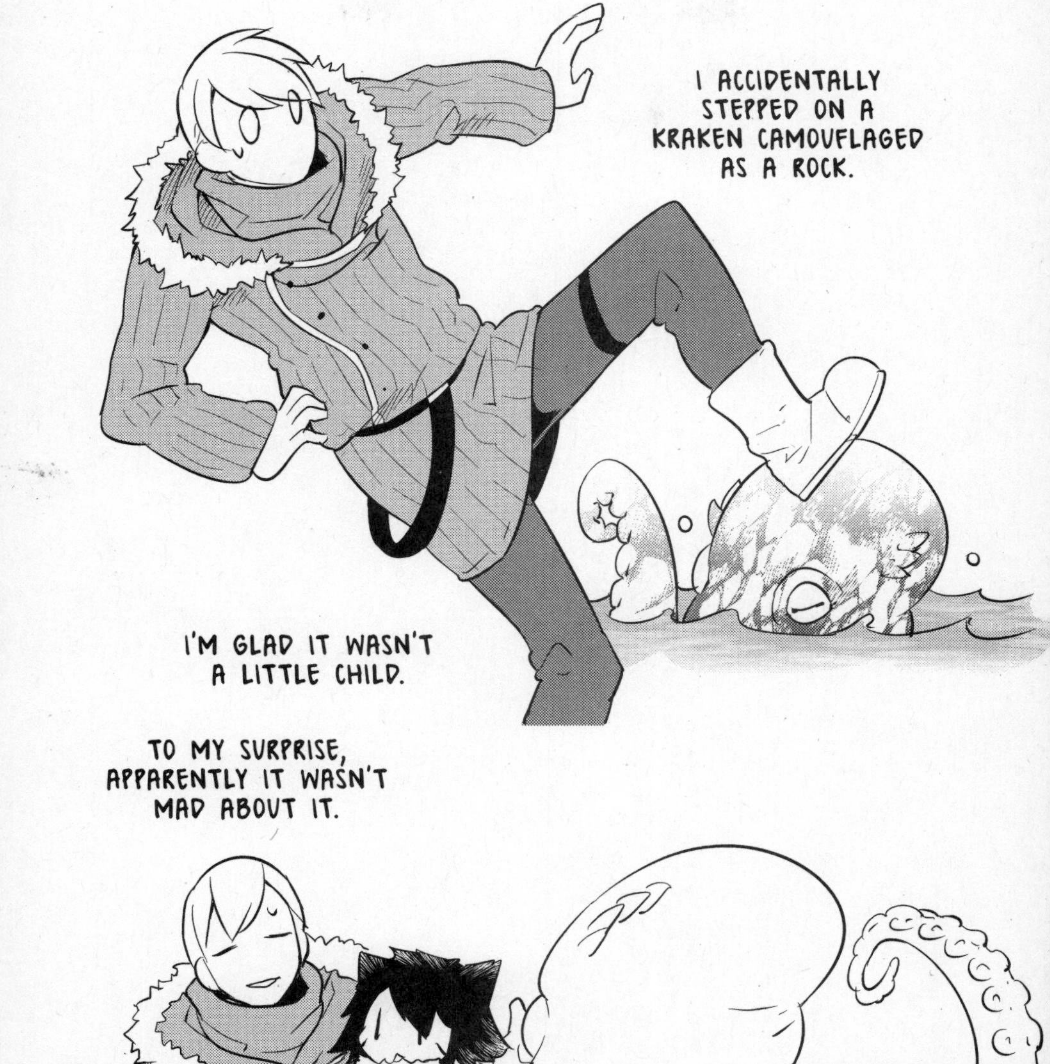
I ACCIDENTALLY STEPPED ON A KRAKEN CAMOUFLAGED AS A ROCK.
I'M GLAD IT WASN'T A LITTLE CHILD.
TO MY SURPRISE, APPARENTLY IT WASN'T MAD ABOUT IT.

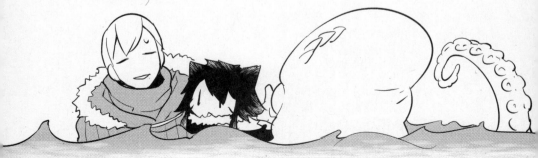

A WEREWOLF CHILD AND
A LIZARDFOLK CHILD
FOUND A KRAKEN CHILD
CAMOUFLAGED AS A ROCK.

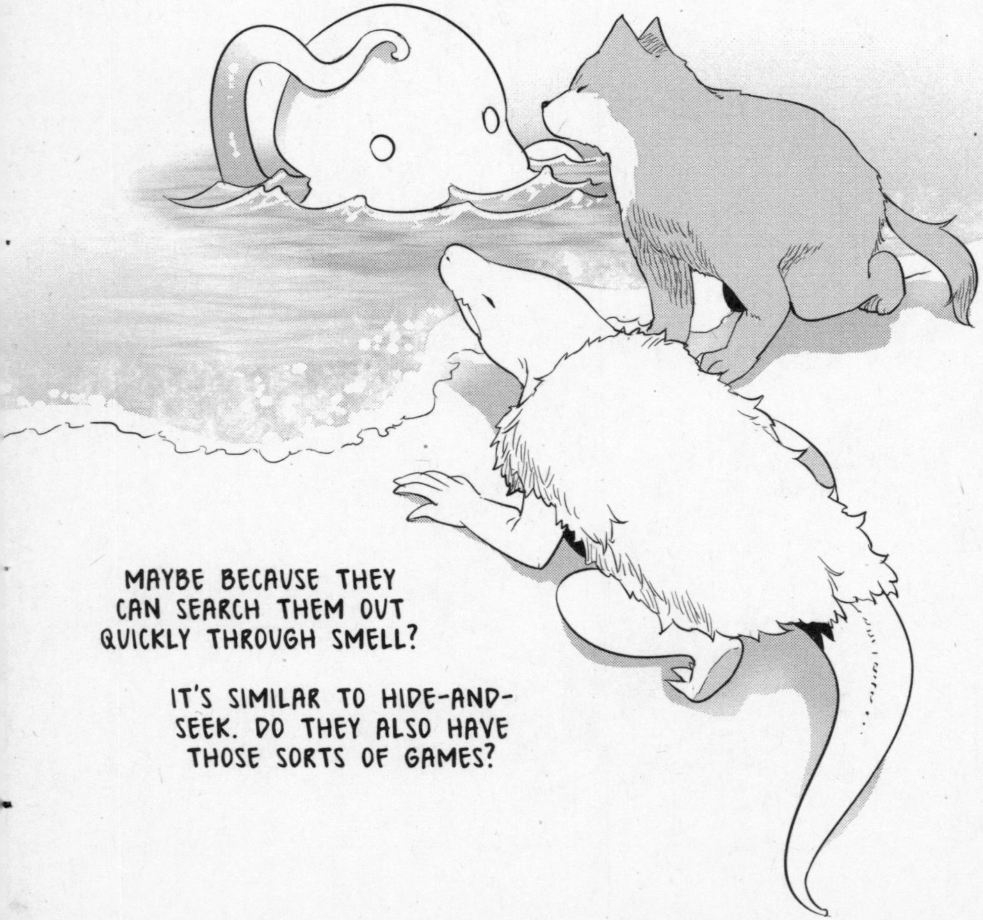

MAYBE BECAUSE THEY
CAN SEARCH THEM OUT
QUICKLY THROUGH SMELL?

IT'S SIMILAR TO HIDE-AND-
SEEK. DO THEY ALSO HAVE
THOSE SORTS OF GAMES?

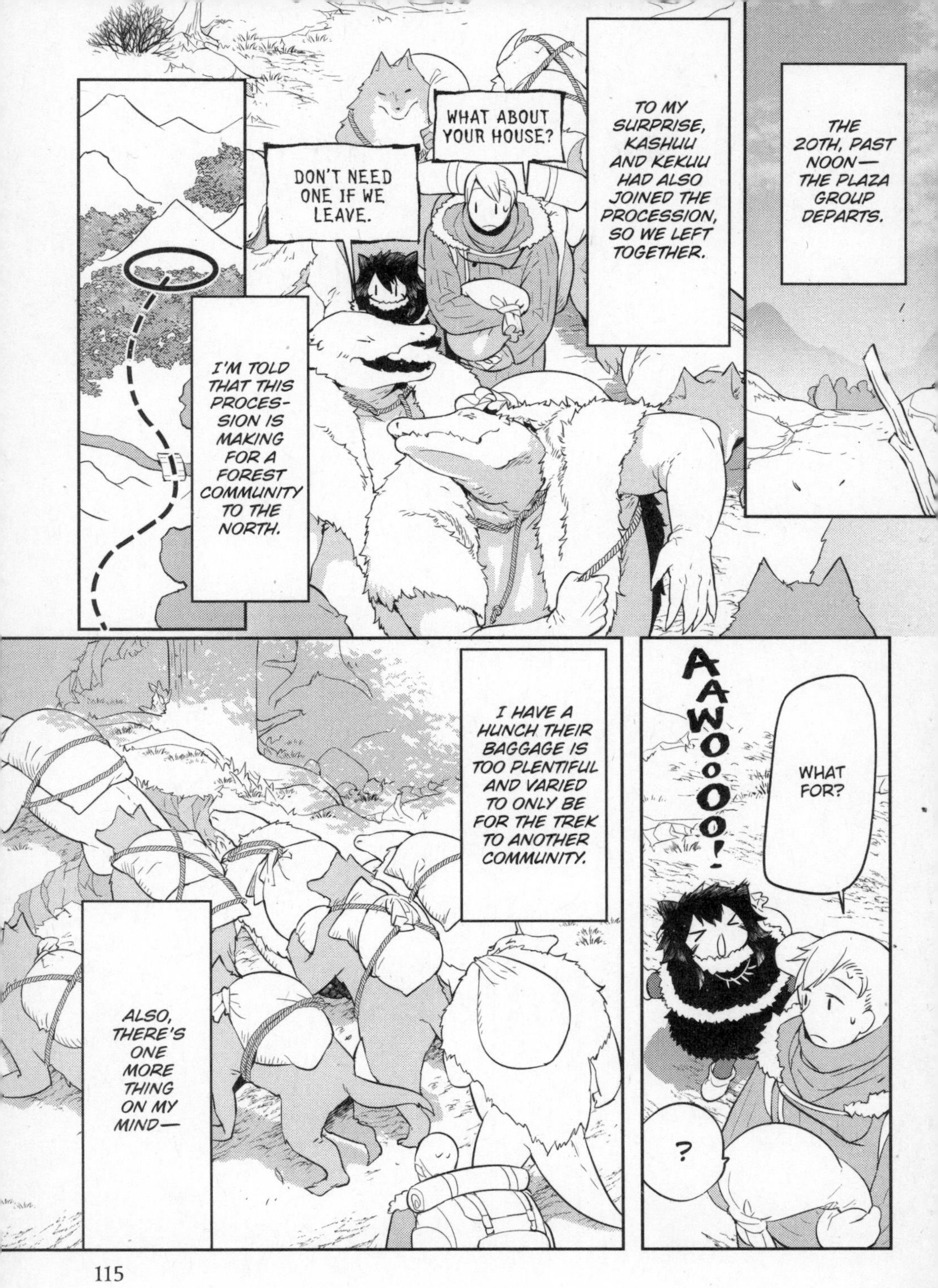
THE 20TH, PAST NOON— THE PLAZA GROUP DEPARTS.
TO MY SURPRISE, KASHUU AND KEKUU HAD ALSO JOINED THE PROCESSION, SO WE LEFT TOGETHER.
WHAT ABOUT YOUR HOUSE?
DON'T NEED ONE IF WE LEAVE.
I'M TOLD THAT THIS PROCES-SION IS MAKING FOR A FOREST COMMUNITY TO THE NORTH.
AAWOOOO!
WHAT FOR?
?
I HAVE A HUNCH THEIR BAGGAGE IS TOO PLENTIFUL AND VARIED TO ONLY BE FOR THE TREK TO ANOTHER COMMUNITY.
ALSO, THERE'S ONE MORE THING ON MY MIND—

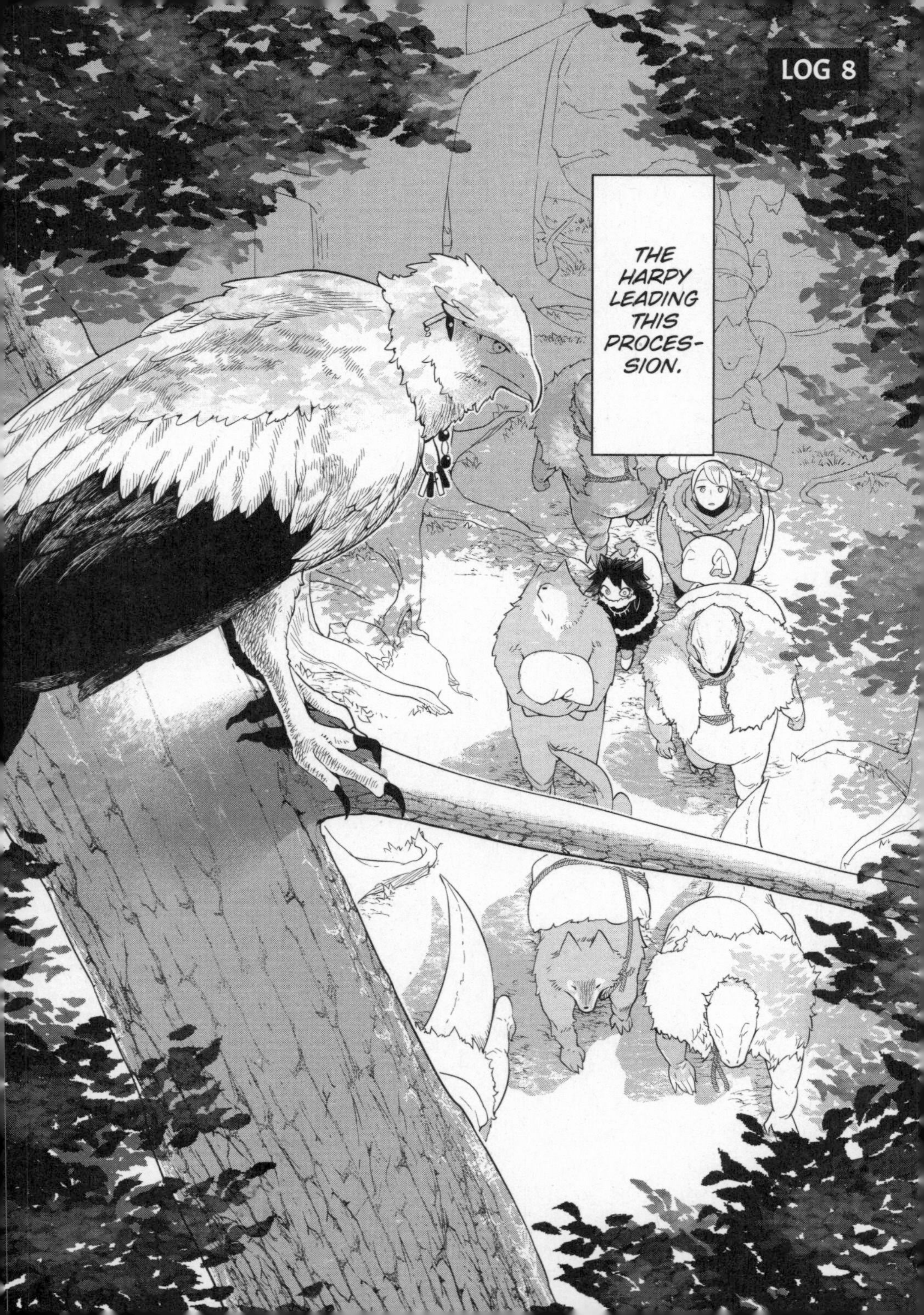
LOG 8
THE HARPY LEADING THIS PROCES-SION.

Their Name

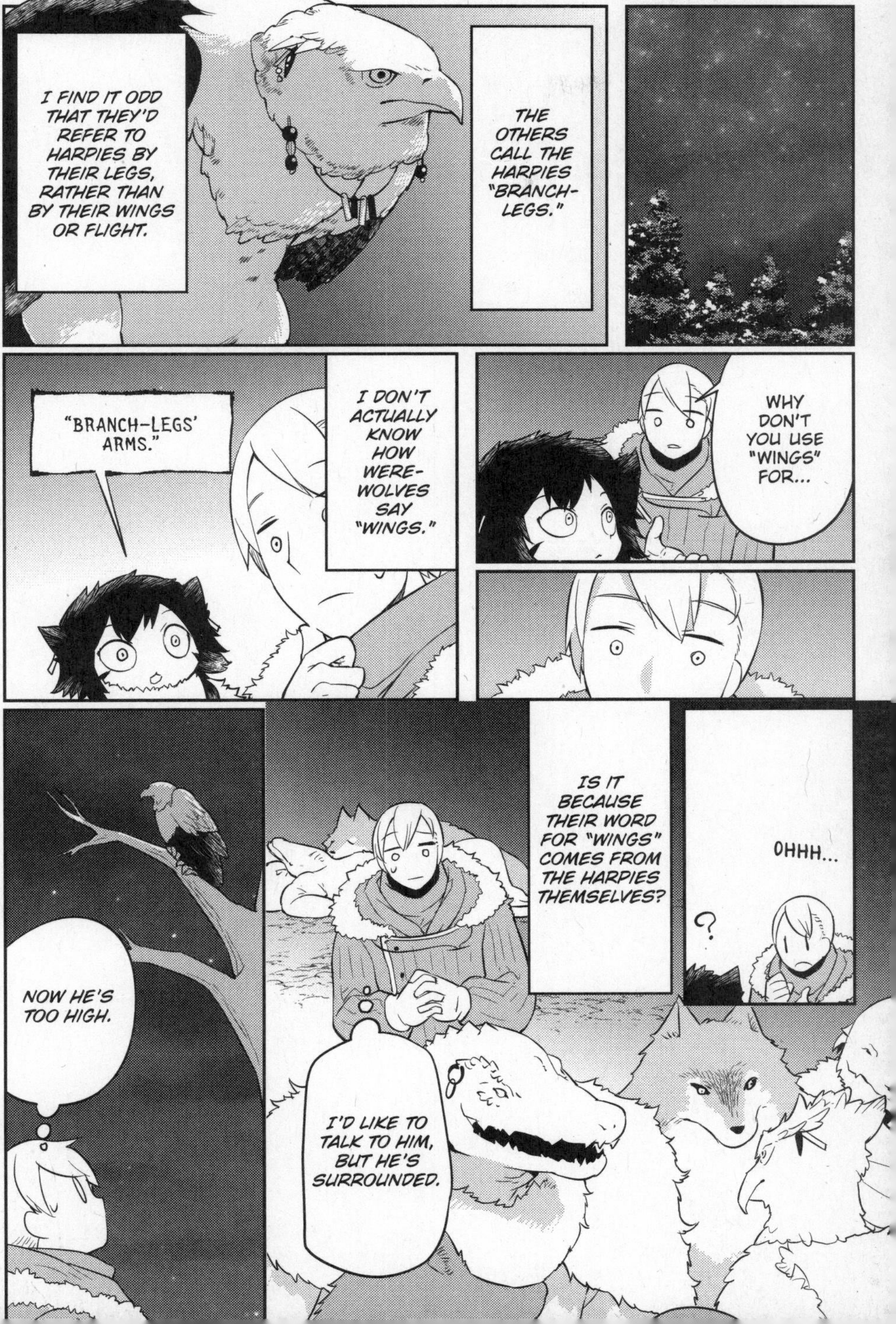
THE OTHERS CALL THE HARPIES "BRANCH-LEGS."
I FIND IT ODD THAT THEY'D REFER TO HARPIES BY THEIR LEGS, RATHER THAN BY THEIR WINGS OR FLIGHT.
WHY DON'T YOU USE "WINGS" FOR...
I DON'T ACTUALLY KNOW HOW WEREWOLVES SAY "WINGS."
"BRANCH-LEGS' ARMS."
OHHH...
?
IS IT BECAUSE THEIR WORD FOR "WINGS" COMES FROM THE HARPIES THEMSELVES?
I'D LIKE TO TALK TO HIM, BUT HE'S SURROUNDED.
NOW HE'S TOO HIGH.

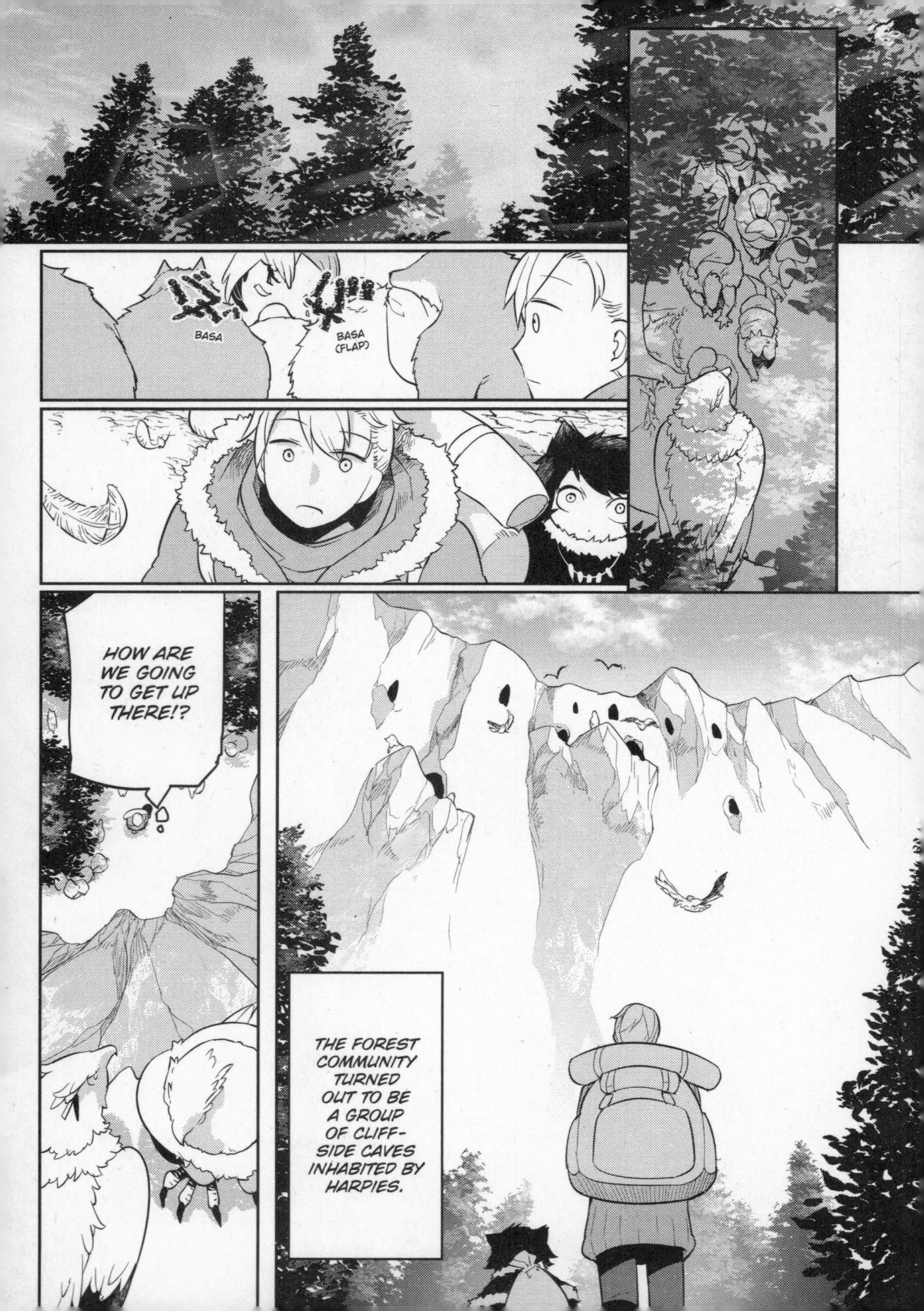
BASA (FLAP)
BASA
HOW ARE WE GOING TO GET UP THERE!?
THE FOREST COMMUNITY TURNED OUT TO BE A GROUP OF CLIFF-SIDE CAVES INHABITED BY HARPIES.

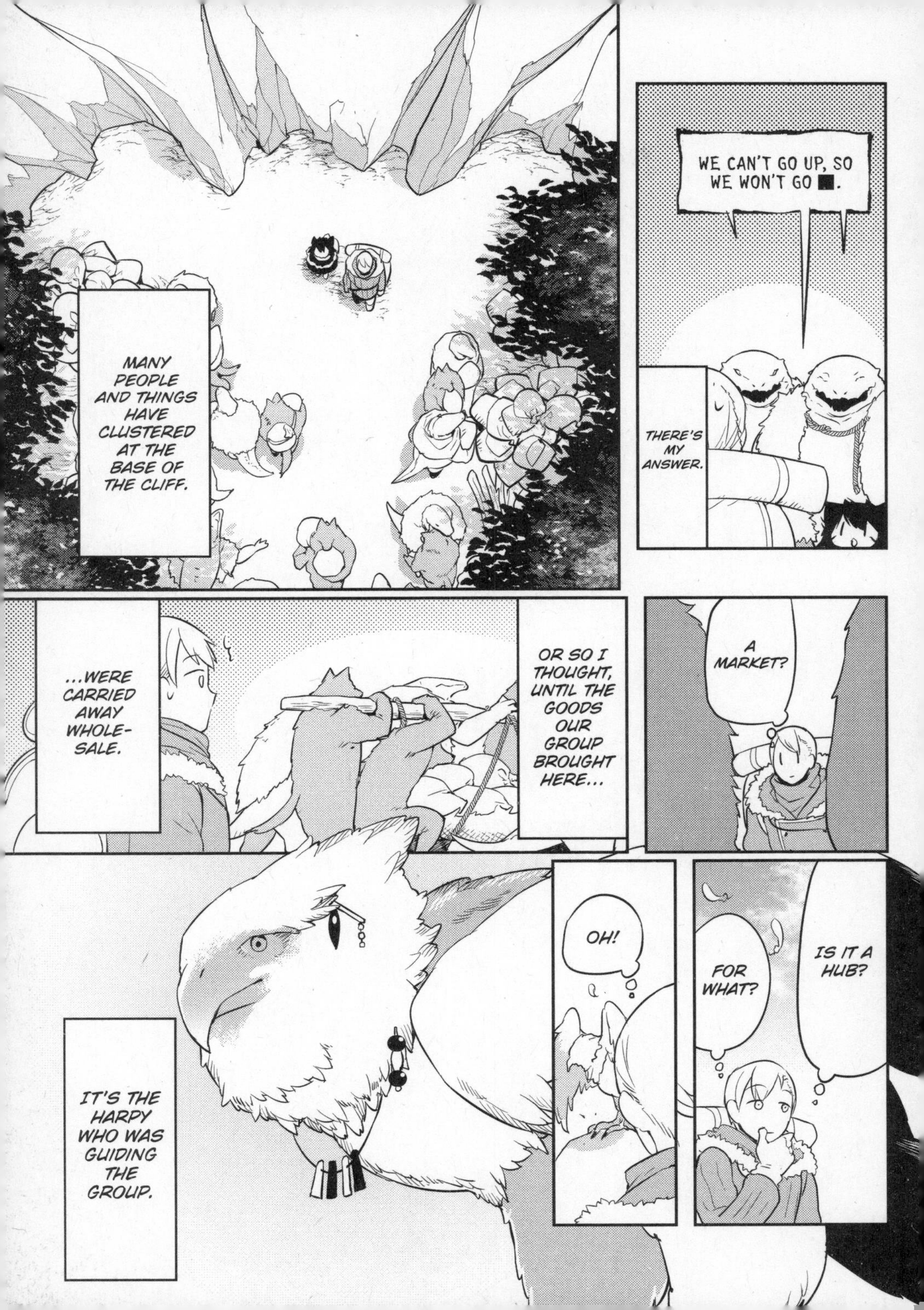
WE CAN'T GO UP, SO WE WON'T GO [redacted].
THERE'S MY ANSWER.
MANY PEOPLE AND THINGS HAVE CLUSTERED AT THE BASE OF THE CLIFF.
A MARKET?
OR SO I THOUGHT, UNTIL THE GOODS OUR GROUP BROUGHT HERE...
...WERE CARRIED AWAY WHOLE-SALE.
IS IT A HUB?
FOR WHAT?
OH!
IT'S THE HARPY WHO WAS GUIDING THE GROUP.

Two Views

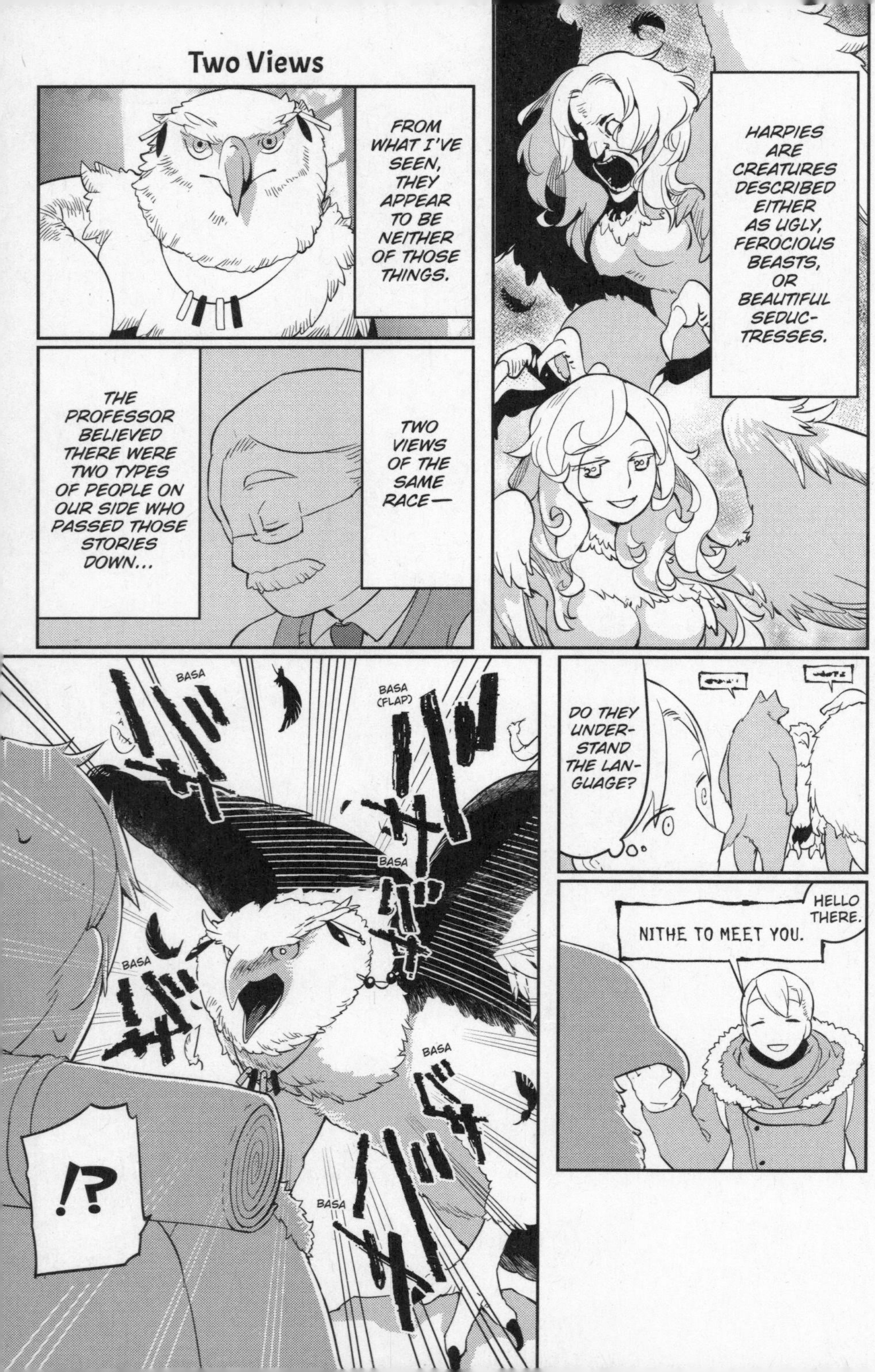
HARPIES ARE CREATURES DESCRIBED EITHER AS UGLY, FEROCIOUS BEASTS, OR BEAUTIFUL SEDUC-TRESSES.
FROM WHAT I'VE SEEN, THEY APPEAR TO BE NEITHER OF THOSE THINGS.
TWO VIEWS OF THE SAME RACE—
THE PROFESSOR BELIEVED THERE WERE TWO TYPES OF PEOPLE ON OUR SIDE WHO PASSED THOSE STORIES DOWN...
DO THEY UNDER-STAND THE LAN-GUAGE?
HELLO THERE.
NITHE TO MEET YOU.
BASA (FLAP)
BASA
BASA
BASA
BASA
BASA
!?

Harpy's Reply

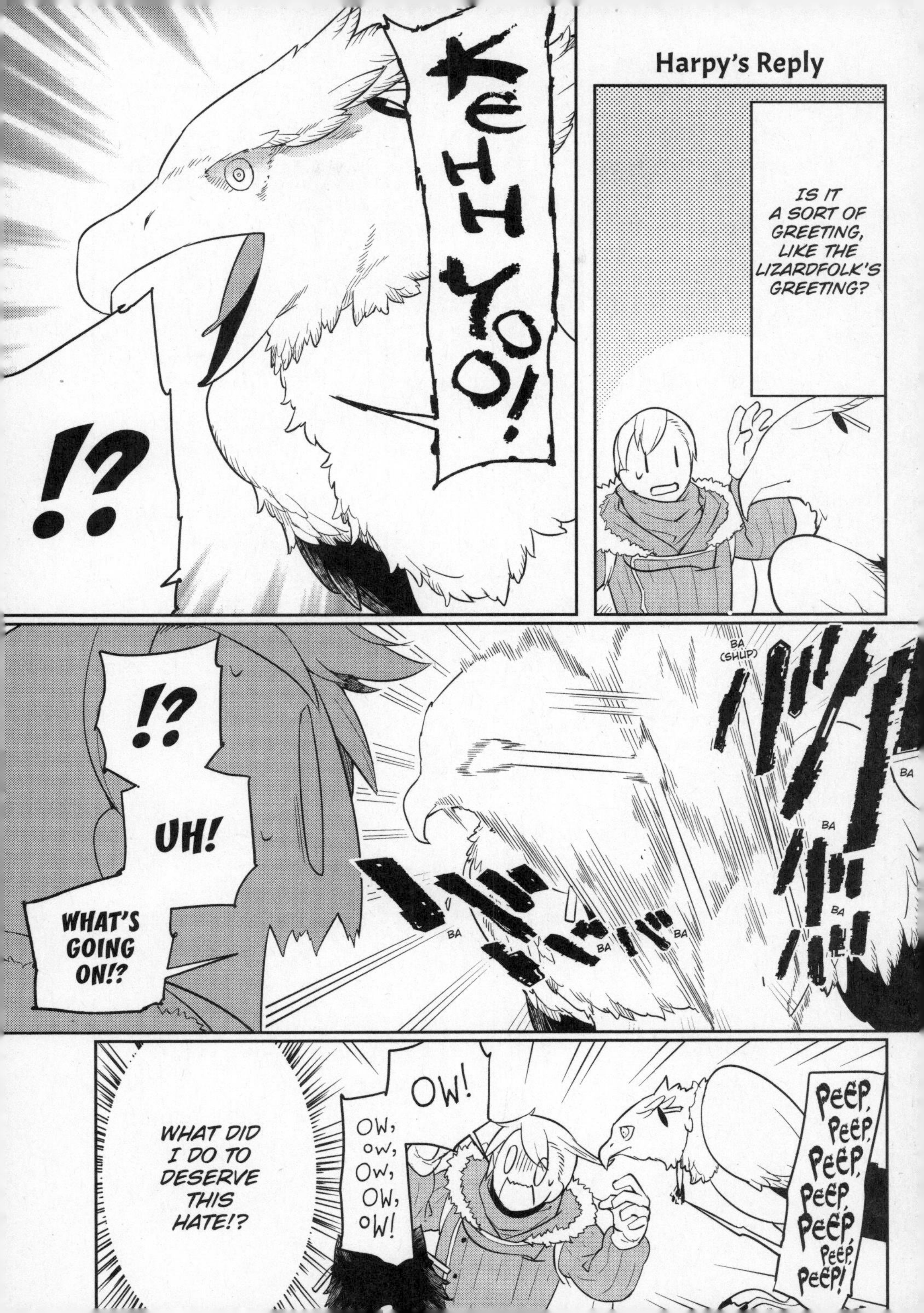

IS IT A SORT OF GREETING, LIKE THE LIZARDFOLK'S GREETING?
KEHH YOOO!
!?
BA (SHUP)
BA
BA
BA
BA
BA
BA
!?
UH!
WHAT'S GOING ON!?
PEEP, PEEP, PEEP, PEEP, PEEP, PEEP, PEEP!
OW!
OW, OW, OW, OW, OW!
WHAT DID I DO TO DESERVE THIS HATE!?

Mysterious Motion

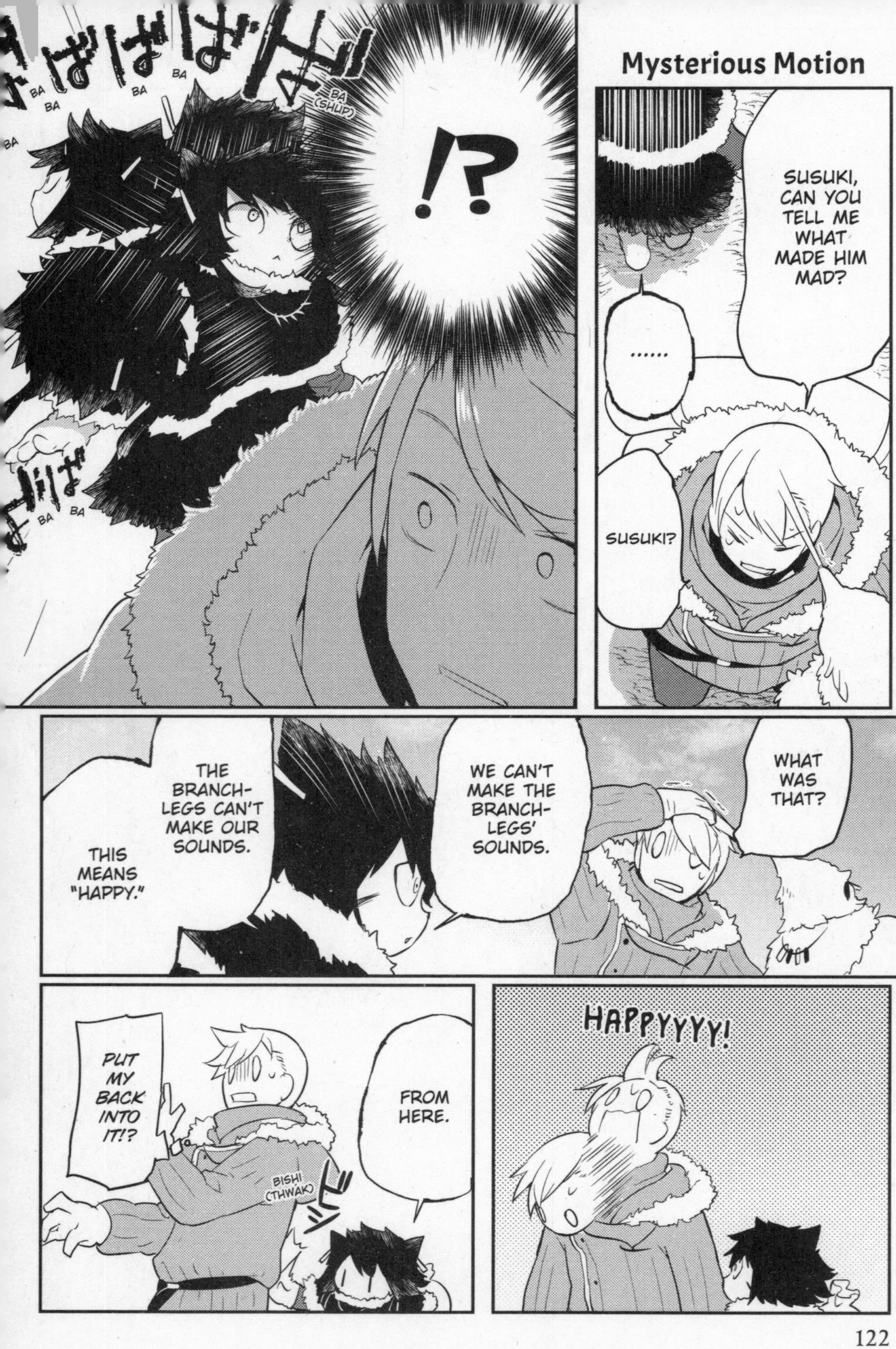
SUSUKI, CAN YOU TELL ME WHAT MADE HIM MAD?
......
SUSUKI?
BA BA BA BA BA (SHUP)
BA BA
!?
WHAT WAS THAT?
WE CAN'T MAKE THE BRANCH-LEGS' SOUNDS.
THE BRANCH-LEGS CAN'T MAKE OUR SOUNDS.
THIS MEANS "HAPPY."
HAPPYYYY!
FROM HERE.
PUT MY BACK INTO IT!?
BISHI (THWAK)

Arcane

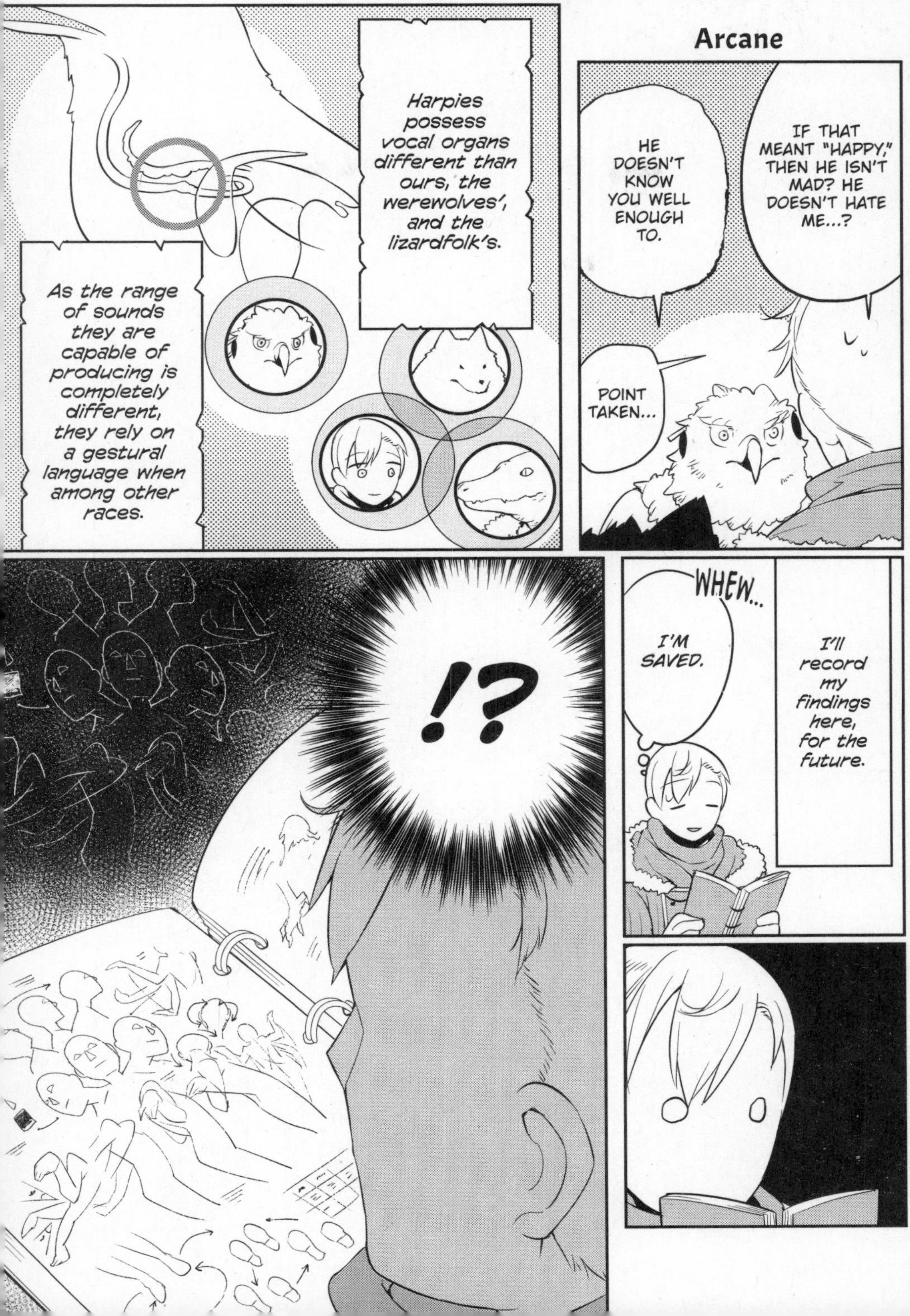
IF THAT MEANT "HAPPY," THEN HE ISN'T MAD? HE DOESN'T HATE ME...?
HE DOESN'T KNOW YOU WELL ENOUGH TO.
POINT TAKEN...
WHEW...
I'll record my findings here, for the future.
I'M SAVED.
Harpies possess vocal organs different than ours, the werewolves', and the lizardfolk's.
As the range of sounds they are capable of producing is completely different, they rely on a gestural language when among other races.
!?

The Faster Way

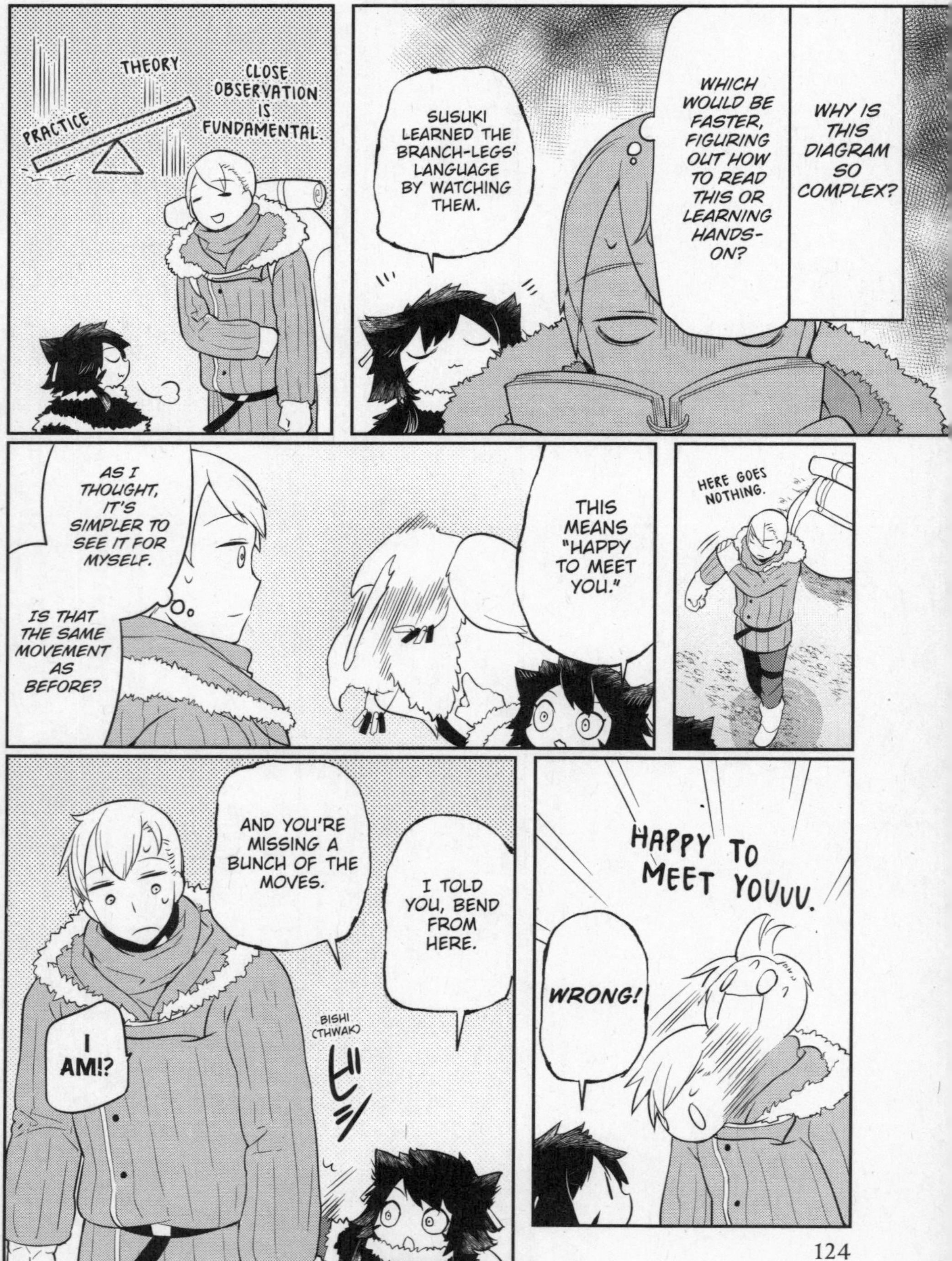
WHY IS THIS DIAGRAM SO COMPLEX?
WHICH WOULD BE FASTER, FIGURING OUT HOW TO READ THIS OR LEARNING HANDS-ON?
SUSUKI LEARNED THE BRANCH-LEGS' LANGUAGE BY WATCHING THEM.
CLOSE OBSERVATION IS FUNDAMENTAL.
THEORY
PRACTICE
HERE GOES NOTHING.
THIS MEANS "HAPPY TO MEET YOU."
AS I THOUGHT, IT'S SIMPLER TO SEE IT FOR MYSELF.
IS THAT THE SAME MOVEMENT AS BEFORE?
HAPPY TO MEET YOUUU.
WRONG!
I TOLD YOU, BEND FROM HERE.
AND YOU'RE MISSING A BUNCH OF THE MOVES.
BISHI (THWAK)
I AM!?

Ultra-High Difficulty

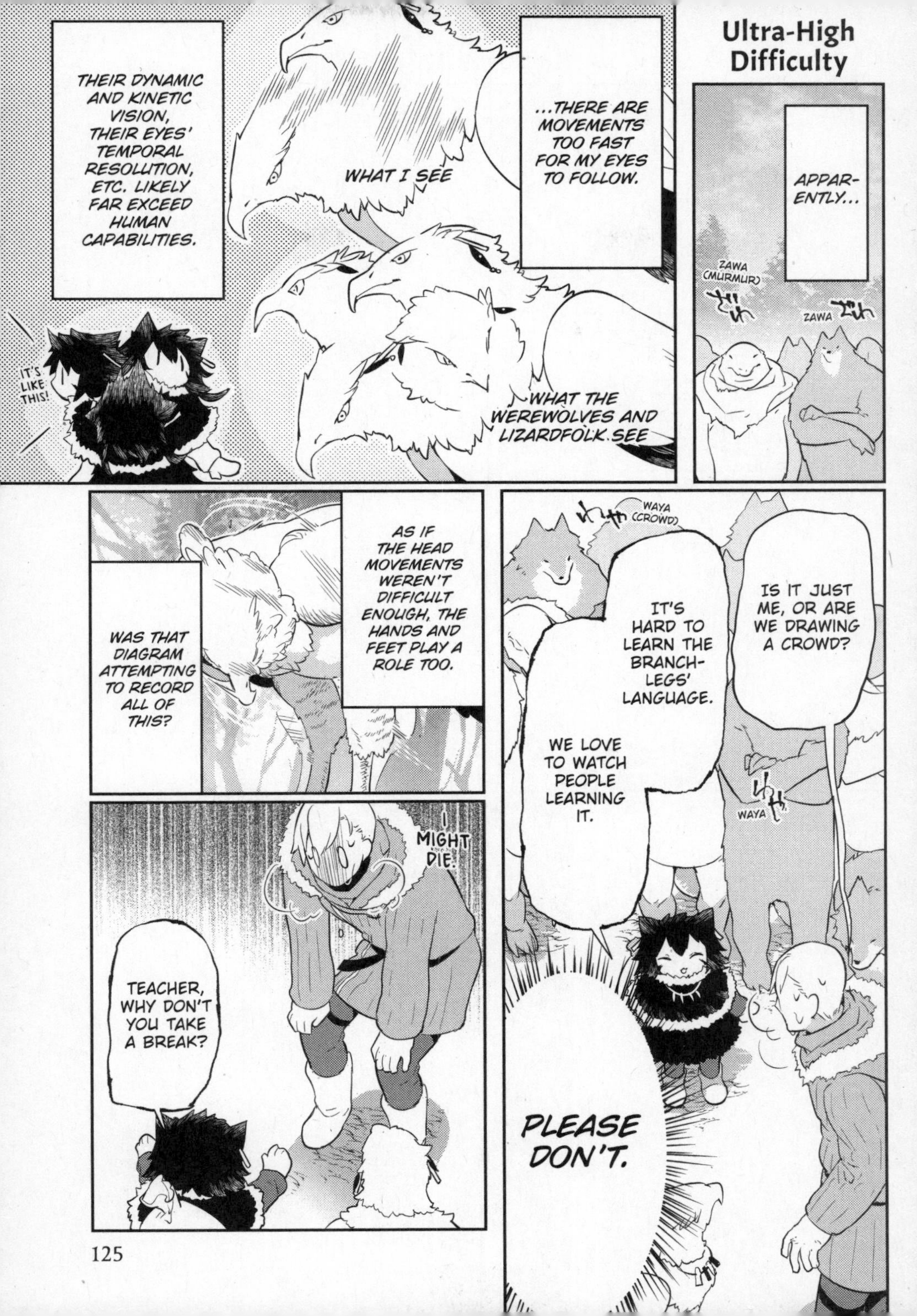
APPAR-ENTLY...
ZAWA (MURMUR)
ZAWA
...THERE ARE MOVEMENTS TOO FAST FOR MY EYES TO FOLLOW.
THEIR DYNAMIC AND KINETIC VISION, THEIR EYES' TEMPORAL RESOLUTION, ETC. LIKELY FAR EXCEED HUMAN CAPABILITIES.
WHAT I SEE
WHAT THE WEREWOLVES AND LIZARDFOLK SEE
IT'S LIKE THIS!
WAYA (CROWD)
IS IT JUST ME, OR ARE WE DRAWING A CROWD?
IT'S HARD TO LEARN THE BRANCH-LEGS' LANGUAGE.
WE LOVE TO WATCH PEOPLE LEARNING IT.
WAYA
PLEASE DON'T.
AS IF THE HEAD MOVEMENTS WEREN'T DIFFICULT ENOUGH, THE HANDS AND FEET PLAY A ROLE TOO.
WAS THAT DIAGRAM ATTEMPTING TO RECORD ALL OF THIS?
I MIGHT DIE.
TEACHER, WHY DON'T YOU TAKE A BREAK?

No Joke

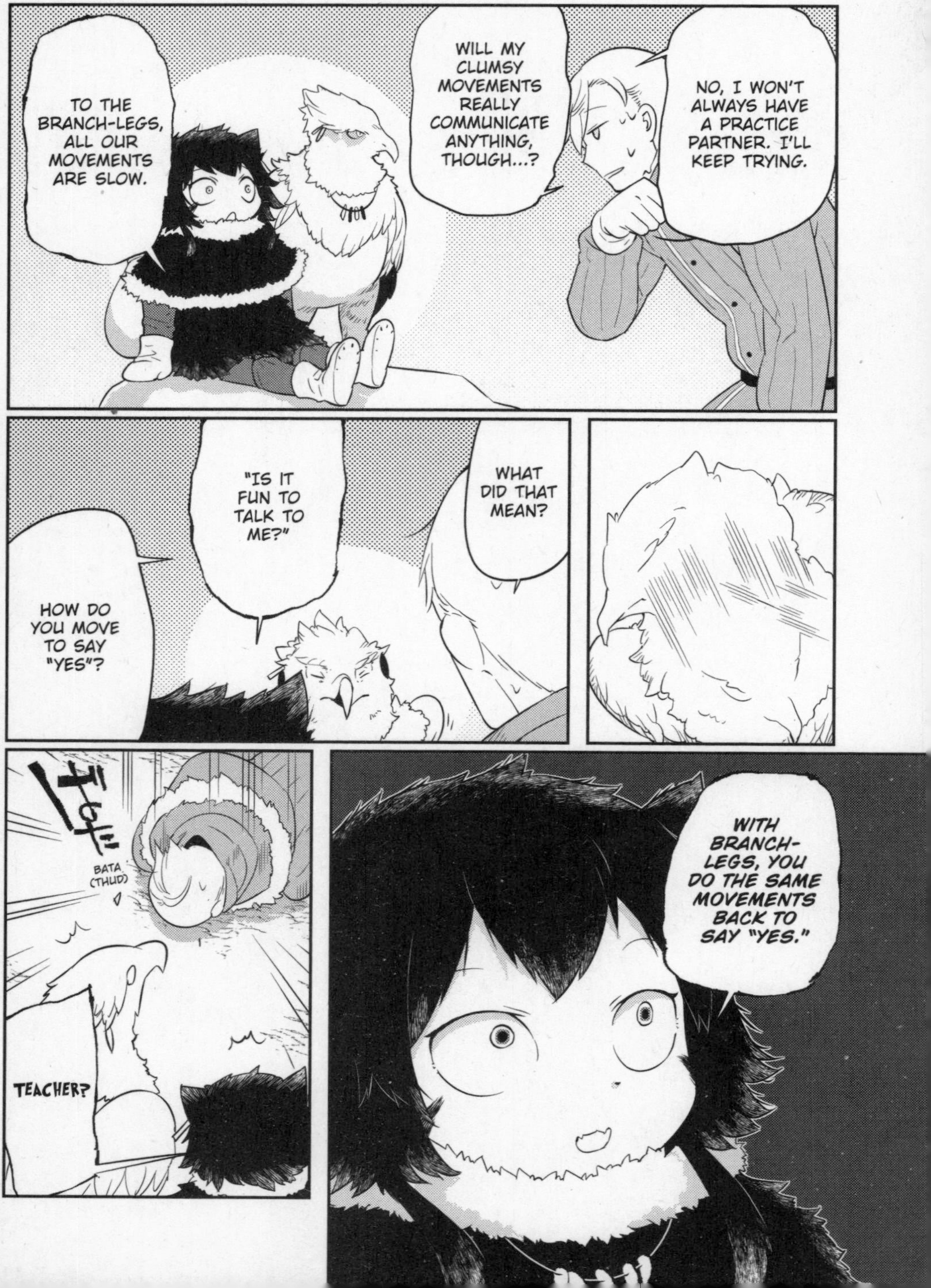
NO, I WON'T ALWAYS HAVE A PRACTICE PARTNER. I'LL KEEP TRYING.
WILL MY CLUMSY MOVEMENTS REALLY COMMUNICATE ANYTHING, THOUGH...?
TO THE BRANCH-LEGS, ALL OUR MOVEMENTS ARE SLOW.
WHAT DID THAT MEAN?
"IS IT FUN TO TALK TO ME?"
HOW DO YOU MOVE TO SAY "YES"?
WITH BRANCH-LEGS, YOU DO THE SAME MOVEMENTS BACK TO SAY "YES."
BATA (THUD)
TEACHER?

Happens All the Time

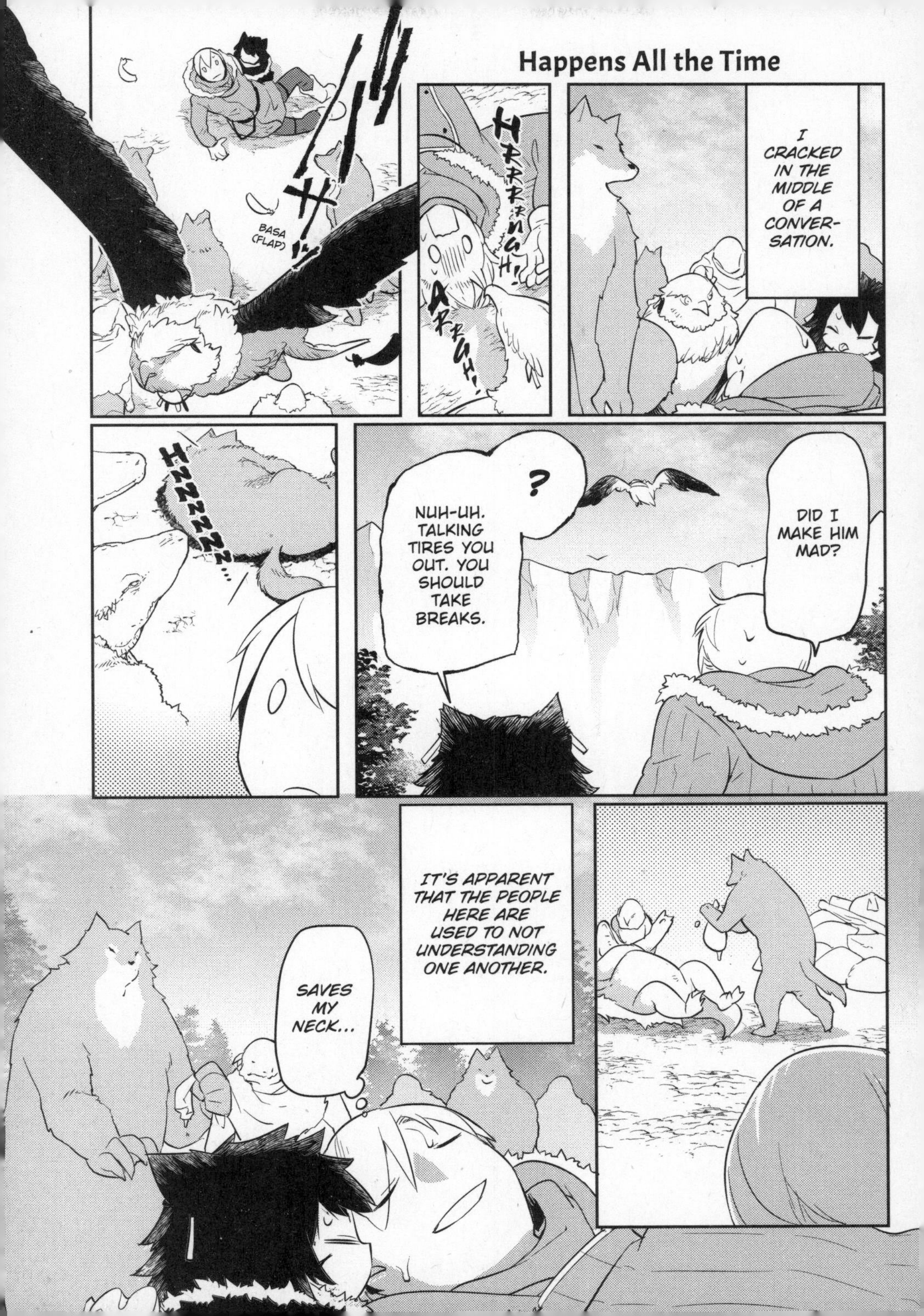
I CRACKED IN THE MIDDLE OF A CONVERSATION.
HRRRRNGH!
ARRGH!
BASA (FLAP)
DID I MAKE HIM MAD?
?
NUH-UH. TALKING TIRES YOU OUT. YOU SHOULD TAKE BREAKS.
HNNNNZZ...
IT'S APPARENT THAT THE PEOPLE HERE ARE USED TO NOT UNDERSTANDING ONE ANOTHER.
SAVES MY NECK...

Destination

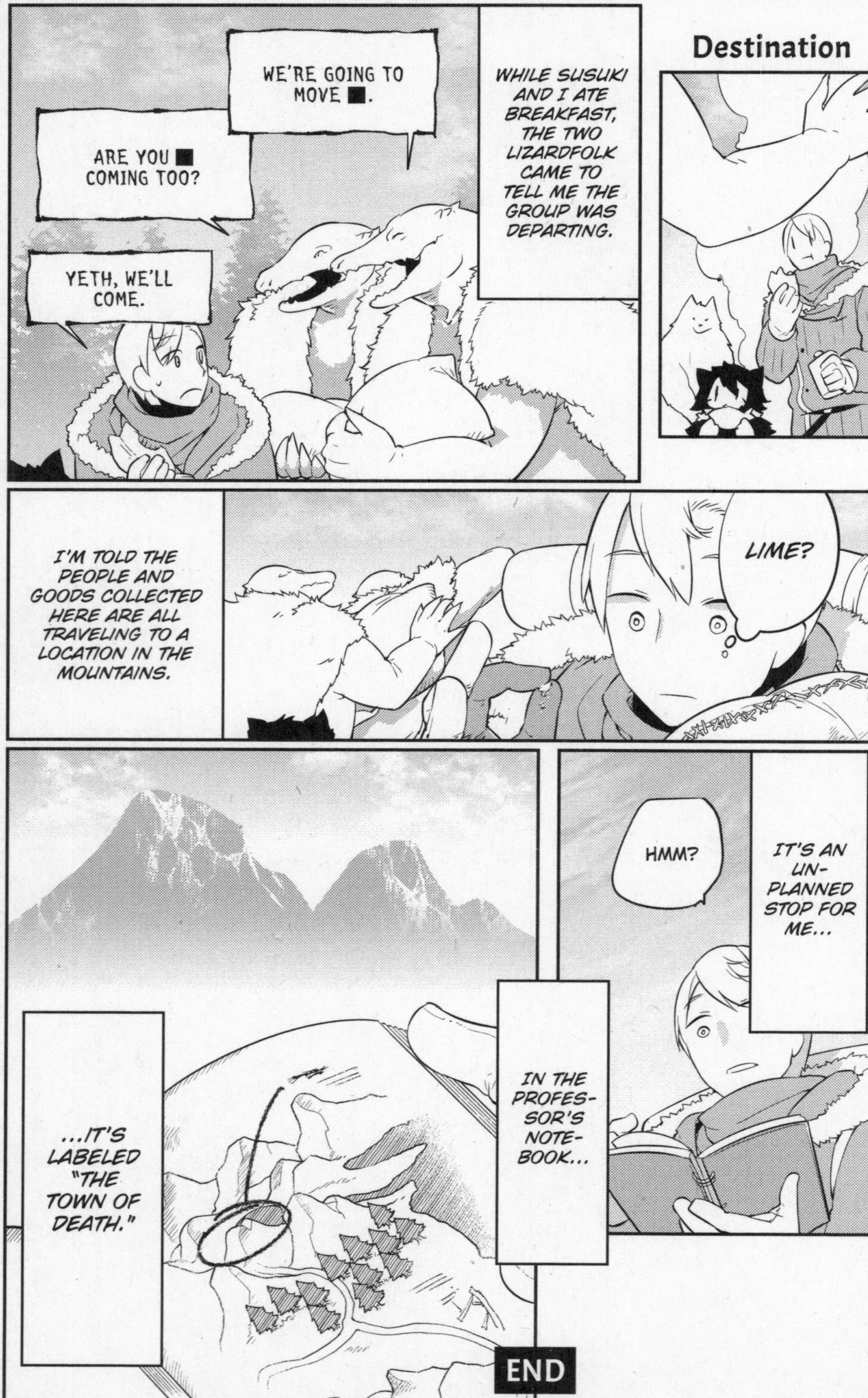
WHILE SUSUKI AND I ATE BREAKFAST, THE TWO LIZARDFOLK CAME TO TELL ME THE GROUP WAS DEPARTING.
WE'RE GOING TO MOVE [redacted].
ARE YOU [redacted] COMING TOO?
YETH, WE'LL COME.
LIME?
I'M TOLD THE PEOPLE AND GOODS COLLECTED HERE ARE ALL TRAVELING TO A LOCATION IN THE MOUNTAINS.
IT'S AN UN-PLANNED STOP FOR ME...
HMM?
IN THE PROFES-SOR'S NOTE-BOOK...
...IT'S LABELED "THE TOWN OF DEATH."
END

THE HARPIES RETURN TO
THE CLIFF BEFORE DARK.

NIGHT

DAY

IT WAS EXPLAINED TO ME THAT THE
WIND DIRECTION SHIFTS AT NIGHT, MAKING
IT DIFFICULT FOR THEM TO ASCEND.

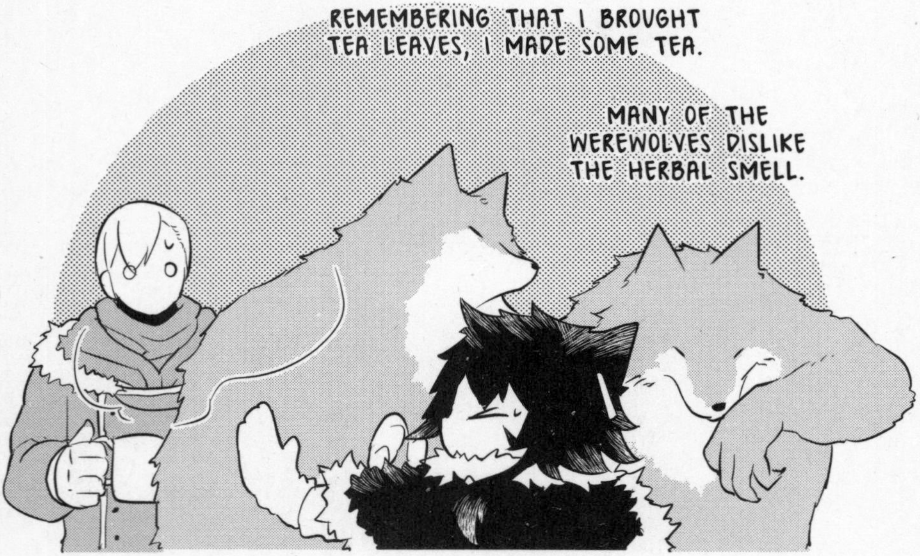
REMEMBERING THAT I BROUGHT TEA LEAVES, I MADE SOME TEA.
MANY OF THE WEREWOLVES DISLIKE THE HERBAL SMELL.

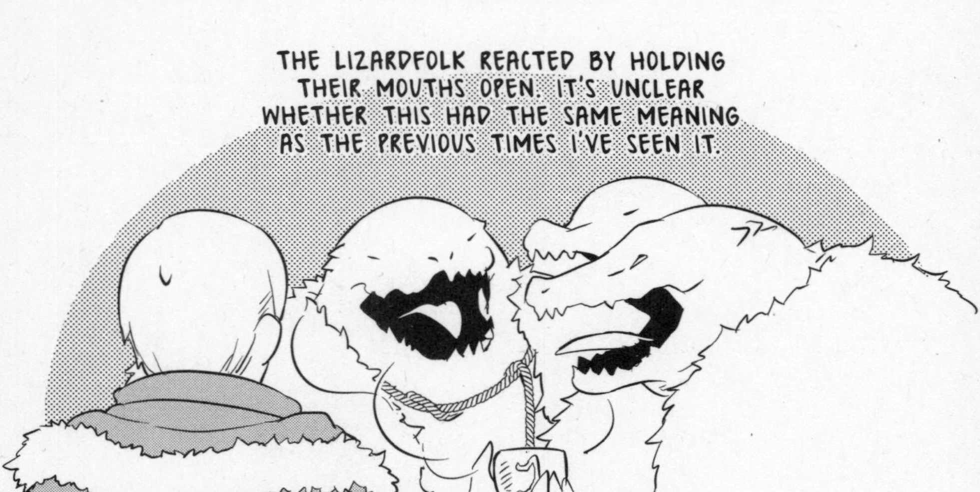
THE LIZARDFOLK REACTED BY HOLDING THEIR MOUTHS OPEN. IT'S UNCLEAR WHETHER THIS HAD THE SAME MEANING AS THE PREVIOUS TIMES I'VE SEEN IT.

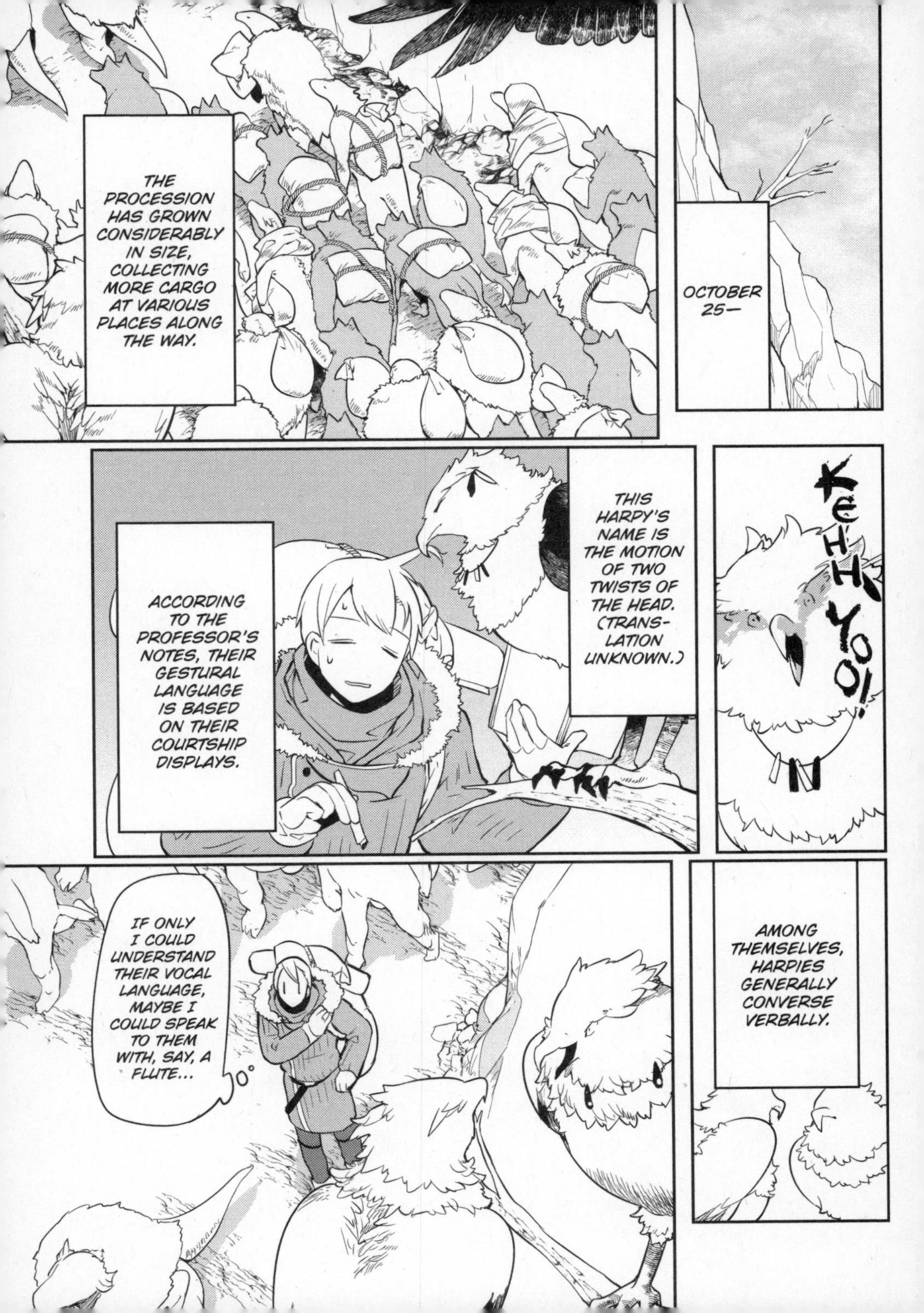
OCTOBER 25—
THE PROCESSION HAS GROWN CONSIDERABLY IN SIZE, COLLECTING MORE CARGO AT VARIOUS PLACES ALONG THE WAY.
KEH HYOO!N
THIS HARPY'S NAME IS THE MOTION OF TWO TWISTS OF THE HEAD. (TRANSLATION UNKNOWN.)
ACCORDING TO THE PROFESSOR'S NOTES, THEIR GESTURAL LANGUAGE IS BASED ON THEIR COURTSHIP DISPLAYS.
AMONG THEMSELVES, HARPIES GENERALLY CONVERSE VERBALLY.
IF ONLY I COULD UNDERSTAND THEIR VOCAL LANGUAGE, MAYBE I COULD SPEAK TO THEM WITH, SAY, A FLUTE...

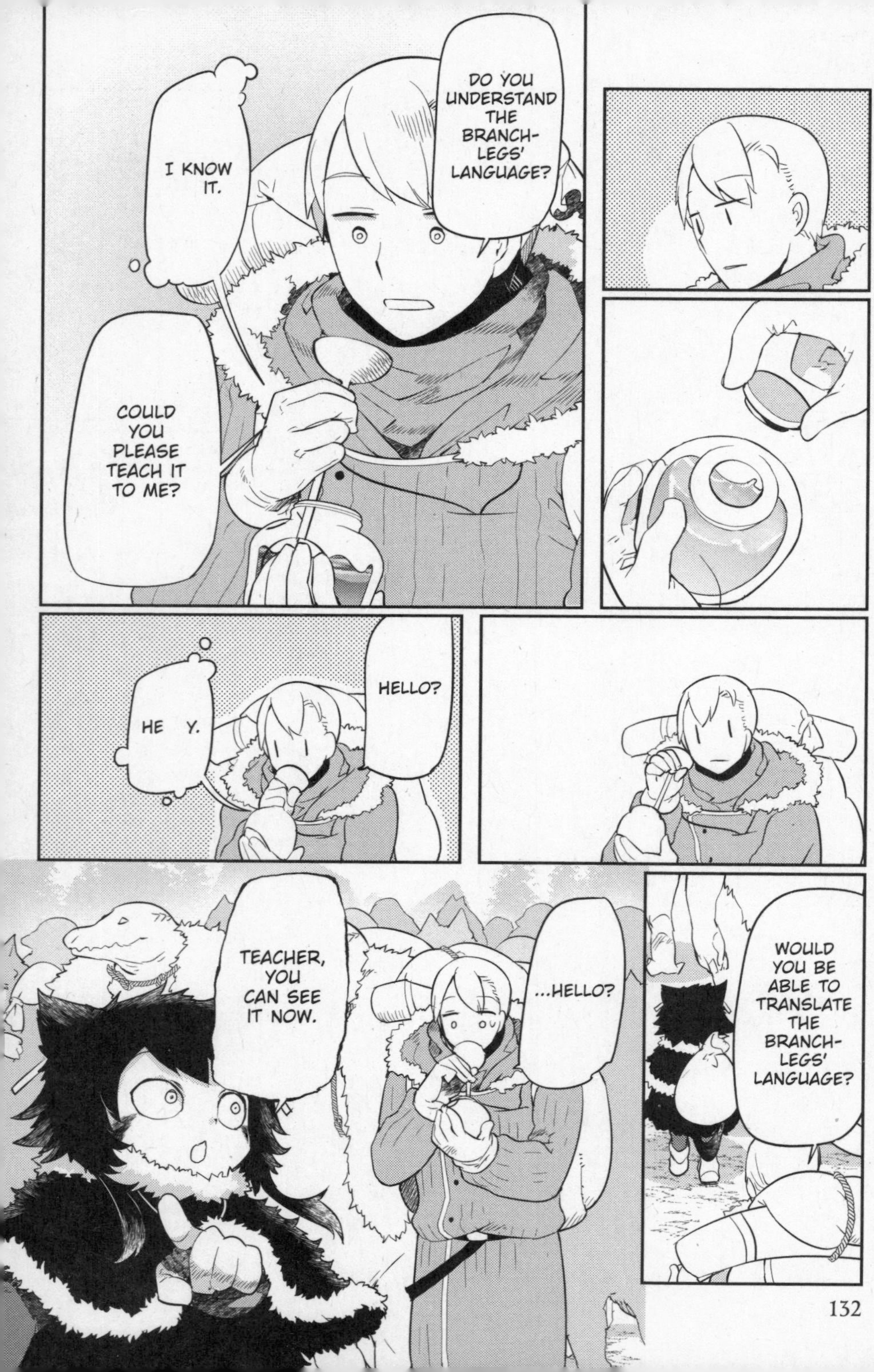
DO YOU UNDERSTAND THE BRANCH-LEGS' LANGUAGE?
I KNOW IT.
COULD YOU PLEASE TEACH IT TO ME?
HELLO?
HE Y.
WOULD YOU BE ABLE TO TRANSLATE THE BRANCH-LEGS' LANGUAGE?
...HELLO?
TEACHER, YOU CAN SEE IT NOW.

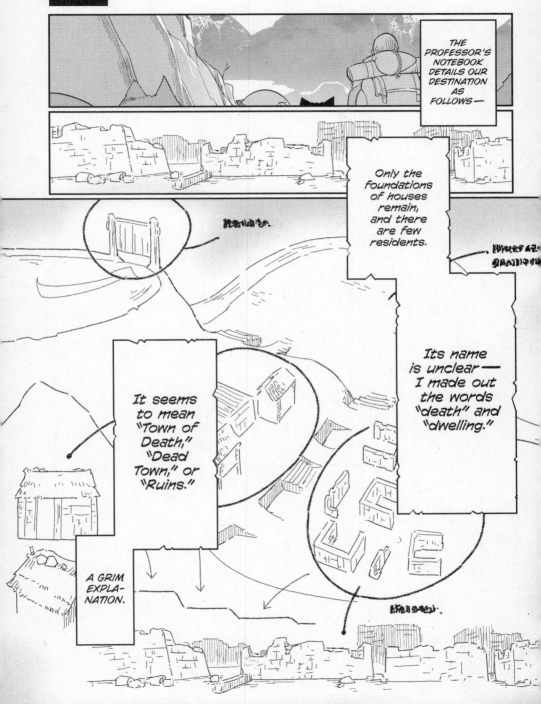

LOG 9

THE PROFESSOR'S NOTEBOOK DETAILS OUR DESTINATION AS FOLLOWS—

Only the foundations of houses remain, and there are few residents.

Its name is unclear— I made out the words "death" and "dwelling."

It seems to mean "Town of Death," "Dead Town," or "Ruins."

A GRIM EXPLANATION.

In Actuality

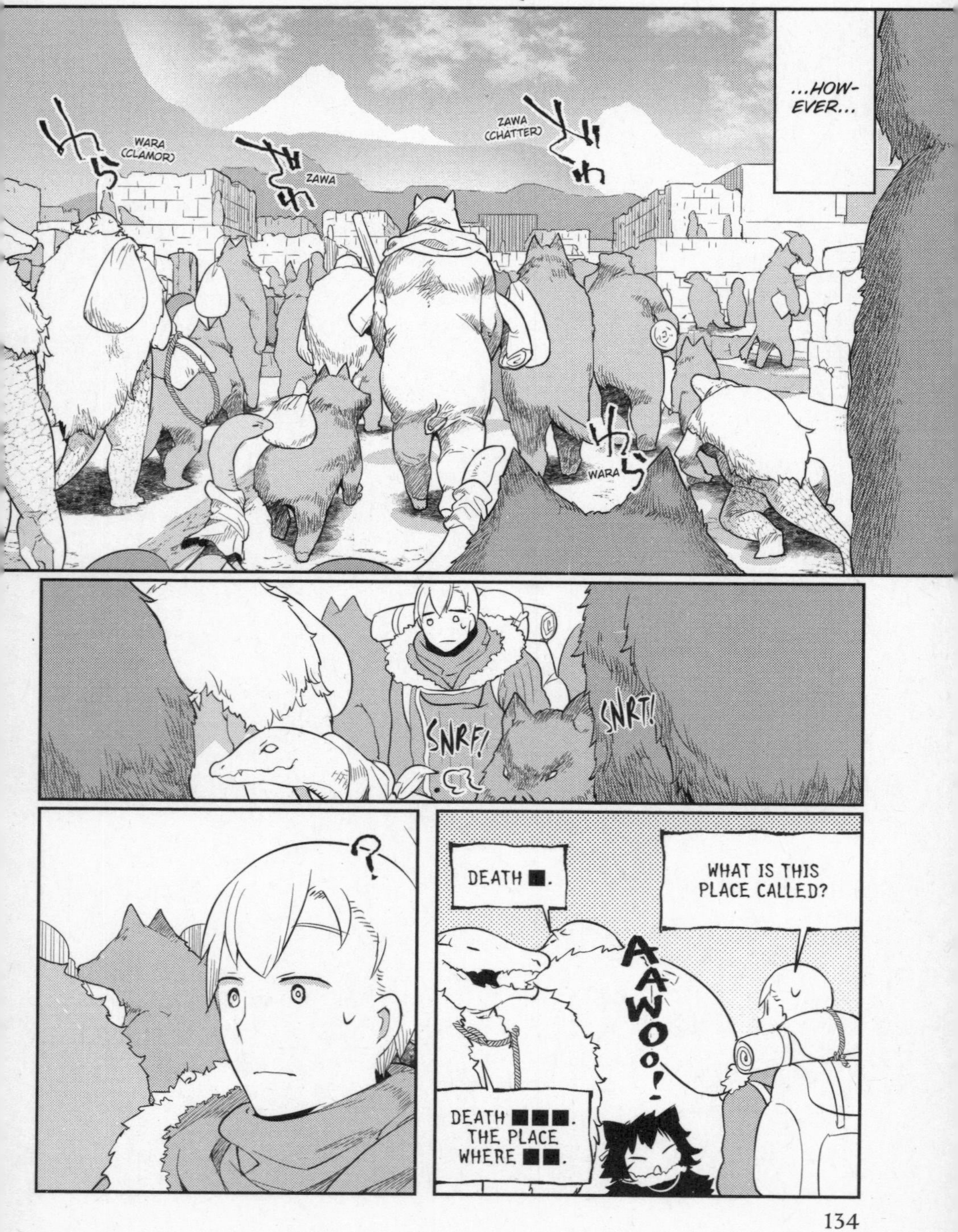

...HOW-EVER...
ZAWA (CHATTER)
ZAWA
WARA (CLAMOR)
WARA
SNRT!
SNRF!
WHAT IS THIS PLACE CALLED?
DEATH [redacted].
AAWOO!
DEATH [redacted]. THE PLACE WHERE [redacted].
?

Remains of a Dwelling

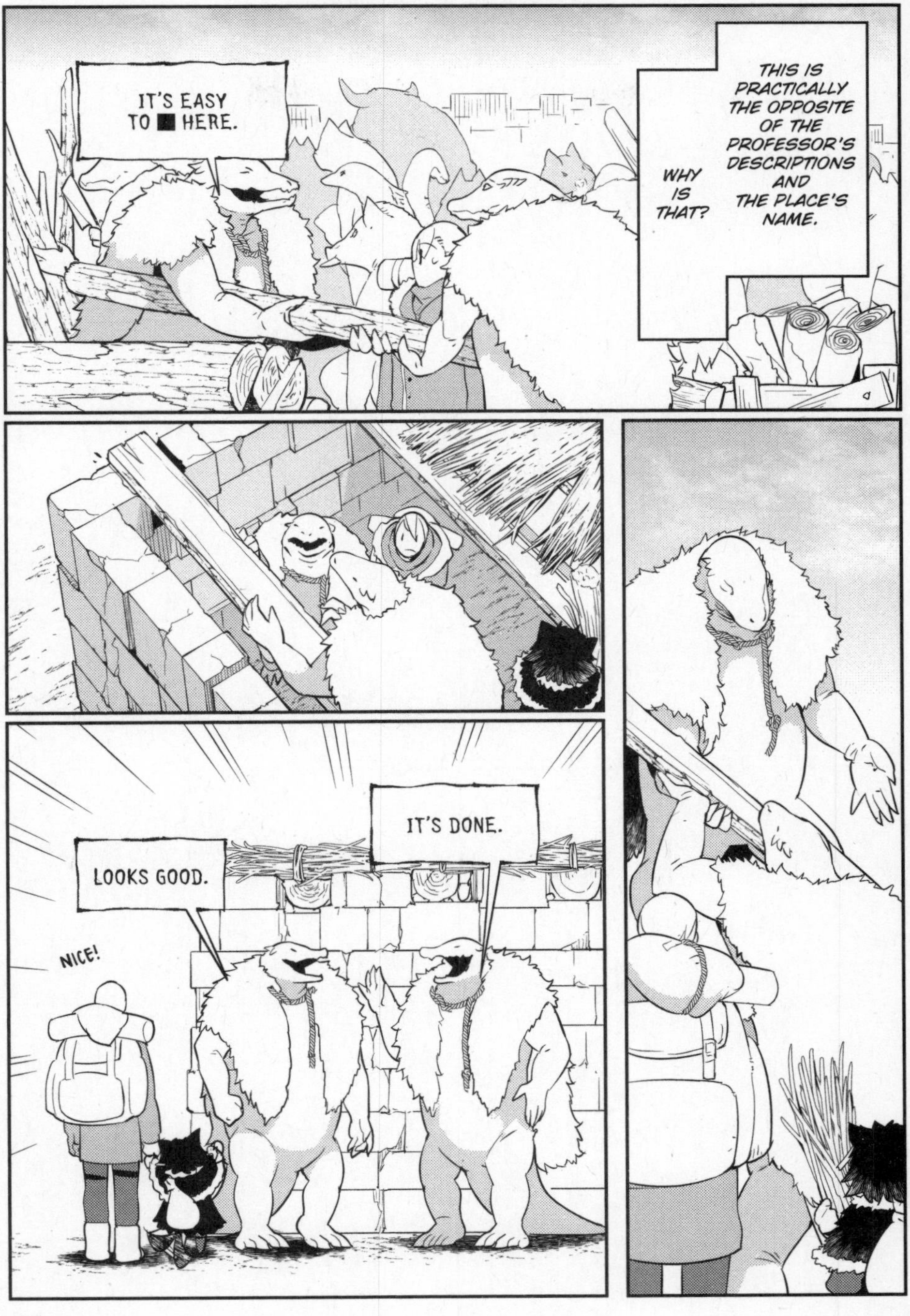
THIS IS PRACTICALLY THE OPPOSITE OF THE PROFESSOR'S DESCRIPTIONS AND THE PLACE'S NAME.
WHY IS THAT?
IT'S EASY TO [redacted] HERE.
IT'S DONE.
LOOKS GOOD.
NICE!

Ruins?

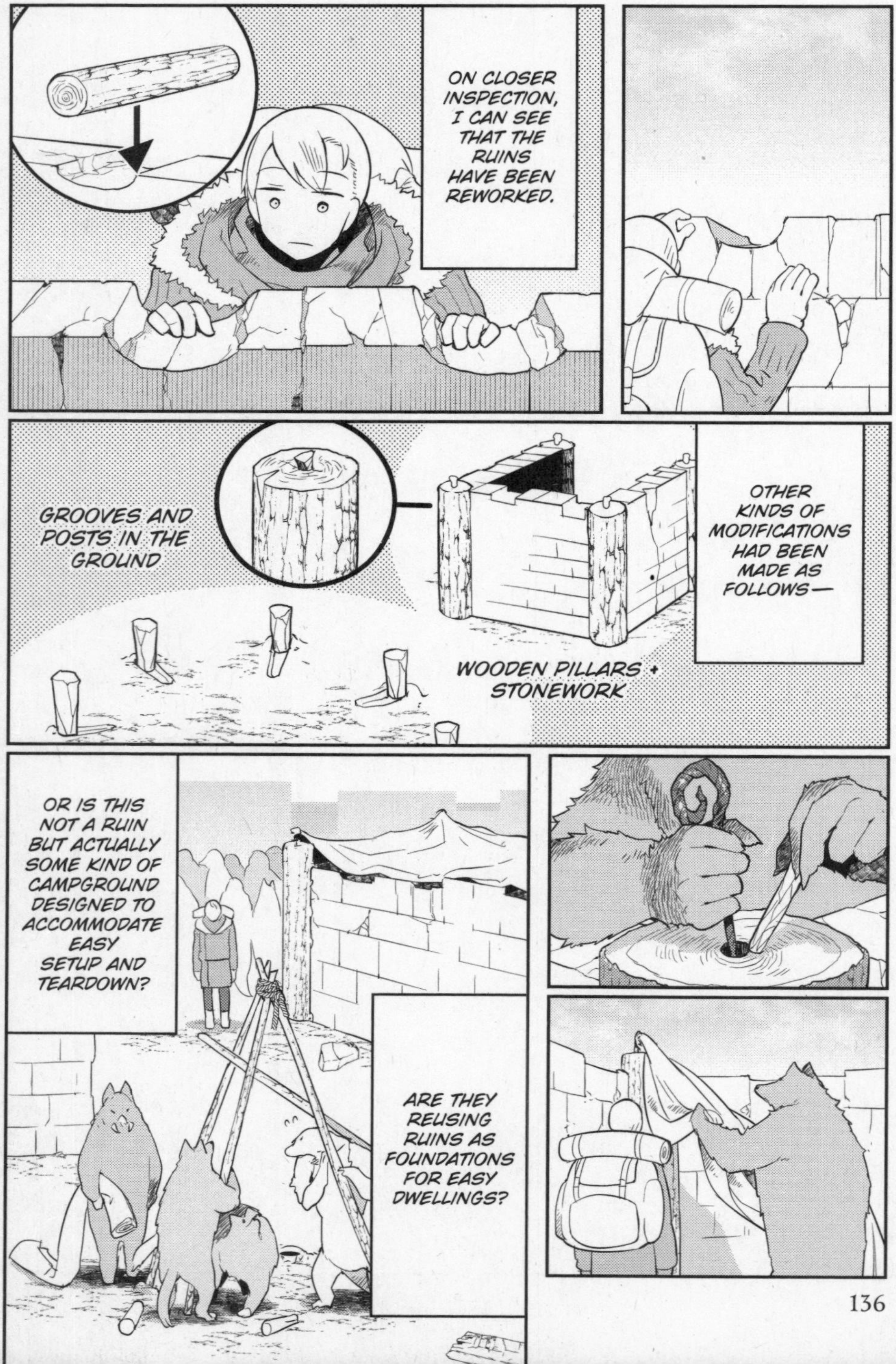

ON CLOSER INSPECTION, I CAN SEE THAT THE RUINS HAVE BEEN REWORKED.
OTHER KINDS OF MODIFICATIONS HAD BEEN MADE AS FOLLOWS—
WOODEN PILLARS + STONEWORK
GROOVES AND POSTS IN THE GROUND
OR IS THIS NOT A RUIN BUT ACTUALLY SOME KIND OF CAMPGROUND DESIGNED TO ACCOMMODATE EASY SETUP AND TEARDOWN?
ARE THEY REUSING RUINS AS FOUNDATIONS FOR EASY DWELLINGS?

Not in the Notebook

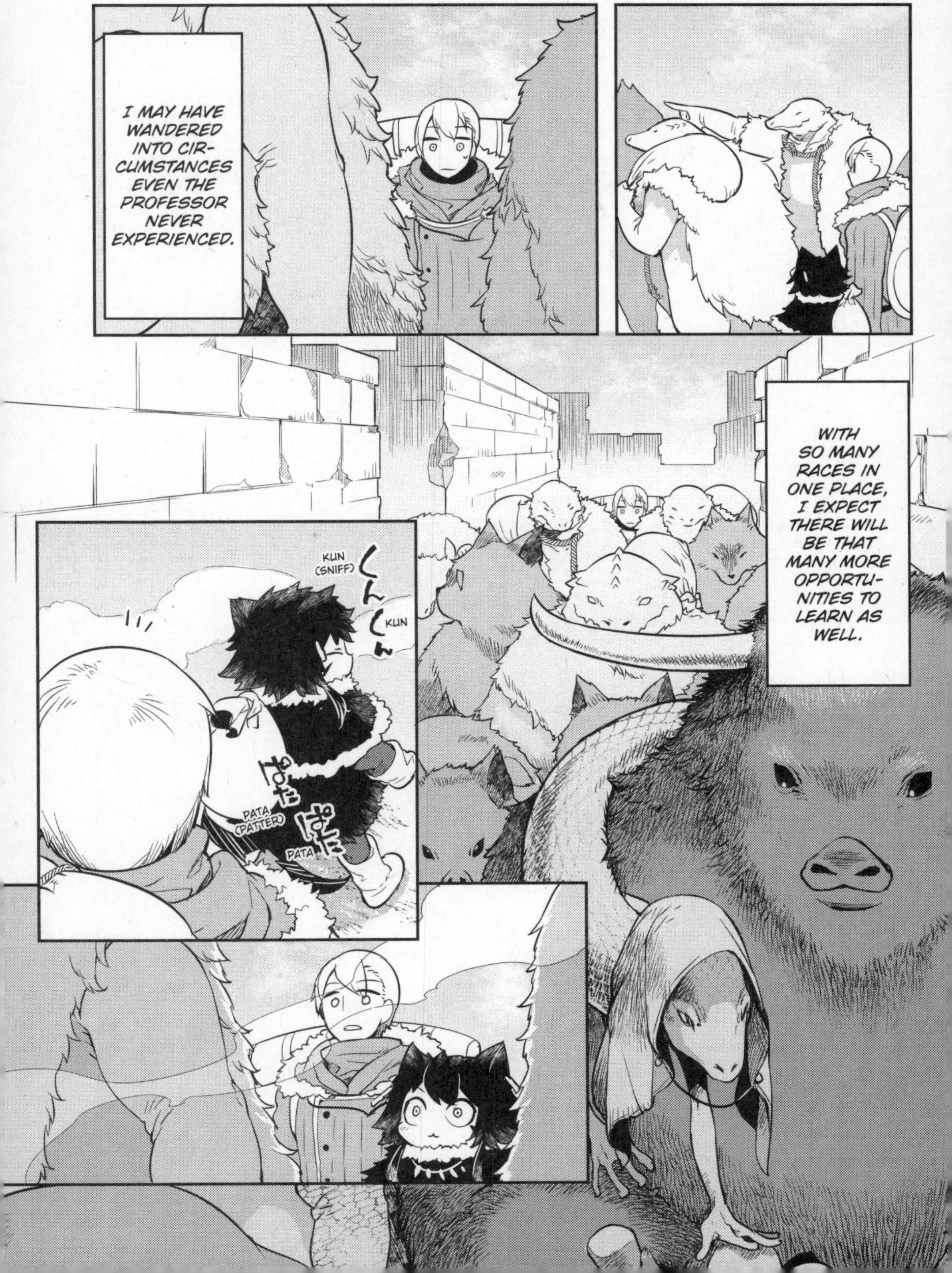

I MAY HAVE WANDERED INTO CIRCUMSTANCES EVEN THE PROFESSOR NEVER EXPERIENCED.
WITH SO MANY RACES IN ONE PLACE, I EXPECT THERE WILL BE THAT MANY MORE OPPORTUNITIES TO LEARN AS WELL.
くん
KUN (SNIFF)
くん
KUN
ぱた
PATA (PATTER)
ぱた
PATA

Town Square

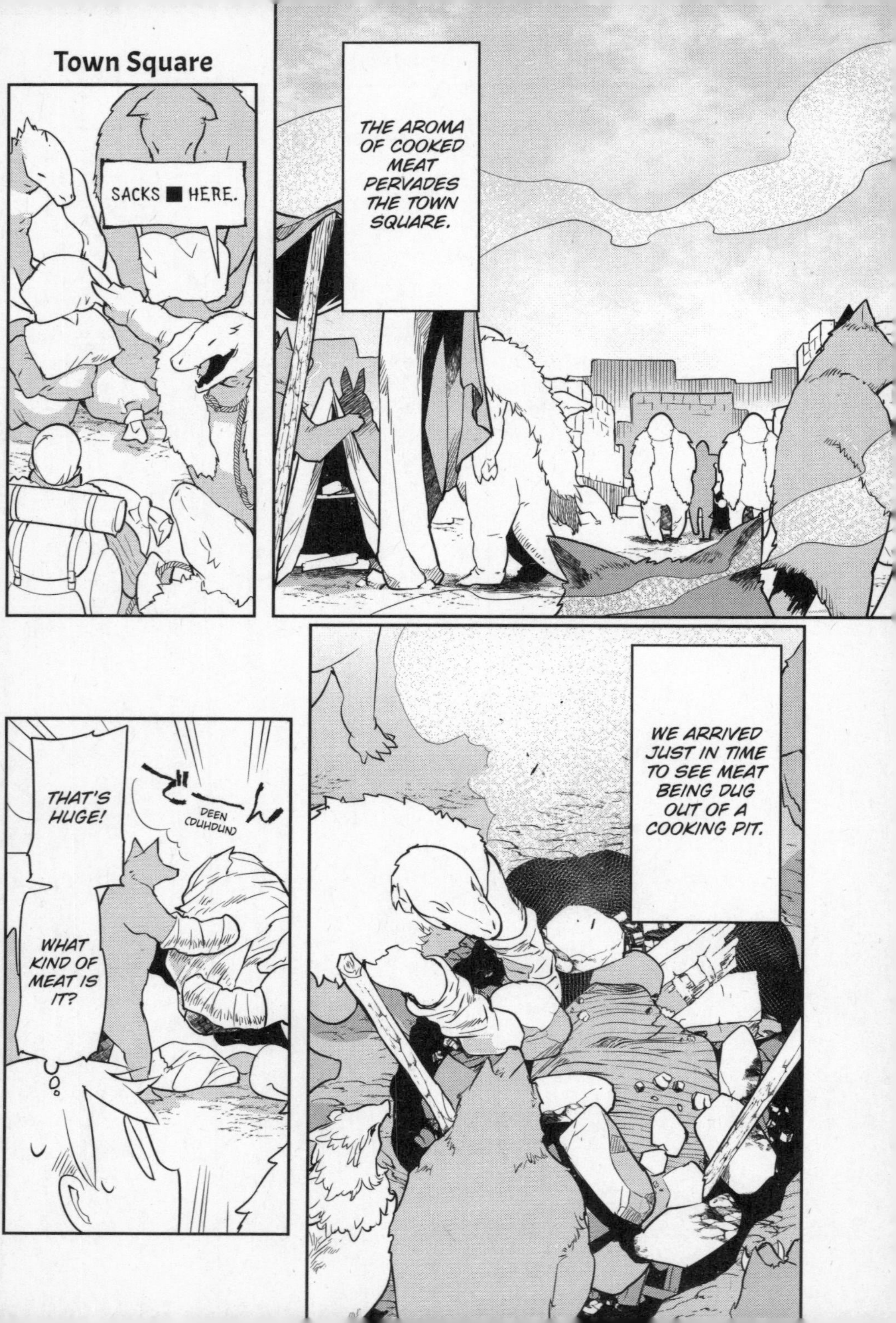
THE AROMA OF COOKED MEAT PERVADES THE TOWN SQUARE.
SACKS [redacted] HERE.
WE ARRIVED JUST IN TIME TO SEE MEAT BEING DUG OUT OF A COOKING PIT.
THAT'S HUGE!
DEEN (DUHDUND)
WHAT KIND OF MEAT IS IT?

Large Meat

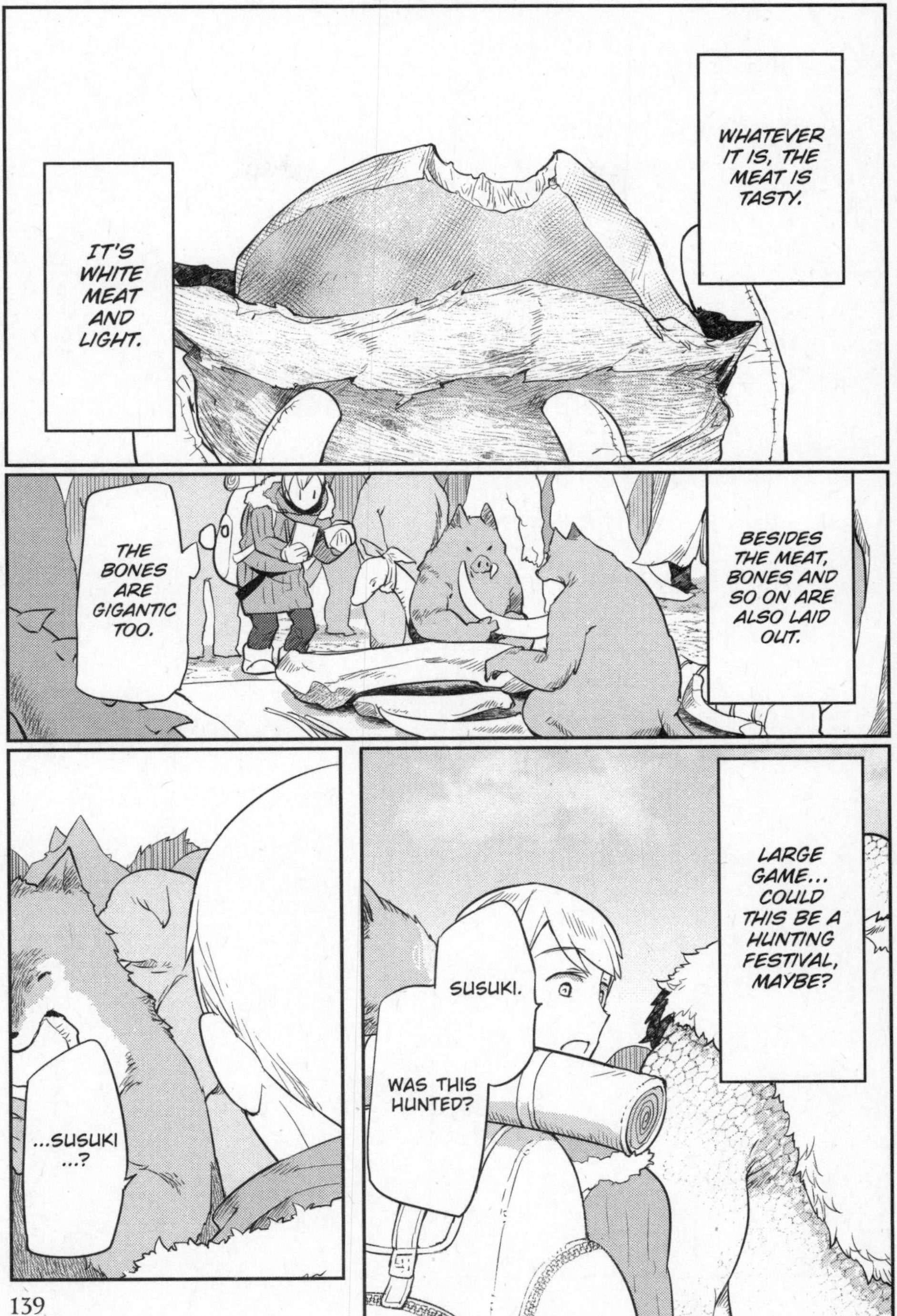
WHATEVER IT IS, THE MEAT IS TASTY.
IT'S WHITE MEAT AND LIGHT.
BESIDES THE MEAT, BONES AND SO ON ARE ALSO LAID OUT.
THE BONES ARE GIGANTIC TOO.
LARGE GAME... COULD THIS BE A HUNTING FESTIVAL, MAYBE?
SUSUKI.
WAS THIS HUNTED?
...SUSUKI ...?

Separated

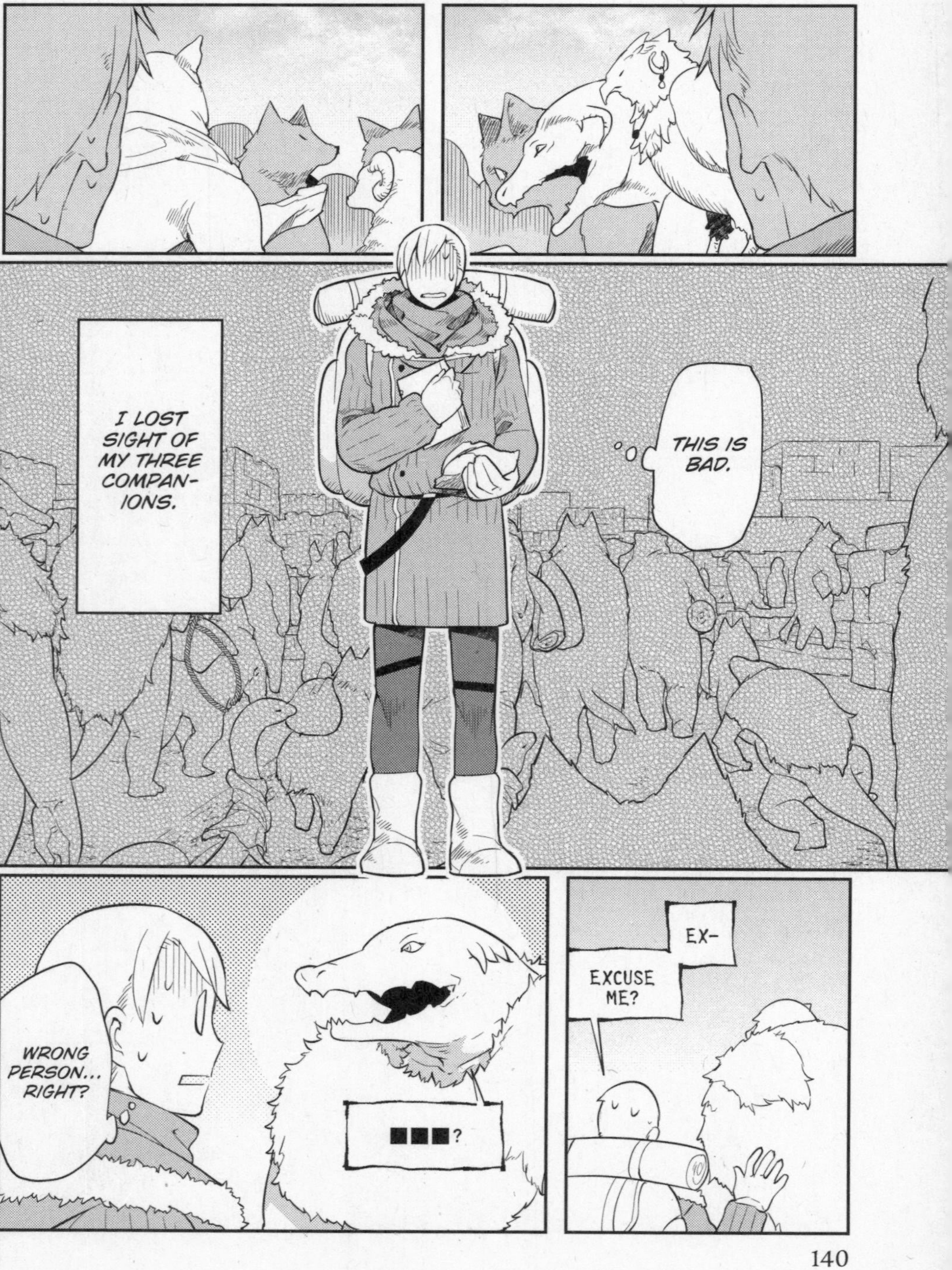
THIS IS BAD.
I LOST SIGHT OF MY THREE COMPANIONS.
EX-
EXCUSE ME?
■■■?
WRONG PERSON... RIGHT?

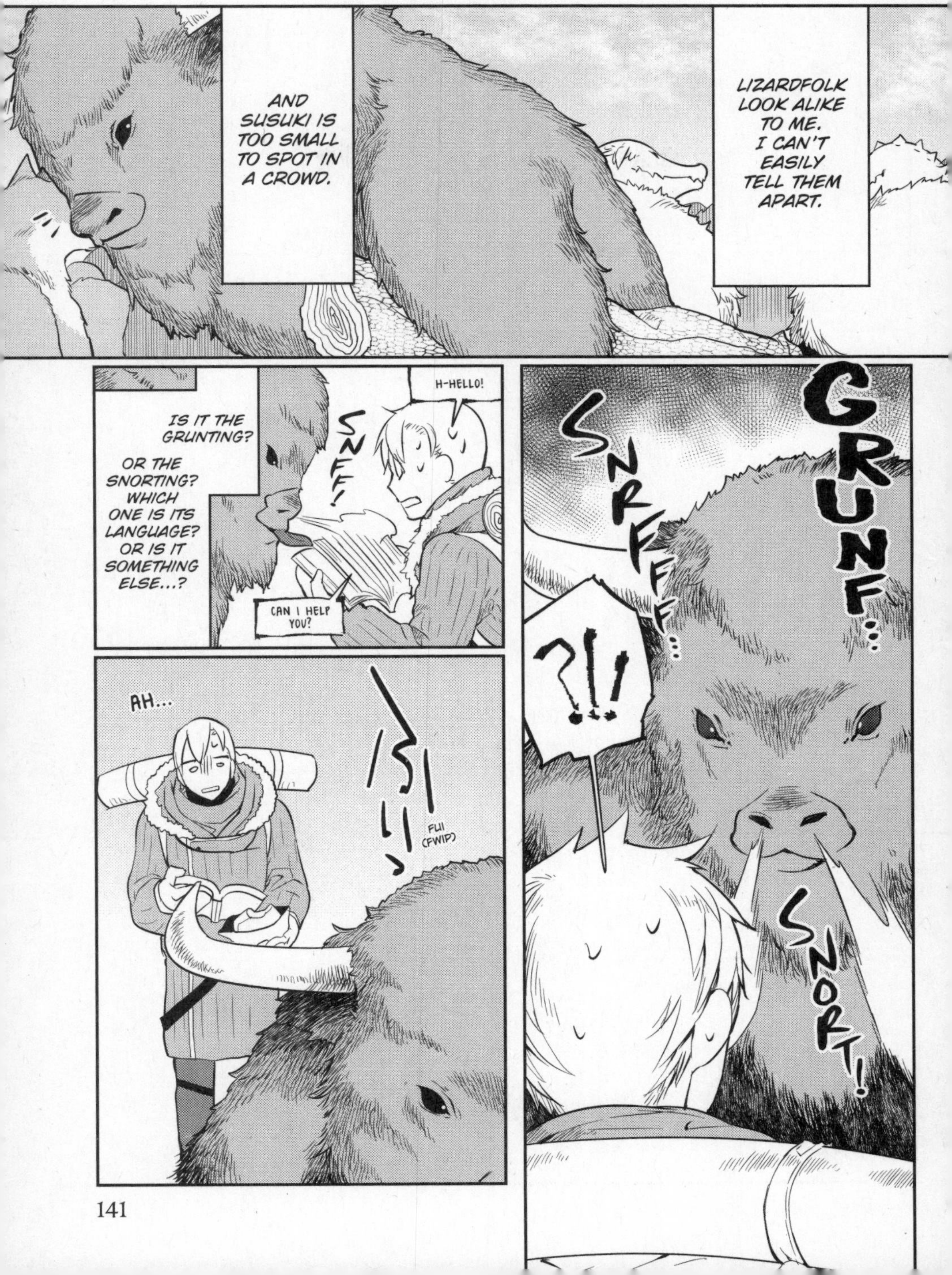
LIZARDFOLK LOOK ALIKE TO ME. I CAN'T EASILY TELL THEM APART.
AND SUSUKI IS TOO SMALL TO SPOT IN A CROWD.
GRUNF...
SNRFFFF...
?!!
SNORT!
H-HELLO!
SNFF!
IS IT THE GRUNTING?
OR THE SNORTING? WHICH ONE IS ITS LANGUAGE? OR IS IT SOMETHING ELSE...?
CAN I HELP YOU?
FUI (FWIP)
AH...

The Unknown

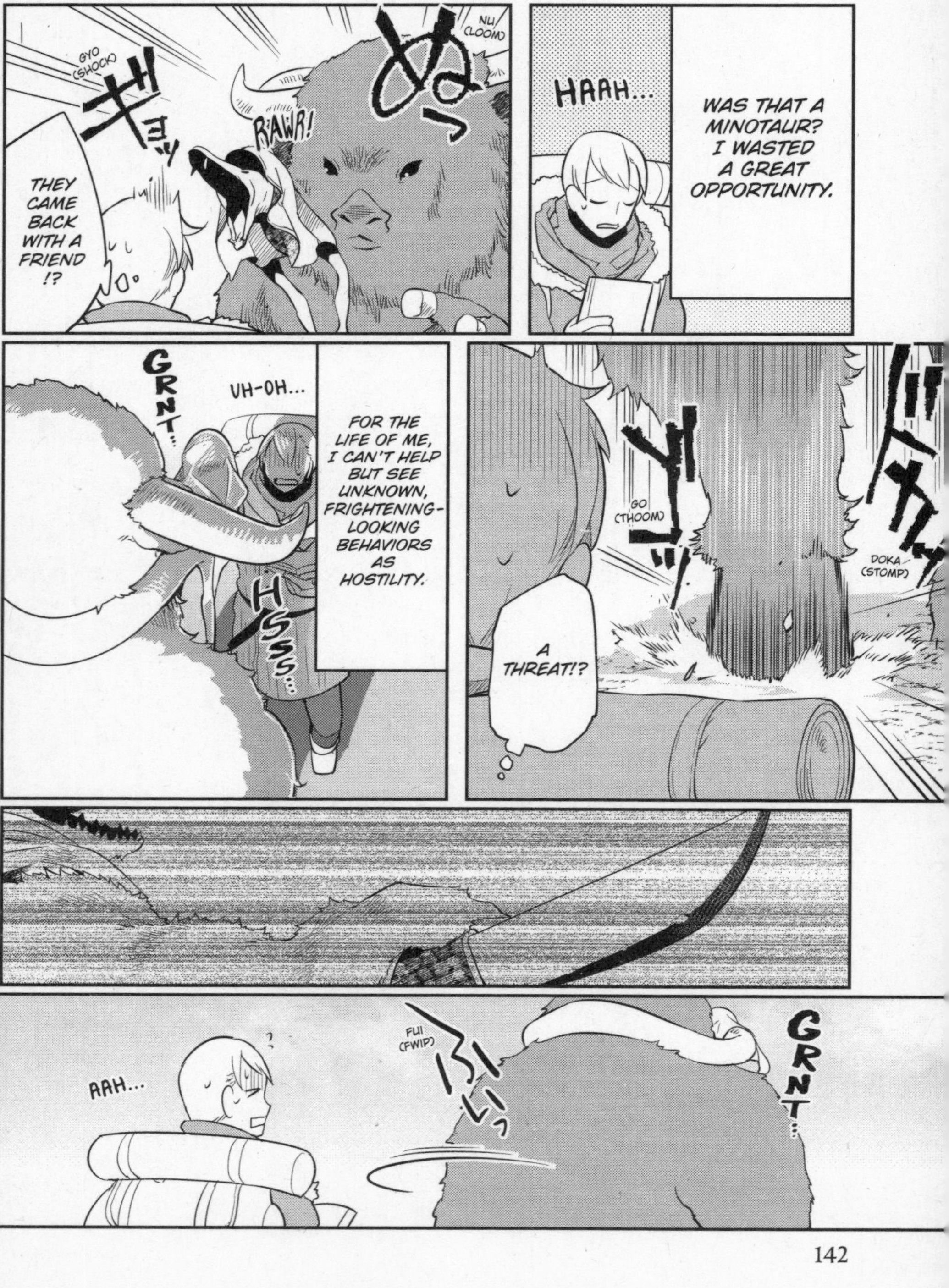
HAAH...
WAS THAT A MINOTAUR? I WASTED A GREAT OPPORTUNITY.
NU (LOOM)
GYO (SHOCK)
RAWR!
THEY CAME BACK WITH A FRIEND!?
DOKA (STOMP)
GO (THOOM)
A THREAT!?
FOR THE LIFE OF ME, I CAN'T HELP BUT SEE UNKNOWN, FRIGHTENING-LOOKING BEHAVIORS AS HOSTILITY.
UH-OH...
GRNT...
HSSS...
GRNT...
FUI (FWIP)
AAH...

Personal Limits

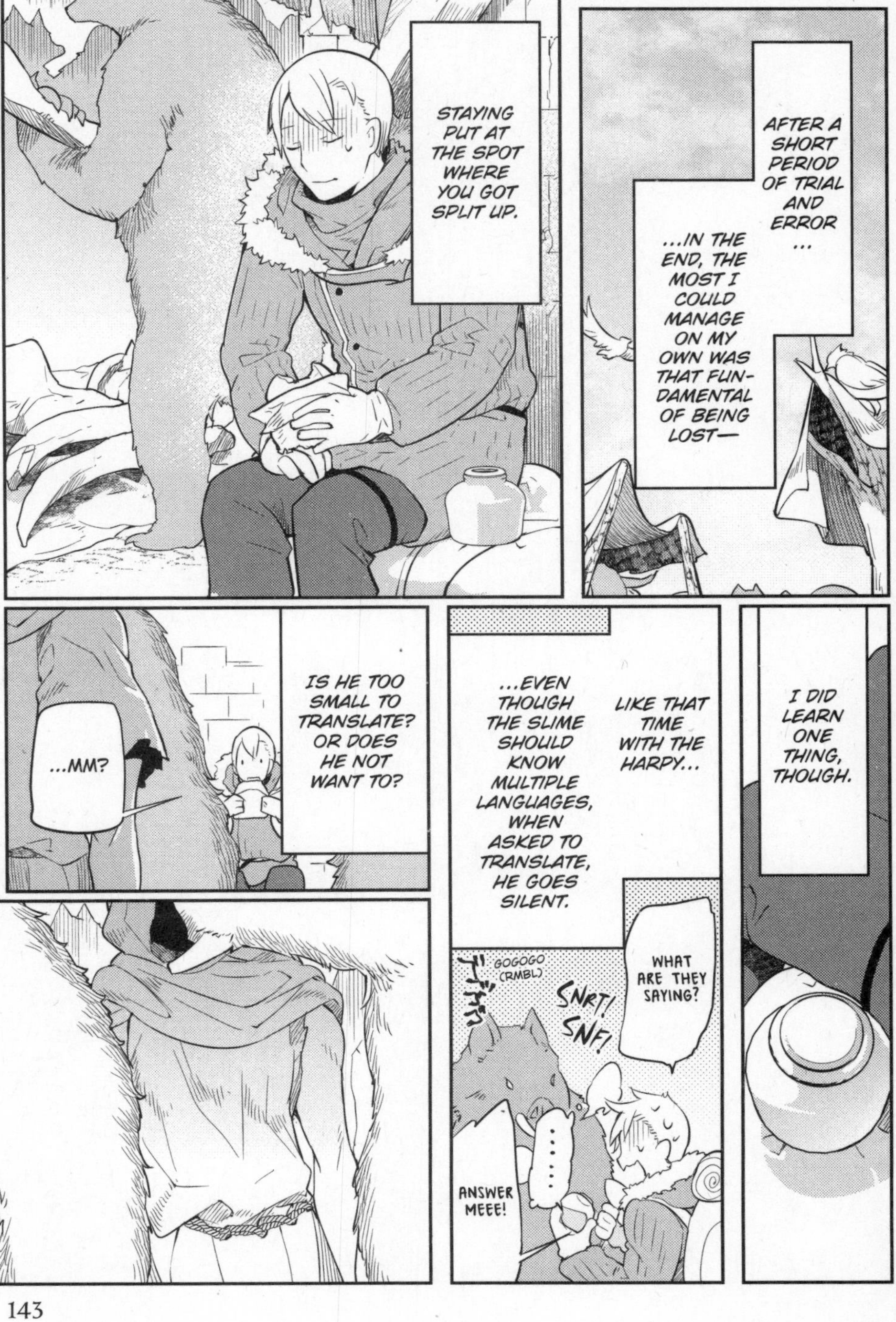
AFTER A SHORT PERIOD OF TRIAL AND ERROR ...
...IN THE END, THE MOST I COULD MANAGE ON MY OWN WAS THAT FUN-DAMENTAL OF BEING LOST—
STAYING PUT AT THE SPOT WHERE YOU GOT SPLIT UP.
I DID LEARN ONE THING, THOUGH.
LIKE THAT TIME WITH THE HARPY...
...EVEN THOUGH THE SLIME SHOULD KNOW MULTIPLE LANGUAGES, WHEN ASKED TO TRANSLATE, HE GOES SILENT.
WHAT ARE THEY SAYING?
SNRT! SNF!
GOGOGO (RMBL)
......
ANSWER MEEE!
IS HE TOO SMALL TO TRANSLATE? OR DOES HE NOT WANT TO?
...MM?

Losing Sight

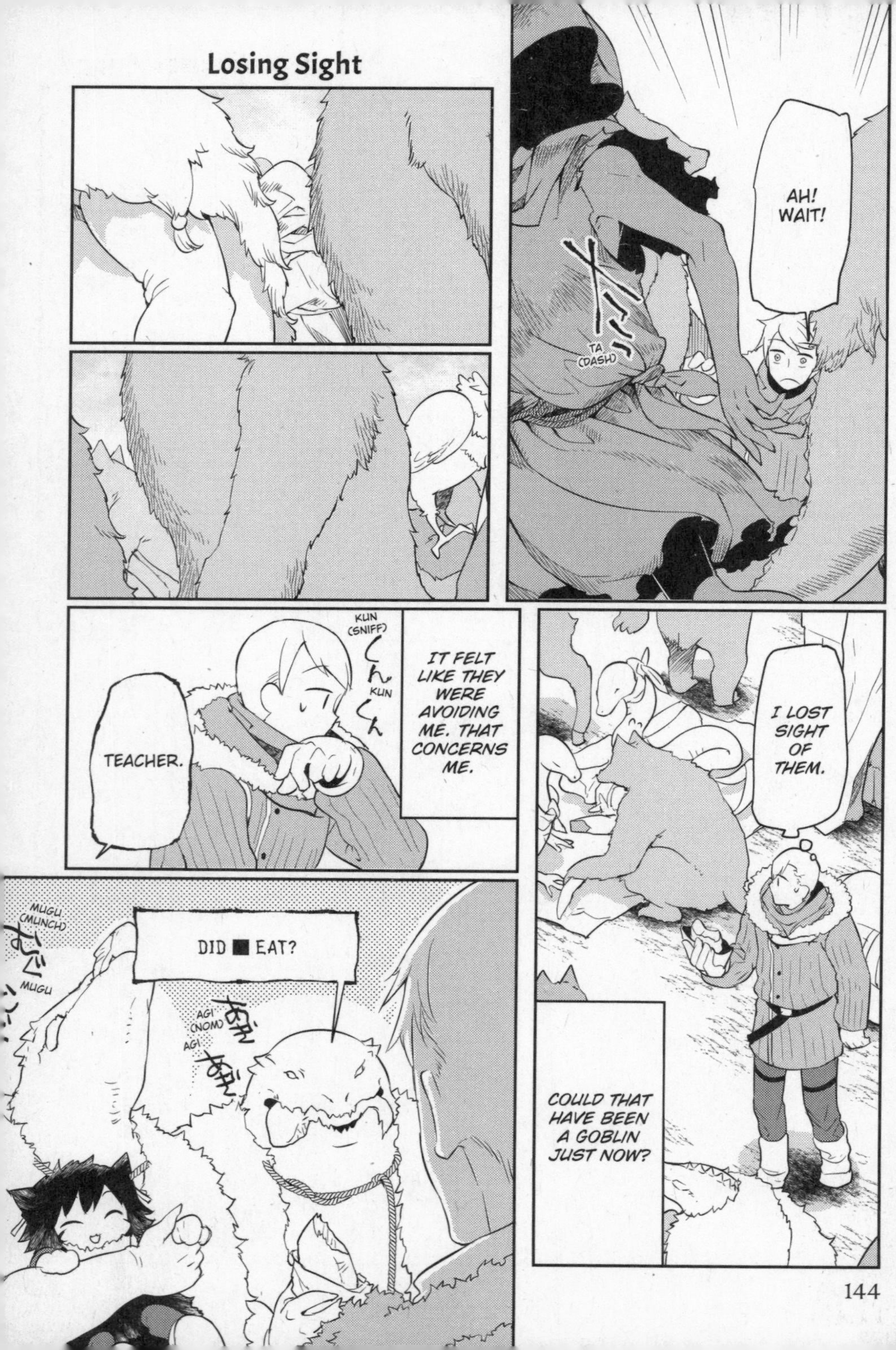
AH! WAIT!
TA (DASH)
I LOST SIGHT OF THEM.
COULD THAT HAVE BEEN A GOBLIN JUST NOW?
IT FELT LIKE THEY WERE AVOIDING ME. THAT CONCERNS ME.
KUN (SNIFF) KUN
TEACHER.
DID ■ EAT?
AGI (NOM) AGI
MUGU (MUNCH) MUGU

The Siblings' Friend

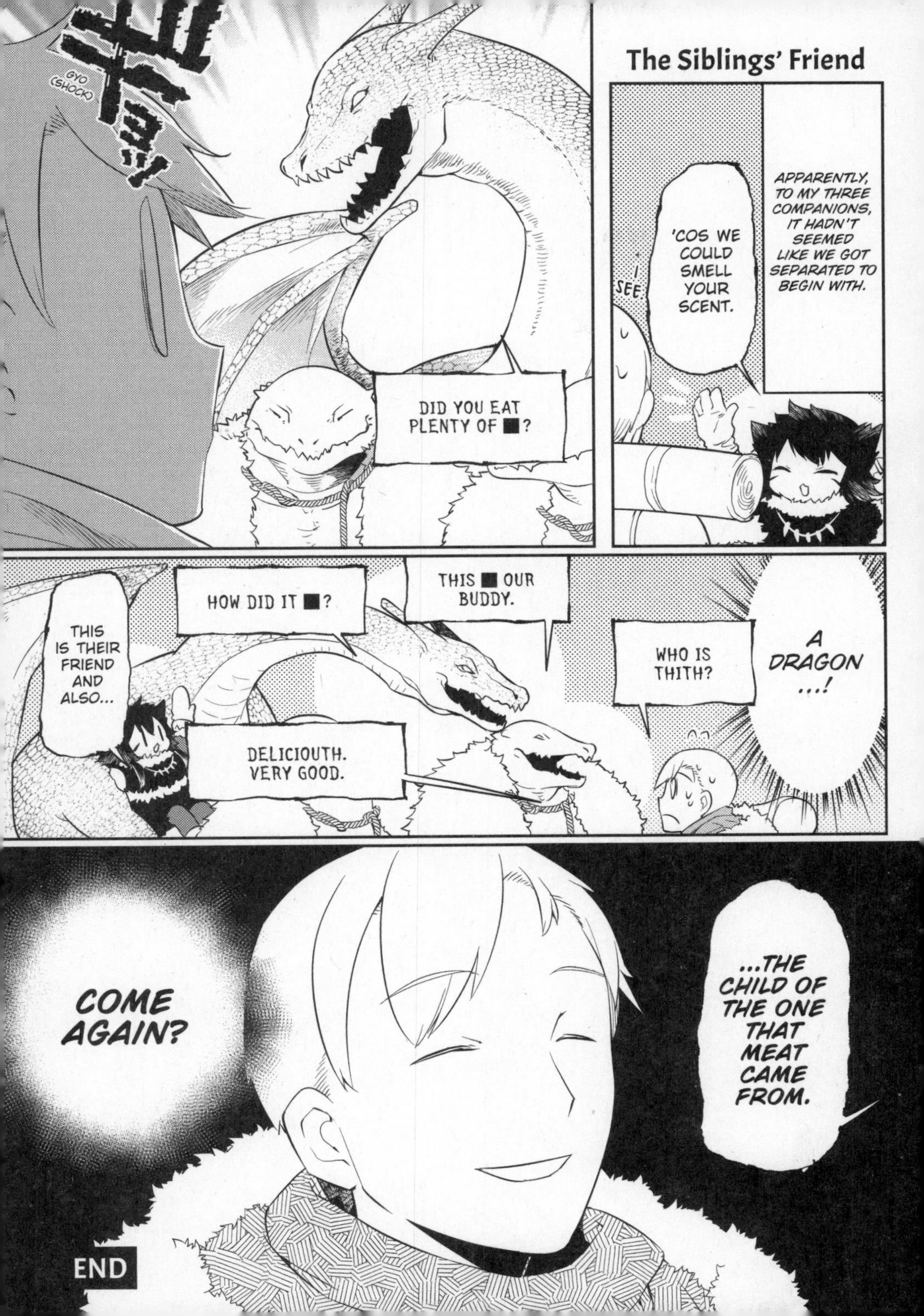
APPARENTLY, TO MY THREE COMPANIONS, IT HADN'T SEEMED LIKE WE GOT SEPARATED TO BEGIN WITH.
'COS WE COULD SMELL YOUR SCENT.
I SEE.
GYO (SHOCK)
DID YOU EAT PLENTY OF ■?
A DRAGON...!
WHO IS THITH?
THIS ■ OUR BUDDY.
HOW DID IT ■?
DELICIOUTH. VERY GOOD.
THIS IS THEIR FRIEND AND ALSO...
...THE CHILD OF THE ONE THAT MEAT CAME FROM.
COME AGAIN?
END

KASHUU WILL OFTEN BE
PLAYING WITH SUSUKI.

IN KASHUU'S OWN WORDS,
IT'S BECAUSE SUSUKI IS WARM.

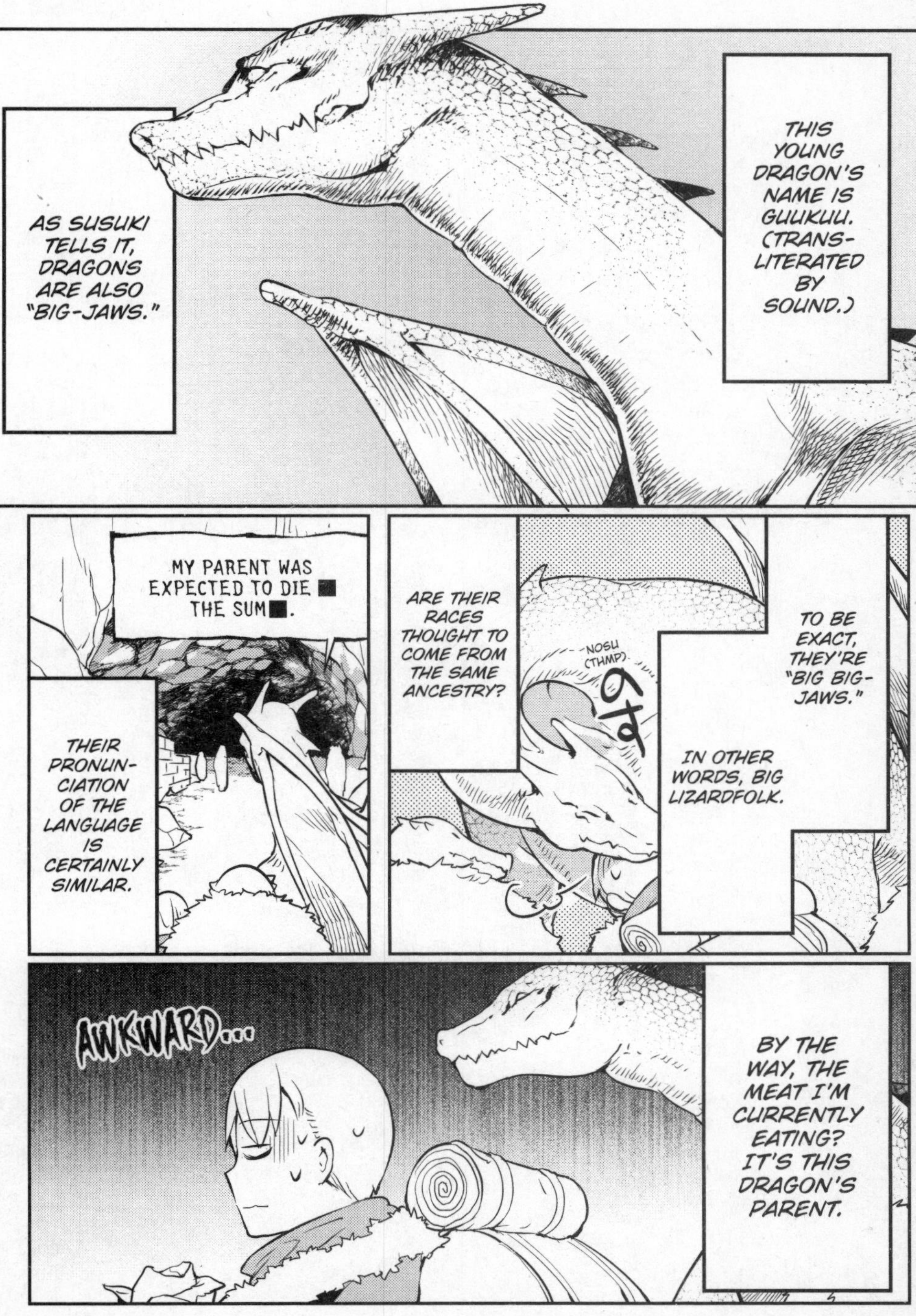

THIS YOUNG DRAGON'S NAME IS GUUKUU. (TRANS-LITERATED BY SOUND.)
AS SUSUKI TELLS IT, DRAGONS ARE ALSO "BIG-JAWS."
TO BE EXACT, THEY'RE "BIG BIG-JAWS."
ARE THEIR RACES THOUGHT TO COME FROM THE SAME ANCESTRY?
NOSU (THMP)
IN OTHER WORDS, BIG LIZARDFOLK.
MY PARENT WAS EXPECTED TO DIE ■ THE SUM■.
THEIR PRONUN-CIATION OF THE LANGUAGE IS CERTAINLY SIMILAR.
BY THE WAY, THE MEAT I'M CURRENTLY EATING? IT'S THIS DRAGON'S PARENT.
AWKWARD...

LOG 10

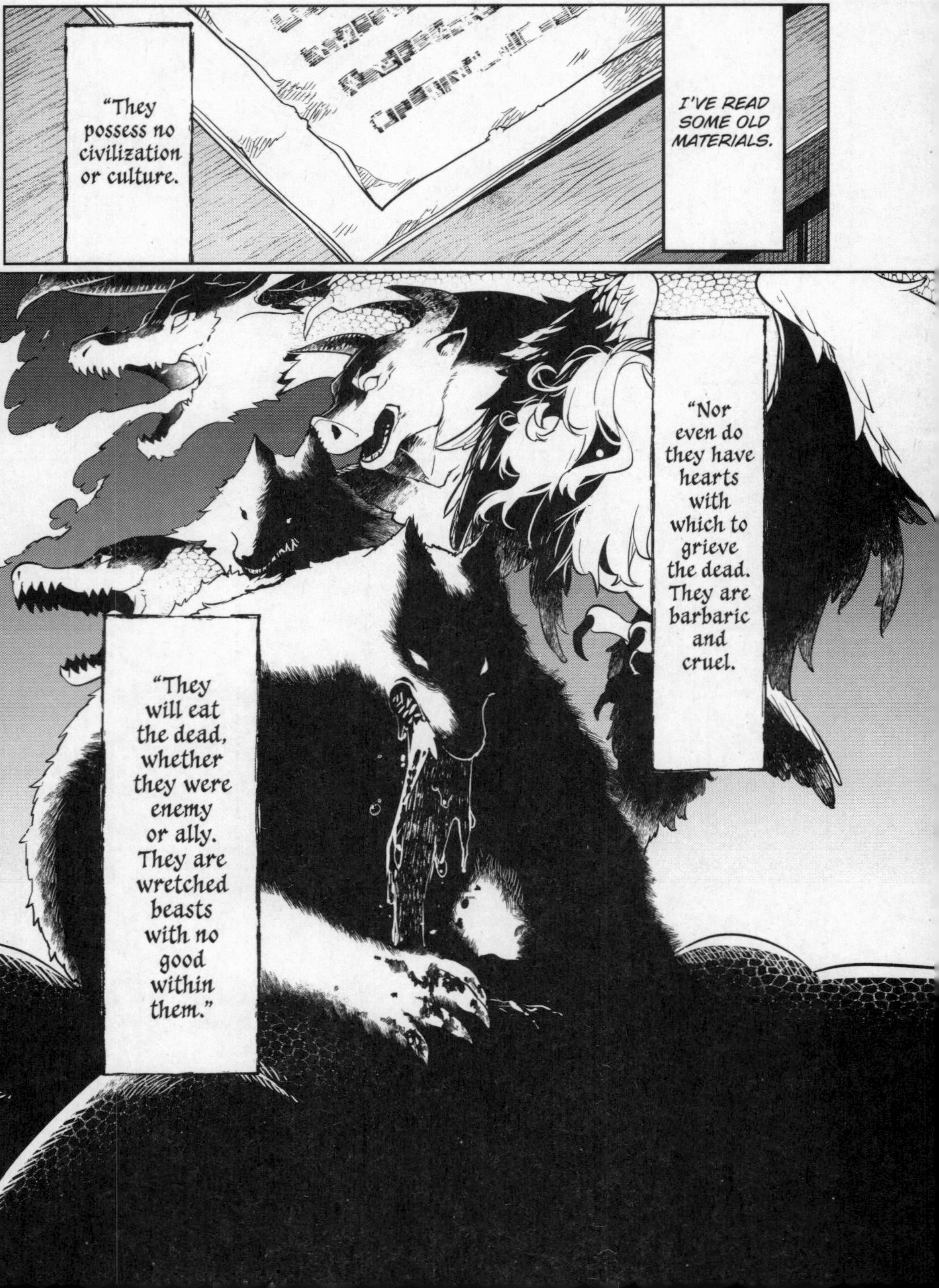
I'VE READ SOME OLD MATERIALS.
"They possess no civilization or culture.
"Nor even do they have hearts with which to grieve the dead. They are barbaric and cruel.
"They will eat the dead, whether they were enemy or ally. They are wretched beasts with no good within them."

Inside the Cave

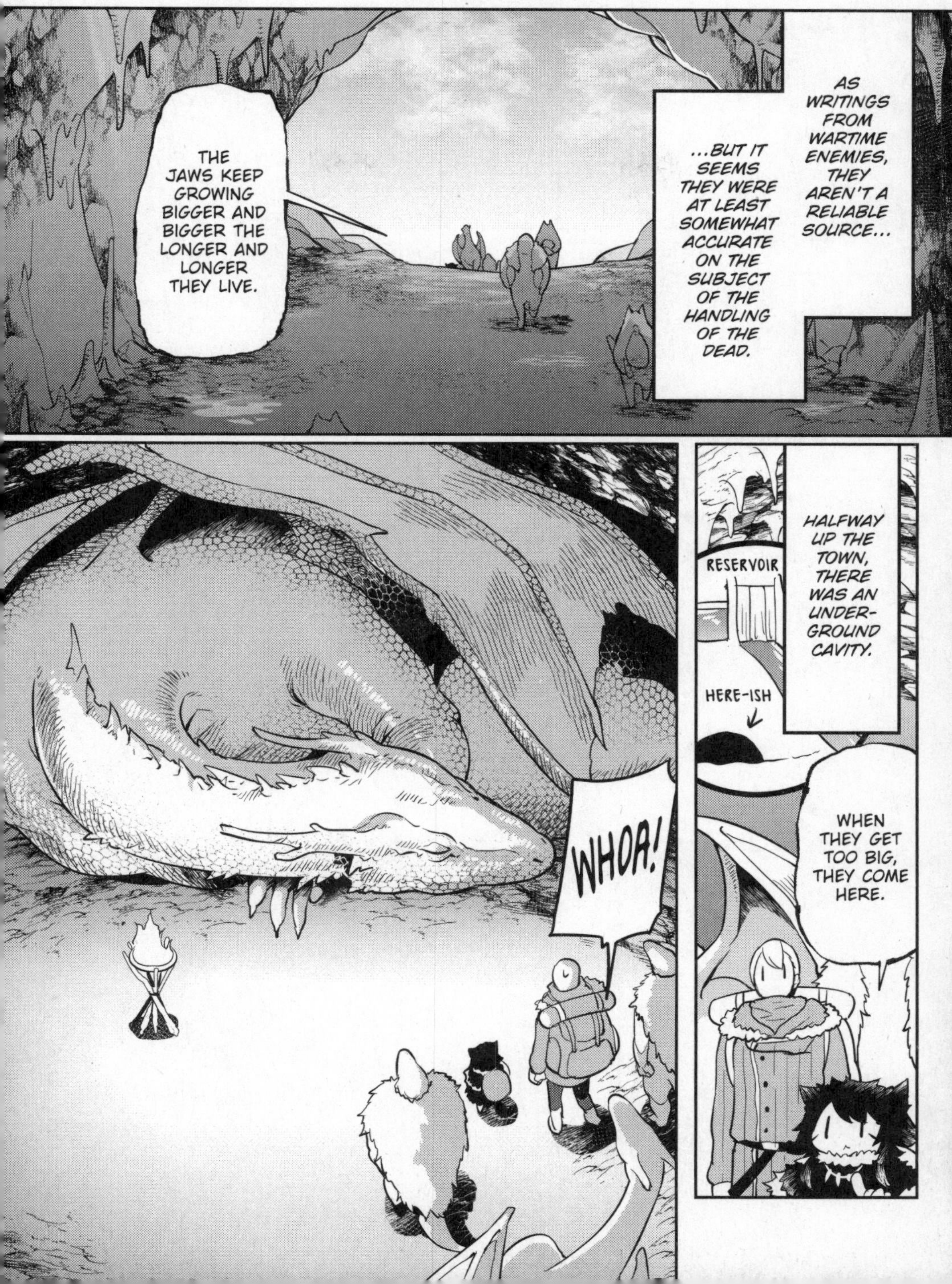
AS WRITINGS FROM WARTIME ENEMIES, THEY AREN'T A RELIABLE SOURCE...
...BUT IT SEEMS THEY WERE AT LEAST SOMEWHAT ACCURATE ON THE SUBJECT OF THE HANDLING OF THE DEAD.
THE JAWS KEEP GROWING BIGGER AND BIGGER THE LONGER AND LONGER THEY LIVE.
HALFWAY UP THE TOWN, THERE WAS AN UNDERGROUND CAVITY.
RESERVOIR
HERE-ISH
WHEN THEY GET TOO BIG, THEY COME HERE.
WHOR!

Big Dragon

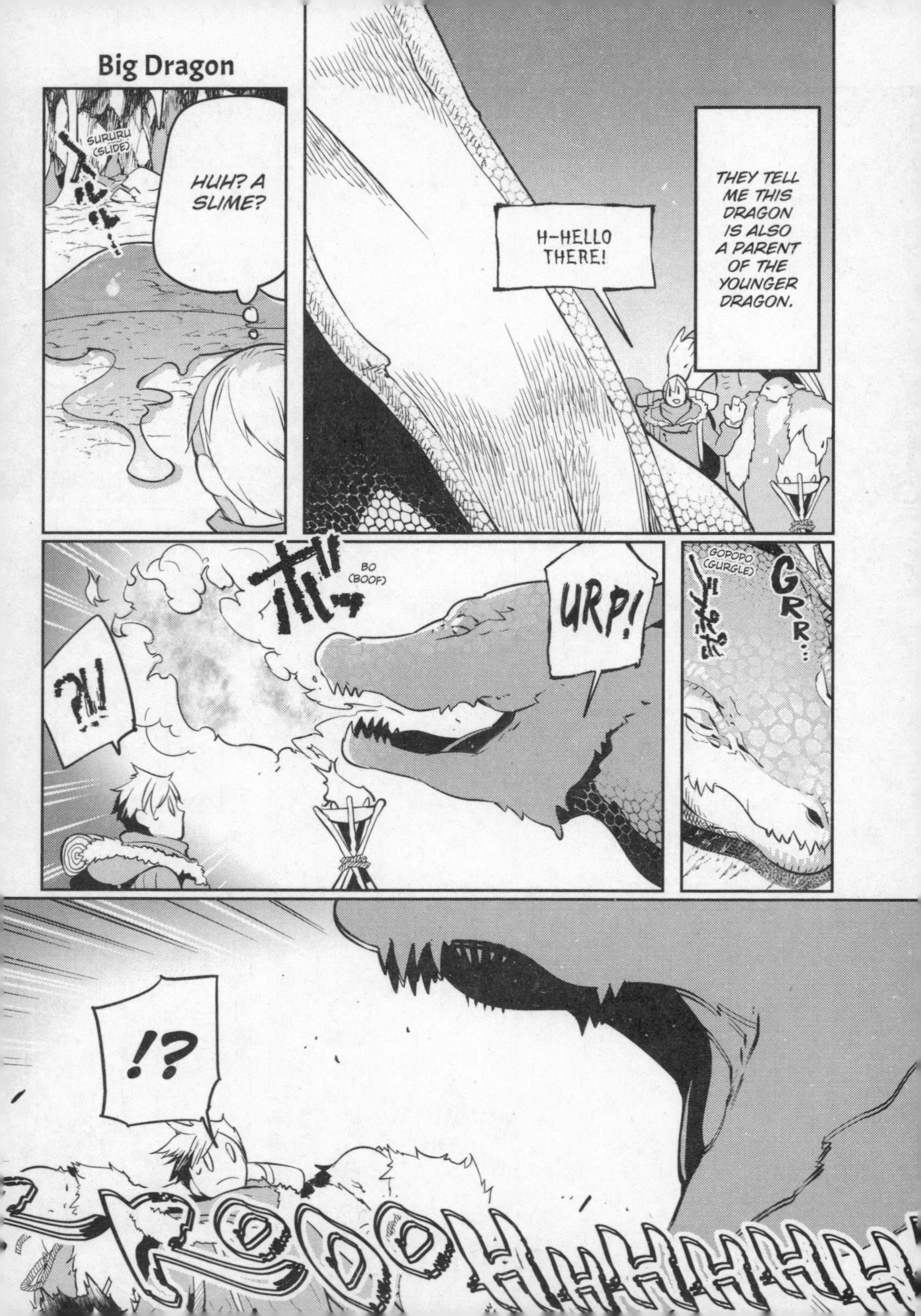
THEY TELL ME THIS DRAGON IS ALSO A PARENT OF THE YOUNGER DRAGON.
H-HELLO THERE!
SURURU (SLIDE)
HUH? A SLIME?
GOPOPO (GURGLE)
GRR...
URP!
BO (BOOF)
?!
!?

Can't Hear

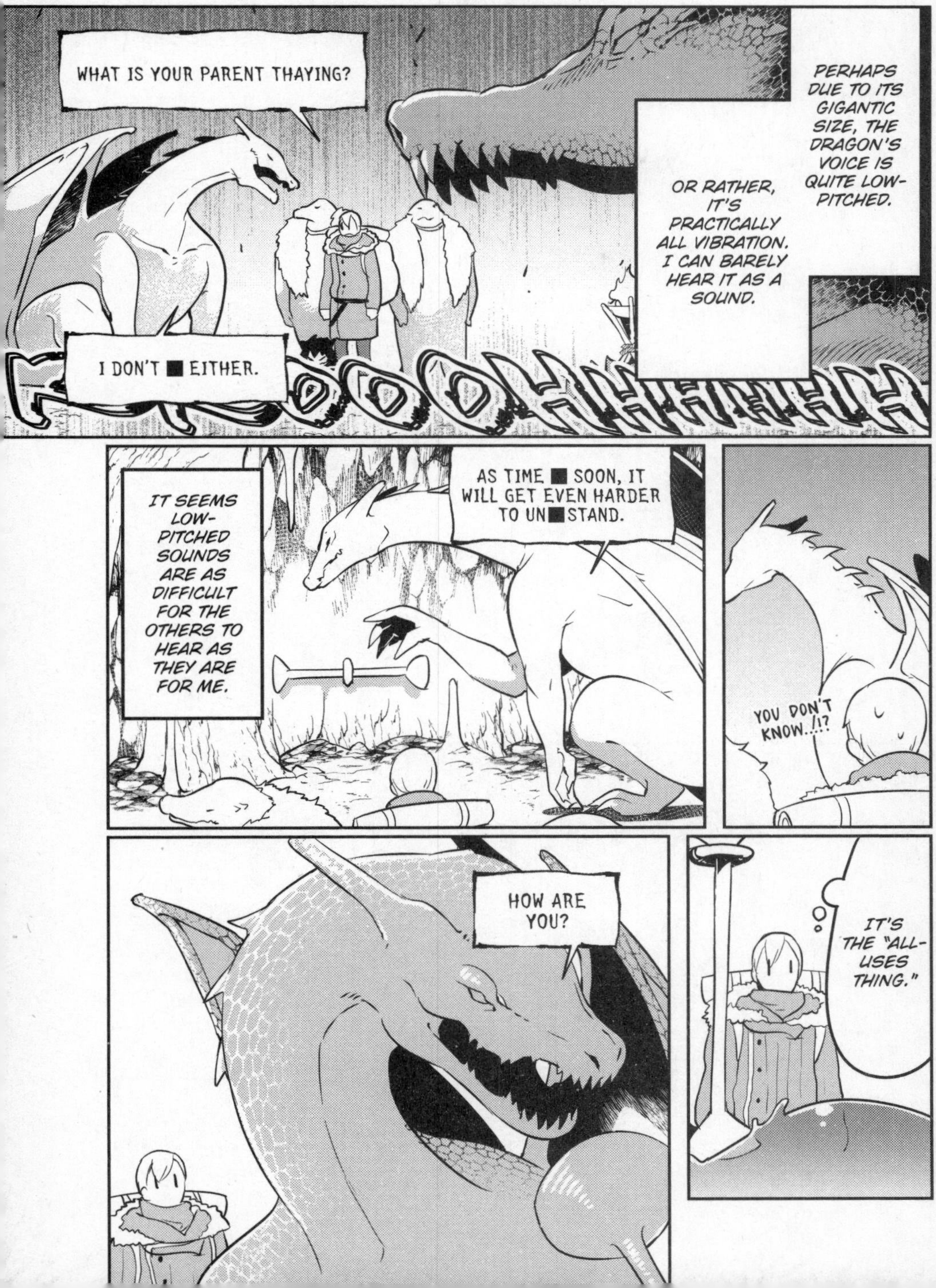
PERHAPS DUE TO ITS GIGANTIC SIZE, THE DRAGON'S VOICE IS QUITE LOW-PITCHED.
OR RATHER, IT'S PRACTICALLY ALL VIBRATION. I CAN BARELY HEAR IT AS A SOUND.
WHAT IS YOUR PARENT THAYING?
I DON'T ■ EITHER.
YOU DON'T KNOW...!?
AS TIME ■ SOON, IT WILL GET EVEN HARDER TO UN■STAND.
IT SEEMS LOW-PITCHED SOUNDS ARE AS DIFFICULT FOR THE OTHERS TO HEAR AS THEY ARE FOR ME.
IT'S THE "ALL-USES THING."
HOW ARE YOU?

Interpretation?

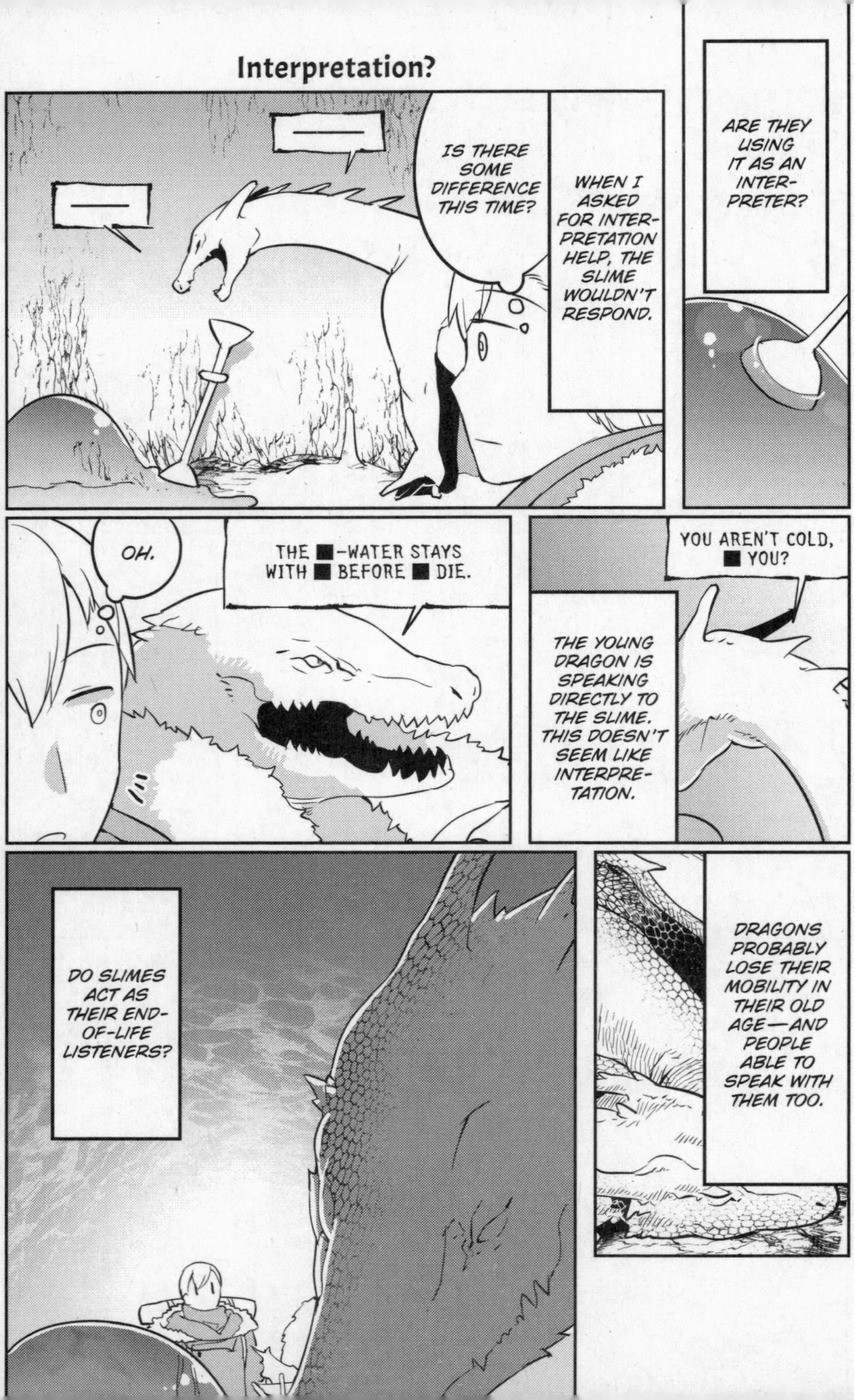
ARE THEY USING IT AS AN INTER-PRETER?
WHEN I ASKED FOR INTER-PRETATION HELP, THE SLIME WOULDN'T RESPOND.
IS THERE SOME DIFFERENCE THIS TIME?
——
——
YOU AREN'T COLD, [redacted] YOU?
THE YOUNG DRAGON IS SPEAKING DIRECTLY TO THE SLIME. THIS DOESN'T SEEM LIKE INTERPRE-TATION.
THE [redacted]-WATER STAYS WITH [redacted] BEFORE [redacted] DIE.
OH.
DRAGONS PROBABLY LOSE THEIR MOBILITY IN THEIR OLD AGE—AND PEOPLE ABLE TO SPEAK WITH THEM TOO.
DO SLIMES ACT AS THEIR END-OF-LIFE LISTENERS?

Participatory

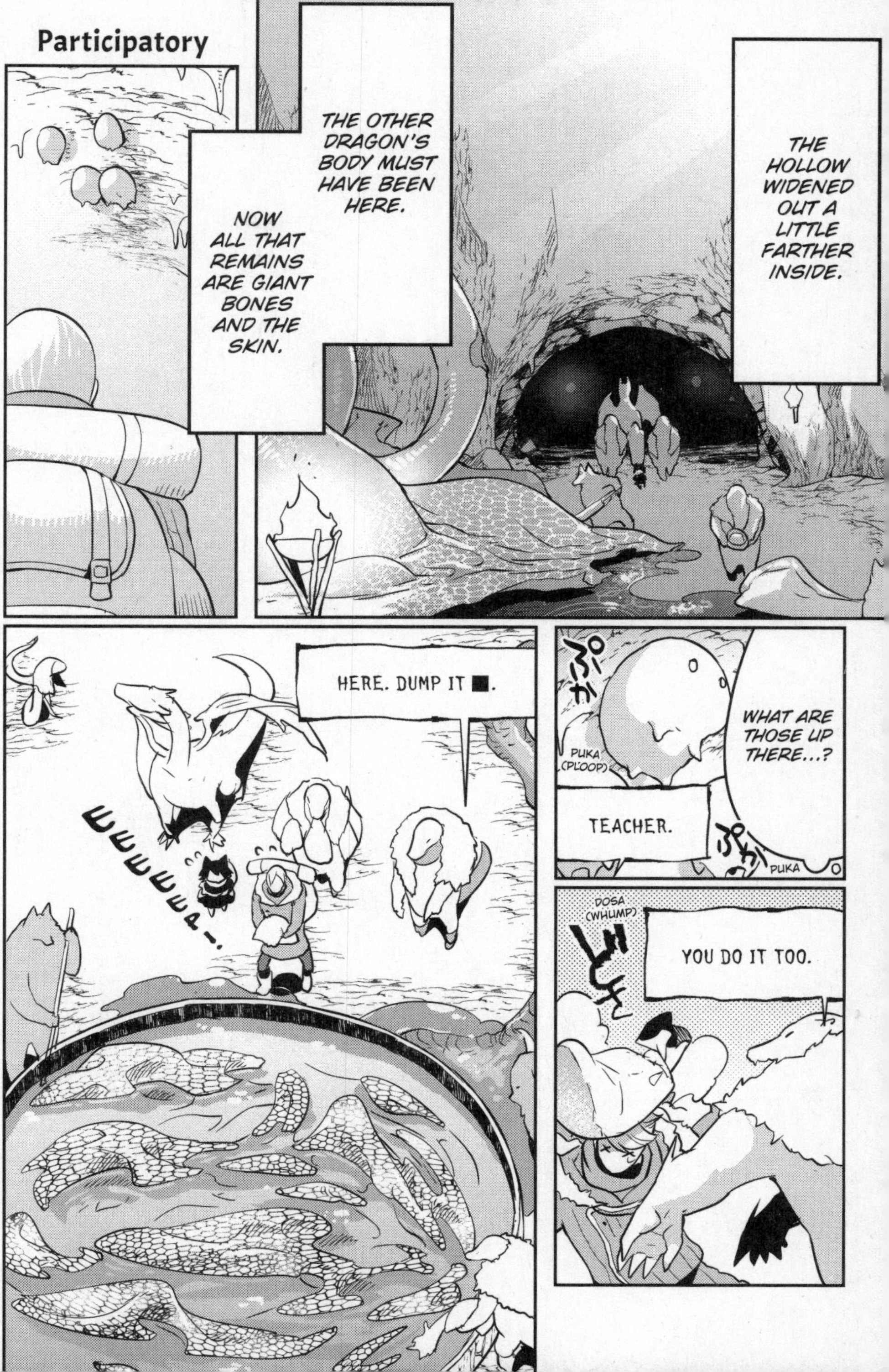
THE HOLLOW WIDENED OUT A LITTLE FARTHER INSIDE.
THE OTHER DRAGON'S BODY MUST HAVE BEEN HERE.
NOW ALL THAT REMAINS ARE GIANT BONES AND THE SKIN.
PUKA (PLOOP)
WHAT ARE THOSE UP THERE...?
TEACHER.
PUKA
DOSA (WHUMP)
YOU DO IT TOO.
HERE. DUMP IT ■.
EEEEEEA!!

An Unknown

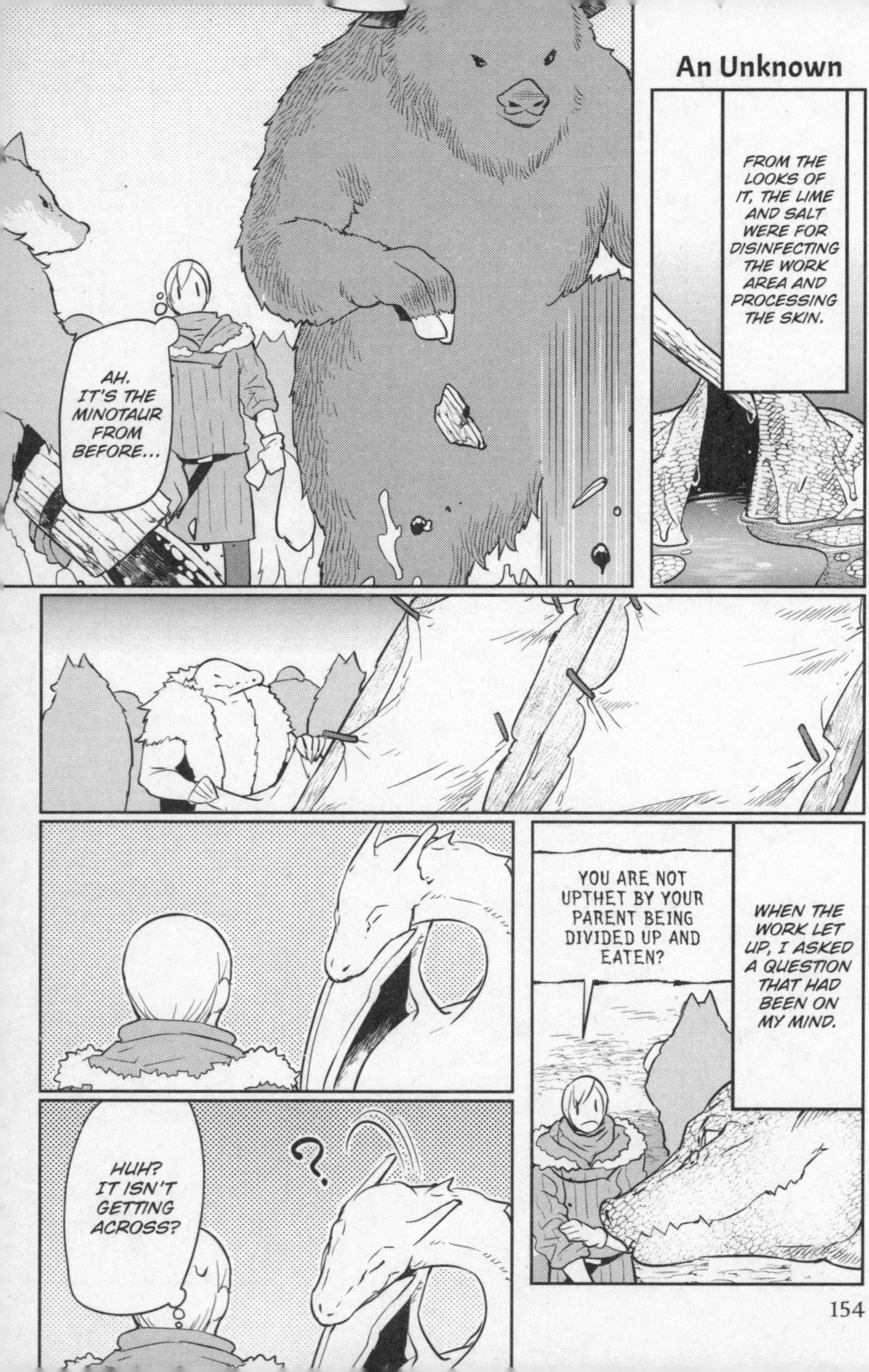
FROM THE LOOKS OF IT, THE LIME AND SALT WERE FOR DISINFECTING THE WORK AREA AND PROCESSING THE SKIN.
AH. IT'S THE MINOTAUR FROM BEFORE...
WHEN THE WORK LET UP, I ASKED A QUESTION THAT HAD BEEN ON MY MIND.
YOU ARE NOT UPTHET BY YOUR PARENT BEING DIVIDED UP AND EATEN?
?
HUH? IT ISN'T GETTING ACROSS?

Hypothetical

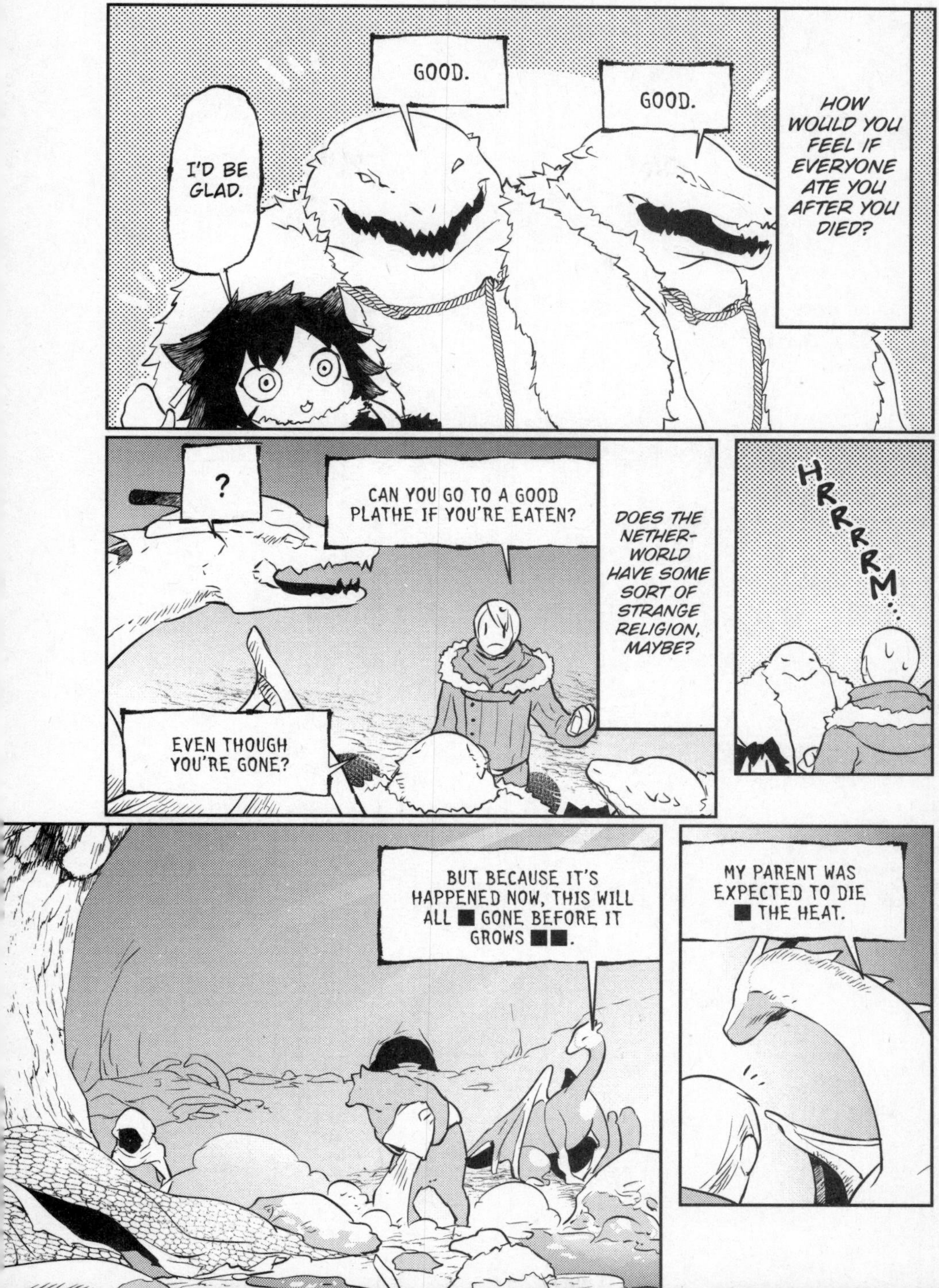
HOW WOULD YOU FEEL IF EVERYONE ATE YOU AFTER YOU DIED?
GOOD.
GOOD.
I'D BE GLAD.
HRRRRM...
DOES THE NETHER-WORLD HAVE SOME SORT OF STRANGE RELIGION, MAYBE?
CAN YOU GO TO A GOOD PLATHE IF YOU'RE EATEN?
?
EVEN THOUGH YOU'RE GONE?
MY PARENT WAS EXPECTED TO DIE [redacted] THE HEAT.
BUT BECAUSE IT'S HAPPENED NOW, THIS WILL ALL [redacted] GONE BEFORE IT GROWS [redacted].

Town of Death: Night

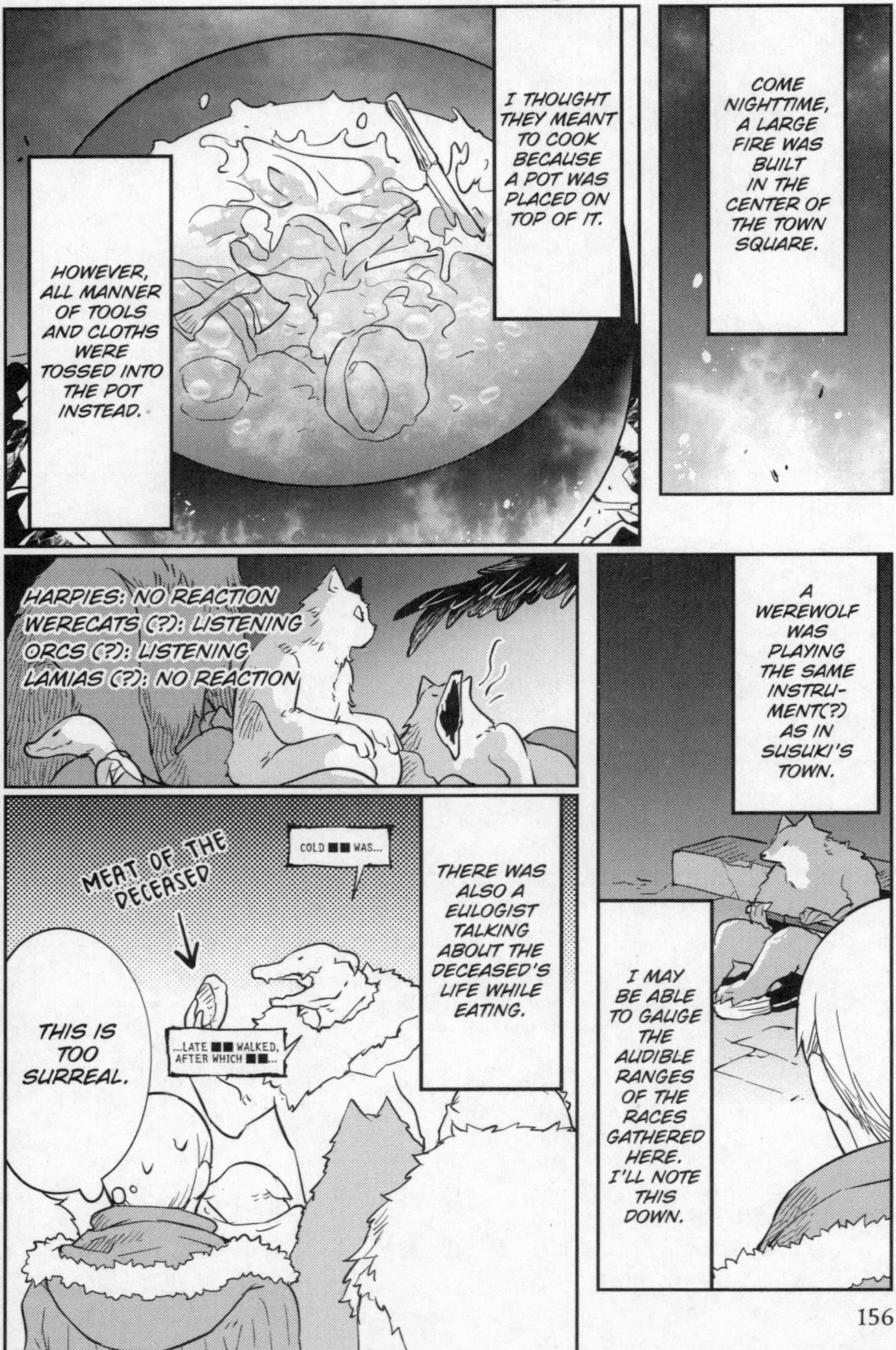
COME NIGHTTIME, A LARGE FIRE WAS BUILT IN THE CENTER OF THE TOWN SQUARE.
I THOUGHT THEY MEANT TO COOK BECAUSE A POT WAS PLACED ON TOP OF IT.
HOWEVER, ALL MANNER OF TOOLS AND CLOTHS WERE TOSSED INTO THE POT INSTEAD.
A WEREWOLF WAS PLAYING THE SAME INSTRU-MENT(?) AS IN SUSUKI'S TOWN.
I MAY BE ABLE TO GAUGE THE AUDIBLE RANGES OF THE RACES GATHERED HERE. I'LL NOTE THIS DOWN.
HARPIES: NO REACTION
WERECATS (?): LISTENING
ORCS (?): LISTENING
LAMIAS (?): NO REACTION
THERE WAS ALSO A EULOGIST TALKING ABOUT THE DECEASED'S LIFE WHILE EATING.
COLD [redacted] WAS...
MEAT OF THE DECEASED
...LATE [redacted] WALKED, AFTER WHICH [redacted]...
THIS IS TOO SURREAL.

Way to Convey

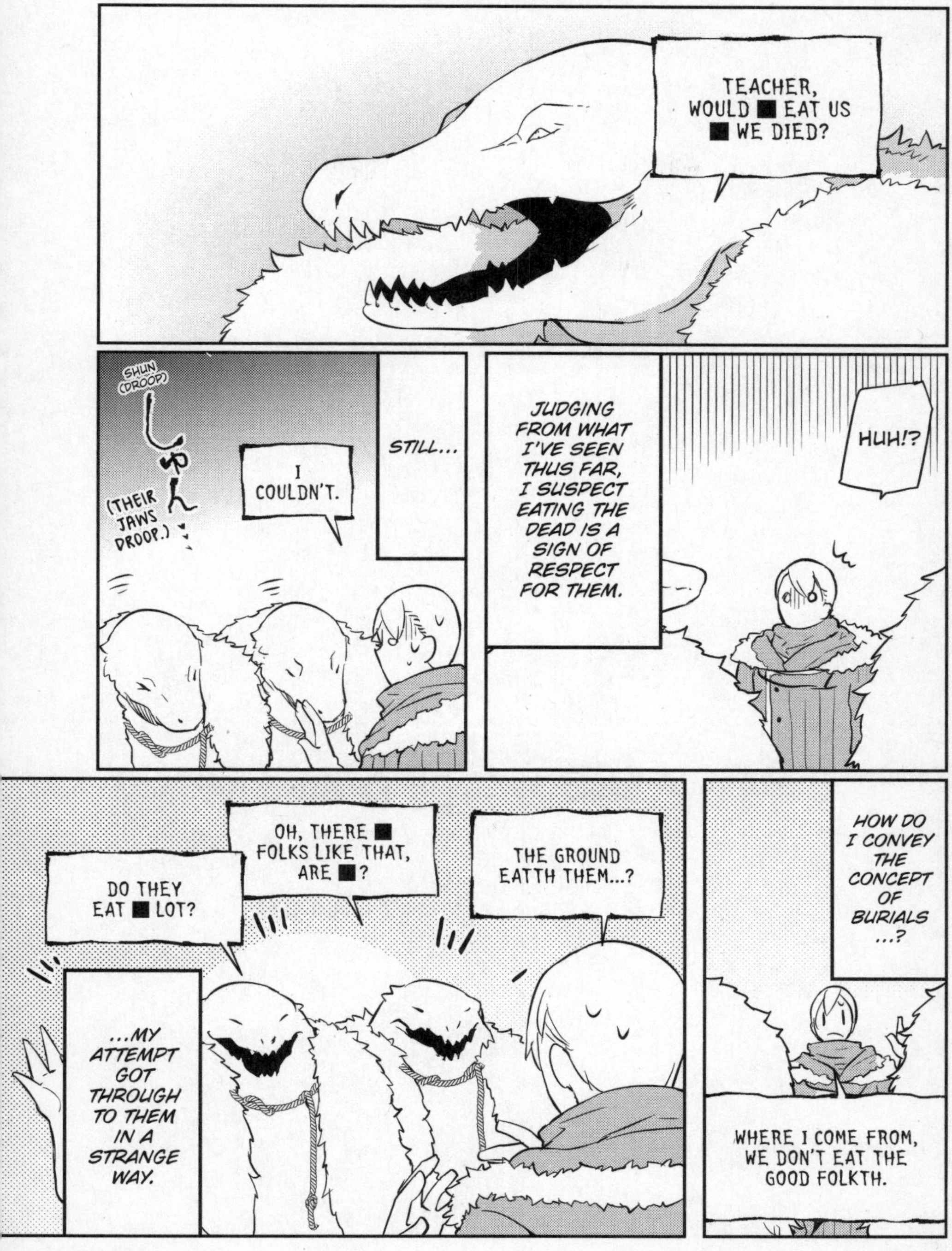
TEACHER, WOULD [redacted] EAT US [redacted] WE DIED?
HUH!?
JUDGING FROM WHAT I'VE SEEN THUS FAR, I SUSPECT EATING THE DEAD IS A SIGN OF RESPECT FOR THEM.
STILL...
I COULDN'T.
SHUN (DROOP)
しゅん
(THEIR JAWS DROOP.)
HOW DO I CONVEY THE CONCEPT OF BURIALS ...?
WHERE I COME FROM, WE DON'T EAT THE GOOD FOLKTH.
THE GROUND EATTH THEM...?
OH, THERE [redacted] FOLKS LIKE THAT, ARE [redacted]?
DO THEY EAT [redacted] LOT?
...MY ATTEMPT GOT THROUGH TO THEM IN A STRANGE WAY.

What About Susuki?

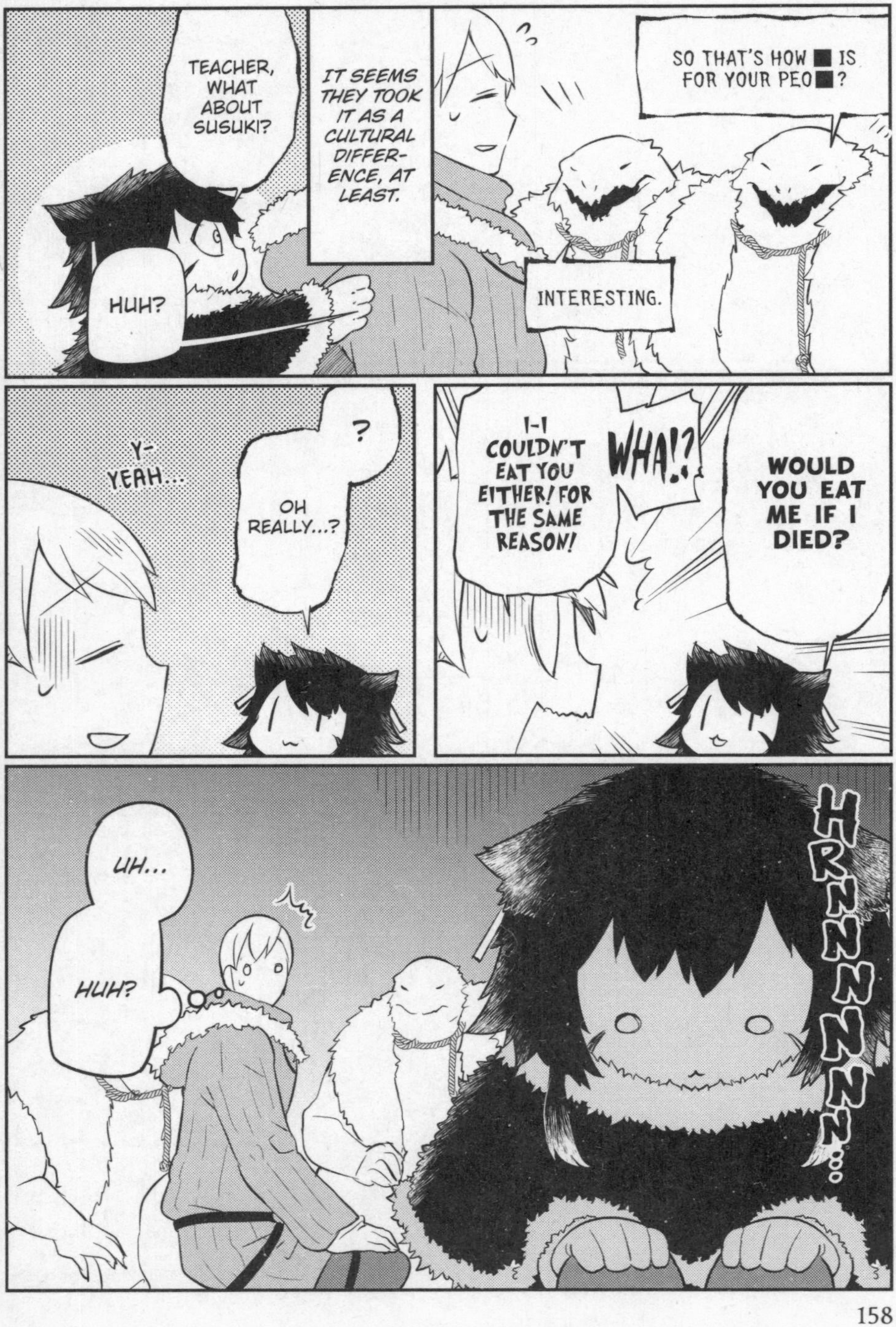
SO THAT'S HOW ■ IS FOR YOUR PEO■?
INTERESTING.
IT SEEMS THEY TOOK IT AS A CULTURAL DIFFER-ENCE, AT LEAST.
TEACHER, WHAT ABOUT SUSUKI?
HUH?
WOULD YOU EAT ME IF I DIED?
WHA!?
I-I COULDN'T EAT YOU EITHER! FOR THE SAME REASON!
?
OH REALLY...?
Y-YEAH...
HRNNNNNNN...
UH...
HUH?

Still Small Susuki?

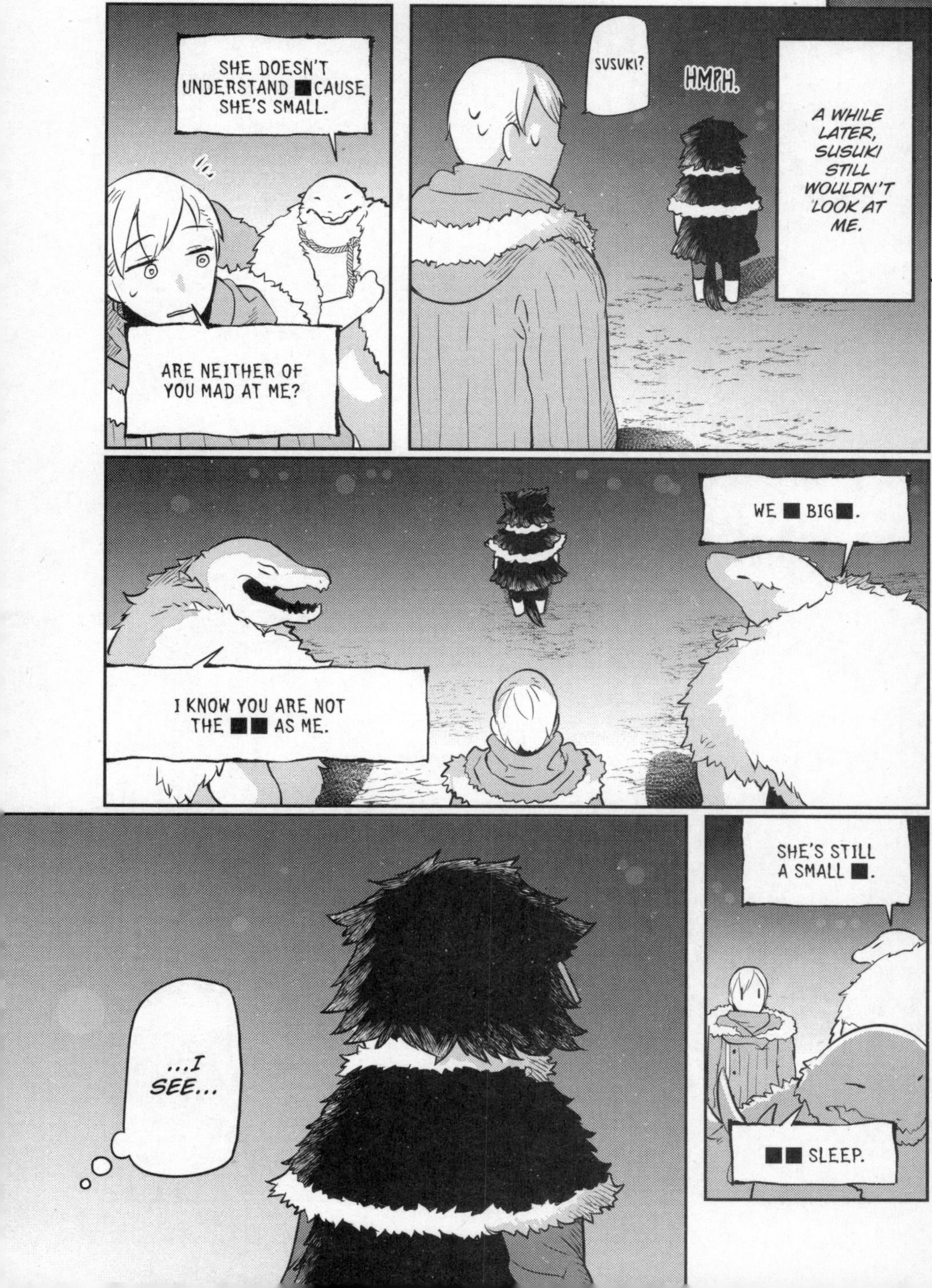
A WHILE LATER, SUSUKI STILL WOULDN'T LOOK AT ME.
HMPH.
SUSUKI?
SHE DOESN'T UNDERSTAND ■CAUSE SHE'S SMALL.
ARE NEITHER OF YOU MAD AT ME?
WE ■ BIG■.
I KNOW YOU ARE NOT THE ■■ AS ME.
SHE'S STILL A SMALL ■.
■■ SLEEP.
...I SEE...

Show of Affection

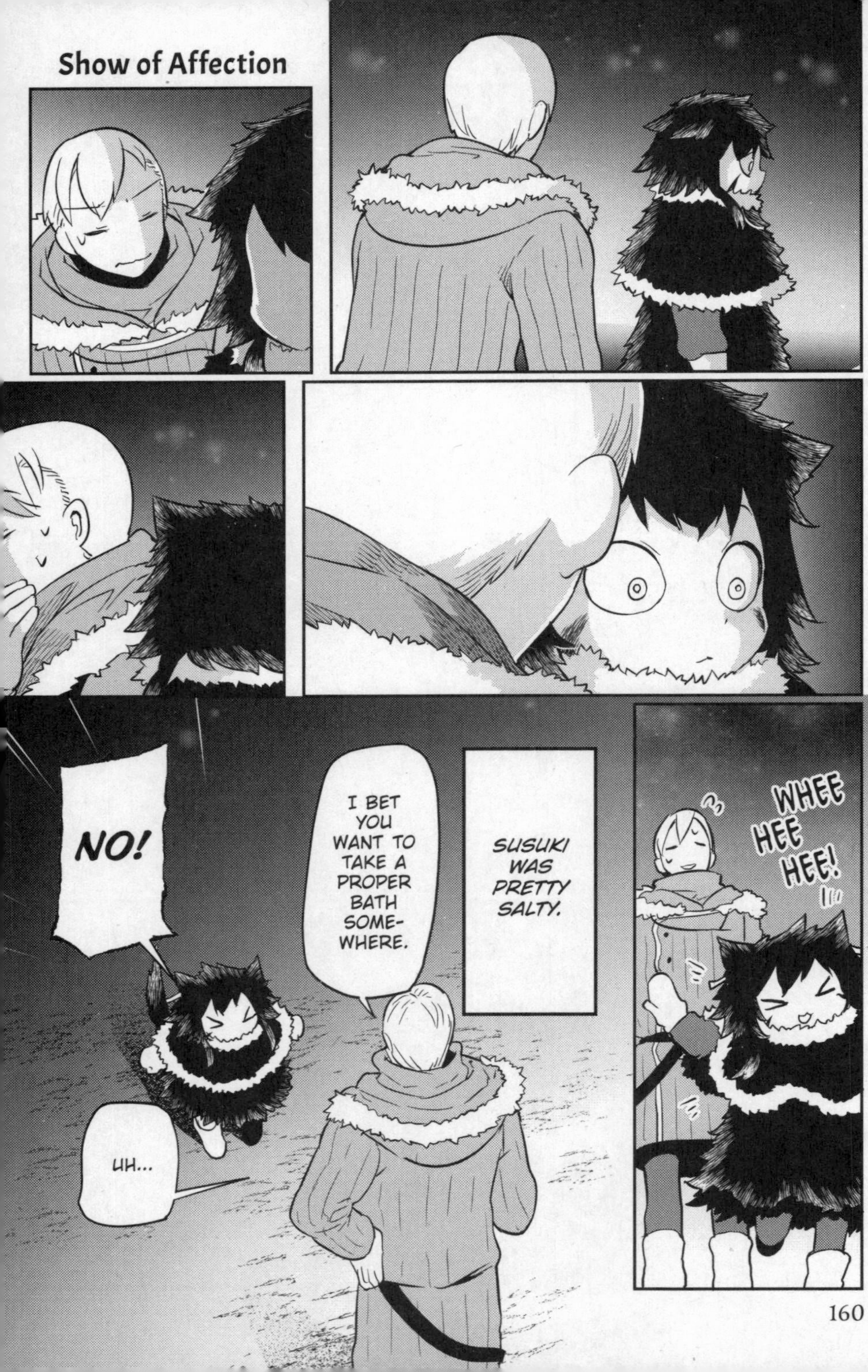

WHEE HEE HEE!
SUSUKI WAS PRETTY SALTY.
I BET YOU WANT TO TAKE A PROPER BATH SOMEWHERE.
NO!
UH...

Not an Understanding

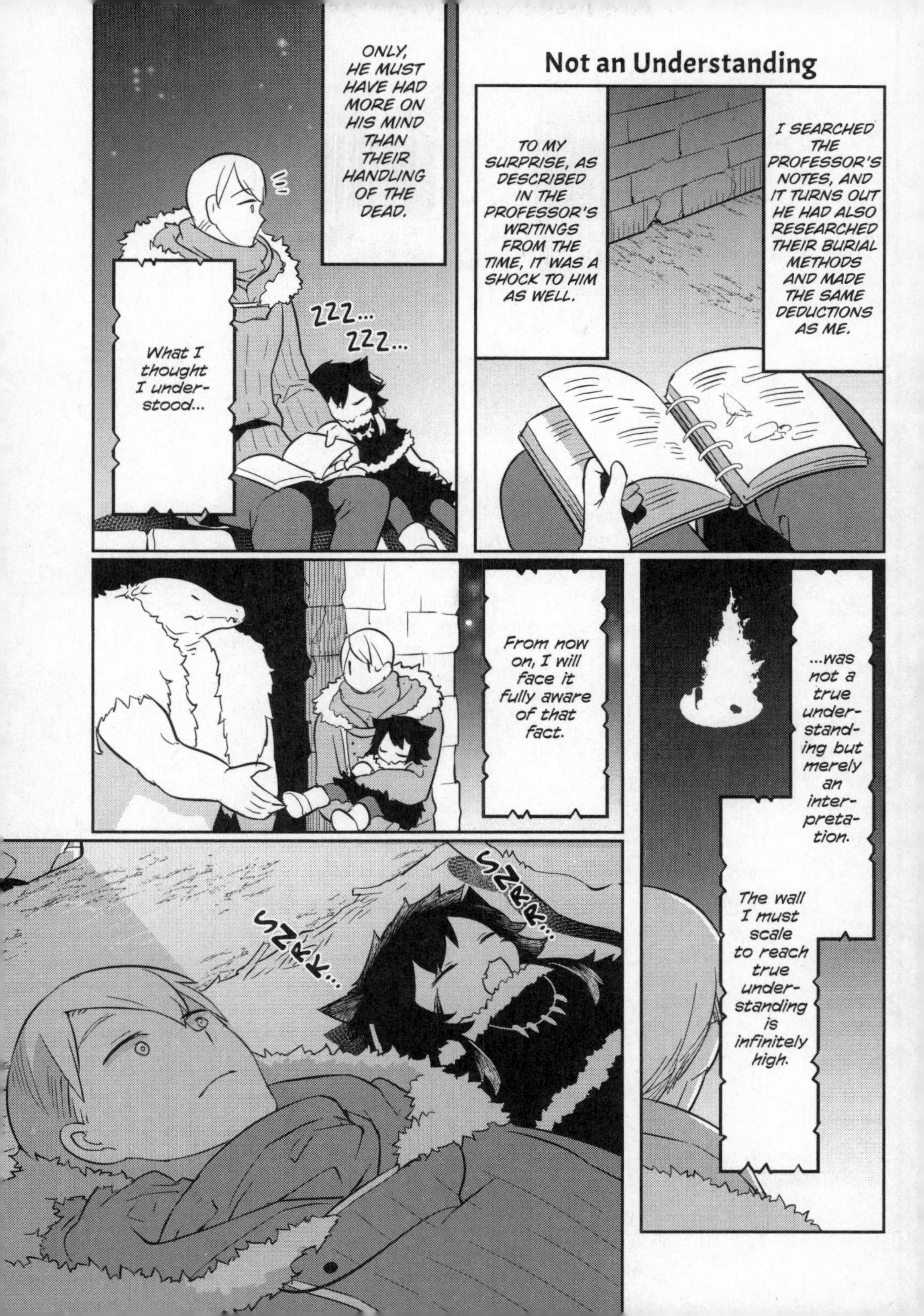
I SEARCHED THE PROFESSOR'S NOTES, AND IT TURNS OUT HE HAD ALSO RESEARCHED THEIR BURIAL METHODS AND MADE THE SAME DEDUCTIONS AS ME.
TO MY SURPRISE, AS DESCRIBED IN THE PROFESSOR'S WRITINGS FROM THE TIME, IT WAS A SHOCK TO HIM AS WELL.
ONLY, HE MUST HAVE HAD MORE ON HIS MIND THAN THEIR HANDLING OF THE DEAD.
ZZZ... ZZZ...
What I thought I understood...
...was not a true understanding but merely an interpretation.
From now on, I will face it fully aware of that fact.
The wall I must scale to reach true understanding is infinitely high.
SZRR...
SZRR...

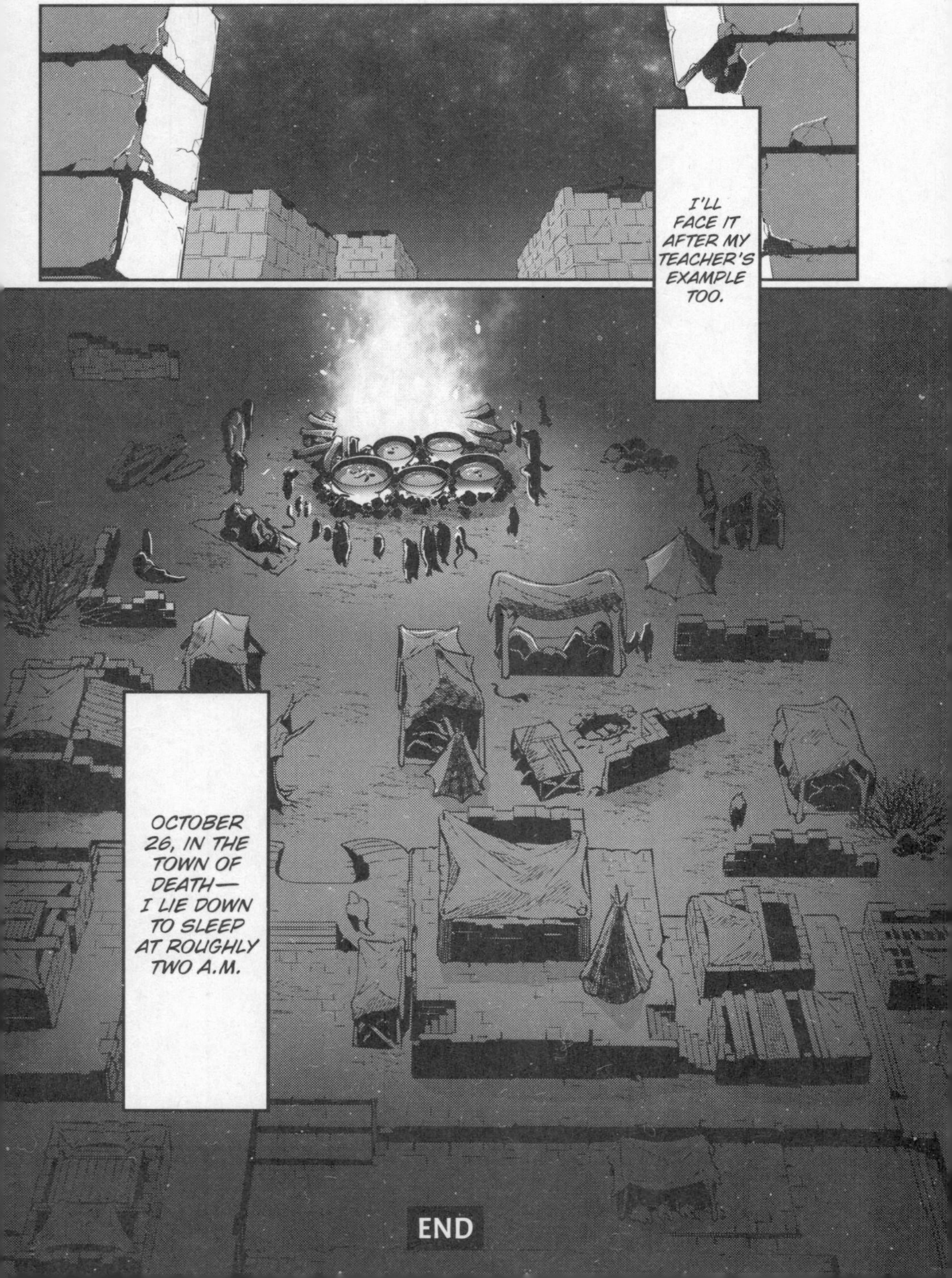
I'LL FACE IT AFTER MY TEACHER'S EXAMPLE TOO.
OCTOBER 26, IN THE TOWN OF DEATH— I LIE DOWN TO SLEEP AT ROUGHLY TWO A.M.
END

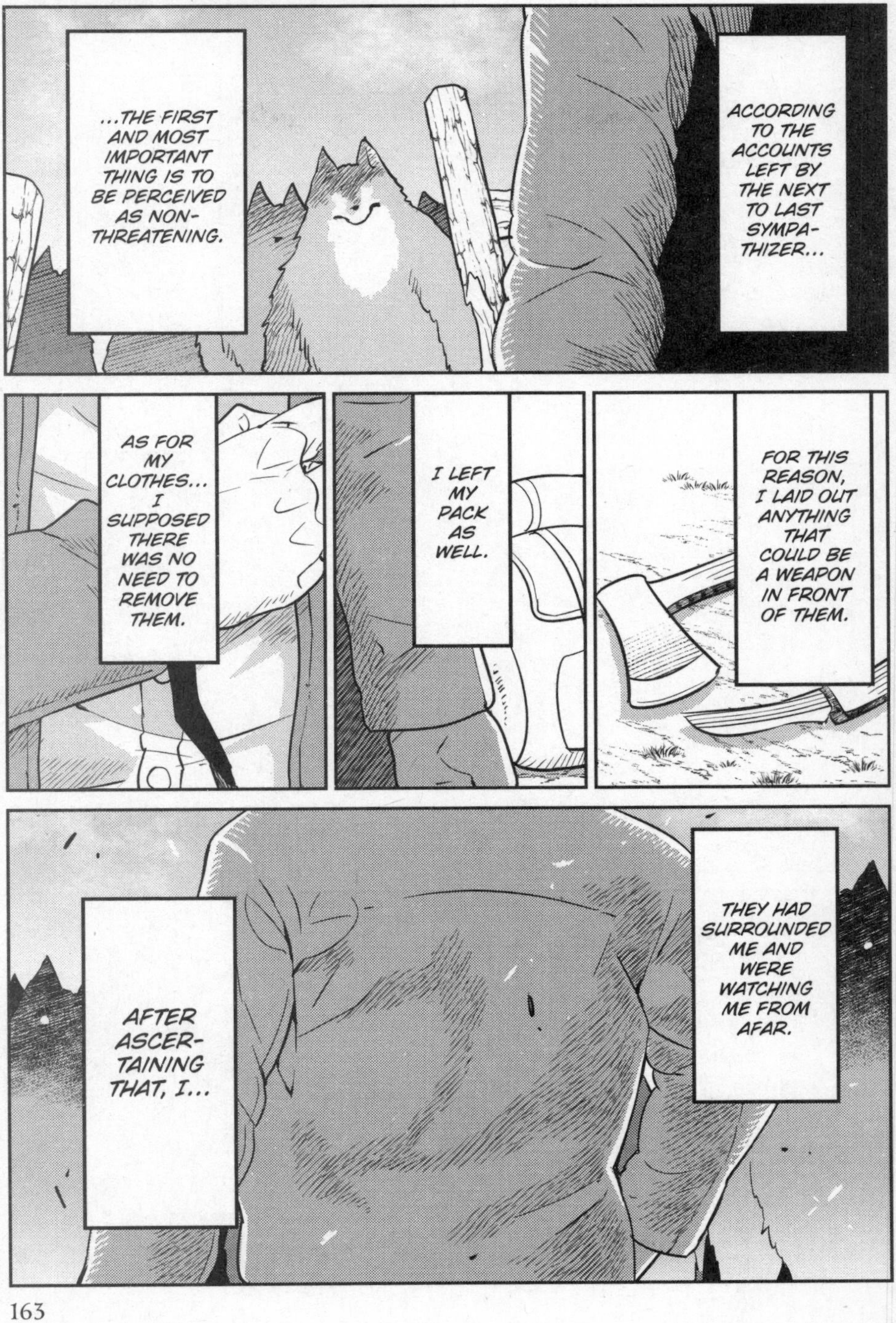
ACCORDING TO THE ACCOUNTS LEFT BY THE NEXT TO LAST SYMPATHIZER...
...THE FIRST AND MOST IMPORTANT THING IS TO BE PERCEIVED AS NON-THREATENING.
FOR THIS REASON, I LAID OUT ANYTHING THAT COULD BE A WEAPON IN FRONT OF THEM.
I LEFT MY PACK AS WELL.
AS FOR MY CLOTHES... I SUPPOSED THERE WAS NO NEED TO REMOVE THEM.
THEY HAD SURROUNDED ME AND WERE WATCHING ME FROM AFAR.
AFTER ASCERTAINING THAT, I...

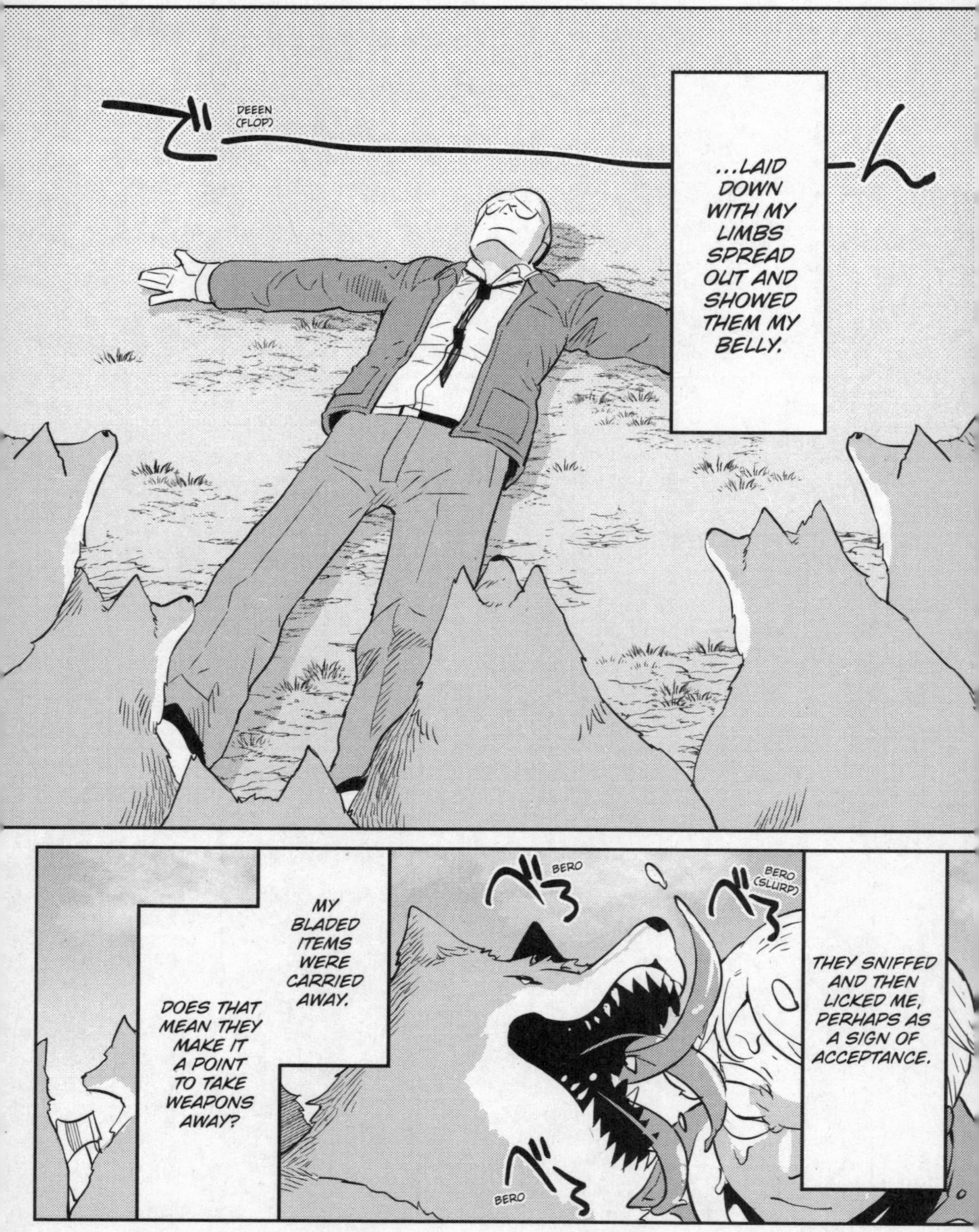
...LAID DOWN WITH MY LIMBS SPREAD OUT AND SHOWED THEM MY BELLY.
DEEEN (FLOP)
THEY SNIFFED AND THEN LICKED ME, PERHAPS AS A SIGN OF ACCEPTANCE.
BERO (SLURP)
BERO
BERO
MY BLADED ITEMS WERE CARRIED AWAY.
DOES THAT MEAN THEY MAKE IT A POINT TO TAKE WEAPONS AWAY?

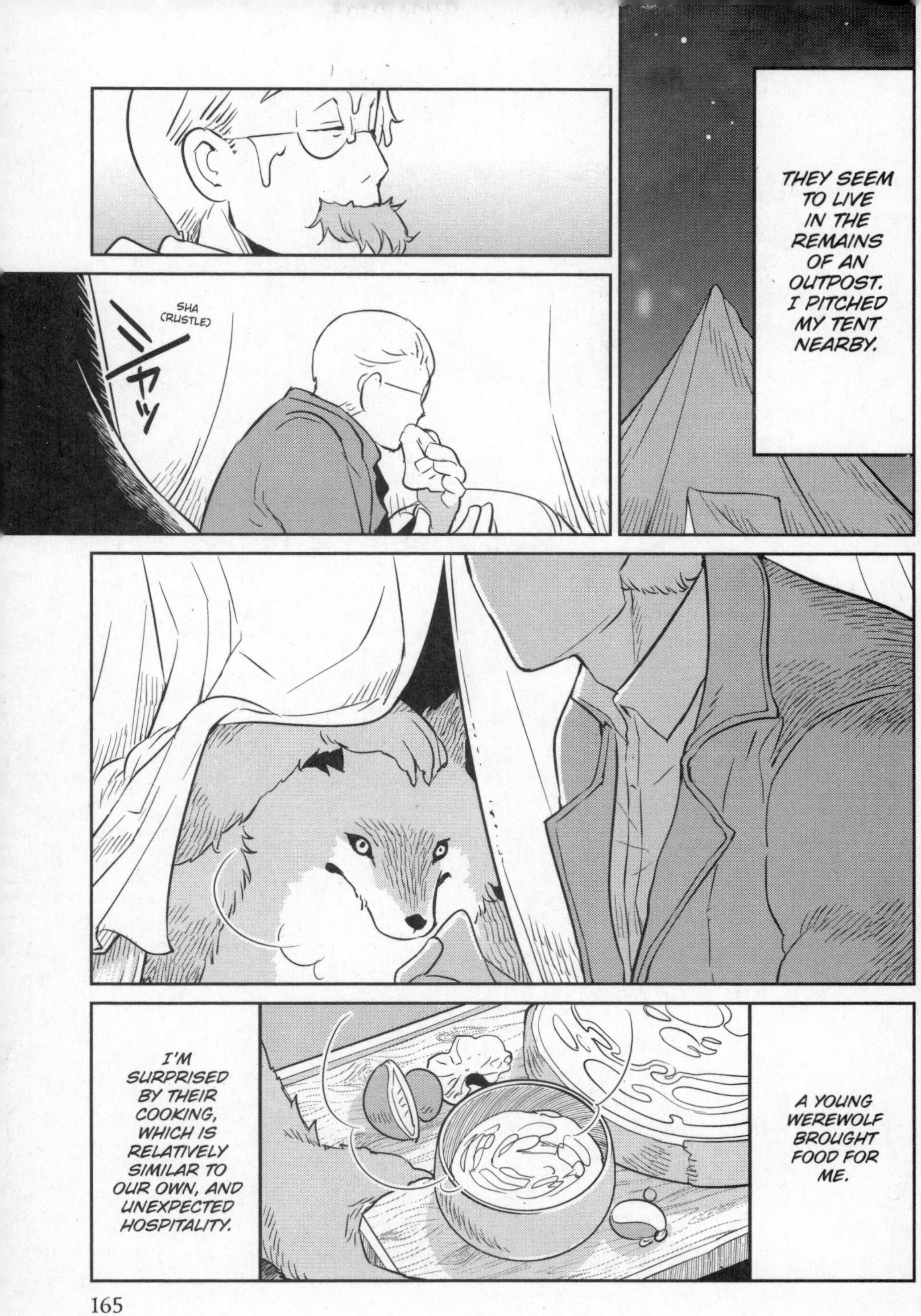
THEY SEEM TO LIVE IN THE REMAINS OF AN OUTPOST. I PITCHED MY TENT NEARBY.
SHA (RUSTLE)
シャッ
A YOUNG WEREWOLF BROUGHT FOOD FOR ME.
I'M SURPRISED BY THEIR COOKING, WHICH IS RELATIVELY SIMILAR TO OUR OWN, AND UNEXPECTED HOSPITALITY.

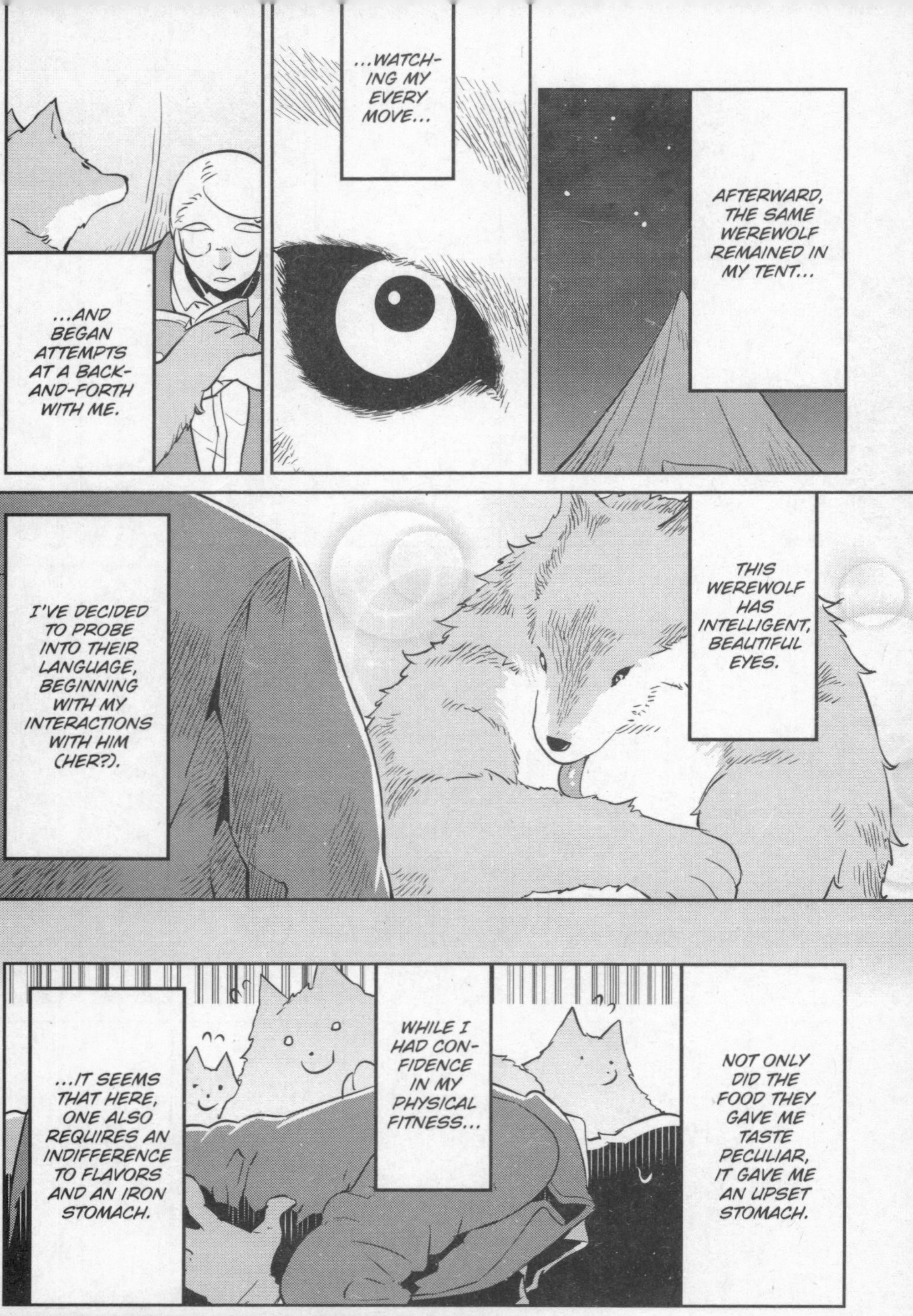
AFTERWARD, THE SAME WEREWOLF REMAINED IN MY TENT...
...WATCHING MY EVERY MOVE...
...AND BEGAN ATTEMPTS AT A BACK-AND-FORTH WITH ME.
THIS WEREWOLF HAS INTELLIGENT, BEAUTIFUL EYES.
I'VE DECIDED TO PROBE INTO THEIR LANGUAGE, BEGINNING WITH MY INTERACTIONS WITH HIM (HER?).
NOT ONLY DID THE FOOD THEY GAVE ME TASTE PECULIAR, IT GAVE ME AN UPSET STOMACH.
WHILE I HAD CONFIDENCE IN MY PHYSICAL FITNESS...
...IT SEEMS THAT HERE, ONE ALSO REQUIRES AN INDIFFERENCE TO FLAVORS AND AN IRON STOMACH.

Heterogenia Linguistico Volume 1 END

HETEROGENIA LINGUISTICO
An Introduction to Interspecies Linguistics

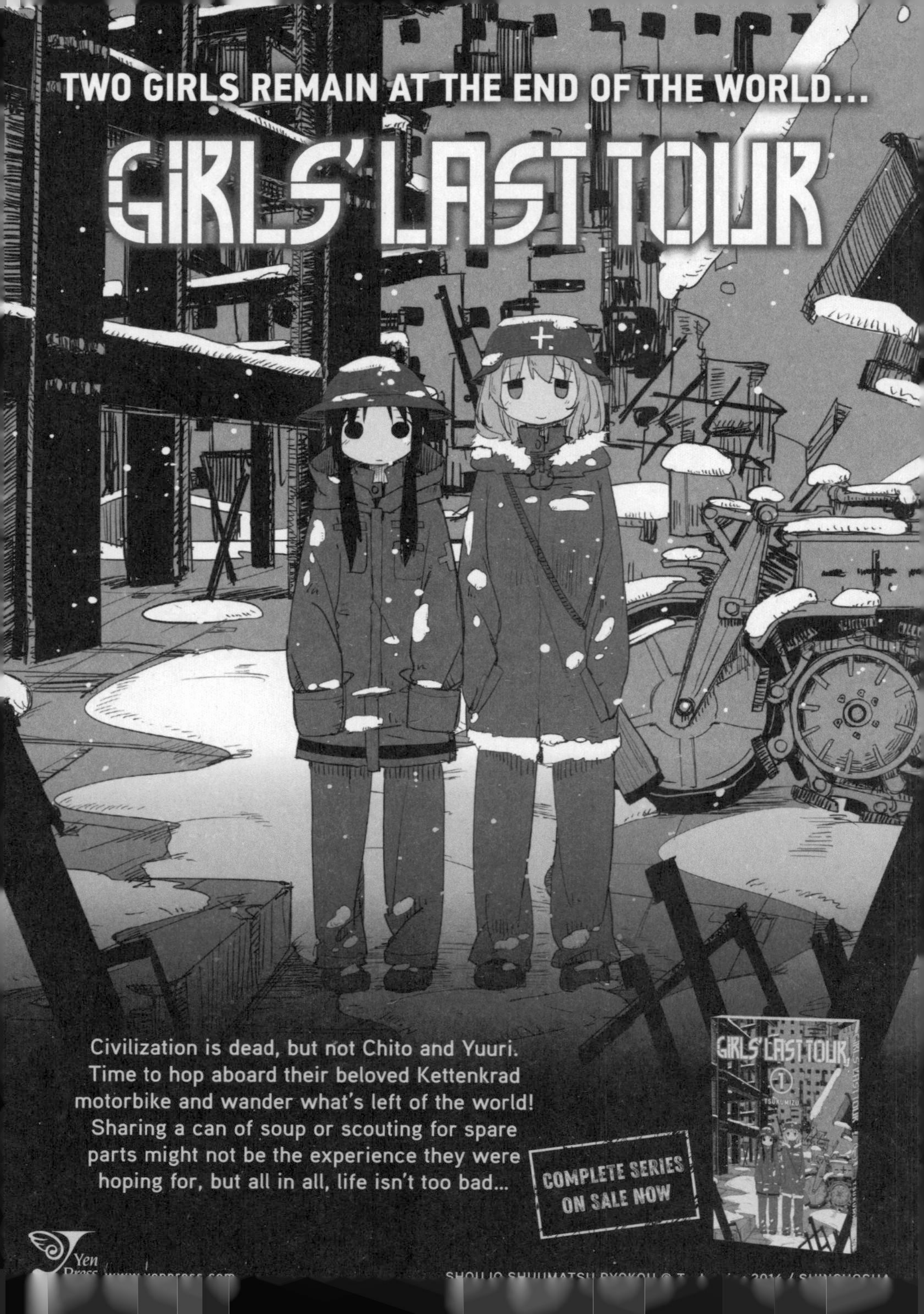
TWO GIRLS REMAIN AT THE END OF THE WORLD...
GIRLS' LAST TOUR
Civilization is dead, but not Chito and Yuuri. Time to hop aboard their beloved Kettenkrad motorbike and wander what's left of the world! Sharing a can of soup or scouting for spare parts might not be the experience they were hoping for, but all in all, life isn't too bad...
COMPLETE SERIES ON SALE NOW
GIRLS' LAST TOUR
1
TSUKUMIZU
Yen Press

BUNGO
STRAY DOGS

Volumes I–16
available now

**If you've already seen
the anime, it's time to
read the manga!**

Having been kicked out of the
orphanage, Atsushi Nakajima rescues
a strange man from a suicide attempt—
Osamu Dazai. Turns out that Dazai is
part of a detective agency staffed by
individuals whose supernatural powers
take on a literary bent!

www.yenpress.com

Everything made sense...
until the penguins showed up!

Tomihiko Morimi, celebrated author of *The Night Is Short, Walk On Girl*, invites readers on another enchanting adventure involving mystery, science, and...penguins?!

PENGUIN HIGHWAY

Tomihiko Morimi

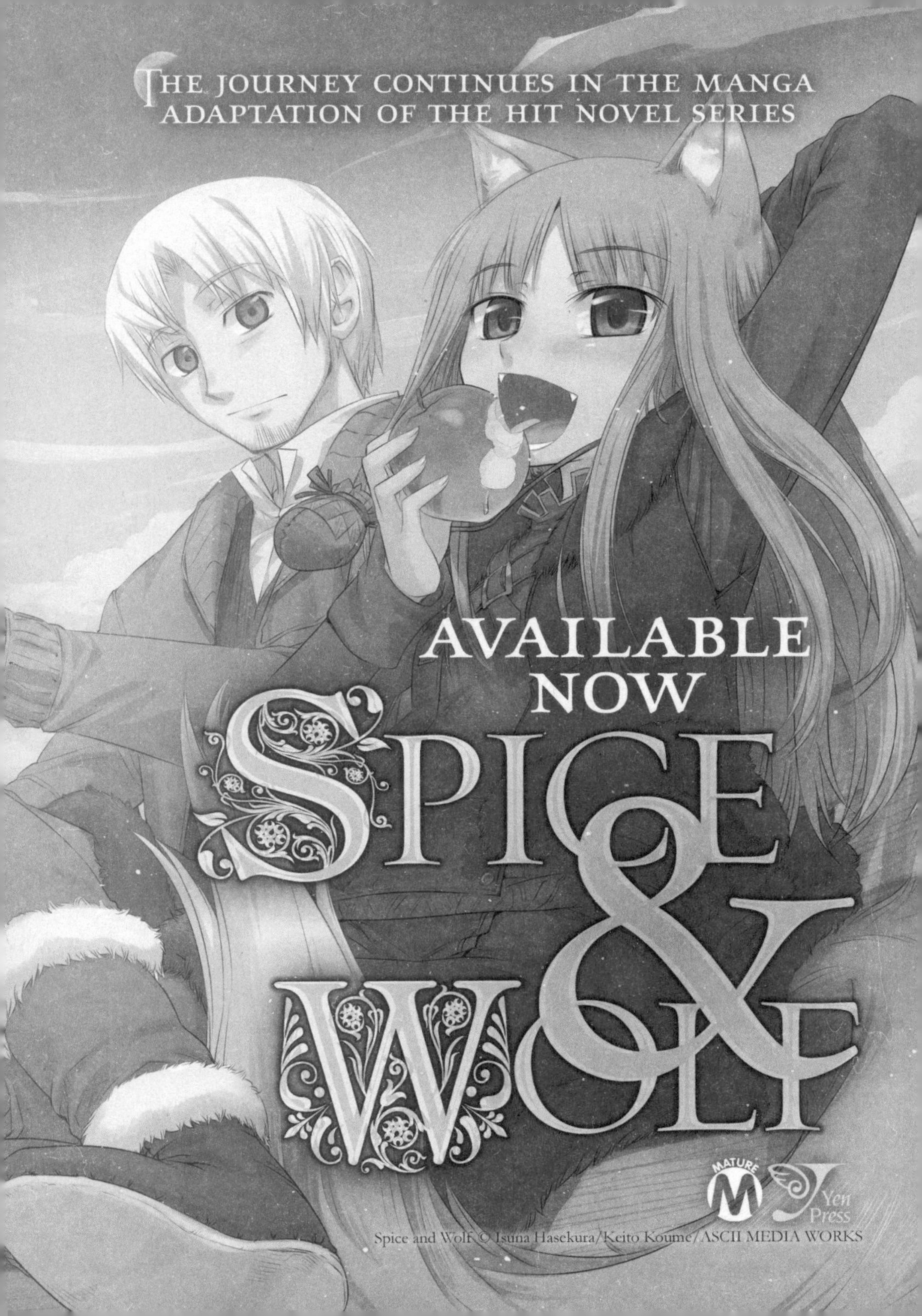
THE JOURNEY CONTINUES IN THE MANGA
ADAPTATION OF THE HIT NOVEL SERIES
AVAILABLE
NOW
SPICE & WOLF
MATURE
M
Yen
Press
Spice and Wolf © Isuna Hasekura/Keito Koume/ASCII MEDIA WORKS

ENJOY EVERYTHING.

Hello! This is YOTSUBA!

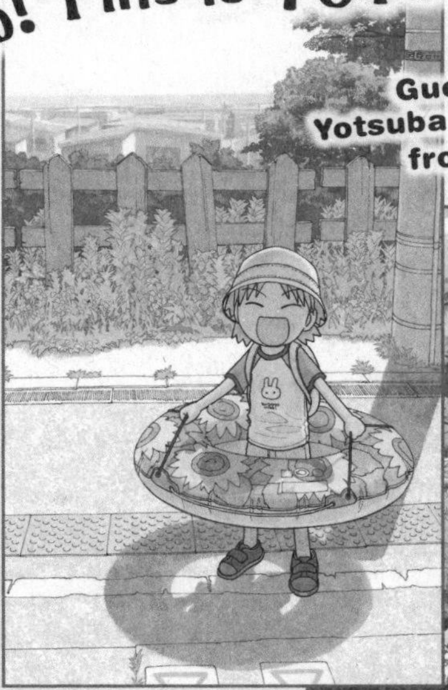

Guess what? Guess what?
Yotsuba and Daddy just moved here
from waaaay over there!

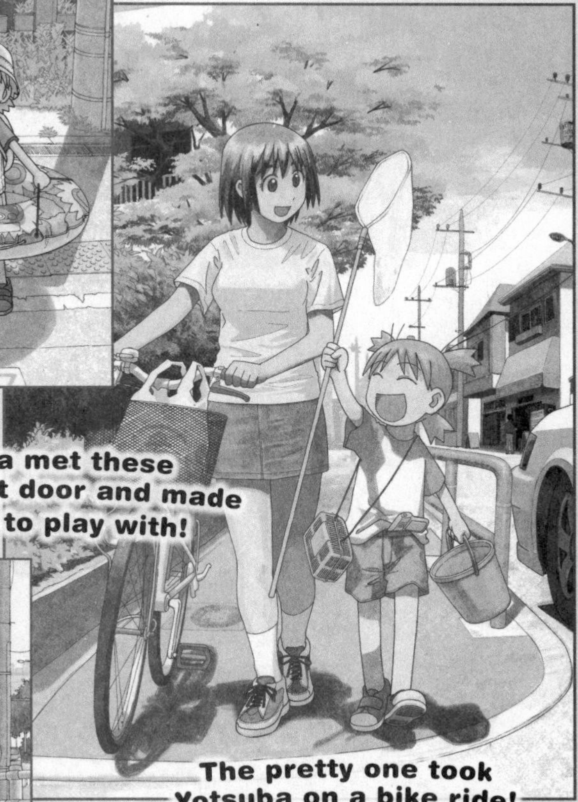

And Yotsuba met these
nice people next door and made
new friends to play with!

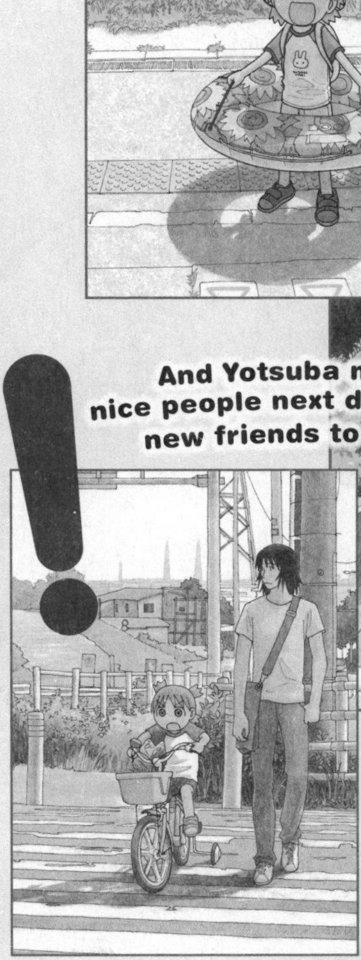

The pretty one took
Yotsuba on a bike ride!
(Whoooa! There was a big hill!)

And Ena's a good drawer!
(Almost as good as Yotsuba!)

And their mom always
gives Yotsuba ice cream!
(Yummy!)

And...
And...
OHHHH!

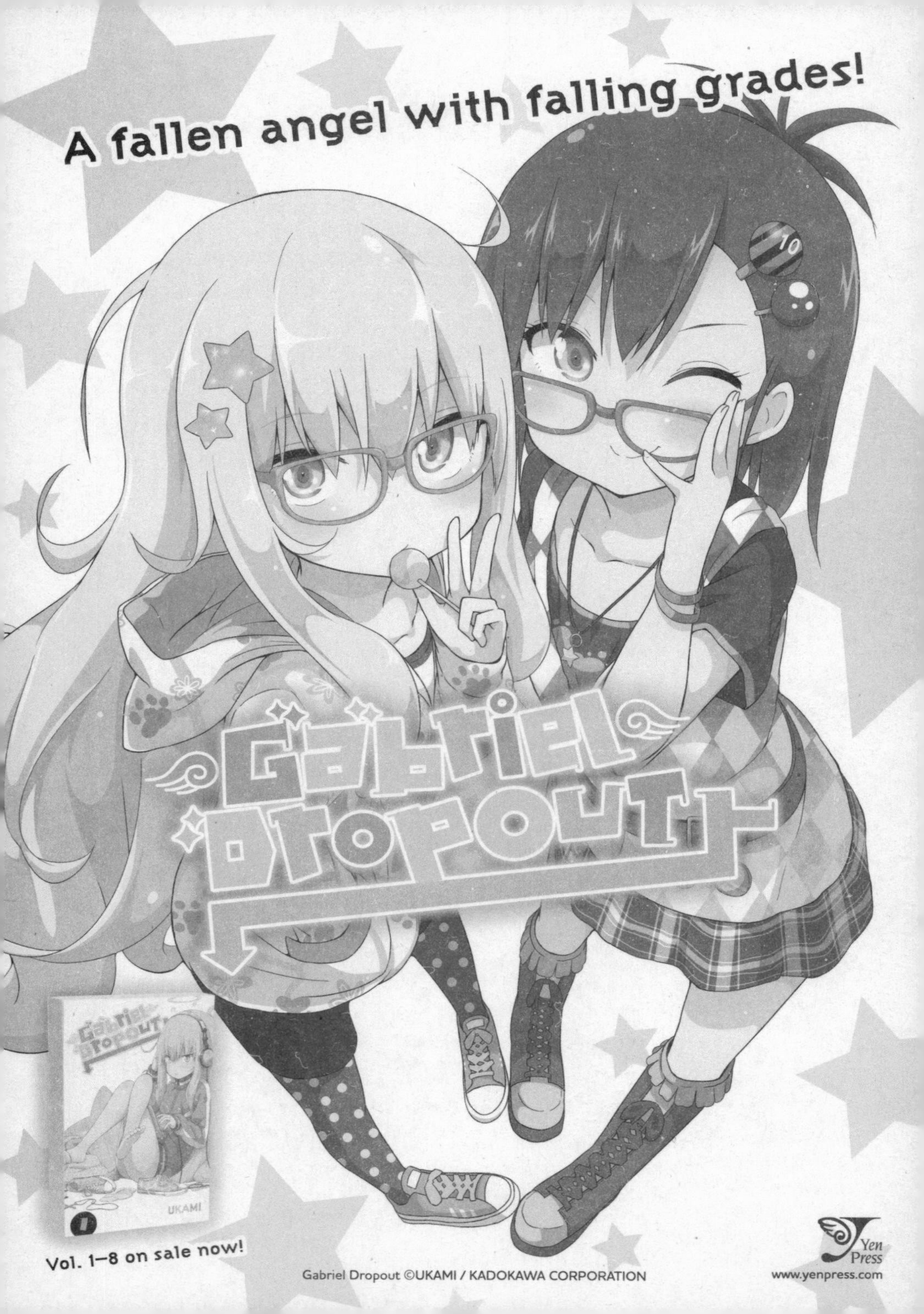
A fallen angel with falling grades!
Gabriel Dropout
Gabriel Dropout
UKAMI
Vol. 1–8 on sale now!
Gabriel Dropout ©UKAMI / KADOKAWA CORPORATION
Yen Press
www.yenpress.com

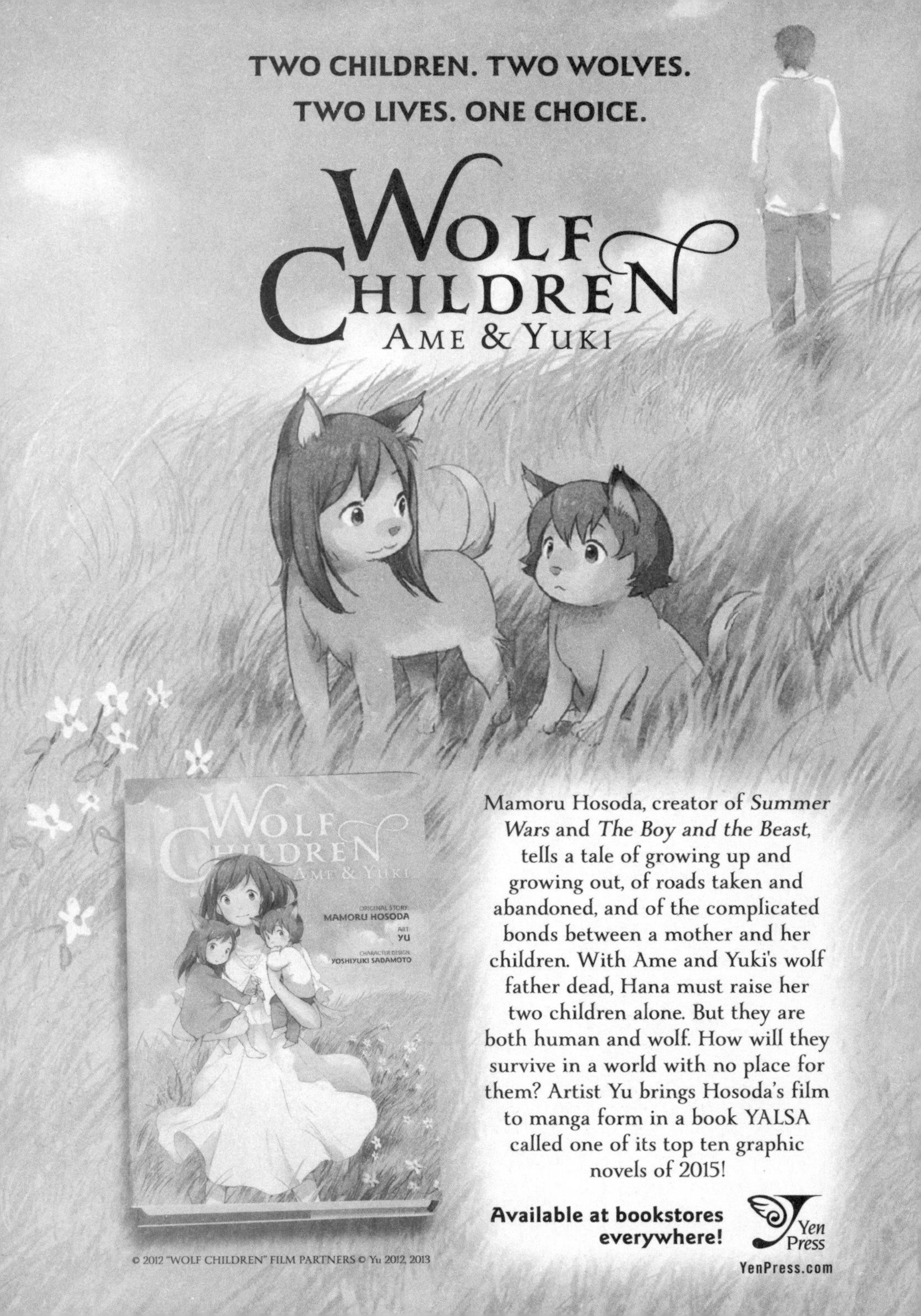
TWO CHILDREN. TWO WOLVES.
TWO LIVES. ONE CHOICE.
WOLF CHILDREN
AME & YUKI
WOLF CHILDREN
AME & YUKI
ORIGINAL STORY:
MAMORU HOSODA
ART:
YU
CHARACTER DESIGN
YOSHIYUKI SADAMOTO
Mamoru Hosoda, creator of *Summer Wars* and *The Boy and the Beast*, tells a tale of growing up and growing out, of roads taken and abandoned, and of the complicated bonds between a mother and her children. With Ame and Yuki's wolf father dead, Hana must raise her two children alone. But they are both human and wolf. How will they survive in a world with no place for them? Artist Yu brings Hosoda's film to manga form in a book YALSA called one of its top ten graphic novels of 2015!
Available at bookstores everywhere!
Yen Press
YenPress.com
© 2012 "WOLF CHILDREN" FILM PARTNERS © Yu 2012, 2013

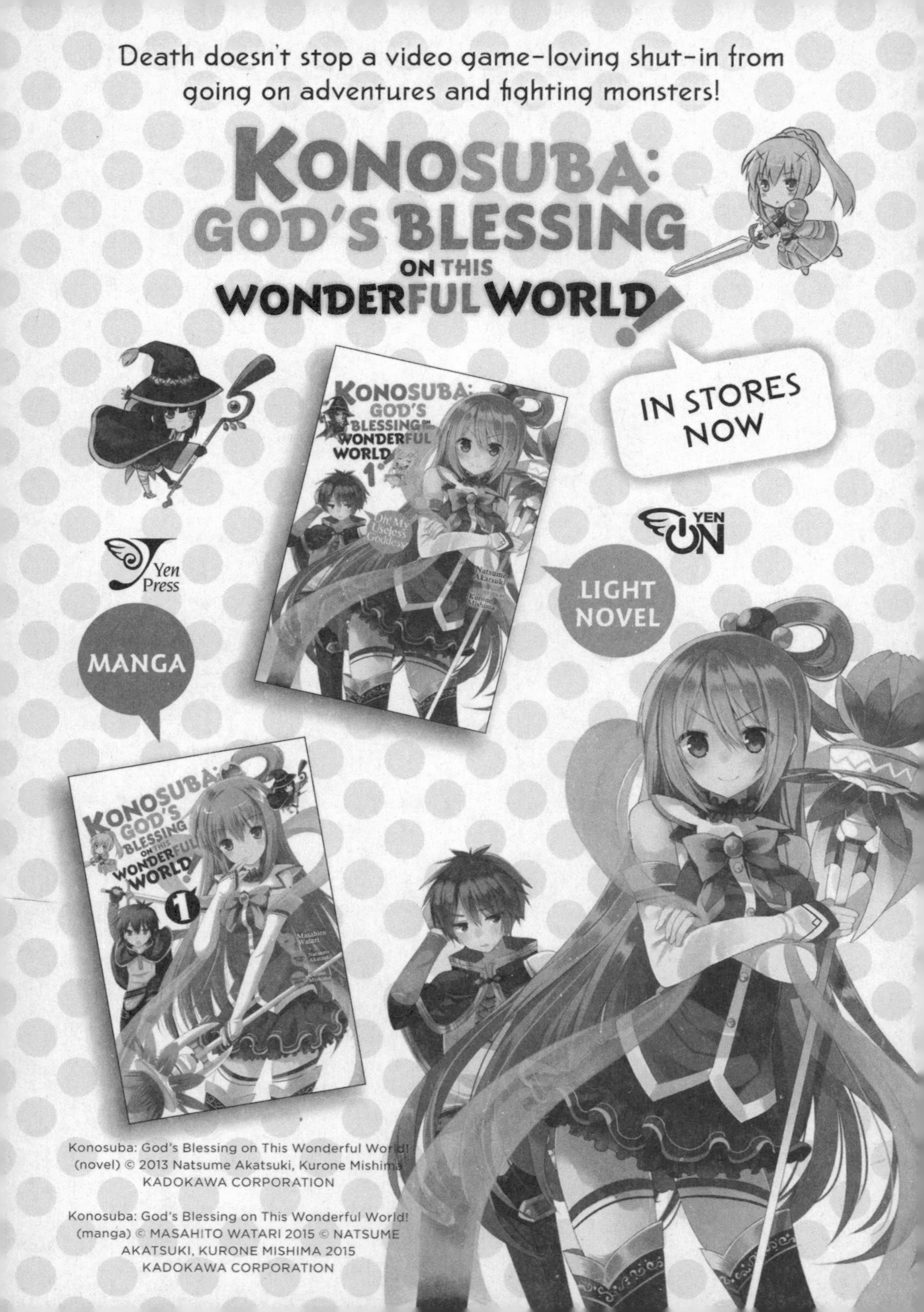
Death doesn't stop a video game–loving shut-in from going on adventures and fighting monsters!
KONOSUBA: GOD'S BLESSING ON THIS WONDERFUL WORLD!
IN STORES NOW
YEN ON
Yen Press
LIGHT NOVEL
MANGA
Konosuba: God's Blessing on This Wonderful World! (novel) © 2013 Natsume Akatsuki, Kurone Mishima KADOKAWA CORPORATION
Konosuba: God's Blessing on This Wonderful World! (manga) © MASAHITO WATARI 2015 © NATSUME AKATSUKI, KURONE MISHIMA 2015 KADOKAWA CORPORATION

HETEROGENIA LINGUISTICO

An Introduction to Interspecies Linguistics

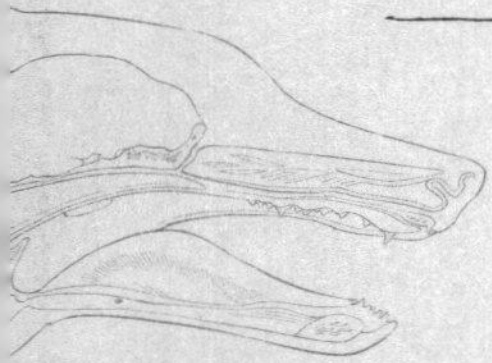

SALT SENO

1

Translation: **Amanda Haley** ┊ Lettering: **Abigail Blackman**

HETEROGENIA LINGUISTICO ISHUZOKU GENGOGAKU NYUUMON Volume 1
© Salt Seno 2018
First published in Japan in 2018 by KADOKAWA CORPORATION, Tokyo. English translation rights arranged with KADOKAWA CORPORATION, Tokyo through Tuttle-Mori Agency, Inc., Tokyo.

English translation © 2020 by Yen Press, LLC

Yen Press
150 West 30th Street, 19th Floor
New York, NY 10001

Withdrawn

Visit us at yenpress.com • facebook.com/yenpress • twitter.com/yenpress • yenpress.tumblr.com • instagram.com/yenpress

First Yen Press Edition: October 2020

Yen Press is an imprint of Yen Press, LLC.
The Yen Press name and logo are trademarks of Yen Press, LLC.

Library of Congress Control Number: 2020942576

ISBNs: 978-1-9753-1807-9 (print)
       978-1-9753-1808-6 (ebook)

10 9 8 7 6 5 4 3 2 1

WOR   Withdrawn

Printed in the United States of America